Cora L. V. Scott

LIFE WORK

OF

MRS. CORA L. V. RICHMOND.

COMPILED AND EDITED BY

HARRISON D. BARRETT.

PUBLISHED UNDER THE AUSPICES OF THE

NATIONAL SPIRITUALISTS ASSOCIATION

OF THE U. S. A.

CHICAGO:
HACK & ANDERSON, PRINTERS.
1895.

DEDICATION.

ILLUSTRATIONS.

OUTLINE OF CONTENTS.

(v.)

INTRODUCTION.

It is impossible to measure the value of an individual life to the outward world until that life has closed, and its records have become history, so that it can be judged by its effects upon humanity at large. No strong character in history has ever been fully appreciated nor his work judged impartially during his or her own lifetime. It is only after that life has ceased to express itself through mortal form, perhaps after long centuries, that the full value of what was said or done through that instrumentality, is appreciated and taken up by the world outside.

What was said of the Nazarene is true today. His work and influence affected but very few during the few years of his earthly pilgrimage, yet, in after time, the influence of that life has been almost measureless upon millions of human beings; although the effects of His teachings have been to separate families, and to shed oceans of blood, these results were through the mistaken application of what He taught. They have also been instrumental in accomplishing much of good to the human family, according to the ability of those receiving them to apply them to their own lives and to the lives of others in a just manner. The philosophers of all the ages found but few followers in their own time, but their thoughts were placed upon the pages of history, and their philosophies are now eagerly read by the thousands of students in all quarters of the globe, who appreciate the sublime teachings that were given through their minds so many years, perhaps centuries, ago.

In the world of politics, the same thing is true. The political leaders who endeavored to work out something of good for their fellow men found martyr's graves in defense of what they believed to be the truth. The Gracchi yielded up their lives for the good of the people, to be apotheosized after centuries had rolled away, as friends of the people and martyrs to the cause of truth. Plato's political economy, as well as that of Sir Thomas Moore, was laughed to scorn in their day, but these have received a new impetus at the hands of modern writers, and they are now applauded as having been seers of that better day that is in store for our humanity everywhere. Brutus, "the noblest Roman of them all," wished people to be free, yet, owing to the inability of the people around him to appreciate his thought, he was called a rebel, and fell at last a martyr to liberty.

There is but little difference between the terms rebel and patriot. The Gracchi, Brutus, Washington, Emmett, were all rebels. They are now considered heroes because the people can see that what they taught and what they strove to do was just and right. Success made some leaders *patriots* at once, like Washington; failure made the Gracchi, Kossuth, and others *rebels*, to become patriots and heroes after the lapse of centuries. As Clarence Hawkes so well says:

" A hero rose in armor bright,
    To drive a tyrant from the land.
    The monarch brought his armed band
And crushed him in a single fight;
And wrong still triumphed over right.

" The rebel died, his honored name
    Was branded with a traitor's shame.
Another rose in greater might,
    With armed men at his command,
    And drove the tyrant from the land.
The people cheered his noble deed,
    And placed the crown upon his head—
    The crown of him who first had bled
In freedom's cause, and sowed the seed."

In the religious world, the same line of argument will hold true, as can be shown by the work of Jesus of Nazareth. The same is true of Zoroaster, Confucius, Buddha, and all other religious teachers in all ages of the world. The effect of the writings and work of the Apostle Paul, of the Apostolic Fathers, of Chrysostrom, of Augustine, of Jerome, of Abelard, the Schoolmen, Bossuet, the Wesleys, the Priestleys, Murray, Channing, Robert Dale Owen, John W. Edmonds, and countless hosts of others, whose lives have been lived in their own way, whose teachings have been applied by millions of human beings, can only be measured to their full extent now that these individuals have passed on to spirit life. Their works can now be studied and the value of their labors realized by those who read the records of their lives in an impartial spirit. Not in the life-

time of any great leader can there be a complete
realization of what that one life is to the race, owing
to the fact of the proximity of the people to the individual whose life is before them.

> " 'Tis distance lends enchantment to the view,
>   And robes each sober mountain in its azure hue."

So with the lives of men and women, distance
brings out the finer points in their teachings, the
nobler attributes of their characters into bolder
relief, and, as often has been the case, their faults
and weaknesses as human beings have been lost sight
of or merged in their better qualities by their biographers. In their lifetimes, it is probable that these
same people were excoriated and villified by writers
who were unfriendly to them and their interests.
Witness the assaults upon the lives and characters of
our most prominent politicians, such as Webster,
Sumner, Lincoln, Grant, and others, and yet, when
they passed from earth, all those things that revealed
the humanity of the men seemed to be forgotten in
the glowing tributes of praise that their biographers
and followers would fain heap upon the altars of
their memories.

But it is not the life of any one individual man or
woman that makes up the history of any movement,
or makes it of value to the race. Therefore, it takes
the records of the united lives of the brightest thinkers of the world to reveal the philosophy of history
in its true light. In Spiritualism, there are many
whose lives and works make up a noble record of
achievements in the way of good deeds done for the
race. We cannot measure in full the influence of

any one of those individual lives apart from the
whole, and especially is it hard to determine the influence of the one whose life is depicted upon the
pages that are to follow. We are too near the scenes
herein described, and many who read these pages,
because of that very nearness, will fail to appreciate
the wonderful work she has done until after the eyes
of our esteemed co-worker and beloved friend have
been kissed by the sweet soft lips of death, and her
willing spirit wafted to its home in spheres immortal.

In conversations with us, Mrs. Richmond has said
repeatedly: "Spiritualism would have been if I had
never existed, and its great work could have been
done without me. Even if my gifts were entirely
blotted out of its record, there would be left such a
vast record of fact and inspiration that the labors of
my individual self might not be greatly missed by the
vast majority. Yet, I recognize that my mediumship
is an integral part of Spiritualism, and, as such, entitled to a place in the annals of its history." These
words can be said with truth of, perhaps, every
worker in the religious world of whatever period or
dispensation, yet no history of any movement is complete unless it comprises the work of its most eminent
teachers and thinkers. Consequently, as our subject
truly says, her work is an integral part of Spiritualism,
and will be so considered in this volume.

Our readers are invited to scan the pages of this
record with great care, to note the developments that
each succeeding decade has brought forth in the social, political and religious worlds, so that the general
effect of what our subject has said and done may be

set forth in a way that will show what can be accomplished through the instrumentality of a willing servant of the higher powers from the spirit side of life.
In years to come, when her life work shall have been
completed, and the people of that distant day are
permitted to read with unbiased eyes, the records of
her life, its *full* measure can be taken, and its *real*
worth to the world will be proved by the enlarged
views, better lives and clearer thinking of the people
of the future.

It is not our object to apotheosize our subject, nor
to claim all the encomiums of praise, all the honors
of the world for her. We only claim that she has
done a noble work in her own way, and, having done
it wisely and well, having exerted a helpful influence
over thousands of human beings, having endeavored
to make the world better because she has lived in it
as a part of its great machinery, she is entitled to
due credit for all her efforts, and should receive her
full meed of praise. She never has arrogated to
herself the credit for the work that she has done.
She has modestly disclaimed the world's plaudits,
and placed the credit and responsibility of her work
upon the guides who have prompted her speech, the
teachers who have directed her thoughts, from the
higher spheres. These pages contain but an imperfect record of the work those guides have accomplished through her organism. They show what one
frail body can be made to do with the assistance of
the vitalizing forces and soulful influences of the
spirit. Volumes could be filled, should we go into
the minutiæ of her work. We have endeavored to

present in this history the leading features of her mediumistic labor, its effects upon the thousands to whom she has ministered, and the results that have come from the seed that was sown by her in the early days of the history of our movement.

So interwoven with the history of Spiritualism itself is the life-work of our subject, who has been for forty-three years a willing instrument in the hands of her guides, that we are able to give much valuable data not heretofore presented to the world in any history of Spiritualism. It is interesting to note the names of some of her contemporaries upon the Spiritualistic platform during those years, and we cannot refrain from mentioning at this point the names of the gifted Ralph Waldo Emerson, Thomas Wentworth Higginson, and William Lloyd Garrison, who were prominent speakers upon the Spiritualistic platform thirty years ago. We feel especially grateful to the thinkers and writers of those early days for the valuable literature that has been given to us through their inspired teachings, and feel that their legacy to the world is one so rich in intrinsic value that it can not be fully appreciated by the general mass of the human race, nor even of Spiritualists at the present time. Spiritual illumination alone can bring a realization of this to the minds of men. It has been the aim of such workers as our subject to make this Spiritual illumination possible, and to enable humanity to hold larger views and to receive yet higher instructions in the days that are to come.

We have examined no less than thirty volumes of literature for data in connection with our work. Hundreds of letters have been written to and received from personal friends of our subject, and many weeks and months of careful study devoted to the preparation of our manuscript and to the compilation of historical facts germane to this biography. We have endeavored to verify every statement made, and feel that we have dealt impartially with the subject matter, so far as was in our power so to do. We have endeavored to make our statements concise, and sought to avoid prolixity in all of our chapters. That which has been deemed to be of the greatest interest to the public we have culled with careful hand, and written from the standpoint of appreciation as a co-worker with Mrs. Richmond, and a student of her guides.

We offer this work to a generous public without a misgiving, as the product of thoughtful study and calm inspiration. As we send this volume forth upon the sea of literature, we trust that it will find many quiet harbors in which it can rest to give light and knowledge to those whose faces are forever turned toward the rising sun.

We are indebted to scores of friends for information that we have gleaned from their letters. We must especially return thanks to Marie Countess of Caithness, Duchesse de Pomar, W. J. Colville, James Burns, Emma Hardinge Britten, John C. Ward, Mrs. Adelaide Slater and Mrs. William Tebb, of England; William Richmond, S. H. Wortmann, Mrs. Helen O. Richmond, Mrs. C. Catlin, F. E. Ormsby, Dr. L. Bushnell, Mrs. Fred Ashton, Frederick F. Cook, Dr. H. B. Storer, Mrs. C. C. Coleman, Mrs. Abbey Heywood, Hon. Wendell C. Warner (United States

Consul, Burslem, England), Mrs. M. H. Skidmore, Hon. A. Gaston, Mrs. T. C. Gaston, Dr. E. C. Hyde, Geo. H. Jones, John A. Wilson and wife, Col. H. J. Horn, C. M. Plumb, Hon. George A. Bacon, Mrs. Orpha E. Tousey, Hon. Thomas M. Locke, A. M. Griffin, Andrew Cross, Dr. James E. De Wolf, Mrs. Anna Orvis, and to all of the guides of Mrs. Richmond, especially the spirit control, A. A. Ballou, and the gentle Ouina, who have ably assisted us in this work.

We must especially return thanks to Messrs. Colby & Rich, the courteous and considerate proprietors of the "Banner of Light," for many favors received from their hands. Their valuable histories have ever been open to us, and the privileges of their editorial sanctum have uniformly been extended to us. Much of the success that has attended our efforts has been due to the assistance they have rendered us.

Such as our work is, we give it to the public, and calmly await its unbiased verdict.

LIFE WORK OF

Mrs. Cora L. V. Richmond.

CHAPTER I.

CHILDHOOD

THROUGHOUT all ages of the world, the lives of representative men have made up all there was and is in the history of nations. Eliminate personalities from the history of any movement in civil or religious affairs, and only empty shells would be left, mere outlines of what these eminent personages had made great and glorious. Clustered around historical names are grouped the pre-eminent virtues that charm the minds of the readers, and lead them almost to idealize the ages that are no more. Everywhere we find the names of prominent men connected with important epochs in history. Warriors and statesmen mingle freely in the rapidly changing scenes of the great panorama of human life as painted upon the pages of history. All great men simply serve to make the nations they represent glow with life and emotion as we read of what they did, what they said, and of the effects of their words upon those who followed their teachings.

We are struck, however, by the one-sidedness of historians as they write of the great personalities that make up the history of nations. Representative men are alone given prominence, and the names and works of representative women find but little place in the glowing tributes paid by the vast majority of writers to the eminent characters in history. Even our own American history is somewhat faulty in this respect, and we have been prone to boast of the prowess of our forefathers, but have failed at the same time to render a just tribute to the foremothers of our republic. In all political movements this is also true, and doubly true of the religious reforms that have been given the world during the past ages. The Jews may refer to Deborah, Esther, Hannah, and the Christians to Mary, Martha and Elizabeth; but both unite in sinking or merging the individualities of their women into the personalities of their husbands, generally giving the latter credit for what their wives have accomplished. But we need not dwell upon these points longer, as the evidence presented would hereafter be merely cumulative.

It was reserved for the youngest and greatest nation on earth, about the middle of the nineteenth century, to usher in a movement that was destined to overturn the ancient order of things, and to cause the rewriting of the history of the world. It was also destined to change the entire current of thought concerning woman, and give to her her true place in the category of human events. Clouds of bigotry and theological darkness had long enveloped the globe. Cold Materialism with its pitiless edict of annihilation was on the one side, and the horrible pictures, the fearful mandates of Partialism were on the other. Hope seemed lost in doubt and fear, while Love was fettered hand and foot by creed, dogma, and the gloom of Christian pessimism. At this hour when the human soul cried out for succor, the angels of God, in the persons of our arisen loved ones, bent near and from their radiant forms threw a hallowed light over all the earth that caused all humanity to smile again, because knowledge of the future had been given by means of this very light. This new dispensation came unheralded by the blare of trumpets, by ceremonials and pomp; but, through the instrumentality of little girls, in an humble home among the plain farmers of western New York, was the tidings of angel ministry proclaimed to a hungering world. The pendulum of thought had oscillated far to one side, and the mystic rap at Hydesville was the call to halt, a signal for it to turn in the opposite direction, but only so far as to evenly balance between the male and female influence in life.

This work was ushered in in the year 1848, which should evermore be called "The year of the new Declaration of Independence," because it marks the beginning of an attempt to do justice to woman.

After the first manifestation what more fitting instrument could be found by the heavenly messengers to confound the wise and to reveal the things of the spirit than innocent children, little girls whose souls reflected the truths as the perfect mirror does its surrounding objects? As we stated at the outset, it is the personalities, around which cluster the associations and events comprising any movement, so in this new dispensation of 1848 we must consider the persons who have proclaimed it to a listening world in order to fully understand its scope and power. A little girl was the first apostle chosen to do the work designed by the spirit world. It is to the life and work of that little girl, the one chosen in that memorable period, that we shall invite our readers' attention as they peruse the following pages.

Cora L. V. Scott, now so well and favorably known as Mrs. Cora L. V. Richmond, was born in 1840, near Cuba in Allegany County, New York. Her father, David W. Scott, at that time owned and was running a lumber mill on the hills between the villages of Cuba and Friendship. When Cora was two years of age her parents moved to Cadytown, now North Cuba, where the next seven years of her life were spent. Could the parents have foreseen the brilliant future in store for their little daughter, how their hearts would have thrilled with pardonable pride as they viewed it! Yet what was in store for Cora Scott was also in store, in part, for other children who first saw the light of day among the hills of western New York. Here were born many of the now eminent workers in the ranks of modern Spiritualism: Margerhetta and Katherine Fox, Lyman C. Howe, Mrs. A. H. Colby Luther, George P. Colby, Mrs. Elizabeth Lowe Watson, Mrs. R. S. Lillie, Mrs. H. S. Lake, Harry Bastion and the Davenport brothers. Of these, the Fox sisters began their work in 1848, aged respectively eight and ten years, while that of Cora Scott began in 1851 in her eleventh year, and all of the others named, save Mrs. Luther, Mrs. Lillie and Mrs. Lake, were but children when their public work began; yet the appearance of them all was subsequent to that of the subject of this sketch, hence not contemporaneous with it, except in later years.

David W. Scott was an independent in his religious views, and at the present day would probably be known as a free thinker. In his younger days he had read Thomas Paine's works surreptitiously, and the impression left by that great man's thoughts had been lasting. Mr. Scott was always philosophical in his line of argument, and determined to sift matters to the very bottom. He was a searcher for truth in all directions, and was willing to receive it from any and all sources whatever they might be. Cora's mother, Lodensy Butterfield, was of a religious turn of mind, her parents being Presbyterians and quite strict in their views; but she was also a truth-seeker, and her religious opinions had been materially modified when Cora's wonderful mediumship was first discovered. She was, therefore, quite prepared to receive the teachings of the spirit world, and made no strenuous opposition to the manifestations when they appeared in her home. It will be seen from these statements that the atmosphere of the home of the Scotts was entirely free from the sulphurous fumes of orthodoxy before Spiritual-ism came to it; hence, Cora's mind had not been biased by partialistic teachings and dogmatic theology. Mr. Scott endeavored to keep pace with the leading reforms of the times, and was deeply interested in the "Hopedale Colony," established by the late Rev. Adin Ballou, near Milford, Mass. Mr. Scott spent one summer and winter, 1850–1, at Hopedale, and firmly be-lieved in Mr. Ballou's plans; but, feeling that

they did not have land enough in Hopedale for
the future growth of their colony, it was determined to organize a branch division in Wisconsin. To carry this plan into execution, Mr.
Scott moved to Waterloo, Wis., in the spring of
1851. During his stay at Hopedale he had attended one Spiritual seance and was interested
in the phenomena he witnessed, but his removal
to the West prevented him from continuing his
investigations.

During the summer of 1851 he was busy per-
fecting his plans relative to the colony, but in
the early autumn an event occurred that made
a complete change in all of his plans and led
him to abandon that line of work forever. The
event was Cora's mediumship. From the very
first he accepted the wonderful teachings that
fell like pearls from his daughter's lips, for he
was ready for the truths of Spiritualism, having
prepared himself through his own logical reasoning for the light of liberal thought. He was
heard to say on one occasion to his wife, after
their daughter began her public work: "Well,
ma, I have now found my religion." Indeed he
had and so had hundreds, yes, thousands of
others, who have been permitted to slake their
spiritual thirst at the same never failing fountain.

Soon after Cora's mediumship was made
known, Mr. Scott returned with his daughter to
their former home near Cuba, N. Y. Prior to

their return Cora had begun her public work as a platform speaker, her first appearance being at Lake Mills, Wis., during her eleventh year. She went to Waterloo, to Milwaukee and to many other places in Wisconsin, and on many occasions was interviewed by college professors and teachers who were nonplussed by her wonderful flow of language and the scholarship of her utterances.

When her first mediumistic experience came to her, Cora knew nothing of Spiritualism. She had never heard, save in rumor, of the "Rochester Knockings", and had no idea of what they might mean. She was then eleven years of age and presented no unusual appearance. She was not over-precocious for her age nor over-studious, but she was fond of school and of play as most children are. She had never been the subject of any unusual visions or indications in her life. She was, however, unusually sensitive, but not more so, perhaps, than hundreds of others of similar temperaments; yet a word, a look, or an unusual sight or sound of any kind affected her keenly. Beyond these and an extreme diffidence she was in no way different from any country girl, reared and educated as country girls are.

In the fall of 1851 the first visitation came to this household. The young girl was seated in an arbor fashioned of young oak trees that were growing in the garden, they having been purposely left to form this arbor. She was preparing in her crude way, as a girl of eleven years will, her composition upon her slate for school, intending to copy it afterwards. As she supposed, she fell asleep, and on her return to consciousness found the slate was covered with writing not her own. Supposing some one had been there and done the writing in sport or as a joke, she hastened to the house to show the slate to her mother and to tell her that some one had been there writing while she was asleep. The mother was slightly shocked when she told her this, for the little children playing around had come in a short time before and told her that "Cora was in the arbor writing in her sleep." Thinking this mere play she had said nothing about it, but when the slate was presented covered with writing, which commenced, "My dear sister," and was signed with the name of a deceased sister of the mother whom Cora had never seen nor scarcely heard of, as she had passed away in early childhood, the mother became frightened, put the slate away and said nothing to Cora of what the children had told her.

A few days later Cora was seated at the feet of her mother sewing when again sleep overcame her, and the mother thinking she had fainted or was ill, applied the usual restoratives;

but meanwhile discovered a trembling motion of
the right hand, and instantly remembered the
slate.   As soon as she placed slate and pencil in
her hands, Cora began to write, this time before
the very eyes of her mother.   She rapidly wrote
one message after another signed by different
members of the family who had departed to
spirit life, all of whom united in saying: "We
are not dead." They also assured the anxious
mother that they would not harm the child, for
they had found through her a means of com-
municating with those on earth, and wished her
to aid them in carrying out this work.   The influence at intervals continued, sometimes once
in two or three days, until at last the house was
thronged with curious friends and neighbors who
came in to see "Cora write in her sleep." There
was no knowledge of Spiritualism in the neighborhood, no realization of what these manifestations might mean on the part of the people, yet
persons of all creeds alike came and not infrequently received messages from their own friends.
They were often called upon to ask questions,
mentally or otherwise, which would be promptly
answered in writing and the answers handed to
them.   Of course the sensitive organism of the
child, the unusual surroundings and the excitement incident to these occurrences must have
brought about serious results to the medium had
there not been a strong band of influences around

her who had complete control of her organism
and were able to dictate what her line of work
should be. These guides would not permit the
child-medium to overtax her physical strength,
and made such conditions possible through the
unconscious trance state as would least affect the
medium's health and general power of endurance.
By taking complete possession of the medium
the maximum effort had to be made from the
spirit side, which left but little for the medium
to do herself. The volume of work that has
been done can be better appreciated when our
reader sees for himself that no one mortal in his
or her normal state could have performed all
this labor without breaking down, unless outside help had been given him. It is a strong
test of spirit aid to find so full a record of long
years of active labor as the one we are to give of
Cora L. V. Scott.

A few months after Cora's first mediumistic experience, Adin Agustus Ballou, son of Rev. Adin
Ballou, of whom an extended account will be
given in the succeeding chapter, passed to spirit
life. As he had been deeply interested in the reforms of the day, and an enthusiastic Spiritualist, he was especially fitted for and ardently
desirous of continuing his reform labors from the
higher side of life. He was taken to the Wisconsin home of the Scotts by a spirit guide, who
told him he was to control the daughter, Cora,

whom he had seen playing in his father's garden
in Hopedale one year previous, of whom he had
never subsequently heard save that with her
parents, she had removed to the West. Spirit
Ballou speaks of his relation to the medium at
that time as follows :

"I had never seen a medium of the type of
Cora Scott. I was requested by the friends and
relatives of the family, who were in spirit life, to
give my aid in developing her powers and shield-
ing her from the throng of spirit influences that
were so anxious to communicate that they, perhaps, might do her injury, as they did not know
much of the power of control. I soon discovered that these were higher guides, guardian
spirits of the medium, who knew her power, and
had requested my presence there to be their
spirit instrument in controlling this child. I
very reluctantly undertook the task. As a mortal I was young in years ; as a spirit I was still
younger. I had been in spirit life but a few days,
when this request came to me, and it was undertaking a most solemn responsibility. I knew,
it is true, of this method of communication between the spirit world and yours ; I knew somewhat of the import it conveyed to humanity, but
I had very little knowledge of governing another
person, very little knowledge of the laws of psychology, and of the influence necessary to be
adapted to the frail instrumentality that I was

called upon to control. However, I was told
that I would not be alone in my control, but that
there were certain powers and functions that I
might more promptly develop than other persons or spirits, and that I would in that way be
enabled at the same time to gain knowledge of
spirit life, and to impart knowledge to others.
I hailed with delight the idea of being useful to
my fellow beings ; I hailed with delight the idea
of receiving additional knowledge of spirit life,
but I shrank from controlling an organism, from
taking possession of a human life in any way
whatever to be its guiding power. I was admonished, however, by spirits above me, that it was
not in my power to alter the destiny of a human
being, that I might avail myself of this organism
for the facility of acquiring knowledge and imparting it, but that I could not, in any way, alter
her life course, for that was in higher hands than
my own."

About the same time that Spirit Ballou first
controlled Cora, a German physician, who always
withheld his name, controlled her at intervals
for the purpose of healing the sick. As soon as
he could do so (which was in a few weeks),
Spirit Ballou controlled the brain and vocal organs for the purpose of speaking, instead of controlling the hand to write, as had been done by
the other controls at first. He controlled her
first experimentally, and afterwards as a teacher;

then by the advice of the spirits beyond him, formed a circle of a certain number of persons, no strangers being admitted. Spirit Ballou soon found that it was much easier to control his medium in an unconscious trance than in a semi-conscious or inspirational state. By so doing the danger of undue exhaustion of the medium's physical powers was obviated, and the guides could much more clearly express their own views, and do their work in their own way.

From the very first of her being controlled by spirits, the subject of this sketch has always been unconscious of all outward occurrences, and from her own pen, later in this work, will be found a brief account of her experiences while in these deep trances.

During the first three or four years of her work, Cora was controlled by the German physician at a given hour each day to heal those who came to her father's house for that purpose. This work often occupied her two, three and sometimes six hours per day, without the least harm to the child. She would occasionally go in a deep trance to the homes of the neighbors who were too ill to come to her, and then treat them with astonishing results. A few well attested instances of the healing powers of our medium will be of interest at this time.

Capt. Pratt, a most worthy and estimable gentleman, was in command of the steamer Globe, on which the Scott family had taken passage to Wisconsin. One year later, when Mr. Scott and Cora were on their way to their former home in New York, they again met the genial captain, who had been for some years more or less of an invalid. He had been deeply interested in Cora's mediumship from the very first, and was finally converted through her to Spiritualism. He became a patient of the German doctor who controlled Cora. In a deep trance she would treat him, and would always relieve him of the keenest agony with which he was suffering. She never knew until after Capt. Pratt's transition what the disease was that she had treated so effectually, and was astounded to learn that it was an ulcerous fever sore. A child would of course naturally shrink from coming in contact with such a disease, much less treat it, but so perfect was the control of the German doctor, that she performed this task daily, and left the patient entirely free from pain and suffering. Capt. Pratt was kept alive by these treatments several years, and finally succumbed to pulmonary trouble that took him into spirit life. It is certain, however, that no child of the age of Cora Scott could, unaided, bandage, dress and otherwise attend upon a limb of that sort in her normal state.

Another important, because difficult case, was that of a carpenter in Lake Mills by the name of Keyes, who had run a large splinter under the

nail of the third finger of his right hand. It was
very painful, because of the sensitiveness of the
part affected. The finger had become badly
swollen, and Mr. Keyes called a physician, who
had lanced the finger, which did but little good,
and caused mortification to take place rapidly.
Mr. Keyes, in his great agony, asked his family
to send for Cora. They were strict church members, and, believing the power to be Satanic,
would not yield to his request. The spirit doctor, however, was on the alert. He, without
any knowledge on the part of Cora's family of
the man's suffering, proceeded to awaken Cora
at midnight, made her go to her father's bed, and
say that she must go to the house of this gentleman, as he was suffering greatly and needed her.
Her father accordingly arose and went with her
on this errand of mercy. Before they reached
Mr. Keyes' door, Mr. Scott could hear the groans
of anguish from the afflicted man. Entering the
house, the physician, seeing who had come, departed in anger. The wife fled to another department, leaving them alone with the sick man.
Cora's father obeyed the instructions given by the
spirit physician, brought bandages, warm water,
and such other appliances as he requested. The
physician, who had fled so hastily, had left his
case of surgical instruments behind him. Directed by the spirit surgeon, Cora walked to the
case, selected a particular instrument, and pro-

ceeded to unbandage the suffering man's hand.
She then, with as much precision as becomes the
practiced surgeon, proceeded to cut away the
proud or mortified flesh, applied the soothing
remedies that Mr. Scott had prepared under the
directions of the spirit guide, and in one short
hour left the patient asleep. He recovered in
less than two weeks, with only the loss of the
use of a joint, the one that the physician had
lanced in his ignorance at the beginning of the
difficulty. Mr. Keyes lived many years to attest
the truth of this story, and there are probably
those living today in Lake Mills, Wis., who can
testify to the facts set forth in the above mentioned cases.

The German physician remained with Cora
about four years, during which period he performed many remarkable cures through her organism. This spirit made his power as a healer
manifest everywhere Cora went. He was an
educated, polished gentleman, and conducted
himself with singular politeness and suavity of
manner. He possessed the most intimate knowledge of surgery, was perfectly fearless in performing difficult operations, and could give a
correct analysis of human diseases of every kind.
He spoke three languages fluently, two of which
he used in controlling Cora, although she had no
knowledge whatever of any language except the
English.

Before we turn from this all too brief sketch of
Cora's power as a healer, we must refer to a most
interesting event connected therewith, involving
the mediumship of a lady who at one time had
been Cora's teacher at school.   This lady, Miss
Mary Folsom, afterwards Mrs. Hayes of Waterloo, Wis., and now Mrs. Chenowith of Eagle
Vale, Cal., was very sensitive, and deeply religious ; hence, had been deeply shocked at the
singular influence that had come over Cora, who
was one of her favorite pupils.   This lady had
prayed earnestly that the evil influence might be
removed from her protege, but finding that it did
not diminish, but multiplied its remarkable works,
Miss Folsom besought the spirits to teach her the
truths—to make her a medium, so that she might
also be the means of doing good to her fellow
beings.   One evening at Mr. Scott's residence,
Miss Folsom witnessed the manifestations that
came through Cora's mediumship—the writing
and speaking—when she was suddenly controlled
by a German, who spoke that language fluently
through her lips, greatly to her own surprise, as
well as that of Mr. Scott and family.   From that
time on she was one of the best healing mediums
ever found in the ranks of followers of Spiritualism.   This lady was an early friend of the Scott
family, and can testify to the many remarkable
cures wrought through her own and Cora's mediumship.   She was a devoted follower of Spir-

itualism for many years, and today is an honored resident of the state of California, where we feel certain she is living the religion of Spiritualism, and enjoying a well earned rest from the arduous labor of former years. Miss Folsom and Cora soon aroused the antagonism of the regular physicians, and clergymen of the neighborhood. The former were without patients, and the latter lacked audiences. They resorted to a religious revival, which was speedily followed by a greater development of mediums. People would insist upon getting well, and staying well, while the sycophant clergy soon learned that their flocks were doing their own thinking. That village in Wisconsin soon became the center of a spiritual circle that had greater power than all the professionals taken together. Churches were abandoned, and the physicians sought other fields of labor, where the light of spiritual knowledge had not yet penetrated. This left the friends of progress to enjoy what the ministers chose to call their "delusions" in peace.

From the very first it was stated that Cora's mission was to be that of a platform speaker, and these years devoted to the art of healing were but experiences to fit her for the work. Spirit Ballou knew what his own mission was to be, and while he did not relinquish his control of the child medium during the four years of labor as a healer, he yet permitted his German friend to prepare the way for his own work that was to follow. Spirit Ballou spent those years in gathering up his own forces, and with the assistance of the higher guides, laid his plans for the future years that were destined to be so full of useful labor for him and his instrument. During the entire four years he controlled Cora frequently and gave weekly addresses of a longer or shorter duration to the select circle to which we have referred above. Every Sunday as Cora's development progressed, meetings were held at her father's house for such friends and neighbors as choose to come to listen to the utterances from the other side of life. At first Spirit Ballou did not control her longer than thirty minutes at one time, but as her strength increased and brain developed, he extended the time to forty minutes, then to an hour or longer, during which time he could use her vocal organs with perfect ease. He did not tax the child's brain to the extent of full and entire exercise of power, but he had no difficulty in expressing facts that were within his knowledge, and *not* within hers. The most judicious care seems to have been exercised by the spirit guides during all those years of growth, for the effect of the control of the spirit was beneficial to Cora in every instance. In thus guiding and guarding her, Spirit Ballou says he was in his turn directed by wise spirits far beyond him.

In order that the guides might not be trammeled in their work, with and through Cora, they directed that she should cease to attend school, which she did in her twelfth year. From that time down to the present, Cora L. V. Scott has never entered a school room as a pupil, nor has she studied any book, listened to any master, pursued any course of study, save those given by her spirit guides while she was in the trance state. We refer our readers to some of the residents of Lake Mills, Wis., who can testify, if they will, to the early life of our heroine in that place.

About the time that the German doctor and Spirit Ballou first came to our medium, a little Indian girl, (then known as "Shenandoah," whose later name is "Ouina") also appeared as one of her guides. Ouina's history will be given in full on the subsequent pages of this book. We mention her advent at this time as marking one of the most important events connected with the life of our subject, for "Ouina's work," says Spirit Ballou, "has been greater than mine, as she is far above me in the scale of progression." We have stated that Cora's public work, *i. e.*, platform speaking, began when she was eleven years of age, but it was not until she was fifteen that her actual spiritual teaching before large audiences commenced. Up to this time, although she was constantly engaged in speaking, it was in smaller towns and villages, or local

circles that had been formed for the purpose.
These meetings awakened a great deal of interest
among all classes of people, and soon attracted
the attention of people residing at a distance
from Cora's home. Probably no physical phenomena could have had the deep and lasting influence upon the minds of the people as did these
mental phenomena that were constantly occur-
ring in the presence of our medium. This statement is also true of the other child mediums
who were developed later in the history of Spiritualism.

It is well at this time to answer a few questions in regard to the ideas advanced by the
guides in those earlier years. Are they consistent or in keeping with those given the same
medium today? Entirely so, for the guides
have simply endeavored to adapt their teachings
to the progressive thought of the age by being
always in advance of the received opinions of
the world. They have advanced step by step in
their teachings as the minds of men through
evolution have been fitted to receive the knowledge of modern times. The thought of today, or
the new thought, is merely built upon the old, or
the thought of yesterday; hence with the mental
unfoldment of our race, our spiritual teachers
have had much to do by bringing to bear upon
humanity the progressive thoughts that were
most needed for the growth of all mankind.

Are the ideas given known to the medium or originated by her ? By no means ; she is and always has been entirely unconscious while uttering these lofty ideas, and her first knowledge of what she said has been given her when one of her addresses has been repeated to her after its delivery.

Are these ideas the personal views of Ouina, the German doctor, or Spirit Ballou ? Sometimes, but in the majority of instances, they are the views of teachers who have progressed much further than Spirit Ballou, (as he himself states), although he is the instrument through which those advanced souls come en rapport with the medium. Spirit Ballou, then, is a medium on the spirit side of life, connecting the higher spheres of thought and action with the mortals yet in the form. In order that there may be no misunderstanding, the guides always state whether they are giving their own personal views or merely repeating the thoughts of others.

In the earlier years of her mediumship, Cora was controlled by many different spirits, the first one being her mother's oldest sister, who wrote the communication on the slate while Cora was preparing her composition, to which event we have already referred. After Spirit Ballou, or "Augustus," as he was familiarly called by Cora's family, became the leader of the controls around her, nearly all communications were given by him and Ouina, in the deep trance state, for the purpose of protecting the medium against all inimical magnetic forces, as well as from such physical exhaustion as might follow heterogeneous controlling of her organism. On several occasions later in life strong individualities have been permitted to control her for specific purposes. Abraham Lincoln, J. A. Garfield, H. W. Beecher, and a few others, who were interested in political and social reforms, were permitted to act in their individual capacities, as controlling influences.

We have found it difficult to trace year by year the early history of our subject, for the records were imperfectly kept, and the subject matter must be of necessity largely made up from the personal reminiscences of her friends and immediate relatives. We have taken pains to verify every statement made, hence our readers can rest assured that what is given in this chapter is an accurate statement of facts, which is far more important, in our estimation, than platitudes and an exhaustive recount of incidentals and unimportant details.

We here introduce extracts from a few letters from Cora's relatives concerning her early life. So many of the parties connected with the events of those important years, 1851-1856, have passed to spirit life, that many interesting circumstances relative to her childhood cannot be obtained. These letters show the esteem in which she was then, and is now, held by her kindred who know her best, hence love her most.

Her Aunt Louisa Vreeland writes, under date of October 15, 1890, as follows :

"My father and mother (Cora's grandparents) were members of the Baptist Church for some years, but it was too close for their liberal views, and they began going to the meetings of the Free Will Baptists. They became acquainted with an Elder Folsom, who held meetings at the Cadytown school house, who was called a 'Patchinite.' *   *   *

"Our folks, also Cora's parents, attended his meetings, and when her parents moved to Wisconsin, the Folsoms went with them, and the Elder's daughters, three in number, all became mediums. It was by the raps given through the mediumship of Lucina Folsom that myself and husband became converted to Spiritualism."

"Cora's mother was also a good medium. I have heard her when controlled by Lorenzo Dow, give the circle a good scolding for not being punctual at the time the meeting should have been called to order. She was also controlled by an Indian girl, who always gave us good advice in a most enjoyable manner. *   *   *
Cora's mother was much respected in the neighborhood, for she was ever ready to lend a help-

ing hand in time of need, and to do a neighborly
kindness for any one who sought a favor at her
hands.   Cora's father was just as ready and
willing to do for his friends and neighbors as was
his wife.   When he passed away, I have heard
Cora state that she saw his spirit as it took its
flight.   *   *   *   Her childhood was largely
spent in Cuba.   As she went to Hopedale, Massachusetts, at an early age, thence West, I am unable to give any particulars of her girlhood
years."

"Later, I know she was controlled by a German physician, who wrought many wonderful
cures.   One of these cures was that of George
Keller, who had a consumptive cough, of which
he could not be cured by the old school physicians.   He had had this cough for some time,
and could get no relief until Cora treated him
for it.   The result of her treatment was Mr. K's
complete recovery.   She also treated my mother,
who was an invalid for some years, and always
gave relief by simply making passes over her.

"We used to sit with Cora at the stand and get
the so-called spirit raps, by means of which we
heard from our friends on the other side.   Many
people scoffed at us, and said we were deluded,
but we let them alone and continued to partake
of the Bread of Life.   Perhaps Lewis and I
were prejudiced in favor of Cora's mediumship,
for the traveling was never so bad but what

Lewis would take his team and go many miles to hear her. I hope she will remain with us many years yet on this earth, as an instrument for the spirit world to work through."

The perusal of these excerpts from her Aunt Louisa's letter, shows very plainly the high esti- mate that was placed, by her relatives, upon her work in these early years. Reminiscences of one's childhood are hard to obtain at any time, in view of the fact that each one feels that an- other can do much better than he or she can, in writing up the events of another's life. So, in this instance, we have had to depend solely upon such reminiscences as have been voluntarily offered by those who were most intimate with Cora during her earlier years. Volumes could be written, without doubt, if we could but obtain the data connected with her childhood from all of those who knew her. This is impossible, as many of them have gone to Spirit life.

It is well at this point to state that one of her teachers, Luthan Hammond by name, now resid- ing in Corry, Pennsylvania, states that he never saw a pupil of such a peculiar disposition as Cora's was, when she attended his school. She was extremely diffident, yet she never seemed to be obliged to study her lessons as other scholars did, but could recite page after page, and lesson after lesson, as readily as if she had committed them to memory, although he was aware of the

fact that she had not glanced at her book.   This
rare intuitive power was but an index of the
wonderful mediumship that came to her later.

Another aunt, Mrs. Jerusha Vreeland, writes
October 21st, 1890, as follows :

"I know that Cora was controlled by an unseen power at a very early age.   She was thought,
by many people, at that time, to be a great
wonder.   I know for one, while in my family
and only a mere child she would be amusing herself around the yard or veranda, when she would
suddenly be controlled by this unseen power and
give us a beautiful message from some one of
the spirit friends who had gone on before.   She
had no college education ; it was something more
than of this earth, and every one who was attracted to her by these messages were made
happy by their receipt, and not infrequently became Spiritualists."

Another relative :

"Cora's grandfather, Scott, was a native of
Vermont.   He was a Methodist in his early life,
but was so liberal in his views that the church
refused to fellowship with him, also with his wife,
who kept pace with his progressive views. None
of his children were ever church members, and
the only religion taught them was truthfulness,
honesty, charitableness and to do right.   One of
her grandfather's sayings was, ' If you would not
do a person any good, do him no harm.'   His

wife was more or less of a medium, although her powers were then imperfectly understood. She would be told in her dreams what to do, and many a time has been known to awaken her husband in the night to go to the sick, sometimes at great distances. Sometimes she saved the lives of those who were pronounced incurable by the regular physicians.

" Cora's father was considered one of the best mathematicians of the day. After his parents moved to Cuba, New York, he found employment as a book-keeper in one of the village stores, where he remained several years."

"David Scott, Jr.'s early married life was spent in Cuba, where four children were born to him and his good wife, Lodensa, who was very religious. The doctrine to which she was attached was taught by Reverends Patchen and Folsom, who were known as Patchinites; but after Cora's wonderful mediumship was discovered, from a long-faced church member the mother became a cheerful, happy-faced Spiritualist. Her father was a very eccentric man — liberal, just, and charitable. He was never so poor that his doors were not open to all needy people. When Cora was quite young, the family removed to Wisconsin. When she returned as a medium, it caused a great sensation, as it was beyond anything the people had ever seen or heard. Her relatives were nearly all convinced of spirit control by seeing how her powers were used by the unseen forces. Her eloquence and thoughts were far beyond anything that was taught in any of the schools or colleges, or in any branch of science in those days. Many remarkable prophecies were given by her when a child, that have since been fulfilled. People were often so excited that her relatives were obliged to collect around her to guard her from insult and injury. There was so much excitement in public places that her Uncle Abel Scott having completed a new barn, arranged for her to speak there so that she could be better protected. Her meetings were always attended by throngs of people, from far and near, who came to listen to the great wonder of the day.

"It was soon discovered that there were several mediums in the family besides Cora. Her grandmother, her aunts Olive, Catherine and Cordelia, and her Uncle Edwin being among the number. Cora's teachings resulted in the conversion of the whole Scott family, and a great many people in the surrounding towns."

In connection with the lives of Cora's parents, her brother, Mr. E. T. Scott, writes as follows : "Our father started to Hopedale, Massachusetts, with our family, from Cuba, New York, April 1, 1851, to join a general stock community, members of which styled themselves 'Practical Christians' or 'Non-Resistants.' I think father's attention was called to this community by a notice of their organ, 'The Practical Christian' in the New York Tribune, to which paper father was a constant subscriber. After a short correspondence with Rev. Adin Ballou, the founder, he decided to move to Hopedale. Having previously visited the West, particularly the State of Wisconsin, his mind was constantly recurring to its broad and fertile lands, and frequent comparisons with the sterility of New England soil, as well as other incidents, induced him to move to that State. We started in August, 1851, going from Buffalo, New York by the Great Lakes. We reached Wisconsin sometime in September, and located on a farm nine miles from Lake Mills, where we lived one year. It was during our sojourn on this farm that Cora's mediumship commenced. Her first meetings at Lake Mills, commenced in the early part of the Winter of 1852-3, and continued until the following Spring. These meetings were reported by our father, but I have not the records at hand, hence my own impressions would be irrelevant to your proposed biography, unless I had these records in father's hand to refer to."

Mrs. Mary Morgan, Nov. 28, 1890, feelingly refers to Cora's girlhood in a most interesting manner, hence we have introduced the letter intact.

"My first recollections of Cora Scott were

soon after she was three years of age; when one
day she came to school with her brother, and I
think after that she came every day, and from
that time until she was nine years old, or nearly
ten, she attended school in this district (North
Cuba) and was considered one of the best
scholars of her age, in her classes. It is but
just to say, however, that when she left school
she was, by education, in no wise prepared
to address an audience, or anything like it.
* * * One peculiarity of Cora's childhood
days was her extreme sensitiveness and liability
to cry. She was also quite given to mirthful-
ness, so that tears and smiles were often very
near each other. As a scholar in school, she
gave her teachers no trouble. I do not remember one instance where she was ever found contending with any scholar in an unpleasant manner. On one occasion only, she strove for and
won, the prize in her class, which she gave to a
girl who had but one arm. The last winter
term in our school, she and I sat together at the
same desk, and I listened with admiration to her
recitations, and her rapid improvement in reading was gratifying. She visited me often, remaining two or three weeks sometimes, and was
much loved by every member of our family.
When she returned to this place, from Wisconsin, her friends here hastened to the school house
when they learned that she was to be there on a

certain evening. * * * No one outside of her father had ever seen her enter the trance state, and one can readily imagine what her audiences must have been in the matter of curiosity to see how the thing was done. An opposing party, led by Rev. I. B. Sharp, a Universalist minister, was on the ground. This gentleman had gained a hearing in this place, because many of the people had outgrown their belief in hell and damnation. He was considered one of the best possible scholars in this neighborhood, but Cora in her trance state confounded him immediately by quoting scripture readily, and defeated him utterly. This sent conviction to the consistent hearers, for they saw something beyond Cora's ability to enable her to engage in such a discussion. * * * In Cora's childhood days, we saw nothing in her to make us think she was different from other intelligent and lovable children. If there was anything, we were not sufficiently unfolded ourselves to discover it. We only saw a difference, as one child essentially differs from other children, in that no two are exactly alike. When I think of her now as she came to school the first time tenderly and carefully led by her brother, who was very proud of ''Sis,'' as he called her, I can think just how she looked with her little face framed in her pink and white sun-bonnet, her cheeks vying in their pink glow with the color of that bonnet, and her fair hair almost as white as the white in the same. I am led to wonder if there are any today among the dear little children in our schools who will be unfolded as she has been."

Mrs. T. C. Gaston, of Meadville, Pa., a cousin of Mrs. David W. Scott, was acquainted with Cora in her childhood, and speaks of her in terms of impartial, discriminative praise. Mrs. Gaston says: "Cora was a very bright scholar, and did not seem to have to study her lessons at all. She attended my brother's school for a time and I remember hearing him say, when I was a very little girl, that he never saw such a remarkable scholar as Cora was. 'She seems to take her lessons in without studying,' were his exact words. I remember that I wondered what it was to 'take lessons in without studying.' Cora was quite diffident and much given to crying, not especially attractive in appearance, but she was particularly so in her scholarship, yet she was not very precocious for her years. When she moved to Hopedale, Miss Ballou, a half sister of Spirit Ballou, who controls her, was her teacher, and wrote very glowing accounts of Cora or Cora-linn, as she was then called, by us in our New York home. Miss Ballou said that she had the best organism for public speaking she ever knew a child to possess. They had some little theatricals in the school in which Cora took part.

Cousin David wrote of her success in them and how much she was made of by all the friends in Hopedale. All of her teachers thought her quite remarkable in her studies. They said she would make her mark some day. She was most amiable and pleasant in all her ways in school and was very well behaved. I heard first of her mediumship when she was about thirteen years old. She was then living in Wisconsin. We all thought her mediumship wonderful, and after we heard of it we began sitting by ourselves. Her mother was a very religious woman, and when she was asked why she did not go to see and hear the spirit rappings, she replied: 'If there is anything in them they will come to me; if we need them they will certainly be given us.'

"While her people were living in Wisconsin, six members of the family passed to spirit life—her father, her grandparents, an aunt, an uncle and a cousin. Cora and her Aunt Minerva (who was only three or four years older than Cora) took all the care of the invalids, and, strange to relate, remained perfectly well through it all. This I consider remarkable, as the disease was cholera. Cora's mother was ill at the time, but recovered and remained in the form until about the year 1869.

"I first heard Cora lecture when she was a young girl in short dresses, but did not hear her again until about the time she came to Meadville,

Pa. I always thought her addresses above the average ; her literary works I consider very able. My brother-in-law, Mr. A. B. Gaston, considers her book, ' The Soul,' one of the ablest works he ever read, and I have heard this same opinion passed upon her works by others equally competent to judge."

Dr. E. C. Hyde, an eminent physician, of Lily Dale, Chautauqua county, N. Y., who was born and reared in Friendship, N. Y., about five miles from Cora's birthplace, gives some very interesting reminiscences of her early life :

"I can remember distinctly the great sensation caused by Cora when she was first brought out as a medium. We thought she was influenced by Satan, the Evil One himself, and that evil spirits had taken possession of her to make her talk and act as she did. The first anecdote of interest that I remember was when she was about three or four years of age, when her mother first permitted her to go about alone. They lost her for some little time, and discovered her on an island in the middle of the river that flows through Cadytown. No one knew how she got there, as the river was too wide for her to ford it, and there was no boat nor log, nor anything else by which she could have crossed over alone. How she could have reached that island was a mystery to every one until the phenomena of Spiritualism came to unlock the mystery. In my

opinion she was carried there by unseen forces.*
She was first brought to my notice as a medium
by a good old man whom we all called Uncle
Sherman. Her appearance created great excitement, and people would drive forty miles to hear
her. Some of them were ministers, lawyers and
doctors, who came to confound her and to exor-
cise the evil spirit controlling her, but they always
went back with their mouths shut. They could
say nothing at all."

" Precepta Ann Austin, who afterward became
my brother's wife, used to sit with Cora at the
table, where they received raps and tippings.
They could not get men enough to hold the table
down. At one time the weight of the men upon
the table broke it into small pieces. The power
was so strong that Miss Austin was frightened so
that she let Spiritualism alone for a time and
joined the Methodist church, but she afterward
became an outspoken Spiritualist ; in fact, both
girls were so frightened for a time that neither
of them would go into dark rooms alone.

" I did not know where to place this influence
that controlled Cora at first. I remember having
a very peculiar feeling the first time I ever heard
her speak. It was an uncanny, wierd sensation

*This must have been confounded by Dr. Hyde with an in-
cident that took place in Lake Mills, Wis , shortly after Cora's
development as a medium, the circumstances being as related
by the doctor, except that the island and lake were in Wisconsin.—ED.

that troubled me not a little while I was listening to her, but passed away as soon as I was out of her sight, leaving me crazy to hear her again. She converted many people to Spiritualism, and her meetings had the effect of emptying nearly every church in Friendship and North Cuba, and the towns in the vicinity of the place where she lived.

"She was always held in the very highest esteem, and is yet, by all of the people in that section where we were born. She is a pure, true, noble woman, and one of the best teachers we have upon the platform."

As a fitting close to these reminiscences of her early years, we here introduce a letter from Mrs. Abbie E. Heywood, daughter of Rev. Adin Ballou, and half sister of A. A. Ballou, Cora's leading control. This letter shows the deep interest taken in our subject by the Ballou family, and the sincere affection they entertained for her. This letter is too valuable to be omitted, hence we give it intact, although portions of it would apply in other connections in this work of ours. These opinions of Mrs. Heywood's will be read with interest when our readers peruse the subsequent pages to which her references would apply in regard to her literary work and the discourses that have come from her brother, A. A. Ballou.

STERLING, March 14, 1894.

DEAR MR. BARRETT :

In response to yours of March 2, I will say, I shall be glad to serve you to the best of my ability ; but exactness of detail I cannot supply as I have no means of securing the data required. My impression is that Cora came to Hopedale with with her parents first, when about ten or eleven years of age. At that time an interest in the subject of Spiritualism was beginning to be felt in the community from various rumors of what was transpiring in distant places, which deepened when unaccountable sounds, table movings, and the playing upon musical instruments, by unseen hands, became more or less common in their own midst. Thus the spirit of investigation was aroused, and many were led to inquire what all these signs meant.

It so happened that her parents, with Cora, were guests at my father's, on her arrival at Hopedale, and she and I occupied the same bed. While she was quietly sleeping, what was my surprise to hear raps upon the headboard ! I became quite excited and curious to know if she were, indeed, a medium for spirits. I began to call the alphabet, when distinct, unmistakable raps, at certain letters, assured me that such was the case. The names of two brothers, long before called hence, and several friends were spelled out. It was a revelation to me, and I hoped something might come of it to verify the statement beyond a doubt, that the departed spirit can and does return to those clad in mortal form, to bless, guide and guard them in the walks of time.   But in the morning I reported what I had heard to her mother and to my parents. They did not question the correctness of my report; but her mother was evidently disturbed by it and urged me to say no more about it, as it would make her timid if no other harm came of it. Thus the matter was dropped, and of her mediumship I knew no more till some time after her people returned to New York, when the slate writing in the arbor occurred, purporting to come from her aunt, and her subsequent development as a healing physician found a place in the public journals.   Of course I was greatly interested, and on her mother's second visit to Hopedale, soon after her father's decease, made many inquiries as to the reliability of what had reached us concerning her wonderful gift, not only to have that confirmed to our minds, but other evidences of Spiritual agency, brought strikingly before us.

As I recall her, a little girl in my school, for several months, nothing so impresses itself upon my mind as her recitations of pathetic, sacred poetry.   I especially remember her rendering of the little poem, "We Are Seven," so touchingly spoken as to invest the sweet lines with a significance unfelt before, even by those familiar with its words. Tears filled to overflowing the eyes of those in attendance, and I felt that back of all the spoken utterance was a rare inspiration that was prophetic of a future yet to be revealed. My brother Augustus was a pupil, and later, a teacher at the Bridgeport Normal School, when Cora was first in Hopedale, and also, when Hopedale people were alive with the newness of Spiritualism. He had little knowledge of what was then transpiring in respect to it, being engrossed in study. I never knew of his expressing any positive opinion in regard to it. Personally he had had no opportunity to test its merits or its actuality, and soon after he entered into that light, which became knowledge. My father, always open to conviction when any new truth, even in the seeming, presented itself for his consideration, lost no occasion for examining the claims put forth for Spiritualism, and for verifying, so far as he could, that which purported to come from the unseen realm. The final result of his investigations he summed up in his work on "Spirit Manifestations," which, late in life, he declared to be in all essentials his abiding faith. In respect to the hopes he cherished for his son, I would say they were heaven-high, as were his own. He would have him a bright and shining example of christian excellence, a true disciple of Christ. His great aim was that his time, talent and mental culture should be devoted to the same philanthropic objects which his own long and noble life had sought before all else. Just before he was called to leave this world, my father had in view "The Hopedale Home School," which should be based on the loftiest principles of moral excellence, comprehensive in its scope, largely philanthropic, and withal should stand as high intellectually as any institution in the land. Over this my brother was to preside as the ruling genius. I might enlarge, but have only time to indicate the course marked for one, whom I am sure, could any have filled so exalted a position, he would have been equal to it. You well know these ardent hopes were blasted when the dear son passed to other scenes of activity. The summons were sudden and the event saddening beyond words, to both my parents ; but, with beautiful trust, they came to accept God's will as their own. The discourses and messages which have purported to come from my brother, as the central control, through Cora, have always had an unusual interest for us, some of them containing passages so strikingly like himself as to need no other confirmation of their origin. He was, like his father, practically alive to philanthropic pursuits, and that this element still characterizes his efforts I can never question; could we have mingled freely, I feel that our communion would have been attended with many choice benedictions.

Her book, "The Soul and Its Embodiments," is rich in suggestion, and when it receives the necessary study required to its understanding, opens a new realm of thought and has a most expanding influence over the reader. I shall anticipate the next volume on the same theme. Its publication, and also the biography, I doubt not will be a valuable acquisition to our Spiritual literature.

Wishing that your request might have been met with a more satisfactory reply, I am,

Yours most cordially,

ABBIE B. HEYWOOD.

CHAPTER II.

WE now invite the attention of our readers to a movement that antedates Modern Spiritualism some years, yet is directly connected with the ethical and religious teachings of it. We refer to the Hopedale Colony, established by the late Rev. Adin Ballou, in the town of Milford, Massachusetts, in the year 1841.

Mr. Ballou was a relative of Rev. Hosea Ballou, one of the founders of Universalism, hence a devoted Universalist in his religious belief, and an able expounder of the doctrines of his church. His mind was too broad to be kept within sectarian boundaries, and his philanthropic spirit soon led him to consider the welfare of his fellowmen as his own. He was an extensive teacher, a deep, logical thinker, possessed of an indomitable will, remarkable courage, and was strikingly original in thought upon every question presented to him.

Mr. Ballou was twice married. Two children, a daughter, now Mrs. Wm. S. Heywood, and a son, the late A. A. Ballou, were the fruits of these unions.

When March 31st, 1848, ushered in the famous "Rochester knockings" whose sounds soon echoed around the world, Rev. Adin Ballou heard them first in amazement, then gladly, because of the revelations of truth which they gave him. He made a most careful investigation of every phase of manifestation presented to him, and was soon convinced that Modern Spiritualism was a truth. He led his wife and children into the seance room, where they, too, were all convinced of the truth of its claim. It is but fair to state that Mr. Ballou's mind was thoroughly prepared for the coming of Spiritualism, and the principles underlying his Hopedale Colony will show our readers that he was far in advance of his age on every question then before the people. Mr. Ballou did not hesitate to proclaim his convictions of the truth of Spiritualism, and contributed valuable articles on the subject to the "Gospel Banner," and other Universalist journals.

In June, 1852, only a few weeks after the transition of his only son, he published a book entitled, "Spirit Manifestations," in which he takes strong ground in favor of Spiritualism, and proves its claims, both by the finest logic and by citing phenomena of the most convincing character. Of his first communications with the Spirit world, he speaks in his "Spirit Manifestations," as follows :

"First, they came to me through a medium
morally incapable of intentional deceit, who was
unconscious of originating the ideas or any volition to express them in writing, but that simultaneously the ideas were strongly impressed on
her mind and written out with her hand by a
spiritual intelligence, distinct from and superior
to her own.   Second, that I have no good reason
to doubt the *substantial genuineness* of the communications, but many for accepting them as
entirely reliable ; yet, that, so long as there remains even a possibility of the contrary, I have
to confess a frequently rising anxiety to receive
some absolute demonstration.   Third, I am
wholly unconscious of originating a single idea
in these communications, and cannot see one
particle of evidence for believing that they were
psychologically derived from my own mind, as
many of the ideas are unlike any that I had
previously formed, and those fundamental ones
in which my son was educated by me are expressed as independently as he ever *could* have
uttered them had he remained in the form."

This book should be in the library of every
Spiritualist for two reasons—first, its own value
as a literary work ; second, the fact that it was
one of the earliest, if not the earliest book published in behalf of Spiritualism, hence it is an
important historical work.   In this book Mr.
Ballou cites many instructive communications

that he received from his son Augustus. Within one week after his son's transition, and before the Scott family had heard of the sad event, Augustus Ballou controlled Cora Scott for the first time. This was in March, 1852, but Cora's mediumship had come to her the previous autumn.

Mr. Ballou was thoroughly conscientious in all of his views, and as constantly sought to instil them unto the minds of his children. He looked upon his son as his successor in his work at Hopedale, and had him most carefully educated at the best schools in Massachusetts. The boy was an apt student and made rapid progress in all of his studies. He accepted his father's views in all of their essential features, although his quick eye did not fail to observe the small cloud in the distance that was destined to overthrow his father's most cherished hope — the colony.

In the autumn of 1850, Mr. Scott visited Hopedale in response to an invitation from Mr. Ballou, with whom he had been for some time corresponding. He was much pleased with what he saw and determined to unite his fortunes with those of the Hopedale Colony. Accordingly, in the spring of 1851, Mr. Scott, with his family, moved to Massachusetts with the full intention of remaining there ; but the limited amount of land owned by the colonists, and the

indicated rapid growth of the settlement, led
Mr. Scott to suggest to Mr. Ballou the necessity
of forming a colony on the same basis in one of
the Western States.   As Mr. Scott had visited
Wisconsin previously, he was led to suggest that
State as the one in which the western Hopedale
should be located.   Mr. Ballou left the matter
entirely to the judgment of Mr. Scott, who
moved to Wisconsin in the autumn of 1851,
traveling *via* the Great Lakes, in company with
Captain Pratt, to whom we have already referred
in a former chapter.

During the summer of 1851, in Hopedale, A.
A. Ballou, then a boy of eighteen years, was
home from school, and on one occasion only did
he look upon the face of Cora Scott.   This was
in his father's garden, into which Cora had been
sent to play and to gather some currants for her
mother.   Young Ballou chanced to pass through
the garden where he saw Cora industriously filling her basket with the ripe fruit from the cur-
rant bushes.   He spoke kindly to her, and was
most amazed when he saw the child flee away
like a frightened deer and disappear before his
very eyes.   He never saw Cora with his mortal
vision again, for, as we have already stated, her
parents took her to Wisconsin the following
autumn.

During the winter of 1851-52, young Ballou
was taken seriously ill, and on the 8th of March,

1852, went up to his immortality. His transition was a terrible blow to his father, and affected every member of the colony as a personal bereavement. It was, indeed, hard to see a young life so full of promise, so suddenly shut out forever, and would have been a cruel blow had not the Infinite had designs for a future work for this bright young spirit. As we have already stated, Augustus was an apt scholar, a fine logician and an eloquent orator. He was argumentative, and always had a good reason for everything he said or did. He possessed an even temper and never allowed himself to be worried by the annoyances incident to every-day life. He was deeply sympathetic, kind and obliging to all whom he met, and made friends wherever he went. He was especially fitted to be a leader in reform work, and his great ambition to be of service to others endeared him to all classes alike. We shall see how this gifted spirit continued to progress in the Spirit world, doing faithfully the work of reform in which he had intended to engage had he remained on earth; therefore, his work was not estopped by his transition, but only changed so that enlarged opportunities for doing good were opened unto him. What these enlarged opportunities were we shall see as we study the work of our subject.

Adin Bailou read with much interest accounts of the experiments of Robert Owen and George

Ripley, studied Fourier, and carefully investigated the teachings of John Humphrey Noyes, the founder of the Oneida Community in New York, and Wallingford, Connecticut.

He recognized that these movements, especially Owen's and the Brook Farm, had each a modicum of truth at its foundation, but he also saw their defects. He then set himself to the task of remedying these defects by building upon the truth in a way that would avoid the pitfalls into which these other reformers had fallen. It is not necessary for us to present the arguments by means of which Adin Ballou proved the errors of Fourierism, Owenism and Noyesism, and showed the chimera involved in the beautiful Utopia of the Brook Farm. This, Mr. Ballou had done for himself in his logical and exceedingly interesting work entitled, "Practical Christian Socialism," published in 1854. We have only to deal with the outcome of his studies, and with the effects of his teachings upon his followers.

As soon as he saw that the co-operative principle was the true one, he began to publish a paper setting forth his views, *viz.*: "The Practical Christian." This paper found its way into the home of nearly every Universalist in the United States. As Horace Greeley, of the New York Tribune was a Universalist, and a believer in the principles of "Christian Socialism," as

the new doctrines were called, it is not strange
that copies of "The Practical Christian" found
their way into many homes in company with the
Tribune. At any rate, David W. Scott one day
received a copy of this paper enclosed in the
"New York Tribune." He was deeply interested
in its contents, at once subscribed for it, opened
a correspondence with Mr. Ballou and was his
warm, personal friend ever afterwards.

Mr. Ballou had early perfected his plans to
such an extent as to appeal to the readers of his
paper to join him in establishing a Christian
colony at Milford, Massachusetts. Several families responded to his appeal. Mr. Ballou was
made president of the Colony, and other officers,
peculiar to any village, were also chosen. The
citizens paid State, County and Town taxes, but
they also had their own local government, to
which they felt their allegiance was first due. It
was really an "imperium in imperio."

We shall present the views of Spirit Ballou
upon the effort made by his father at Hopedale,
subjoined to which will be found an interesting
account of Hopedale, from the pen of John
Humphrey Noyes.

"The word, 'Socialism,'" says Spirit Ballou,
in an able lecture in 1890 through Mrs. Richmond, "has come to mean something very different today from what it meant fifty or seventy-
five years ago. It was first discussed in the

early portion of the present century, and the
particular activity in this direction to which I
refer was in the years between 1825 and 1850.
There were at that time many singular elements
that combined to make this activity possible in
the world. The old lines of severe religious
thought and sectarian discipline and monarchial
influence had all become somewhat shaken.
German philosophy was encroaching upon English conservatism and the poetry and literature
of the first quarter of the Nineteenth century
promised to yield a great harvest of reform. The
abolition of slavery was well-nigh accomplished
in all the English colonies, while Shelley and his
contemporary poets were breathing forth their
liberal religious ideas and projecting their reformatory measures, despite the sneers and
ostracism of society, church and state. Between
the year of 1830 and 1840 a *coterie* of brilliant
literary minds received the same impetus from
this liberal thought. In the East there was a
movement toward the solution of the problem of
social life in the communistic idea. We do not
mean French Communism, nor the Socialism of
Germany, nor the Red Republicanism that demanded the blood of all ruling classes, but in
the kind of intellectual social life which Margaret
Fuller introduced that enabled her to gather
around her the brilliant minds of that period,
when Horace Greeley was the literary, socialistic

and reform editor of the New York Tribune, all
of whom seemed to have anticipated a half or
even a full century of growth by leaping forward
to the fulfillment of it.

" It was under the stimulus of these intellectual ideas that Adin Ballou, though not a college
graduate, a disciple of the then unpopular Universalist religion, appeared upon the scene of
his destined labors. He knew of the Shakers
and their work, and he believed their utter
seclusion and social ideas were wholly at variance with the natural requirements of mankind.
He also knew about other communistic movements and found them lacking in some essentials,
yet he felt that somewhere there must be found
an absolute basis of true life. Without being
bigoted in any degree, he was a thorough student
of the Sermon on the Mount and the Golden
Rule. The prevailing thought which took possession of his mind, even while he was still in
the twenties, was the practicability of the
Golden Rule. He believed it possible to live the
life and carry forward the teachings of Christ
the Exemplar, and he believed that had it not
been possible that the life could be lived, and
these teachings made practicable, Jesus would
never have come into the world. However mistaken in the period of time in which these
things could be generally applied, he certainly
was not inconsistent in supposing that all who

accepted Christ as their Exemplar were bound
to illustrate those teachings in their lives. So
from being equally a Universalist and reformer
in many ways, as he early espoused the cause of
the abolition of slavery, he grew into something
more, a practical Christian.

"The thought entered his mind and finally
absorbed his entire nature, which he opened to a
few of his friends, of an associated life in which
practical christianity could be demonstrated as
the essential principle of life. He knew all
about church history and church organizations,
but he believed in none of them. As the first
basis of this practical christianity he adopted
the principle of non-resistance to evil, *i. e.*, non-
resistance by force. He was an essential non-
resistant; he believed in the advocacy of a
cause; but he believed in no violence to overcome a wrong. He accepted as the basis of
life, the absolute nature of truth, and that even
though the human mind is obscured in its acceptance of truth, the truth itself is not only final,
but an absolute perception of it is possible. He
believed also in the essential responsibility of
each individual according to his or her life and,
replacing the responsibility from church, and
state, and society, upon the individual, he made
each one's moral nature responsible unto itself
for the highest good. He believed that upon
this basis social reform was possible, and he be-

lieved to the fullest extent in the final triumph of these principles in the world.

"When you consider that the nation was then struggling, or the advanced minds of the nation, with the problem of human slavery ; when you consider that not one of the social reforms now being carried forward, had a foothold in the predominating thought of this country ; when you consider that not until ten, fifteen, or twenty years later was there anything resembling a perception of modern Spiritualism in the world— albeit he was one of the first to recognize its presence—you will not think it strange that such a mind that could seize upon these absolute principles and bear them forward into practical life is certainly deserving of the name of sage, possibly prophet. The fact that in the midst of the first half of the nineteenth century a dream could be dreamed and partially realized which would nearly express the fulfillment of the christian prophecy, and would solve all the problems of life, was certainly a noticeable fact, a fact prophetic for the world.

"The dreamer of this dream was Adin Ballou and he called his little community Hopedale, which expressed his aspirations. A few people, some of whom were practical business men, conceived the idea of establishing a community of social interests by abrogating all individual titles to property, by refusing in any way to partici-

pate in a government that sustained a standing
army, or forcibly taxed its people, by living individually pure lives, by preserving the sanctity of
the family altar, but making all financial enter-
prises and monetary affairs co-operative or general only.   At first the community lived, as there
were but few families, in one dwelling, a unitary
home.   After the numbers increased the families
had separate dwellings, but no separate land or
property interests.   The financial affairs were
managed for the benefit of the whole by those
who had ability in that direction, while the thinking and teaching were done by those who had
ability in those directions.   It is needless to say
that Adin Ballou was the thinker and teacher, as
he was the founder essentially of this practical
scheme for carrying forward the religious teachings of Practical Christian Socialism.   At first
there were small industries carried on in common.   Then came a scarcity of land.   Then it
was deemed advisable for some one to go into
the Western States to see if more lands, which
would open up a better field of industry for the
young people, could be procured.

"Adin Ballou led the minds of this little community for nearly two generations.   But the
younger lives heard the rumblings of the world
outside, the world of excitement, turmoil and
struggle ; they felt the limitations of the small
existence and the narrow opportunities that were

theirs, and the second and third generations gradually fell away. Mammon was all around, in the
outer world the government with its system of
forcible laws came, and took by force, what was
required from those peaceable people, they
never giving and never resisting ; and when at
last it was found that the steadily encroaching
tide of individual experience took away the
younger life, it was also found that even in the
assistance which the business minds in the community rendered and in which they endeavored
to be impartial, there was always the result that
a certain portion of power which profit brought
seemed to go into their hands. Gradually the
society became indebted to individuals thus aiding financially, and gradually these individuals
absorbed the possessions of the association.
Although Adin Ballou saw this with ever increasing sadness, he still maintained and believed until
the date of his passing away, in the month of
August, 1890, that somewhere and sometime this
dream would be realized.

"There never was an officer of the law required at Hopedale ; there never was anything
that partook of the nature of violence or disturb-
ance ; no one ever stole anything ; no crime was
ever committed there ; the moral atmosphere of
the place pervaded even those who came to sneer
and scoff" (an anticipation evidently of Cassadaga Camp). "Hopedale was in the world many

years ahead of its time, a day-dream, a blossom, an illustration of what will come. Undoubtedly, had Hopedale been sufficiently successful to have flushed Adin Ballou with consciousness of fulfillment ; had there been a sufficient number to have borne forward the enterprise to financial success under the system then adopted, of unitary capital ; had there been anything other than the peaceful and delightful moral influence and the wonderful integrity of the people who clustered there, probably the world would not see the fulfillment of that prophecy so soon as now. Could it have crystalized into a living form of thought, if even in a limited extent, it could have gone forward, yet not have swept out into the world, could there have been any worldly prosperity attained, or could there have been a sufficient number of people imbued with the stern asceticism and absolute enthusiasm of the founder, very likely they would have become separated from the rest of mankind and crystalized, possibly, into a perfect moral community, but not bearing the fruitage thereof unto the world.

"Adin Ballou's life was the best illustration of his principles. It was not so much what he did for others, although he imbued them with such hope and promise, as it was the sincerity and integrity of his purpose from beginning to end. While he experienced two severe disappointments there was still in the latter part of his life a serenity and calmness, a great activity in good deeds, a social influence, a widespread moral influence that more than compensated for the two disappointments. The first great disappointment was that Hopedale did not yield the results which he had expected. Had he been a little more of a prophet, he would have known from the beginning that it could not. The second disappointment was that his son was taken into spirit life at the age of nineteen, when he had fondly hoped that that son would be his successor to carry forward the plans which he had in view. Had the son remained on earth, however, Adin Ballou would have been doomed to a still greater disappointment; for even at that early age it was visible to the son's mind that the world was not ready for that social plan; that the life inaugurated and incorporated there was for another period of human history, was for a race of people that had not yet passed through the primary discipline leading to such result; that not for realization, but for prophecy, an individual illustration, did Adin Ballou come into the world at that particular time. He bore his disappointments as all great natures must; peacefully and camly, without bitterness; but the essential hope, the essential ardor, and the efficient progress of his life hope ceased at the failure of the colony.

"The fact that in such an age a society could exist without law, without officials, without a

creed, without a ritual or form of any kind, only
that which connected them by principle, which
was based upon the highest standard of human
thought, is surely a divine prophecy, and there
are not many persons in the world today who are
clearly penetrated by this essential light. There are
in all the nations of the world, especially in this
nation, people who lean towards the same ideas,
who long for them with outstretched hands, who
look toward the future for their fulfillment, who
under various names that bear reproach, or honor,
are leading the world to the realization of what
that fulfillment is, *i. e.*, the most wonderful realization of the dream of Adin Ballou. It is better
to have his thought in the world today scattered
broadcast, as it is, existing here and there in
shining, central minds, than one little, peaceful
village, though its inmates were ever so righteous
and happy. The latter would be like the limited
Paradise of the Ancients, light never could radiate from that, but the leaven that is in the world,
the leaven of highest human thought, must go on
until it reaches all the kingdoms of the earth.

"Socialism in its highest, practical, Christian
sense is the abrogation of all individual possessions in any of the common and general things
that belong to the world. Of course each human
being is entitled to his or her individual life, but
to suppose that anything is a possession which
can be had at the expense of another is to put as

a predicate that which is not in the nature of things possible — the individual possessorship of that which is the common inheritance of all, the sunshine and pure air, the earth which you occupy, all things that can and must be shared in common by humanity, must be set aside for the idea of the general possession of all. It was on this basis that the societary interests at Hopedale were founded; but the chief basis was not physical, the external was only secondary or less, and the entire moral nature as a basis was an absolute necessity; the recognition of truth an absolute necessity; the individual illustration of it an absolute necessity; the individual responsibility equally a necessity, and in this way the absolute fulfillment of every duty an obligation in life.

"Of course all people look to the millenium for the fulfillment of these propositions; but between Hopedale and Adin Ballou, and that millenium we have a right to expect as many stages of human progress as will be required to attain their fulfillment. We must be blind morally and spiritually not to see that the present tendency of the world in its highest thought is in that direction more and more as the century goes on. Ultimately there will grow out of the ideas and efforts in the direction of co-operation in the external world, such results morally and spiritually, as will serve as a perfect illustration of the fulfillment of this prophecy of Adin Ballou.

"Truth comes into the world in this manner and comes always to stay ; soon or late, within ten years or ten centuries, it overtakes mankind as its need and proclaims itself in the world. It will not come by patching here and there the present fabric of church, or state, or society, it will come with an absolute and entire change of the social fabric, beginning with the moral responsibility of the individual, which has been wrested from man by false theology, and ending with the solution of the labor and all political questions. The world has well nigh reached the turning point. Ere this century is complete many of the problems now perplexing you will be solved, although nearly two thousand years of christian civilization have signally failed to solve them. Causes not effects must be sounded. The moral basis of this Association, small though it was, will be found to be the keynote that will echo around the world; and although people may cry out for reform in many directions of human injustice and wrong, yet the keynote of all reform will be found in the individual moral growth of the people and there only."

HOPEDALE.

This community was another anticipation of Fourierism, put forth by Massachusetts. It was similar in many respects to Brook Farm, and in its origin nearly contemporaneous. As Brook

Farm was the blossom of Unitarianism, so Hopedale was the blossom of Universalism. Milford, the site of the community, was the scene of Dr. Whittemore's ministerial labors, one of the founders of Universalism.

Hopedale held on its way through the Fourier revival, solitary and independent, and consequently never attained so much public distinction as the Brook Farm and other associations that affiliated themselves with Fourierism; but considered by itself as a Yankee attempt to solve the socialistic problem, it deserves more attention than any of them. Our judgment of it, after some study, may be summed up thus: As it came nearest to being a religious community, so it commenced earlier, lasted longer, and was really more scientific and sensible than any of the other experiments of the Fourier epoch.

Brook Farm was talked about in 1840, but we find no evidence of its organization till the fall of 1841, whereas, Mr. Ballou's community dates its first compact from January, 1841, though it did not commence operations at Hopedale until April, 1842.

The North American Phalanx is reputed to have outlived all other associations of the Fourier epoch; but we find, on closer examination of dates, that Hopedale was not only born before it, but lived after it. The North American commenced in 1843 and dissolved in 1855. Hopedale commenced in 1841, and lasted certainly until 1856 or '57. Ballou published an elaborate exposition of it in the winter of 1854-55, and at that time Hopedale was at its highest point of success and promise. We cannot find the exact date of its dissolution, but it is reported to have attained its seventeenth year, which would carry it to 1858. Indeed it is said there is a shell of an organization there now, which has continued from the community, having a president, secretary, etc., and holding occasional meetings, but its principal function at present is the care of the village cemetery.

As to the theory and constitutional merits of the Hopedale Community, the reader shall judge for himself. Here is an exposition published in tract form by Mr. Ballou in 1851, outlining the scheme which was fully elaborated in his subsequent book:

"This estate they named Hopedale—joining the word 'Hope' to its ancient designation, as significant of the great things they hoped for from a very humble and unpropitious beginning. About the first of April, 1842, a part of the members took possession of their farm, and commenced operations under as many disadvantages as can well be imagined. Their present domain (Dec. 1, 1851), including all the lands purchased at different times, contains about 500 acres. Their village consists of about thirty new dwelling-houses, three mechanic shops, with water-power, carpentering and other machinery, a small chapel, used also for the purpose of education, and the old domicile, with the barns and outbuildings much improved. There are now at Hopedale some thirty-six families, besides single persons, youth and children, making in all a population of about 175 souls.

" It is often asked, What are the peculiarities, and what are the advantages of the Hopedale Community ? Its leading peculiarities are the fo lowing:

" 1. It is a church of Christ (so far as any human organization of professed Christians, within a particular locality, have the right to claim that title), based on a simple declaration of faith in the religion of Jesus Christ, as he taught and exemplified it, according to the Scriptures of the New Testament, and of acknowledged subjection to all the moral obligations of that religion. No person can be a member, who does not cordially assent to this comprehensive declaration. Having given sufficient evidence of truthfulness in making such a profession, each individual is left to judge for him or her self, with entire freedom, what abstract doctrines are taught, and also what external religious rites are enjoined in the religion of Christ. No precise theological dogmas, ordinances or ceremonies are prescribed or prohibited. In

such matters all members are free, with mutual
love and toleration, to follow their own highest
convictions of truth and religious duty, answer-
able only to the great Head of the true Church
Universal. But in practical Christianity this
church is precise and strict. There its essentials
are specific. It insists on supreme love to God
and man—that love which 'worketh no ill' to
friend or foe. It enjoins total abstinence from
all God-contemning words and deeds; all un-
chastity; all intoxicating beverages; all oath-
taking; all slave-holding and pro-slavery compro-
mises; all war and preparations for war; all
capital and other vindictive punishments; all in-
surrectionary, seditious, mobocratic, and personal violence against any government, society,
family or individual; all voluntary participation
in any anti-Christian government, under promise
of unqualified support—whether by doing military service, commencing actions at law, holding
office, voting, petitioning for penal laws, aiding
a legal posse by injurious force, or asking public
interference for protection which can be given
only by such force; all resistance of evil with
evil; in fine, from all things known to be sinful
against God or human nature. This is its acknowledged obligatory righteousness. It does
not expect immediate and exact perfection of its
members, but holds up this practical Christian
standard, that all may do their utmost to reach

it, and at least be made sensible of their shortcomings. Such are the peculiarities of the Hopedale Community as a church.

"2. It is a civil state, a miniature Christian
republic, existing within, peaceably subject to,
and tolerated by the governments of Massachusetts and the United States, but otherwise a
commonwealth complete within itself. Those
governments tax and control its property, according to their own laws, returning less to it
than they exact from it. It makes them no
criminals to punish, no disorders to repress, no
paupers to support, burdens to bear. It asks of
them no corporate powers, no military or penal
protection. It has its constitution, laws, regula-
tions and municipal police, its own legislative,
judiciary and executive authorities; its own
educational system of operations; its own
methods of aid and relief; its own moral and religious safeguards; its own fire insurance and
savings institutions; its own internal arrange-
ment for the holding of property; the management of industry, and the raising of revenue; in
fact, all the elements and organic constituents of
a Christian Republic, on a miniature scale.
There is no Red Republicanism in it, because it
eschews blood; yet it is the seedling of the true
Democratic and Social Republic, wherein neither
caste, color, sex, nor age stands proscribed, but
every human being shares justly in Liberty,

Equality, and Fraternity. Such is the Hopedale Community as a civil state.

" 3. It is a universal, religious, moral, philanthropic, and social reform Association. It is a Missionary Society, for the promulgation of New Testament Christianity, the reformation of the nominal church, and the conversion of the world. It has a moral suasion Temperance Society on the teetotal basis. It is a moral power Anti-slavery Society, radical and without compromise. It is a Peace Society on the only impregnable foundation of Christian non-resistance. It is a sound theoretical and practical Woman's Rights Association. It is a charitable society for the relief of suffering humanity, to the extent of its human ability. It is an educational society, preparing to act an important part in the training of the young. It is a socialistic community successfully actualizing, as well as promulgating, practical Christian socialism— the only kind of socialism likely to establish a true social state on earth. The members of this community are not under the necessity of importing from abroad any of these valuable reforms, or of keeping up a distinct organization for each of them, or of transporting themselves to other places in search of sympathizers. Their own Newcastle can furnish coal for home-consumption, and some to supply the wants of its neighbors. Such is the Hopedale Community

as a Universal Reform Association on Christian
principles.

"What are its advantages?

"1. It affords a theoretical and practical
illustration of the way whereby all human beings, willing to adopt it, may become individually and socially happy. It clearly sets forth
the principles to be received, the righteousness
to be exemplified, and the social arrangements
to be entered into, in order to obtain this happiness. It is in itself a capital school for self-
correction and improvement. Nowhere else on
earth is there a more explicit, understandable,
practicable system of ways and means for those
who really desire to enter into usefulness, peace,
and rational enjoyment. This will one day be
seen and acknowledged by multitudes who now
know nothing of it, or knowing, despise it, or
conceding its excellence are unwilling to bow to
its wholesome requisitions. 'Yet the willing and
obedient shall eat the good of the land.'

"2. It guarantees to all its members and
dependents employment at least adequate to a
comfortable subsistence; relief in want, sickness
or distress; decent opportunities for religious,
moral and intellectual culture; an orderly, well
regulated neighborhood; fraternal counsel, fellowship and protection under all circumstances;
and a suitable sphere of individual enterprise and
responsibility, in which each one may, by due

self-exertion, elevate himself to the highest point
of his capabilities.

"3.   It solves the problem which so long puzzled socialists, the harmonization of just individual freedom with social co-operation.   Here exists
a system of arrangements, simple and effective,
under which all capital, industry, trade, talent,
skill and peculiar gifts may freely operate and˙
co-operate, with no restrictions other than those
which Christian morality everywhere rightfully
imposes, constantly to the advantage of each and
all.   All may thrive together as individuals and
as a community, without degrading or impover-
ishing any.   This excellent system of arrangements in its present completeness is the result of
various and wisely improved experiences.

"4.   It affords a peaceful and congenial home
for all conscientious persons, of whatever religious sect, class or description heretofore, who
now embrace practical Christianity, substantially
as this community holds it, and can no longer
fellowship the popular religionists and politicians.
Such as need sympathy, co-operation and fraternal association, without undue interference in
relation to non-essential peculiarities.   Here they
may find what they need.   Here they may give
and receive strength by rational, liberal Christian
union.

"5.   It affords a most desirable opportunity
for those who mean to be practical Christians in

the use of property, talent, skill or productive
industry, to invest them. Here these goods and
gift may all be employed so as to benefit their
possessors to the full extent -of justice, while
at the same time they afford aid to the less fortunate, help build up a social state free from the
follies of irreligion, ignorance, poverty and vice,
promote the regeneration of the race, and thus
resolve themselves into treasure laid up where
neither moth, nor rust, nor thieves can reach
them. Here property is pre-eminently safe,
useful and beneficent. It is christianized. So,
in a good degree, are talent, skill, and productive industry.

"6. It affords small scope, place or encouragement for the unprincipled, corrupt, supremely
selfish, proud, ambitious, miserly, sordid, quarrel-
some, brutal, violent, lawless, fickle, high-flying,
loaferish, idle, vicious, envious and mischief-
making. It is no paradise for such; unless they
voluntarily make it a moral penitentiary first.
Such will hasten to more congenial localities;
thus making room for the upright, useful and
peaceful.

"7. It affords a beginning, a specimen and
presage of a new and glorious social christendom—
a grand confederation of similar communities—a
world ultimately regenerated and Edenized. All
this shall be in the forthcoming future.

"The Hopedale Community was born in obscurity, cradled in poverty, trained in adversity and has grown to a promising childhood, under the Divine guardianship, in spite of numberless detriments. The bold predictions of many who despised its puny infancy have proved false. The fears of timid and compassionate friends that it would certainly fail have been put to rest. Even the repeated desertion of professed friends, disheartened by its imperfections, or alienated by too heavy trials of their patience, has scarce retarded its progress. God willed otherwise. It has still many defects to outgrow, much impurity to put away, and a great deal of improvement to make—moral, intellectual and physical. But it will prevail and triumph. The Most High will be glorified by making it the parent of numerous progeny of practical Christian Communities. Write, saith the spirit, and let this prediction be registered against the time to come, for it shall be fulfilled."

For a specimen, take the following: Mr. Ballou finds all man's wants, rights and duties in seven spheres, viz.: 1, Individuality; 2, Connubiality; 3, Consanguinity; 4, Congeniality; 5, Federality; 6, Humanity; 7, Universality. These correspond very nearly to the series of spheres tabulated by Comtists. On the basis of this philosophy of human nature, Mr. Ballou proposes not a mere monotony of phalanxes, or commu-

nities all alike, but an ascending series of four
distinct kinds of communities, viz.: 1, the Par-
ochial Community, which is nearly the same as a
common parish church; 2, the Rural Community, which is a social body occupying a distinct
territorial domain, but not otherwise consoli-
dated; 3, the Joint-Stock Community, consoli-
dating capital and labor, and paying dividends
and wages, of which Hopedale itself was a specimen, and 4, the Common-Stock Community,
holding property in common and paying no dividends or wages, which is Communism proper.
Mr. Ballou provides elaborate constitutional
forms for all of these social states, and shows
their harmonious relation to each other. Then
he builds them up into larger combinations, viz.:
1, Communal Municipalities, consisting of the
two or more communities making a town or city;
2, Communal States; 3, Communal Nations, and
lastly, the grand Fraternity of Nations, represented by Senators of the Supreme Unitary
Council. Moreover he embroiders on all this an
ascending series of categories for individual character. Citizens of the great Republic are expected
to arrange themselves in seven circles, viz.: 1,
the Adoptive Circle, consisting of members whose
connections with the world preclude their joining
any integral community; 2, Unitive Circle, consisting of those who join in building up Rural
and Joint-Stock Communities; 3, the Perceptive

Circle, consisting of persons devoted to teaching in any of its branches; 4, the Communistic Circle, consisting of persons devoted to extending the Republic by founding new communities; 6, the Charitive Circle, consisting of the most worthy and reliable counselors—the fathers and mothers of Israel.

This is only a skeleton. In the book all is worked into harmonized beauty. All is founded on religion; all is deduced from the Bible. We confess that if it were our doom to attempt community building by paper programme, we should choose Adin Ballou's scheme in preference to anything we have ever been able to find in the lucubrations of Fourier or Owen.

(Read the preface to Mr. Ballou's elaborate work, Practical Christian Socialism, to find what pure and highly religious tone pervaded his entire system.)

Let it not be thought that Ballou was a mere theorizer. Unlike Owen and Fourier, he worked as well as wrote. Originally a clergyman and a gentleman, he gave up his salary and slaved in the ranks as a common laborer for his cause. In conversation with one who reported to us, he said, that oftentimes in the early days of Hopedale, he would be so tired at his work in the ditch or on the mill-dam, that he would go to a neighboring haystack and lie down on the sunny side of it, wishing that he might go to sleep and never wake again! Then he would recuperate and go back to his work. Nearly all the recreation he had in those days was to go out occasionally into the neighborhood and preach a funeral sermon !

And this, by the way, is a fit occasion to say that in our opinion there ought to be a prohibitory duty on the importation of socialistic theories that have not been worked out as well as written out by the inventors themselves. It is certainly cruel to set vast numbers of simple people agog with Utopian projects that will cost them their all, while the inventors, and promulgators do nothing but write and talk. What kind of a theory of chemistry can a man write without a laboratory? What if Napoleon had written out a programme for the battle of Austerlitz and left one of his aides-de-camp to superintend the actual fighting?

Unlike Fourier and Owen, Mr. Ballou confessed that his experiment was a total failure. Fourier was dogmatic and thought himself infallible, while Owen, after a hundred defeats, never doubted the perfection of his scheme and never fairly confessed a failure. As to the cause of Hopedale's failure, Mr. Ballou accounts for it in the old story of general depravity. The timber he got together was not suitable for building a community. The men and women that joined him were very enthusiastic and commenced with great zeal; their devotion to the cause seemed to be sincere, but they did not know themselves. Mr. Ballou was the first president, and was superseded by E. D. Draper. The latter came to Hopedale with great enthusiasm for the cause. He was a sharp, enterprising, business man, and very soon became the manager of the whole concern. He had a brother associated with him in business who had no sympathy with the communistic enterprise. With this brother Draper became deeply engaged in outside operations, which were very lucrative. They gained wealth by these operations, while the inside interests were gradually falling into neglect and bad management. The community lost money from year to year. Draper bought three-fourths of the joint-stock, and so has local control in his hands. At length he became dissatisfied and went to Mr. Ballou, telling him that this thing must not go on any further. Mr. Ballou asked him if that meant the community must come to an end. He replied, yes. "There is no other way," said Mr. Ballou, "but to submit to it." He then said to Mr. Draper that he had but one condition to put to him. That was that he, Mr. D——, should pay all the debts. Mr. Draper consented, the debts were paid, and thus terminated the Hopedale experiment.

It will be of interest here to subjoin an epitomization of Ballou's principles which led to

the establishment of his Hopedale Community,
by giving brief outlines of his theology, principles of personal righteousness, and social order.
We also adduce the advice which he gives to his
followers, and to the world at large, in his teachings, both from the pulpit and through his pen.
His advice to the world is based upon axiomatic
truths :

1st. "Mankind are by nature social beings."

2nd. "No individual alone possesses all the
capabilities of human nature for happiness."

3d "One individual supplies the deficiencies
of another."

4th. "Individuals can realize the highest
good only when rightly associated."

5th. "In true association, all the essential
interests of individuals and families will be harmonized."

6th. "Such an harmonic order of society is
possible here on earth, and ought to be insti-
tuted."

In order to accomplish these six principles in
life, he advises all men, among other things to—

"Study to be useful. Be diligent and persist-
ent in rational endeavors to enlighten, purify
and elevate yourself, your family, your friend,
your neighborhood, society and the world. Live
the right life at home and among your neighbors.
This will exert the most powerful of influences
in the right direction. Be punctilious in attend-

ing to civil and religious duties as citizens. En-
courage every means of improvement. Look
well to education at home and throughout the
sphere of your usefulness. Make no truce with
ignorance. Be not an obtrusive proselyter, and
yet a faithful commender of truth and righteousness. Surround yourselves liberally with the
finest periodicals, books, pamphlets and other
reading obtainable. Employ, patronize and co-
operate with, your fellowmen in all laudable pursuits. Live peaceably with all mankind, but be
sure to compromise no essential divine principles. Remember, that the better people are,
the nearer they can live comfortably together,
and the worse they are, the farther they must be
kept apart. Remember that a bad neighbor always carries one with him, and never finds a
good neighborhood. Remember that fair talk-
ers and writers often turn out to be very *unfair
doers*. Be modest, unassuming, conciliatory,
reasonable and accommodating. Be just, truthful, frank and reliable. Whatever you promise
or undertake, execute with punctilious fidelity, if
within bounds of possibility. Be yielding to the
last degree in non-essentials, but firm, uncom-
promising and inflexible on all points of absolute
principle; but mistake not your own will or self-
interest for principle. Take care to exemplify
the axiom—'It is more blessed to give than to
receive.' Resolve to impose few burdens on

others and to bear many. Be not a grumbler, croaker or panic-maker. Bear patiently with an excuse of mere weakness and imperfections, but reject unmistakably sins without respect of per-·sons. Cultivate common sense and plain good nature. Govern your animal appetites, and passions, and tongue. Preserve your individuality without magnifying it. Confess frankly and amend honorably your own faults. Stickle not for your own rights and dues in little matters, but be very careful to respect those of others. Finally, do all things and bear all things conscientiously. *Be* what you *profess.*"

We have already referred to his theology, principles of personal righteousness, and of social order, which he has given in his excellent work, "Practical Christian Socialism," in the form of statements made in what would now be termed a "dogmatic manner." We subjoin them in order that our readers may see for themselves the close relationship between the teachings evolved by Ballou from his conceptions of man's duties to his God and to his fellowman, which led him to found his colony at Hopedale and those which have been given through our medium. Upon many of these principles have the wonderful lectures of Spirit A. A. Ballou been based, as he has utted them to the world through the mediumship of Cora L. V. Scott. So marked is their relationship to many of the present expressions of thought among many of the advanced teachers in Spiritualism, that we give them a prominent place in this work, in order that our readers may see that the work of the Ballous has been carried grandly on, to a higher state of perfection by the chosen instrument, who was called to assist them in this work. These principles are as follows:

Principles of Theology.

1. "The existence of one all-perfect, infinite God."

2. "The mediatorial manifestation of God through Christ."

3. "Divine revelations given to men."

4. "The immortal existence of human and angelic spirits."

5. "The moral agency and religious obligations of mankind."

6. "The certainty of a perfect divine retribution."

7. "The necessity of man's spiritual regeneration."

8. "The final universal triumph of good over evil."

Principles of Personal Righteousness.

1. "Reverence for the divine and spiritual."

2. "Self-denial for righteousness sake."

3. "Justice to all things."

4. "Truth to all manifestations of mind."

5. "Love in all manifestations of mind."

6. ''Purity in all things.''

7. ''Patience in all right aims and pursuits.''

8. '' Unceasing progress towards perfection.''

Principles of Social Order.

1. '' The supreme fatherhood of God.''

2. '' Universal brotherhood of man.''

3. '' The declared perfect love of God to man.''

4. '' The required perfect love of man to man.''

5. '' The required just reproof and disfellowship of evil doers.''

6. '' The required non-resistance of evil doers with evil.''

7. '' The designed unity of the righteous.''

Our readers will see that his eight principles of theology can, with a single exception, be accepted by all Spiritualists as axiomatic truths. That exception is the second statement, ''The mediatorial manifestation of God through Christ,'' and even this one, many so-called Christian Spiritualist—whatever that term may mean,— would be willing to accept in toto. It is not our province to discuss this particular point pro and con, but leave to our readers to form their own conclusions in regard to the breadth of thought that dominated Mr. Ballou's mind when formulating the eight general statements of his idea of his own relation to his God.

His Principles of Personal Righteousness carry

with them lessons for all mankind.   Some Spiritualists and perhaps agnostics and materialistic
thinkers would object to the first one, "Reverence for the divine and spiritual;" but the spirits
from the higher realms of thought have taught
us to revere spirituality in all things and to hold
the divinity within every man, woman and child
up in its dignity and grandeur as worthy of the
respect, aye, even of the highest regard, of all
living beings.   If we respect the divinity within,
we revere the conception which we have of the
divine nature implanted within ourselves   Therefore, we feel that even this statement is one that
all Spiritualists could accept by interpreting it,
each one from his own standpoint.

His Principles of Social Order contain the
same trenchant truths, and can be accepted, with
possibly two or three exceptions.   The first statement, in the minds of the majority of Spiritualists, should read: "The supreme fatherhood
and motherhood of the Infinite;" and the third
some would object to as entirely irrelevant, but
upon this point each one must come to his own
conclusions through a process of reasoning peculiar to himself.   The fifth, "The required just
reproof and disfellowship of evil doers," is the
standard of the world today, and really is society's only method of protecting itself from the
injustice of the evil-disposed on this earth; yet,
as Spiritualists we would introduce more of the

thought of forgiveness and the idea of checking and reforming the wrong-doer.

Taken as a whole, however, the twenty-four statements are wonderful prophecies of the coming of Spiritualism, for they antedate it some seven years. Therefore, we consider Adin Ballou to be almost the John the Baptist in Spiritualism in his great work at Hopedale, especially as he based it upon such trenchant truths as those which we are now discussing. Spiritualism took up the thoughts in their essentials that were involved in these principles, and its media and teachers have carried them forward with more or less success during the forty-six years that our movement has been before the world.

A. A. Ballou, from the spirit side of life, took up the same line of thought and work that his father had given to the world, broadened some of the conceptions of social order, of religion and personal conduct, and ushered into being a broader conception of a religion for the whole wide world. He chose as his instrument the subject of this sketch, the gifted Cora L. V. Scott, and that work has been most loyally carried on, and all duties laid upon her faithfully discharged by her as a mortal through the aid of the noble guides who have shaped her destiny and protected her through all these years since the ascension of the younger Ballou.

CHAPTER III.

OUINA.

WE now invite the attention of our readers to the work of the sweet spirit, Ouina, the gentle Indian maiden who has given comfort to so many sorrowing hearts. Her story is a poetic romance of the far away past, in which all classes of people will take a deep interest, from the fact that it reveals some matters not mentioned in history, and that it gives a beautiful picture of life among the children of Nature, in the forest primeval.

Ouina, when she first controlled Cora Scott, gave her name as "Shenandoah," that being the name of the valley in Virginia in which her father lived, also of the tribe and of her father. She soon became familiarly known as "Shannie," and made many friends wherever her medium went. "The name, 'Ouina,'" says this loving spirit, "is the name my mother gave me when I entered her sphere of spirit life."

Ouina's history reads like a story of the Orient, and presents many charming pictures to our view. She was born in the lovely vale of the

(84)

Shenandoah river, in Virginia, about four hundred and twenty years ago. Her father was the chief of the tribe that dwelt in that quiet valley, and made many journeys in his birchen canoes to the "Great Waters," or to the Atlantic coast, probably at the point now known as "Hampton Roads." On one of these voyages, after a great storm at sea, the chief was sitting on the beach, when suddenly he saw the form of a woman tied to a spar, floating in the waters. He went into the water, brought the form to the shore, applied a few simple restoratives, and the woman revived. She was looked upon as a visitor from another world; and the children of the forest stood ready to fall down in worship at her feet.

It will be seen by the above statement that this event, the rescue of the mother, occurred prior to the discovery of America by Columbus. Ouina tells us that her mother was a Spanish lady, whose father commanded a band of sea rovers in search of wealth. On one of their voyages, the commander's wife and daughter accompanied them. They sailed southward from Spain, and encountered many storms which took them far out of their course to the west, bringing them, finally, to the coast of Virginia, where they anchored near Hampton Roads. While at anchor another fearful storm arose, in the course of which the vessel was lost, with every soul on board save the commander's daughter, Cliona, who was saved by the chieftain, Shenandoah, as we have described above.

As soon as she had regained her strength, she was taken to the Shenandoah Valley, where she received every kindness at the hands of the Indians, with whom her after life was spent. After one year she married the noble chief, Shenandoah, of whom Ouina speaks, as follows:

> "He was a type of all that manliness
>   With which nature endows
> Her eldest sons; his form was lithe and tall
>   As the proud pine tree's height;
> Erect and firm he stood among his kind,
>   With gentleness and might.
> His courage was undaunted, and his skill
>   At arms or in the chase,
> In counsel, and all their communings,
>   Had won for him this place.
> He reigned and ruled, supreme and mild,
>   And thus, by edicts kind,
> He led his people by his strength, and skill,
>   And gentleness combined.

She soon learned the Indian language, and taught the women some of the arts of civilization that she had left behind her in lordly Spain— cleanliness in their persons and wigwams, and the making of garments being among these. She never taught them her language, but would wander alone in the moonlight beside the river, chanting in her own tongue the sweet songs of her native land, far away over the sea. At such times we may imagine that her heart would grow heavy and her eyes be filled with tears, as she recalled the happy days of her childhood years. Yet she always entered her wigwam with a smile on her face, for she had learned to love her chieftain with all the ardor of her fiery, Spanish nature, and always wished to keep her sorrows from his notice.

One year after the marriage Shenandoah was born, but the mother closed her weary eyes in the restful sleep of death, as the tiny babe opened hers to the sights and songs of that peaceful valley.

" The babe was left; oh, sweetest recompense,
    For death He giveth birth;
The rose must fade, but ever a new germ
    Unfolds from the warm earth."

They buried the mother beneath violet decked soil and, at her request, planted a cross above the mound. Sweet rest, no doubt, the pure soul of the exiled Spanish woman found in her quiet sleep in that lovely valley, with the sweet, wild flowers upon her breast.

Ouina's childhood was made as joyous and pleasant as a father's fond love could make it. As she grew older her face and form became singularly like her mother's, while her voice had the same sweet melody of song. She wandered at will among the forest trees, and sent her light birch canoe flying over the waters with as much skill and dexterity as obtained with any of the

children of the forest in those bygone years.
She seemed to have the power to talk with the
birds in the trees and with the animals that
roamed through the valley. Her people often wondered which was the song of the bird and which
Ouina's, as they listened to them from a distance.
She loved the beautiful in life and was sportive
as a fawn, but she never had the heart to kill
even an insect. She even wept when the warriors would return with slaughtered game or tro-
phies of their latest fray. She accompanied her
father on all of his journeys, and sought by every
means in her power to make bright and cheerful
his wigwam home.

One day when Ouina was about fifteen years
of age, a strange vision appeared to her. She
had had glimpses of strange scenes her mortal
eyes saw not all through life; but this vision was
enrapturing, because intensely real to all her
senses. She saw her mother, and at once broke
forth into song, chanting the same Spanish melody that her mother had often been heard to sing
as she wandered up and down the valley so many
moons before. A strange silence settled over all
her people as they listened, for they felt that the
Great Spirit had sent a messenger to Ouina, and
they wondered what the message might be. As
the hours passed their awe grew greater, for the
child gave no other sign and seemed to be listening in silence to the voice of the Great Spirit

which they could not hear.   At last she came
out from the forest where they had seen her
form and heard her song in the strange tongue
they could not understand.   Straightway she
sought her father and spoke to him in firm, clear
tones, words which we here quote in full:

" Across the stream, where I had wandered oft
    To gather the wild flowers,
I heard a voice like the winds rustling
    Among the leafy bowers;
And then I saw a form so beautiful
    That everything grew fair,
And soon a song, unlike any bird's song,
    Floated upon the air.
The face that I beheld was like my own,
    I've seen it in the stream;
I knew it was my mother's voice I heard,
    And not an idle dream.
I fell into a sleep and saw a cloud
    Arising in the west,
When it came near it seemed a mighty host
    Of warriors; each breast
Was bared, and painted eagles' plumes
    Were on each brow, and bows
Were drawn, while quivering arrows keen
    And clubs sent fearful blows
Among your people.   You went forth in might
    To conquer and to slay,
But then I saw your bravest people fall
    And some were borne away.
That mighty chief ruled o'er the land now yours,
    And you found no relief
From want and woe and all that brings despair,
    Or bows the soul with grief.
Full soon another and a darker cloud
    Arose where the clear eye

Of the Great Spirit looks upon the world,
  Far in the eastern sky;
A cloud like a white bird borne on the wind,
  And flying o'er the sea.
Another and another came, until
  There seemed at least to be
As many as the flocks of birds that fly
  Each year above our home.
They bore strange people with their snowy wings,
  With faces like my own.
Then saw I all your broken scattered tribes
  Fleeing with footsteps fast,
A mighty warrior upon the trail,
  And you, dear sire, at last
In sorrow and despair, perish with those
  Who clung so lovingly
And would not leave you until the latest hope
  Had faded swift away.
At last the western mountains hid their forms.
  From my bewildered sight;
I thought they must have gone to that bright world,
  The hunting grounds of light.
Before one harvest moon has come and gone,
  The first cloud will arise;
A mighty western chieftain comes to claim
  One, who, within the skies,
Treads now a brighter path than you could find,
  Though yours were paved with flowers.
Her wondrous beauty he hath learned and comes
  To bear her to his bowers.
And, after many winters' snows shall pass,
  Those white birds o'er the water
Will bring the people with the pale, white face,
  And you and I, your daughter,
Will dwell with Manitou in that bright home,
  Where all our loved ones are."

The father received these words of ominous
portent in stern silence and with an unwilling

mind. They seemed to bring some strange spell over him, and he lapsed into a profound reverie or meditation, from which he did not arouse himself for seven full days and nights. This vigil was in accordance with a custom that prevailed among the primitive tribes of this land. Whenever a message was given them from their seers, seeresses, or medicine men, their chief men pondered it in silence for seven days and nights, and if the statements were confirmed by additional testimony given them direct, they then advised their people to be governed by what had been given. In this instance the great chief, Shenandoah, ill could brook a prophecy that his loved people were to be overthrown; hence, during his prolonged fast and grim meditations, it occurred to him that his beloved daughter had come in contact with the evil spirit, who had made her to speak falsely to him of the future. He called his wise men into council, and told them what had happened, closing his speech with the words, "Brothers, my child must die." The other chieftains sought to save the maiden, but to no avail. Twenty braves were selected from the strongest warriors in the tribe, were directed to dip their arrows into the surest poison they could distill, and bidden to be ready for the execution of Ouina in seven days' time. Ouina, who was much beloved by all the tribe, knew nothing of what her father had determined to do.

She saw that he was troubled, and kept much
out of his way, but she mingled with the people
freely, singing her choicest songs and seeking to
cheer them as much as possible in her innocent
way. One night as she was quietly sleeping she
was suddenly seized, denuded of all her clothing,
bound firmly to a hemlock tree around which
had been piled a quantity of wood for the purpose of burning her body at the stake when the
arrows had done their fatal work. The fires
were kindled and the warriors commanded to
bend their bows for their terrible deed. One
young brave commanded them not to shoot, and
dashed through the flames to save the gentle
Ouina, but an arrow from the shaft of death had
already touched her young heart, stilling its loving pulsation forever. The angels had called
her, and she had gone to them, even before the
poisoned arrows of man, and the holocaust of
fire had touched her form. The young brave
who tried to save her perished with her. Soon
after this event, the people of the Shenandoah
were attacked by their old time enemies and were
put to flight. Defeat followed defeat, until
Shenandoah himself was slain upon the very
spot where the soul of Ouina had escaped from
its bondage of nature to the hunting grounds
above.

The remnants of the tribe ever after, or until
the tradition was lost among them, when passing

that spot cast a stone upon it as a memorial for the beautiful Ouina. Every year for nearly a century this custom was kept up, until a large hill arose in the middle of what had been a level plain. This hill, in the lapse of time, became covered with trees, and, today, can be found in the Shenandoah Valley, a silent monument to Ouina, the seeress, who foretold the destruction of her people. This hill seems out of place in that valley, and when Ouina was describing the place of her execution to Gen. N. P. Banks, the soldier statesman, now recently ascended, she alluded to this small mound and gave such an accurate description of it that the General recognized it at once. He said he had often gazed upon this mound, wondering how and why it came to be there. This is the story of Ouina's life briefly told, and we must now call our readers' attention to her life and work as a spirit.

(Gen. Banks accepted Ouina's statement as the only reasonable explanation of the origin of the mound, and was sustained in his opinion by many others who are acquainted with this story, and have seen the mound as he has.)

We can see that Ouina was a seeress among her people, and was esteemed as such by them. The tragic fate of the young brave who endeavored to rescue her from the cruel flames is strong evidence that she was almost worshipped by those humble children of the forest, and looked upon as a messenger direct from the Great Spirit, to minister to them in their hours of need. This, Ouina is said to have done most willingly, and she often glided silently into the wigwams where sickness had come, and the magic of her touch would almost restore the sufferers to health. Wherever gaunt famine laid its fatal hand, she, too, went, carrying food and raiment, that none of her people might want while it was in her power to prevent it. "Her life was gentle, and her soul sincere," hence, it is no wonder that the birds in the trees, the animal in the forest, as well as the people in her tribe, should love her most devotedly.

Soon after her entrance into spirit life, she sought again to be of use to her fellowmen by ministering to those whose friends had forsaken them, and to little wanderers from the earth plane who had no one to welcome them to spirit life. She eagerly sought instruction from the advanced teachers in the higher spheres. She rapidly unfolded her own soul's powers, and soon became a teacher in the spirit realms. As a teacher she was permitted to select her own especial field of labor, and gladly did she choose to become the guide and instructor of little children. It was her delight to welcome the little ones who had been wrested from the arms of mother love on earth, to her quiet home among the flowers, in the Morning Land, that she might 'soothe them and cause them to forget the loss of their earthly homes and parental affections, in the higher joys of the supernal world. She often came to the stricken parents and sought to impress them that all was well with their darlings, striving also to still the pain that rankled in their hearts. In this way she became a messenger of peace and love between the two worlds, always breathing a holy benediction over those whom she could reach from the spiritual side of their natures. Of course, it was impossible for her to impress all to whom she thus came, but many homes on earth ceased to be enveloped in the clouds of grief because of the silent visits paid by Ouina to their hearthstones. Many parents were made to feel that their little ones were enwrapped by the tender love of the angels, and somehow they knew that their loved ones lived. This was especially true of those who were susceptible to the influence of the spirit; their hearts would be comforted, the cutting pain would depart and their grief-stricken souls be illumined by a light whose power they felt rather than perceived. When Modern Spiritualism came, this holy work of love became much easier, for people could then perceive this messenger in their midst, and receive directly from her voiceless lips the messages of love she had brought to them from their arisen loved ones.

Of Ouina's home we need not speak at the

present time, as a full account of it will appear in a subsequent chapter, written by Mrs. Richmond under Ouina's own direction.

It is impossible to relate in detail Ouina's experiences as a teacher. From the time the infants came into her sphere, until they became fully developed as men and women, in the spiritual sense, she so sought to instruct them in the essentials of being, and had lessons fitted for every stage of their unfoldment. Those who had been sent to her by the red hand of murder, from the chrysallis state were carefully nurtured and given a holier birth in spiritual consciousness than they could possibly have received on earth. Others, who had gone to her through neglect and cruelty of earthly guardians were given every attention, and shown that love was the predominant power in the spirit world. Many who had been the victims of wrong-doing among men, whose earthly expressions had been marred by passion and sin, were taught that purity and goodness could soften even the hearts of those who had wronged them, and that forgiveness was a divine principle for them to accept.

The thousands of spirits to whom her beneficent instructions have been given, unite in one grand pæan of praise for their loving teacher, their counselor and guide—the gentle Indian maiden, Ouina. Gratitude is considered one of the choicest (because one of the rarest) flowers that bloom in the garden of human affection, and wherever it is shown among men, it is welcomed almost as a message or a blessing from the Over Soul itself. But gratitude among the angels is something so far transcending that which we find among mortals, as to make the latter sink almost into nothingness. The fragrance of the angelic flower is so rich as to shed a perfume over all souls, whose senses are at all awakened to a realization of what perfected love can do. Ouina's garden is full of these flowers, and each flower represents a spirit to whom she has ministered as a teacher in the spirit home. '' Ouina's bouquet '' is a term most familiar to those who have had the privilege of talking with her, for every noble thought, every exalted sentiment, and every ennobling emotion of the human soul, she calls a flower. These flowers, when combined artistically, certainly make up a priceless bouquet of the choicest flowers, culled as they are from the beautiful gardens of immortality.

Ouina's nature is like sunshine, full of life and good cheer. She seems to sustain a most happy relationship to the guides of her medium; being, as she says, an equalizing, vitalizing power—an equilibrium for her medium. She always brings strength and takes away all sense of weariness from her medium, by coming in for a few moments after her deepest and most exhaustive lectures have been given. She has the happy faculty of bringing a smile of joy to all faces whenever she appears, through her vivacity and catching good nature. She has a keen sense of humor, and knows just how to exercise that gift for the highest good of her auditors. She always endeavors to be just, and is severe only when the cause of right demands firmness and decision. While she is full of sparkling wit and vivacity, her instructions are fully as deep and philosophical as those given by any one of the guides. In fact, Spirit Ballou says, as we have already stated, that she goes far beyond him in scholarly wisdom. Her work may be likened to the intermediate state of two existences, partaking of the nature of both. She introduces her hearers to the simpler forms of thought in her own inimitable, happy manner, then leads them on to the more complex by means of the revelation of her own powers. In this way she may be said to link the thought of the two worlds in an endless chain of progression, and to make it possible for her friends on earth to receive instructions from the masters of thought in the world of souls. Her canoe, in which she delights to take passage from one sphere to another, is always filled with these rare bouquets of uplifting thought, to which we have already adverted, taken from celestial mental gardens, in the lovely valleys of Spirit Land. No more fitting symbol than a birchen canoe, filled with flowers of the most

expressive types, can be found to represent
Ouina; and on many occasions where the medium
has gone before the public, a tiny canoe was
there, as a token of loving greeting to the gentle
spirit whose presence is an angel of light to the
sorrowing ones of earth, who thus delight to welcome her.

Ouina's special forte is her "soul readings," as
they are called. This work is totally unlike that
done by the average psychometrist, as it deals
entirely with the spiritual side of life. The nicest
distinctions in mental, moral and spiritual relationships are made by her, independent of the
physical attributes with which psychometry, as
expressed by most mediums, usually deals.
Ouina, however, goes directly into the spiritual,
and does not require the mediumship of any material substance to bring her *en rapport* with her
subject. In this respect, we may here state, she
enters the field of pure psychometry, from the
Greek *psyche* (soul), and *metre* (measure), and
brings out its hidden wonders. To lead mortals into, and to cause them to comprehend
the soul realm is the aim of this gifted spirit.
She finds a purpose in all the phenomena of
Nature, and clearly proves by her wonderful delineations that human lives are but the expression
of a spirit, back of which is the soul. These individual souls are portrayed in a manner that
reveals each one to its own consciousness, which

ultimates in a perception of its spiritual attributes. Some of the most prominent men and women in our Nation's history have received these readings during the past forty-three years, and, whether Spiritualists or not, they have unanimously testified to the marvelous accuracy of the delineations. These soul readings have led many people to investigate Spiritualism, who, otherwise, would not have been interested in it at all.

Ouina has a happy faculty of expressing herself in verse, the meter and rythm of which are usually faultless, hence, the wonder and envy of poets and scholars, as they are often wholly unable to bring their productions into rhetorical or orderly form even with weeks of study. These poems are called "Name Poems," each subject being given some poetic title expressive of the elements found by Ouina in the soul life of her subject. She has been most generous with these Name Poems, having unselfishly given poem after poem, at receptions to herself and medium. These poems have contained some of the rarest gems of thought that have ever emanated from a Spiritual source. The poetic principle has always been recognized and followed with the utmost precision and dignity of speech. Many of these poems have moved their recipients to tears, and have given them new courage with which to meet the battles of life; they have always en-

couraged those who have received them to seek
the higher light of the spirit, and to endeavor to
realize for themselves the truth of the reading.

No one can understand another until he first
understands himself. Not less than thirty thousand of these Name Poems have been given by
Ouina, through her medium's lips, during the
years of her public ministry. Thousands of
them have not been stenographically reported,
hence are lost to the world in toto. Others
have been reported and are now held in stenographic notes, subject to the order of those who
have received them. Mr. William Richmond, of
Rogers Park, Illinois, has at least ten thousand
of these poems, in that form, taken by him as
they were given by Ouina, in all quarters of the
globe, and as many more have been written out
and are in the hands of the people to whom
given. No two of these poems are alike and
one person seldom receives a second reading,
and never until the subject has outgrown the
former. This fact shows the versatility of the
controlling spirit, and proves that the medium
herself is perfectly adapted to the work of revealing the truths of the soul world to the denizens
of earth. It is hoped that these poems will, at
some time in the near future, be collected and
published for the benefit of the thousands to
whom they were given.

In addition to these Name Poems, Ouina has

given at least ten thousand other poems, on subjects taken at random from promiscuous audiences on all sorts of topics.   These poems have
been fully as perfect as the others in their rhetorical nature, and have confounded the would-be
wise man in all of the schools of thought.   These
poems generally follow all of the lectures given
by our medium, and have always been reported
with those lectures.   In a literary sense, these
poems are of great value, and when they are put
into print for the reading public to enjoy, the
poetry of America will be materially richer
thereby.   Let us hope that this wish may be
consummated in the near future.   Ouina has
been the poet among the guides, and the work
done in this sphere has been hers.   Spirit Ballou
says that he could not make a poem even to save
his spiritual life, and has left it to Ouina to lead
her medium into the realm of poetry which is
described hereafter.   This work has been such
as to be considered a complement to what has
been done by the other guides, and must be
studied and judged by itself.

We have given in the foregoing pages a mere
outline of Ouina's work.   One large folio volume
could be more than filled with interesting matter,
pertaining to the experiences of this highly progressive spirit.   What we have given is authentic,
and will lead our readers to a perception of the
fields of thought traversed by Ouina, through

which she has also led her medium, to whom she has ever been a loving friend and companion, as well as teacher and guide. The teachings and work of Ouina cannot fail to be a constant inspiration to all lovers of spiritual truth, and if this brief chapter shall lead but one soul to philanthropic effort, and awaken a desire for soul growth, it will have served Ouina's purpose as well as our own.

CHAPTER IV.

THE OTHER GUIDES.

WE have already given extended accounts of the work of Spirit A. A. Ballou and Ouina, and it now remains for us to notice in detail the work of the other guides who are connected with the band that gathered around Cora L. V. Scott when her mediumship was made known to the world. The marked personalities of each of these controls is worthy of especial note, because of the diversity in the work which they had to perform. This diversity was so great as to completely change the personality of the medium at the various times when these divers controls were in possession of her organism. From the very first it was announced through Cora's own lips that there was a band of spirit controls of those whose mutual attraction and sympathy had drawn them together in this work of controlling and guiding our subject. This band, acting together, under her guides who had charge of the work, would carry forward the message of truth which the spirit world had for humanity, through her organism.

Spirit Ballou never claimed to be the origi-

nator of the work, nor to express his own knowledge and opinions exclusively; but, as far as
he was taught and unfolded in spiritual knowledge, to give that knowledge and to act as the
mouth-piece for the other controls when they
desired him to do so; in other words, when he
gave his own opinion he stated that fact plainly,
saying that he was acting for himself; but whenever this personal explanation was wanting, the
other controls or guides were back of him,
prompting the thought that he was voicing to
the world through Cora's lips.

We have stated that Ouina's work was distinctively her own; yet, even she was subject to
and governed by the band around her, of which
she was and is a most highly valued member,
and perhaps one of the most advanced minds in
that grand galaxy of spirits that have surrounded
our subject during her whole life. But it should
be noted that there is no claim of superiority on
the part of any one of these guides, but that
each one simply states that he or she had a particular niche to fill and an especial line of work
to do, according to his or her adaptability to do
that work; hence, all work in harmony and with
a full understanding of the purposes, each of the
other, so that the perfect equality which we, as
Spiritualists, have always been taught to recognize, is an assured fact in the spirit band around
our subject.

It was announced from the first that there were twelve spirits, having different gifts or phases of knowledge, who would speak as the occasion or theme required: on scientific, philosophical, historical, political, or other topics chosen by or adapted to the audiences. In those early days the subjects were almost always chosen by committees selected from the audiences. The great variety and range of topics called forth the special and, not infrequently, the combined knowledge of the entire band around her. In nearly all of the large cities the committees chosen were always composed of the most scholarly men known to the public, such as presidents of colleges, medical men, doctors of divinity and statesmen. They generally endeavored to select the topic which they deemed most difficult for any speaker to discuss, with which to confound the young girl to whom it was to be given. They even chuckled over their great skill and ingenuity in devising these difficult questions, and their chagrin at the ease with which she treated these difficult problems was much enjoyed by her friends, when these learned personages were forced to admit their discomfiture at the close of her discourse. On one occasion, in New York city, an incident worthy of note at this point took place.

Isaiah Rynders, or ''Capt'n'' as he was called by his followers, was a leader of the ''Bowery

boy" democracy.   One of the early "Tammany
Reds" who never lost an opportunity for fun or
a fight, and who, though a man of considerable
ability, was no judge of *belles lettres* or scientific
investigation.   Still the gallant Captain had a
weakness for the fair sex, and was chivalrous
to a degree that would do credit to many a man
moving in the refined society of the "four hundred."

He was passing down Broadway one evening
with about fifty of his comrades, returning from
or going to some favorite resort, when he espied
the bulletin in front of the Broadway Tabernacle
announcing the lecture that was to be given that
evening, by the "young girl apostle of Spiritualism in a trance state."

"Let's go in here, boys," cried the leader of
the gang, "and break up this ―― nonsense."

In they rushed, to find the place filled to overflowing with the brightest minds of New York.
A little awed at first, they would, perhaps, have
proceeded to have their own fun, had not some
gentleman performed a master-stroke.   The
audience were just choosing the committee to
select the subject for the evening lecture.   There
was a brilliant array of editors, lawyers, doctors
and scientists to choose from, and all the five
except one had been chosen.   The *coup d'etat*
was then performed in nominating and electing
Captain Isaiah Rynders as the fifth member of

the committee. He was compelled to leave his
comrades to go to the committee room to assist (?) in the selection of the subject, to take his
place upon the platform with the other members
of the committee, and to listen to the address.
His followers either remained and listened or
withdrew. At the close of the lecture, which
was a profound one on a deep subject, the chairman of the committee expressed the satisfaction
and amazement with which they had listened to
the lecture; in fact, it was a complete triumph.
Mr. Rynders arose and begged to be allowed to
say a few words, although his voice was tremulous with emotion.

He confessed to having come into the hall for
the purpose of "breaking up the whole business;" said he had never seen nor heard anything
like the lecture they had listened to ; hoped the
audience and the speaker would forgive him, and
said he meant to be a better man. He did not
know what power had spoken to them through
the lips of the young woman, but it had conquered and subdued him. The applause that
followed was tumultuous. The tears were stream-
ing down the face of the man of the world—for
the time, at least, he was moved one degree
nearer the divine.

The New York Herald in its report the next
day, while commenting upon the above incident
said: "It was difficult to tell whether the sub-

ject of the discourse, the lady's eloquence, or
the golden curls had vanquished the Capt'n."

Our readers will wonder how a young girl of
fourteen was able to discuss such a question as
this: "The Influence of the Aryan Philosophy
upon the Philosophy of Modern Times," which
was propounded to her in one place visited by
her soon after she became known to the public
as a speaker. She gave a most eloquent lecture
upon this subject, replete with logic and erudition which men of mature years did not possess,
and showed a knowledge of the subject far transcending that which was possessed by any mortal
at that time. Many abstruse metaphysical
questions were propounded to her, which were
answered with perfect ease and always in the
same scholarly, dignified language. As the audience were permitted to choose their committees to select the topics for the speaker's consideration, it was not unusual to find a great variety
of subjects suggested, which related to all possible questions then occupying the attention of
the public. It is worthy of note at this time,
that the controls of Cora Scott, were the first in
the Spiritualistic field to allow subjects to be
chosen by the audiences. This was done in order that the people might have a more perfect
test of the power of the controls over the medium, and to demonstrate their wonderful ability
to give these marvellous addresses to the public.

In fact, many people, simply by listening to
these erudite discourses were led to acknowledge
Spiritualism as a fact, without witnessing any
other phenomena, because they well knew that
no child of twelve or fourteen years, nor young
woman of sixteen or twenty years could possibly
give lectures upon historical subjects, or scientific questions with such ease and evince such
scholarship as did Cora Scott, during these trying days of her early work upon the rostrum of
Spiritualism. In this especial field, as a child-
worker, Cora was subsequently joined by others,
whose words had a similar effect upon the people,
convincing them of the reality of spirit return,
without recourse to the physical phenomena,
which are now claimed to be so essential to the
conversion of the skeptic, by many of our Spiritualistic friends. This selection of the subjects
by the audiences lasted until the public became
perfectly satisfied that Cora could not have been
prepared by any human training to deliver these
discourses, but this work covered a period of
some years, during which the public was gradually led to acknowledge the fact of the control,
without desiring the repetition of the test at each
separate lecture, then the people manifested a
desire to be instructed upon themes chosen by
the guides themselves. No doubt they felt that
the guides could take a more consecutive line of
thought and follow it out to greater profit to

them than could be done by the selection of subjects at random, on the part of the wonder-
seekers and curiosity-hunters, who were always
to be found at every seance or lecture that was
held or given during the earlier years of Spiritualism.   We wonder if there are none such now
in our ranks to frequent our public assemblies
and to dominate our seance rooms.   It is to be
hoped that the days of seeking signs and wonders will soon be over and that the higher gifts
of the spirit may be permitted to control the
thoughts, or to influence the minds of all classes
and conditions of men.   All classes of phenomena have their use, but they are not the be-all
and the end-all of the philosophy of Spiritualism.
Phenomena are only helps to a clearer understanding of the life they came to demonstrate,
hence they should be sought as we seek the A,
B, C in our primary schools—merely as stepping-
stones to an understanding of the things that lie
beyond them.   Thus the philosophy and phenomena blend into oneness and make up the grand
superstructure which we call Spiritualism.   In
the life of Cora Scott we find this blending made
almost perfect, and that the phenomena of her
trance state, coupled with the profound philosophy and religious thought given by the spirits
through her lips, while in that condition, are indices that the spirits thus recognize the importance of keeping the phenomena, philosophy and
religion united as one whole.

The band of guides and controls have ever remained the same from the time Cora's mediumship was first discovered down to the present
time, but other spirits, according to the needs of
the public and from their own desire were frequently invited to give addresses through the
human instrument thus prepared. Here we
must call our readers' attention to the vast range
of subjects treated by the controls through this
young girl yet in her teens. Metaphysics, philosophy, all branches of science and ancient and
modern history, all came in for treatment at the
hands of this gifted instrument. In fact, every
known theme of human thought or interest was
given to Cora, in various cities in our land, during her pilgrimage up and down the country.
She spoke upon them without a moment's warning, or an instant's hesitation, fluently, eloquently and scholarly, voicing the thoughts that
were given to her from the unseen guides who
were controlling her organism. Prof. J. J. Mapes
and scores of others equally well-known in the
schools of philosophy and science of modern
times, have said they could not have delivered
similar addresses on any one of the topics we
have named, even though they were familiar
with them, without weeks of preparation. This
fact alone is sufficient evidence to prove the
guiding power of wiser and higher minds, far beyond the teachers of earth.

A distinguished writer, Prof. J. J. Mapes, whose mom de plume was *Phœnix*, writing under date of May 11, 1859, in relation to her early work speaks as follows:

"Soon after Abner Lane invented the gyroscope and before it had been generally seen or known in New York, he placed this philosophical toy in Cora's hands, when she was entranced, and her explanation of this instrument was, and still is, the only clear description which has ever been given in relation to this invention."

On another occasion Phœnix says he asked Cora this important question: "What is the difference between absolute momentum and continuous force?" This question had never been answered—our books and philosophers were alike silent upon it—but this child of thirteen years answered it with the greatest clearness, accompanied by explanations which rendered her replies perfectly intelligible to all persons. Her oratory, purity of language, and depth of thought could not be excelled by any teacher or speaker of that day.

Her audiences were always interested in what she was saying, because of the ready flow of language so eloquently uttered, and also owing to the fact that thinking minds were instructed by the lofty thoughts voiced by her in these lectures. In speaking on social and political questions in those days, when the storm cloud, caused

by the existence of slavery, was about to burst
over the land, she seemed to be especially guided
by a prophetic spirit, and pointed out subsequent
events with an unerring finger and most remarkable prescience. She never hesitated to speak
freely upon the subject of emancipation, and
throughout the North questions concerning the
outcome of the anti-slavery agitation were freely
poured in upon her. She had a ready answer,
and even aroused her audiences to great enthusiasm by the patriotic words she spoke. Her
voice was always ·heard on the side of liberty,
and her appeals to the people to be just to the
black man did much towards enlightening the
people upon the all-important question of human
freedom.

In science and philosophy we can say the
same, because she took up questions relative to
each of these departments of knowledge, that
were then mere theories, and showed by conclu-
sive arguments that certain facts could be demonstrated if they would but follow the light the
spirit world was shedding over the minds of men.
So it has proved, and the scientific world is
richer because of the leadership of these guides,
of Cora Scott, who gave to the men of science,
in their laboratories, these new facts and important data, upon which to base their conclusions
and general line of reasoning.

Nearly all of her public lectures have been pre-

ceded by brief answers to a few questions selected
at random from the audience. To all of these
she has had ready answers, and given much positive information upon the points under consideration. On one occasion she was asked—no
doubt, in a spirit of sarcasm—"if the negro was
a human being?" Her answer was, of course, in
the affirmative, and so completely did she turn
the tables upon her interrogator as to cause great
merriment upon the part of all the people present. She said, "he was a human being, else
he could not be cultivated through the influence
of the white man." Thousands of similar ready
answers could be adduced, but they would all go
to prove one and the same thing: that our subject was simply in the hands of higher powers,
who were guiding her destiny as well as her
work.

This diversity of subjects was met by a diversity of minds among her controls. That is to say,
one guide would speak upon the subject of chemistry, another upon physics, still another upon
historical questions, and others upon philosophical or religious topics, but in this diversity there
was an essential unity of effort and of purpose
toward the bringing out of the best thought of
the guides, in the clearest possible manner, for
the comprehension and understanding of her
hearers. As we have already stated there was no
ambition for place or position in this band, each

one sought to do his or her work in the best possible manner for the highest good of all.

Spirit Dr. Rush dealt with questions of hygiene, physiology and anatomy, together with a line of thought upon soul culture or psycopathy, to which our readers' attention will be called later on, as the teachings on psycopathy form an important part of the present work, indeed, it is one of the most important features in the life of our gifted medium. Each subject was treated by the several spirits, as by one who knew that he was master of his theme. This, indeed, was really the case, and carried conviction to the minds of all who listened to these utterances.

The names of the spirit controls were often given, and included several modern thinkers, and others of a more ancient period, yet it was always obvious that the guides did not wish their names to be used as authority for the truth that they were uttering, but that they wished the truth to be its own authority. Whenever it became necessary, however, for any responsibility to be fixed for a particular utterance, or for personal views expressed on a particular subject, the names were always given. For questions in the early '60's and just prior to and after the outbreak of the war of the rebellion, Henry Clay gave many distinctly individual utterances in behalf of the Union, while John C. Calhoun gave all the argument for State Rights. Thomas Paine, Thomas

Jefferson and many other well-known thinkers
gave their individual views upon these particular
questions. The personalities of these several
spirits was so distinct as to be readily recognized
by even the most thinking mind. In fact, the
utterances of Clay, Calhoun and Webster were
readily recognized by some of the people present,
through the knowledge they had of these individuals while in earth life, as this triumvirate had
only a few years prior to that time, gone up to
their immortalities.

On themes of science, as the theories or propositions were distinctly individual, the control-
ing spirit always gave the name of the one whose
ideas were being advanced. As, for instance,
Kepler, Herschel, and later on subjects in connection with general science, Baron Von Humboldt. If the themes were general, however, and
of such a nature that all the controls held similar views, no names were given. The marked
individuality of the several controls at such times
as the names were announced was an especially
convincing feature, as we have already stated in
our reference to Webster, Clay and Calhoun.
When a discourse was announced from the sphere
of Plato, or from the sphere of Swedenborg, it
meant that the ideas would be from those whose
names were given, but that they would be presented or spoken by Spirit Ballou; in other words
the soul of Swedenborg would be dominating the

mind of Spirit Ballou, who was controlling Cora in the unconscious trance state. Later, when Mr. Lincoln spoke, his personality was very marked, which was also the case in the three or four times that James A. Garfield controlled our subject, shortly after his transition. Mr. Lincoln has frequently controlled her organism, and gave some of his characteristic utterances through her lips. Any student who is familiar with Lincoln's state papers, or with his public addresses on any occasion, cannot fail to recognize the similarity of thought in the terse sentences given through our medium, when under his control.

Newly arisen spirits who are desirous of speaking in order that they may make known their condition in spirit life, who are acting under the conviction that if they spoke, their friends and the people who knew them must believe, have been occasionally permitted to control our subject. Sometimes they have been invited to do so, but they soon learned that their friends, like every one else, must grow to a knowledge of spirit communion —such has been the experience of Mr. Garfield, Mr. Beecher and others who have been occasionally visitors at the lecture room of the speaker.

We now come to the higher guides, as they call those whose names have never been given to the world. By the term "Higher Guides" is meant those who by virtue of intelligence and adaptation are fitted to direct a movement of any

sort. Our medium controls were the first to use
the word *guides* as applied to the guardian spirits
or directing intelligences. The usual controls are
not guides, and sometimes are only transient in
their associations with the different mediums.

Neither controls or guides are universally limited to any particular medium, but, in the very
nature of things, may control, direct or guide
many mediums. Instances are on record where
one spirit controlled two mediums at the same
hour in different places. Many other mediums
have been visited by the same spirit, controlled
by that spirit, and made aware of the fact of the
visits paid to others by the one controlling. This
proves that the spirit can come *en rapport* with
many persons whose tastes, dispositions and
characters may be said to be similar to its own,
hence when mediums talk as if they had exclusive
right to any particular spirit or control, it is a great
folly and shows a lamentable human weakness.

It became manifest from the very first that not
only was the life-work of Cora under the guidance of very exalted intelligences behind the controls who spoke through her, but that they early
announced that the whole movement of Spiritual
manifestations, philosophy, ethics and religion
were a unit in the higher spirit states. We want
our meaning on this particular point made clear
to our readers. The real guides are those who
occupy exalted stations in the soul world, who

seldom come in contact with mortals. Controls
are those who prompt or direct the mediums to
whom they come, to give certain utterances or
manifestations, or tests, as they may be called to
others, while the guides of a medium are those who
guide and direct their controls—therefore, govern
and direct the medium, as well, in the absolute.

The latter teachings through our medium have
revealed an especial guidance in her life, and
have more fully admitted those who have heard
or read them into direct contact with the guides.

The names of the advanced guides are wisely
withheld since, if they were great on the earth,
people who believe in Spiritualism would attach
too much importance to them, while unbelievers
would say, "too much is claimed." If unknown
on earth, people would say, "how can we tell
whether this is a wise spirit or not, since the name
is wholly unknown," still wherever the names are
of real value, they do not hesitate to give them.

We have already adverted to the names of
Spirit Ballou, Ouina, Dr. Rush, and one or two
others of the band, but their names are only
given when occasion requires them to prove
their personal identity.

Whether the teachings come from Ouina's
sweetly-scented, flower-decked gardens, in the
sunny fields of immortal life, or from the laboratory of Von Humboldt, or the observatory of
Kepler, the sphere of Beethoven, or of Plato,

of Swedenborg, of Phidias, or of Michael Angelo, whose names are but types of the several spheres and lines of work in which they dwell and have to perform, there is always the same uplifting thought and positive knowledge conveyed to those who listen to this instrument of the Spirit world. The bickerings and clamors, the hatreds and the slanders of mortal life, together with the differences of men upon ethical, religious and philosophical questions are shown to be but transitory in the development of the human soul, and all are made to subserve the high gifts of the spirit emanating from the advanced souls in the supernal realms. Everything given upon any line of thought, be it music, history, art, science, or philosophy, is made to subserve the ultimate truths of Spiritualism, whereby the soul world is shown to be the only real, and that "Expressions of the soul" are but aids to the unfoldment of the soul-unit dominating the millions of personalities expressed in mortal form. These lofty ideas are beautifully expressed in our subject's able work, "The Soul in Human Embodiments," to which attention will be called later on in this work, and which will ever be the greatest monument to our medium's memory. This book and "Psycopathy" are the two works of interest to the reader as bearing upon the higher teachings given by these advanced guides, to whom we pay our humble tribute of praise.

CHAPTER V.

BUFFALO WORK.

WE have now introduced our readers to all of our medium's guides, and presented a brief outline of the work they are striving to accomplish through her organism. We now invite them to go with us to the former home of the Scott family, near Cuba, N. Y. We have seen that Cora was taken by her father back to that place from their Wisconsin home in the spring of 1852, only a few weeks after she was first controlled by Spirit A. A. Ballou. She had given several public addresses to select circles in her Wisconsin home, and had gone out to the school houses in the adjoining villages and country districts semi-occasionally. She had also spoken in Milwaukee, Fond du Lac and other places in that state. Upon her return to her early home she was brought prominently before the people, because she had a large circle of relatives in the vicinity of Cuba, and also because of the fact that her father was well and favorably known to the people of Allegany County. She spoke in district school houses and town halls of the villages in the vicinity of Cuba. These meetings were always largely attended, standing room generally being at a premium. She took subjects from the audience occasionally, and sometimes the guides would select their own topics. These discourses were upon every question then occupying the minds of the people. Think of it, readers, if you can imagine the picture,—a child of twelve years of age standing before crowds of people, discoursing to them upon the most abstruse questions in ethics, philosophy, science and theology, in a scholarly, dignified manner! What did it all mean? This was the question asked by the multitudes who listened to her, and to which the more thoughtful among them could find but one solution— it meant that the spirits of the departed had the power to return to earth, and by means of some psychic law could control the brain of a human being for the purpose of giving their testimony to prove that death was but the gateway to life immortal. Hundreds were converted to Spiritualism by means of these lectures, for the people realized fully that it was impossible for the child, Cora L. V. Scott, to originate these lectures or create the thoughts that fell from her lips. Later on, in the history of Spiritualism, similar phenomena were witnessed through the instrumentalities of Misses Libbie Lowe, Nellie Temple and W. J. Colville, who began their public work as lecturers of great power when they were but children.

In the autumn of 1852, Mr. Scott and Cora returned to Wisconsin, where they spent the winter. Cora continued to give her public addresses to the utter astonishment and discomfiture of the Christian ministers, and to the chagrin of the would-be philosophers who attempted to confound her statements when they were completely baffled in their attempt by her watchful guides.

During her public addresses the timidity, to which we have referred in connection with her childhood, would disappear when she went on the platform, or perhaps a little before, when Spirit Ballou would assume control. Under his wise guidance this diffidence gradually became controllable, and she could carry herself with greater ease; but this never wholly disappeared.

In the summer of 1853 Cora, accompanied by her aunt, again returned to her New York home. Her father, who up to this time had always been her constant companion, had some business to attend to in Wisconsin and could not accompany her. She had been in Cuba but a few days, when her guides told her that she must go back to Wisconsin as she would soon be needed there. She returned almost immediately to witness, one week later, her father's departure to spirit life. Of this period she has herself spoken in fitting terms later in this work.

Cora's mediumship had meant much to Mr. Scott. He gave up his dream of a Western Hopedale to accompany his daughter on her lecture engagements and to assist, as far as he was able, in the development of her wonderful psychic powers. He stood ready to follow the suggestions of the guides on all occasions, and sought to acquaint himself thoroughly with the teachings given from the higher realms. His broad mind saw a wider field of labor and a greater sphere of usefulness for himself and daughter in spreading the truths of Spiritualism, than ever could have been evolved in a second Hopedale — a Hopedale, east or west, could reach but few people; hence, the localization of humanitarian principles could not reach the masses. The new dispensation, while involving the ethics and religion of the Hopedale leaders, was yet much broader and was fitted for the whole world to hear and enjoy. To carry the good news to the world, with the aid of the spirit guides, became the aim of David W. Scott; and his daughter's guides encouraged him in this thought, and he was planning his future in a way that would enable him to do their bidding in every respect. It was his greatest delight in life to listen to the words of wisdom as they fell from Cora's lips, but it was not to be his enjoyment

long. In the month of August, 1853, the silent
messenger visited the Scott homestead in Wisconsin, and called the husband and father to go
with him to the unseen "city where the feet of
mortals have never been." Peacefully, quietly,
and with a loving smile upon his face, did David
W. Scott close his eyes upon this world of sense,
to open them in a happier world when the bright
sunshine of the spirit realms bade him a glad
good morning.

Mr. Scott's transition made many immediate
changes in Cora's work. Mrs. Scott and her
younger daughter, Emma, returned to Western
New York soon after her husband's transition.
Cora, however, remained in Wisconsin at the
home of her aunt, Mrs. Phillips, whose husband
was Cora's guardian and, with the mother, general executor of her father's will.

In the Spring of 1854, Cora returned to Cuba
to be with her mother and other relatives. Cora's
brother, Edwin T. Scott, was at Hopedale attending school at the time of his father's transition, and in 1855 her mother and younger sister,
removed to Hopedale to be with her brother,
where they all remained for two years, near the
Ballou family. Cora, however, was not with
them save for a portion of the period from the
Summer of 1854 until the Spring of 1855. Cora
made visits to Hopedale in 1856 while her mother
resided there and spoke in the little church, and

also in Milford, under the control of Spirit A.
A. Ballou.

Prior to her return to Cuba from Wisconsin,
she had continued her public work, even though
her father had not been with her in bodily form,
to assist her. The same marked series of suc-
cesses were hers as had been at the time of her
first appearance before the public. She made
further engagements in and about Cuba immediately after her return. Her name soon became
known far beyond the limits of her native town
and the ablest minds in Buffalo and other cities
in Western New York soon heard of the phenomenal child, as she was then called. They went
sometimes many miles to listen to her lectures
and marvelled much at the wonderful erudition
she displayed.

During the Summer of 1854 Cora visited Fredonia, Dunkirk and Buffalo, N. Y., and spent
considerable time at the home of Mrs. Palmer,
in Dunkirk, who soon became a most zealous
Spiritualist. These lecture trips soon made
Cora an object of interest everywhere and in the
Fall of 1854 she was invited to lecture in Buffalo,
exclusively. She accepted the invitation and
was located in that city for two full years, during which time she presented the truths of
Spiritualism clearly to the minds of the thousands who flocked to hear her. During the
greater portion of this time, Thomas Gales

Forster, one of the most gifted orators in Spiritualism, was associated with her in her Buffalo work, both speakers being engaged by the same society, and speaking at the same sessions from the same platform. It was a unique spectacle that presented itself to the thinking minds in Buffalo, to see a child of fourteen years officiating in the capacity of pastor of a large and constantly increasing society, yet such was the fact, and nobly did she perform her work, and most acceptably to all did she discharge the duties pertaining to her important office. Of course, she was assisted most efficiently by Mr. Forster, who had certain lines of work to perform. She had the improvisations, invocations and general questions to give and to answer, but occasionally alternated this with Mr. Forster and gave the regular lectures in his stead. If the *savants* in our colleges and churches will but stop to consider for a few moments what this work means, that this child of fourteen summers was performing at that time, what remarkable development of brain did she possess, that in its convolutions there could be stored such a wealth of knowledge that it could come forth at the bidding of promiscuous audiences, on any and all occasions. Was it like the famous mines of Golconda, where the priceless jewels were secreted in a most conspicuous place and mortals unable to find them, or was it a brain sensitized and attuned by angel hands to receive the psychic impressions from the soul world, which were by her to be repeated to the mortals upon this earthly plane? Surely the claim of inspiration needs no further demonstration than the wonderful ability with which Cora L. V. Scott handled all the intricate questions of that troublesome period in the history of our nation, met the scientific agnostics upon their own ground and completely baffled the materialistic casuists and sophists who were determined to prove that there was no such thing as intellect or intelligence in the universe.

We now present a series of communications from personal friends of our medium, in connection with her work in several of the towns we have mentioned above, such as Fredonia, Dunkirk and Buffalo. One of these friends, Mrs. Orpha E. Tousey, writes as follows:

"Our first knowledge of Cora L. V. Scott was when she was about thirteen years of age, when, in company with her father and mother, and ex-Governor Chase, she visited Kiantone, New York, in the capacity of a medium. While there she encountered several professional and scientific persons—doctors, lawyers, etc., and the masterly manner in which the uneducated child handled the most difficult metaphysical and scientific problems won for her at once a wide reputation. Soon after this she was called to Laona and Fredonia, and was an inmate for a time of a sanitarium conducted by Doctors J. F. Carter, Brown and Marion. She was then a little girl in short dresses, with a profusion of golden curls, as playful and unrestrained as the birds and kittens she loved to chase and frolic with. She gave lectures of the highest order, conducted circles and gave sittings, and was the instrument of converting many people to Spiritualism.

"All this time the child medium seemed wholly unconscious of the wonderfully important mission that was hers, and which was the marvel of all who knew her. Often up to the very hour appointed for her lecture, she would be rambling in the fields, chasing the birds and butterflies, or perhaps with some playmates would be dressing dolls. Several times she was thus engrossed and oblivious of the appointment which had been made for her, but her invisible guides would snatch her from her play and bring her to the circle or audience room, and in a twinkling the playful child would be transformed, as it were, into astute sage, philosopher or poet. Once during this time she officiated at the funeral of Mr. Narcross, father of the well-known Dr. Narcross. It was held in the open air, in order that all might have room. The assemblage was a large one, many people coming from curiosity to hear what the little girl could say upon such an occasion. So touching, so beautiful and far-reaching was the discourse that many were moved to tears.   Hon. Hanson Risley, Laurens Risley, Wm. A. Barden and John Mullett, attorneys at law; George C. Rood, Jerry G. Rood, Colonel Forbes, and several prominent physicians of the town, became interested through this discourse in Spiritualism, and the majority of them have been thorough Spiritualists ever since.

"We next met Miss Scott, while we were teaching in the public schools, in Dunkirk. We boarded with S. S. Germond, who was then mayor of Dunkirk, and who was, through Cora's instrumentality, developed as a writing medium, giving tests of a remarkable character, some of which were published in the local papers and will be remembered by all old-time workers. Cora spent a week or more at Mr. Germond's at this time, during which period we became greatly interested in and warmly attached to her. We may say here that our interest and attachment have never become lukewarm during the forty years that have elapsed since that time.

"The next summer, 1854, we met her again while we were still engaged in the same school and were boarding at Alonzo Palmer's, a staunch and worthy veteran in the cause of Spiritualism, who, with his most excellent wife, visits Cassadaga Camp nearly every season. Cora spent much of her time at our boarding place, holding circles and giving public lectures. She spoke several times in our school building, and we well remember a prophecy she made in the course of a very comprehensive political lecture, purporting to come from Spirit George Washington. In speaking of the evils of slavery, she said: 'Slavery is a curse and a disgrace to a republican government, and the spirit world was combining their forces to wipe it out. They would be glad if it could be done without bloodshed, but it had taken such a hold and was so grounded in the selfish and material interests of the slave-holder that it could not be done except through the agency of material force. Therefore, a bloody war between the North and South, waged by the devotees of human rights on the one side, and selfishness and tyrrany on the other was unavoidable.' She said that within ten years a war, which had no parallel in history, would occur. She told where the principal battles would be fought and many particulars which were verified in that terrible struggle which was waged, primarily, for the emancipation of the African slaves. Probably no one who listened to this prophecy, given through the lips of this little girl on that night, seven years before the breaking out of the Rebellion, believed such a thing possible, but they were painfully reminded of it when shot and shell were rained upon Sumter in the spring of 1861, only seven years afterward, when the Rebellion raised its hideous form, and armed warriors began to pour their shot and shell against its brazen face, at which time our fathers, brothers, husbands and friends were one after another, sacrificed in the struggle.

"Many more incidents of an equally remarkable character might be related by us, concerning the gifted woman who is the subject of our sketch, but we are aware that within the forty-four years of her ministrations there would be much to recount, and after bestowing upon her our heartfelt benediction and God-speed, we drop our pen and give way to those whose privilege it is to do her humble justice."

Other interesting letters relative to the early work in Laona, Fredonia and Dunkirk, might be entered here, but as we have already stated, their testimony would merely be cumulative, hence a repetition of what has been so well stated by Mrs. Tousey in her splendid letter.

The personal testimony of Mr. Germond and Mr. Palmer would be of interest if it could be obtained, but the former is now a denizen of the spirit world, and the latter, now far advanced in years and no longer a resident of Dunkirk, is not able to furnish us the data we would desire. The ground he would cover is essentially that which has been given by our correspondent; but we know he would add his personal testimony to the worth of Cora Scott, and give her his benediction of peace and good courage for the great good she wrought in his home, and in the city where he then resided.

From others who were acquainted with our subject at that time we learn that the cause of Spiritualism was advanced rapidly through Cora's ministrations in the places we have named. It reached a class of people that could not have been touched by phenomena of a physical nature, and gave it a standing in Chautauqua County, New York, on a level with all other religious denominations. This social status was largely due to the influence of this child medium, and the noble guides who prompted her thought during the memorable years of 1852-3-4. Reminiscences of this period could be adduced that would fill the pages of this work full to overflowing, were they deemed germane to our text at this point. They are written, however, in the soul affections of those who knew her best at that time, and have known her through all the years that have flown into the eternity of the past, since she came to Chautauqua County, a spiritual messenger, guided by the heavenly hosts who have come to redeem a sorrow-stricken world.

As we have already stated Cora went to Buffalo in 1854 to minister to the Spiritual society in that city. From this point she visited Cleveland, Ohio, occasionally, and of her at this period, Mrs. Helen O. Richmond, 627 Euclid Ave., Cleveland, writes as follows:

"I first knew Cora Scott in Buffalo, in the winter of 1854-55. She was, I think, in her fif-

teenth year, guileless and sweet in disposition,
with long, natural curls floating below her waist,
fond of girlish pursuits, with nothing in her
normal condition to indicate her wonderful mediumship. However doubtful persons may at
present be of her entire unconsciousness when
used by her guides, no one who knew her in her
childhood could, I am positive, have doubted it
then, for those who were intimately acquainted
with her knew that she did not read or study at
that time, but delivered profound and exalted
discourses without a moment's preparation. She
visited my house often, and I saw much of her.
Both in Buffalo and Cleveland she was greeted
by large and intelligent audiences, who listened
to the words of wisdom with rapt attention as
they came from her childish lips. She was often
controlled by Ouina, who was then known as
Shenandoah, and in company with Sarah Brooks
(another fine medium) gave memorable seances,
when they both, dressed in Indian costumes,
made by directions of the spirits—would be controlled by Indian girls, and under their control
convinced many in their audiences of the truth
of Spirit manifestations. It was a brave thing to
do in those days, when to be a Spiritualist was to
be ostracised, and to be a medium, given over
body and soul to the tender mercies of the evil
one by the unbelieving public.

"The Indian seances I have mentioned (given

in costume) were always held at private residences.

"In the two cities I have mentioned, as well as in other places, Cora Scott's lectures were well received by the best minds in the higher classes of society. The more thoughtful became interested in Spiritualism, and I am sure attracted many intellectual people to a consideration of its teachings who otherwise might never have been led to investigate. N. E. Crittendon, my father, Mr. Everett, Mrs. H. F. M. Brown, J. W. Gray, editor and founder of the Cleveland "Plain Dealer," all of whom are now in the spirit world, were much interested in Cora Scott's work, and thought that no intelligent person could doubt that she was controlled by some superior outside power.

"If all of the facts relative to her earlier life could be published they would make a most interesting volume, and so rich a value will her life have that I will gladly subscribe for a copy of her biography, as soon as it is in print."

An interesting account of some of Cora's experiences in Buffalo, from the pen of Samuel H. Wortman, will be of interest here:

"H. D. BARRETT: Dear Sir,—I am glad you have undertaken to write a history of *our* Cora's life-work, in the cause of Spiritualism, and am especially pleased to contribute my mite towards making it of interest to the public. It was my good fortune to know much of her earlier

history in regard to her mediumship, from my
own observation. In 1854, Prof. J. J. Mapes,
of New York city, came to Buffalo to pursue his
investigations of the Spiritual phenomena. At
that time the First Spiritual Society of Buffalo,
holding its meetings in a small hall on Main
Street—circles were held in the forenoon, and
lectures were given in the afternoon and evening.
Prof. Mapes attended the morning circle, and sat
at the same table with Cora Scott, in company
with two or three others. Cora soon went under
the control of Shenandoah, now known as Ouina.
This spirit asked Prof. Mapes if he would speak
in the afternoon for the society. He replied:
'Yes, if you will control your medium, and let
me give the subject that she shall speak upon.'
The Professor had fallen into the very trap Shenandoah had laid for him; the very one which
he thought he had set for her. It was the very
thing—the test of tests that the spirits wanted to
give him. The afternoon came, and the hall was
packed. Cora took the platform, and as soon as
the choir had finished the hymn she came forward with her countenance so illuminated by the
light of the spirit, that the story of Moses having
to wear a veil when he came down from the
mount, I could readily believe. There was an
intellectual and spiritual radiance from her face
that struck all beholders with admiration. Her
guide called for a subject. Was it in the Bible?

No. Prof. Mapes spoke the two words, 'Primary Rocks.' What a subject to give an uneducated girl of fourteen, but it was handled in a manner worthy of the mind of a sage or a scientist of great renown. After the lecture the control called upon Prof. Mapes to speak upon the same subject. Prof. Mapes came upon the stand, and with tears in his eyes, said: 'I am a college educated man, and have been all my long life an investigator of scientific subjects and associated with scientific men, but I stand here this afternoon *dumb* before this young girl.' This was a remarkable tribute to her mediumship and to the power of the spirit world.

"One other instance I will relate to show Cora's wonderful susceptibility to spirit control. The Buffalo Spiritualists, owing to their rapidly increasing numbers, had hired a larger hall and had engaged Cora as one of its regular speakers. In the Summer of 1855 I had, myself, become a subject to Spiritual influences, and was greatly interested in everything pertaining to Spiritualism. I was always the first one at the hall and the last to leave it. One hot day in Summer, on my way to my Spiritual Zion I picked a leaf from an overhanging branch of a tree by the roadside. I wondered for a moment why I had done so, when I suddenly heard a voice saying 'Place that leaf on the speaker's stand.' I did so as soon as I entered the hall. No person

saw me do it, nor could that leaf have been seen
by any one in the audience unless they were
standing on the platform and looking directly
down upon it. Cora came into the hall, partially
under control, as was her usual custom, and
when the singing was over advanced to the
speaker's stand, took up that very leaf, and from
it the controls gave one of the finest discourses
it has ever been my good fortune to hear. After
the discourse, every one, even the medium,
wondered where that leaf came from. I did not
enlighten them, but the next Saturday, at one
of Cora's circles, she was entranced by Shenandoah, who came to me and said, 'I made you
get that leaf, that day. The Ballou brave said
to me, 'Shenandoah, can't you get me a leaf,'
so I looked around and said, 'I thought I could,
I knew a medium just beginning to jump.' So
I watched you as you came under that tree and
made you think you wanted a leaf. Then I impressed you what to do with it, to put it upon
that table.' This was a fine test to me and to
all who knew the circumstances.

"In my opinion, Mrs. Richmond is one of the
best controlled mediums that ever came before a
public audience. Her lectures in Buffalo caused
the greatest interest in Spiritualism, in connection with those given through the organism of
Thomas Gales Forster, especially with the intellectual class of minds, and today, after a lapse

of nearly forty years, I look back to that period
as the golden age of Spiritualism. Many earnest
men and women who loved Spiritualism and
labored for its success, I can remember in connection with the history of our cause in Buffalo.
The majority of them are now basking beneath
the sunlight of eternal love in the supernal
world, and their mansions in the Morning Land
make glad the city of our heavenly home.
Prominent among them come gliding down over
the silken cords of memory the names of Stephen
Albro, editor of 'The Age of Progress;' our
president, Lester Brooks, Jacob Foltz, Thomas
Rathburn, Edwin Scott and his noble wife, Mr.
Maynard and wife, and Mr. Savage, who is well-
known to Cora, H. G. White and Seth Pomeroy,
the latter being the principal in one of our public
schools, who said that he was called upon to ex-
pose Spiritualism, and as a result of his investigations he accepted the presidency of our society;
S. Dudley, Guy Salsbury and wife, Mr. and Mrs.
John Coleman, Capt. Amos Pratt and family,
Capt. Gibson and many others, were Cora's
warm friends, and thought the Spiritual sun had
sunk forever when she left our city. May she be
spared many years to do loyal battle for our
glorious cause."

Besides those already mentioned as warm personal friends there were others who were interested in the work at that time and who were

astonished at the utterances through the little
girl, viz.: Millard Fillmore and his niece Miss
Fuller (the latter always a warm friend of Cora),
Horatio Seymour, Eli Cook (then Mayor of Buffalo) and wife, and many others whom want of
space prevents us from mentioning.

In connection with her Buffalo work, one of
her old-time friends, Mrs. C. A. Coleman, of
Mt. Vernon, N. Y., speaks most feelingly in a
letter of some length concerning Cora's work in
that city. She says, referring to the teachings
through our subject, that they have undergone
some changes in regard to certain points touching the soul teachings, but refers in most glowing
terms to the high philosophical and intellectual
cast of her lectures in those early days in the
city of Buffalo. "She has not lost caste," says
Mrs. Coleman, in comparing her past utterances
with those of the present. "I first met Cora as
a girl of thirteen, when she was brought to Buffalo by Capt. Pratt on a trip of pleasure, on the
first screw propeller on Lake Erie. On this occasion she was most wonderfully controlled by a
German physician, in a dignified manner, pre-
scribing for an invalid lady of the company.
When next I met her, if I mistake not, it was in
the fall of 1855, again in the city of Buffalo,
when she was controlled by Spirit A. A. Ballou.
Through his instrumentality, combined with
other resident spirits she made an engagement

to speak a portion of the day before our society, the first ever formed in Buffalo. Soon after her advent Thomas Gales Forster was also brought to us, both ministering to us, alternating discourses, Cora giving impromptu poems, invocations, lectures and so on, until the following Summer of 1856. From that time on our lives drifted apart, except as we casually met in different localities. Cora came to me under peculiar circumstances, being led by the spirit forces to see the necessity of a change of home relations. They (the spirit forces) brought her to me in order to restore her to health, being at that time threatened with an abscess on the lungs. She remained with me until her recovery was assured. Again that spring she came to me, making one of my family until the pressure became so great in the way of persecution to her and to me, that it was deemed advisable for a change to be made, so she went to the home of a friend in the country.

"During my association with Cora, I found her ever to be most reliable and modest of girls, always ready to answer all demands upon her mediumship, and uniformly agreeable to strangers as well as to friends, never indulging in scandal, cautious in her intercourse with others and very charitable in her comments when called upon to speak of personal actions. I shall ever feel a tender interest in her life, and trust the day is not far distant when life with her will assume all the pleasant aspects she most desires.

"It has never been an ideal task to be a public medium, but when Cora, a young child, taken from her home to roam as directed by the spirit forces, without knowing whither or where to lay her young head from day to day, it, indeed, required great trust in the spirit forces in guiding, and not only that innate trust, but also that philosophical brain that has ever since carried her through the most trying ordeals of life. The *Age of Progress*, published in Buffalo, in 1854, 1855, 1856 and 1857, edited by Stephen G. Albro, contains some of her poems given during her Buffalo engagement, and other items of great interest that were given through her lips."

We deem this letter and subject matter thereof so germane to our work that we give it in its entirety at this point; without it there would be a void in our history of her Buffalo work.

She closed her labors in Buffalo, in 1856, from which point she removed to New York city, where we find her laboring for the cause of Spiritualism, for the next ten years, with occasional visits to all of the large cities east of the Rocky Mountains. This next ten years' work will constitute an important epoch in our subject's life, the subject matter of which will fill the two succeeding chapters of this work.

CHAPTER VI.

NEW YORK WORK, ETC.

AFTER more than two years of constant labor in Buffalo and vicinity, Cora was called to take up a work in New York and other large cities of the Union. This indicates that her fame had grown beyond the confines of even so progressive a city as Buffalo, and that through the influence of such great thinkers as Hon. J. W. Edmonds, Horace H. Day, Horace Greeley, Prof. J. J. Mapes, and Prof. Robert Hare, she was to be introduced to the cultured minds of the older and larger cities of the land.

Horace H. Day was the editor of the "Christian Spiritualist," published in the fifties. He had visited Buffalo, and had listened to the wonderful utterances through the lips of Cora Scott. It was no doubt partly due to his glowing editorials and statements concerning her that Prof. Mapes and Horace Greeley were induced to go to Buffalo and hear for themselves. The editor of the "Spiritual Telegraph," Prof. S. B. Britten, also visited Buffalo as a lecturer, and saw our subject, among her own people, performing the duties of a pastor at the age of fifteen. No wonder that he, trained in scholastic lore and with years of experience as a clergyman, was surprised at the powers of this untutored girl. It was in the rooms of the ''Christian Spiritualist'' that Katie Fox was engaged by the year to give sittings and messages to all who came free of charge, Horace H. Day defraying all the expenses of the medium and her mother that the public might receive this wonderful light of spirit communion.

There also, in those rooms, Cora met Emma Hardinge (now Mrs. Britten), who had a musical institute in the same building. A year or two later Miss Hardinge became a speaker on the Spiritualist platform, her brilliant career being thenceforward contemporaneous with that of our subject.

Horace H. Day wrote of Cora Scott when he saw her at Buffalo:

''With hand crossed upon her breast, and eyes uplifted, she gave forth a prayer that seemed like an inspiration from Heaven itself, so deep, so fervent, so beautiful. The address that followed was upon the Sermon on the Mount, and never has it been my privilege to listen to such words as fell from the lips of this young girl apostle. * * * Let others go and listen, and then let them try to describe her and her utterances.''

We have already seen that Prof. Mapes visited Buffalo to listen to this gifted child of fourteen

years, and we are now to learn that Horace
Greeley made the trip from New York city for
the self same purpose. It is not because our
subject attracted such gifted men as these that
we publish the fact to the world, but merely to
show that her fame is not dependent upon the
men of fame, or women of fame that she called
to her different meetings. It is a pleasing thing
to record, however, that these gifted minds were
interested in Spiritualism, and we can now truthfully state, ardent and earnest believers in this
grand philosophy that we know by the name of
modern Spiritualism.

In the month of September, 1856, we find
Cora located in New York city. Here she was
greeted by crowded houses as she had been in
Buffalo, and each lecture was more largely attended than its predecessor had been. The
thoughts that she gave were appreciated by all
the best writers and thinkers of the time, and the
committees who selected her subjects were composed of the most scholarly men of the literary
clubs of New York city. Upon one occasion,
September 15th, 1856, she was given the subject
"The Philosophy of the Spheres," by a gentleman of education in that city. The following excerpt from this lecture, taken from the
Spiritual Telegraph, will show the beauty of the
thought given through this young girl of sixteen.

"You desire an elucidation of the philosophy

of the 'spheres,' or an explanation of the successive unfolding of the Spirit through different gradations, either embodied or disembodied. The word 'sphere' when applied to any object, simply signifies the orbicular condition or position of *that* object, and does not illustrate or imply any particular location with regard to other objects. But when applied to mind, it represents the compass or power of the mental capacity. The sphere of your material earth comprises all that space in which in which it moves and, atmospherically, all those elements that surround it and are influenced by its revolutionary changes. So the sphere of an individualized soul is the orbit of its revolutions, and the influence of its movements upon its own center of attraction.

"When we speak of the seven spheres or circles of the Spirit-world, we do not intend to convey the idea that our world is divided and subdivided into regular compartments, each separate and distinct in its formation. But that we may bring your capacities in harmonious communion with our own, we are obliged to render an outward or objective distinction, thereby enabling you to realize that we occupy a world as real, as tangible, and positive as your own. Seven is a harmonic number. There are seven great principles in the spiritual identification of mind, and there must be correspondingly seven material principles. There are seven hues in the rainbow,

or prismatic reflections of these hues.   You have
divided your weekly revolutions of time into seven
days.   There are seven grand principles of
melody in the harmonic world of music, and
each distinctive principle is a trinity.   Seven
and three are the combinations of harmonious
numbers ; three and seven are the union of harmonious sounds; and sounds and numbers are
the united representation of spiritual or real existence.

"But before I can proceed to a direct analysis
of spheral harmony, I must distinctly impress
upon your mind that ours is a world of causes, or
the spiritual, and yours is the world of effect or
the material.   And as no effect can exceed or
become superior to the cause, no embodied form
can represent fully the spirit of embodiment.
We see reflected in the drop of water a miniature
image of the whole starry heavens; but remove
the water and we see no stars—yet, does that
destroy the vast myriads of rolling worlds?   No!
We have only to look upward to see the reality.
So in the external world we see, embodied in the
flower, the beauty, the loveliness and odor of its
spiritual existence.   But soon the external flower
is destroyed by the blast, and its petals fall with-
ering to the ground.   But where is the odor, the
color, and the beauty?   Not dead, but blooming
in the atmosphere, more lovely because more refined and purified.

"Thus, my dear friend, it is with the soul you see reflected in the human or outward form, the image of the Spirit; and gazing upon its beauty and perfectness, you bow before the shrine of the exterior, forgetting that, like the drop of water, it must soon pass away. And when it is removed at last, mortals gaze in sorrow and sadness, striving to restore the faded image instead of lifting up their eyes to see the beautiful reality.

"The spheres of the human souls are like the orbits of planets, each perfect in itself, yet distinct and harmonious; and whether that soul exists in the external form, or in the interior and spiritual, it matters not, if it only attain its own orbit and not, like the erratic comet, flash a moment in the mental horizon and disappear. But even the comet occupies its own sphere, and never comes in contact with any other planet however near it may approach.

"Man's sphere is ascertained on earth by the external application of his interior powers. Men rear grand architectural palaces, whose marble halls and lofty turrets are emblazoned with the choicest gems of earth; surround themselves with every treasure of art, science or beauty. The poet weaves for himself the silken robe of song, and sees in all nature a grand lyric of perpetual beauty. The sculptor chisels for himself an embodiment of his ideal of Nature's perfect images. All these are the outbirth of the interior man, and illustrate the spheral or harmonic development of the soul.   The philanthropist creates for himself a pedestal of earnest and perfect love, and with clear and piercing eye traces out the windings of his pathway, gazes on the whole race of souls, and with one loving clasp draws the whole world to his noble heart and bears them on to joy.

"Thus it is in our life.   The architect creates for himself the ideal, yet real images of his interior thought, and sees in the whole universe a grand and perfect temple.   These thoughts are handed down through successive spheres until at last they reach the earth.

"Here the poet sings his lyric rhymes in harmony with eternity's everlasting beauty, and this, like the other, permeates all spheres corresponding with its own, until some soul on earth, catching the inspiration, speaks, and lo! the poem becomes an outward form.

"Here Mozart thrills forever the strings of Nature's lyre, and improvises grandest melodies in harmony with Eternity's glorious voice.   And Rembrandt, through his own ideal and imaginative power, pictures for himself a panoramic scene of Creation's lovely landscapes, presenting to the eye of God the artist power of Nature.

"Thus in the interior and exterior worlds the spheral harmonies of each are combined, while the soul, immortal in its powers, passes from gra-

dation to gradation, from world to world, from
universe to universe, retaining still its own sphere,
and performing still its revolutions around its center, viz., its own interior self."

Early in October following this series of lectures in Gotham, we find our medium in Baltimore. At that time Spiritualism was in a very
healthy condition, both morally and intellectually, which gave it character and influence
among the thinking minds of the people of that
city. Her audience consisted of judges, lawyers,
teachers, naval officers, all of whom were deeply
interested in the lectures given by this young
girl; and if any of these scholarly men felt that
Spiritualism was not worthy of an investigation,
they were at least forced to admit that they did
not have, even among their hoary-headed veterans and teachers, one who, in intellectual philosophy, could cope with this young girl of sixteen.
These thoughts are culled from a letter in the
"Spiritual Telegraph," of October 25, 1856.

Under date of October 14th, the late Washington A. Danskin writes from Baltimore, in reference to our subject, as follows:

"The fair apostle of the Gospel of Truth has
been lecturing in our midst for the past ten days,
and through her instrumentality a new impulse
has been given to the cause of mental freedom.
Her public lectures have been well attended and
produced a decided sensation. In the elucida-

tion of the subjects presented there was exhibited
a profundity of thought, brilliancy of description,
beauty of imagery, and fluency of language,
which even the most determined skeptic could
not attribute to the natural powers of the youthful and unassuming speaker. A still deeper impression was made, however, by the manifestations given in private circles. On one occasion
some twelve or fourteen gentlemen, of legal, scientific and literary attainments, were engaged for
two hours in proposing questions metaphysical,
philosophical, and varied in character, and the
answers were so prompt, so clear, and displayed
so much erudition and logical reasoning, combined with poetical beauty, that all present expressed their wonder and delight. Those who
still fear to avow a belief in the intercourse with
the Spirit world, pronounced it a manifestation
of intellectuality, surpassing all their previous
conceptions."

During the greater portion of the time from
1856 to 1866, our subject made the city of New
York her general headquarters, and from that
place she visited the cities East and West, in the
course of each year. Thus, we find her in the
Fall of 1856 giving a course of lectures in the
city of Baltimore. From that city she returned
to New York, and while it is not permitted to us
to follow her from city to city and review each
lecture, yet we feel it incumbent upon us to give

a general description of the work she performed in each of these cities, if not in a specific sense in a way that will connect each year's work with the one preceding, so that our readers can note the results obtained through her indefatigable labors.

From Baltimore she returned to her New York home and resumed her work in that city. Late in December of 1856, we find her guides writing as follows:

"All truth is ultimate, for truth is a principle. Principles being the attributes of God, are ever ultimate and perfect. The comprehension of truths by mortal minds, we define as facts. For instance, it is a truth that the construction of the solar system is spheral and that planets revolve around the sun in exact proportion, distance, density, etc. But it has been a fact only a few years; therefore we define truth an ultimate principle, unchanging and unchangeable, eternal and all-pervading—an attribute of God. Fact is man's comprehension of truth as manifested in the external development of the human intellect. As a further illustration of our position, let us illustrate. It is a truth that the human mind can be better governed by love than by force, for 'God is love;' but the fact has not become visible to the majority of the human race. Is it less a truth because they do not comprehend it? We answer, No. Finally, let

us say that truth is absolute, a positive (not relative) principle, the entire comprehension of
which is only in the mind of the Deity; therefore, the mind of man can never grasp its fullest
meaning; yet, does that change the truth itself?
No. Facts are the manifestation of truth
through the comprehension of the human intellect. We wish you to remember this and trace
the laws more deeply, and we are quite certain
you will agree with us in opinion."

This communication was signed " Philosophic
Guardian," evidently one of the higher guides,
to whom we have already called our readers' attention. We present such gems of truth as this,
in order that our readers may become familiar
with the wealth of thought that flowed forth
from the hidden mine of Spirit power with which
she was possessed. Wherever she went the
most difficult questions were always conjured up
by some scholar, statesman or politician and presented to her for elucidation. In Baltimore, we
find on one occasion the following subject given:
"The Antiquity of the World as Proved by the
Discovery of Geology; its Consistency, as a
Science, with Biblical History." A big topic for
a young lady not yet seventeen, to speak upon
to college-bred men. We find her here at this
time contending with the ex-Governor of Mary-
land, a man of superior intellectual abilities,
educated for the priesthood, and carefully trained

as a lawyer, a ready debater whose powers in this direction had been tested again and again, and who had never yet come off second best in any contest, yet, when he was brought into an argument with our subject, it was unanimously agreed by his own friends that he was fairly and completely overthrown, that it was not a matter of question but an overwhelming defeat. Our language is that of a friend who gave an interesting account of the controversy, in the "Spiritual Telegraph," early in the year 1857.

During the Winter of 1856-57, as we have already stated, our medium visited all of the large Eastern cities, and her work in Philadelphia is worthy of an especial notice, because of the high intellectual standing of the audiences that greeted her there. She filled the largest hall in the "Quaker City," with audiences who were deeply interested in that which came from her inspired lips. At times (we are told upon the authority of those who attended her lectures) she was greeted by audiences of more than five thousand people, who were not only interested in, but were instructed by the teachings advanced through her lectures. We subjoin a personal letter from Hon. Thomas M. Locke, a prominent citizen of Philadelphia, who speaks of her as follows:

DEAR BROTHER BARRETT : It is with pleasure that I give my personal recollections of Mrs. Rich-

mond's wonderful work in Philadelphia. My
first impression was that of astonishment to hear
from the lips of such a child (for such she appeared to be to me, as she was about sixteen years
of age at that time), such a flow of logic and
powerful reasoning as fell from her lips. The
people of Philadelphia were delighted, as well as
astonished, with her style of speaking and mar-
veled much at her wonderful oratory. The hall
was crowded whenever she lectured here; in fact,
the hall would not begin to seat the people
who flocked to hear her. She attracted the
brightest minds in our city. Such men as John
W. Forney, of the Philadelphia Press; Geo. W.
Childs, recently ascended, the well-known phil-
anthrophist and founder of the Philadelphia
Ledger; Hon. Wm. D. Kelley, who, for thirty
years, represented our state in Congress; Col. S.
P. Kase; Prof. Robert Hare, whose fame as a
scientist was world-wide, and many others of the
brightest minds and best thinkers who were then
living in Philadelphia, crowded the hall during her
stay with us. The secular papers at that time commented freely and favorably upon her lectures,
and regarded her as one of the wonders of the
age—some of them admitted that they had never
heard such lectures before. At nearly every meeting she held on Sundays, for several succeeding
seasons, during which she visited our city, we could
see John W. Forney and George W. Childs sit-

ting at the editorial table in front of the audience, with pencils in hand, ready to take excerpts
from her lectures. Mr. Forney became a thorough Spiritualist, and for many years George W.
Childs was deeply interested in the phenomena
and philosophy of our religion. Her lectures
attracted the attention of the liberal minded and
most intelligent people of our city, and gave Spiritualism an impetus it had never attained prior to
her advent. What puzzled the people most was
the masterly and wonderful manner that she had
in discussing the various questions presented to
her by her audiences. During her stay with us,
a number of scientific gentlemen proposed some
difficult questions, the answers to which were of
such a character as to completely astound them,
for they knew it was impossible for a lady of her
age to comprehend them, much less to answer
them intelligently. The audience was greatly
delighted with the wonderful knowledge she
seemed to possess, and the thorough manner in
which she treated these questions proved that there
was some power outside of herself who was assist-
ing her in her work.

It was not my pleasure to attend all of her lectures, but I am giving you my recollections of
those I did attend. I do know that she drew
immense audiences to listen to her lectures, and
gave those who had the pleasure of attending them
a better idea of Spiritualism than they ever had

previous to that time. Captain Kieffer, Colonel
Kase, Jonathan M. Roberts and many others could
give you more information upon this subject than
I can, but some of them have passed to spirit life,
and I have found it impossible to visit Captain
Kieffer or Colonel Kase in reference to this matter. I regret that I cannot give you more information upon the subject, but it is with pleasure
that I contribute my mite to your proposed biography of this great and gifted teacher in our ranks.
The return of the times and inspiration through
such a child as she was then, to our city, now,
would be an inestimable boon; but Spiritualism
is progressing in the Quaker City, and we shall
ultimately win the good fight for the uplifting of
humanity.

Wishing Mrs. Richmond and yourself unbounded success and prosperity, I am,

Your sincere friend,

THOMAS M. LOCKE.

607 N. 7th st., Philadelphia, Pa.

The month of March, 1857, finds our subject
lecturing before large assemblages of learned
people in Boston, where she created an unusual
sensation. The clergy were invited to attend
her meetings and suggest subjects for discussion.
The report of these meetings in the "Spiritual
Telegraph" says that the hall was densely
crowded, and that hundreds were obliged to go
away for want of a convenient place to stand.

The Boston "Daily Ledger" contained the following interesting paragraph:

"The Spiritual meeting last night, in Horticultural Hall, was a large and attentive one. The speaker certainly performed wonderful things, whether she did it under the influences of higher intelligences or not. The questions that were put directly by several gentlemen in the audience in relation to the teachings of the Scriptures, and in explanation of various texts taken at random from all parts of the sacred volume, were answered without the least hesitation and with a definitiveness and beauty of expression that, to say the least, charmed all who heard her. What gives the character of her answers to questions still greater interest is the fact that she is yet seventeen years of age, has received but a very limited education, and speaks in a strain of beauty and eloquence that is exceedingly impressive."

In her work in New York city her lectures were so popular that ordinary halls would not seat the great crowds that sought to listen to her inspired utterances, so that the largest theater in the city was secured on different occasions, and even this was taxed to its utmost capacity to accommodate the people who rushed in to hear her.

We have already referred to the fact that many of the most gifted literary men and women of the nation were attracted by the lectures. Among these we may mention, at this point, the popular author and editor, the gifted N. P. Willis, who may be ranked among the classic poets of America His impressions of our subject in the "Home Journal," of which he was then the able editor, are as follows:

"The lady speaker was introduced to the audience a few minutes after we took our seats in a pew of the Tabernacle—a delicate-featured blonde of seventeen or eighteen, with flaxen ringlets falling over her shoulders, movements deliberate and self-possessed, voice calm and deep, and eyes and fingers no way nervous. The subject being given her by a gentleman in the crowd ("Whether man is a part of God"), she commenced with a prayer—and very curious it was to see a long-haired young woman standing alone in the pulpit, her face turned upward, her delicate bare arms raised in a clergyman's attitude of devotion, and a church full of people listening attentively while she prayed. A passage in the Bible occurred to me:

" 'Let your women keep silence in the churches, for it is not permitted unto them to speak.

" 'And if they will learn anything, let them ask their husbands at home; for it is a shame for women to speak in the church. Cor. xiv: 34, 35.'

" But my instinctive feeling, I must own, made

no objection to the propriety of the performance. The tone and manner were of an absolute sincerity of devoutness which compelled respect; and, before she closed I was prepared to believe her an exception — either that a male spirit was speaking through her lips or that the relative position of the sexes is not the same as in the days of St. Paul. How was it with the Corinthians? Women are certainly better than we in these latter days, and, as standing far nearer to God, may properly speak for us, even in holy places—or so it seemed to me while listening to her.

"Upon the platform, in the rear of the pulpit, sat three reporters; and the daily papers have given outlines of the argument between the fair 'medium' and an antagonistic clergyman who was present. No report can give any fair idea of the 'spirit presence,' however,—I mean of the self-possessed dignity, clearness, promptness and undeniable superiority of the female reasoner. Believe what you will of her source of inspiration — whether she speaks her own thoughts or those of other spirits — it is as nearly supernatural eloquence as the most hesitating faith could reasonably require. I am, perhaps, from long study and practice, as good a judge of fitness in the use of language as most men, and in a full hour of close attention I could detect no word that could be altered for the better—none, indeed (and this surprised me still more), which was not used with strict fidelity to its derivative meaning. The practiced scholarship which this last point usually requires, and the curious, un-hesitating and confident fluency with which the beautiful language was delivered was (critically) wonderful. It would have astonished me in an extempore speech by the most accomplished orator in the world.

"The argument was long and, on the clergy-man's part, a warm and sarcastic one. The reverend gentleman (what is commonly described as a 'smart man with high health, a remark-ably large and high forehead, and a lawyer's sub-tlety of logic), alternated speeches with the 'medium' for an hour and a half, leaving the audience, I thought, unanimously on the lady's side. But, what was very curious and amusing, was the difference of scope and dignity in the operation of the two minds. She looked at the subject through an open window, and he through the keyhole. She was severe by the courage, skill and good calm temper with which she met his objections in the full face of their meaning only, disregarding their sneers; and he was severe by twisting her words into constructions not intended, and by feathering the sarcasms thereupon with religious commonplaces. Instead of the sonorous obscurity and rhapsody of which the Spiritualists are commonly accused, her argu-

ment was the directest and coolest possible
specimen (my brother and I thought) of fair,
clear reasoning.

"If you recollect my conversation on this subject, my experience in Spiritualism has always
been unsatisfactory. The 'Fox girls' and others
have tried their spells upon me in vain. It
has seemed to me that I was one of those to
whom was not 'given' (as the Bible says) ' the
discerning of spirits.' But it would be very
bigoted and blind not to see and acknowledge
the wonderful intellectual demonstration made
by this young girl; and how to explain it, with
her age, habits and education, is the true point at
issue. I think we should at least look at it seriously, if only in obedience to the Scripture exhor-
tation which closes the chapter on this very subject: 'Covet earnestly the best gifts.'"

In the Spring and Summer of 1857, she made
an extensive tour of the Western States. The
month of June was passed in the city of Baltimore where she attracted the usual large audiences. On this trip she visited Cleveland, Akron,
O., Chicago, Illinois, and many of the towns
near the large cities to which we have referred.
An anonymous writer speaks of her at this time
as follows:

"To us she seems a bright, pure spirit, endowed with heaven's richest gifts. Her impressive invocations which generally precede her lec-

tures, seem almost to bear one near the highest
courts of Heaven. She is a child of the richest
inspiration. Able critics have spoken in terms of
commendation of her superior talents, captiva-
ting oratory and eloquence. Her lectures were
universally conceded to be profoundly scientific
and philosophical, and were received with much
satisfaction by many who had previously manifested little interest in Spiritualism. None of
the clergy dared to meet this uneducated girl of
seventeen, for they could not accomplish in a
lifetime what she was doing with ease, every day
of her life."

The latter part of July found her in the Western States, where she awakened a great deal of
interest in the subject of Spiritualism. She
created a furore by the remarkable results that
were obtained through her addresses in the city
of Milwaukee. An editorial from Britten's
"Spiritual Age," under date of August, 1857,
contained an excerpt from the "Daily Wisconsin," then published in Milwaukee, and is in
point here. We quote it entire for the benefit of
our readers:

"The lady is but seventeen years of age, of
rather slight figure, with blue eyes, flaxen hair,
and features very animated and spirituelle. The
subjects for her discourses yesterday, were chosen
for her by a committee, selected by the audience,
who had the privilege of selecting anything from

the whole range of philosophy or ethics. The
subject proposed by the committee in the morning, was 'The Creation or Origin of Mankind.'
As soon as the theme was announced, the lady
stepped forward to the desk, offered a most
beautiful and eloquent prayer, and then unfolded
her subject. She spoke over an hour, most
beautifully, without the least hesitation, going
over the whole range of philosophical and theological theories on the matter, analyzing them
and pointing out their supposed fallacies, and
giving her own solution of the subject.

"In the evening quite a large audience assembled to hear the medium. The committee appointed for the selection of a subject were Hon.
Judge Smith, Hon. Judge MacArthur, and S. M.
Booth. The subject selected was "Death—
Man's state after Death, his Destiny, and the
means by which he must reach that Destiny."
The process which the medium exhibits in going
into the trance state is quite interesting. Her
eyes are rolled upward, a slight nervous tremor
is observable through her whole frame, then an
expression of mingled pleasure and surprise flits
across her countenance, lips quiver, and the
tears start in her large blue eyes, and then, with
a spasmodic jerk, her face resumes a natural expression, but all glowing with a new animation
appears to be intently gazing at the Spirits who
are entrancing her.

"We have always felt as though this spiritual mediumship was the sheerest moonshine and humbug, but it is certainly a difficult thing to account, in any ordinary way, for the facility with which this lady, of seventeen years speaks upon subjects which have puzzled the greatest intellects of the world. The mere knowledge which she displays of the theories and speculations of others is wonderful, even in a toiling Crichton—how much more in such a youth. What man in these United States would dare stand up before the audiences of our critics, and announce to speak, extempore, on any subject, scientific and moral, and submit himself to the questioning of his hearers? If any man would dare do it, he would only cover himself with ridicule at the first attempt.

"In whatever way you account for the wonderful knowledge and power of language which she displays, whether as the inspiration of Spirits, the result of devoted and exhausting study, or the intuition of genius, the fact itself, as it stands forth patent to all, is an extraordinary phenomenon."

About the first of September she returned to the State of New York, visited Buffalo, Rochester, Saratoga, Oswego, Syracuse, Albany and Utica on her way to New York city, where she purposed spending the Winter. In all of these cities she was greeted by large and enthusiastic audiences, and in Oswego created no little excitement through the attack made upon her by Rev. W. N. Barber, a prominent clergyman of that city. Her friends immediately challenged the reverend gentleman to a discussion of the points at issue, which he promptly refused to accept. Then the following proposition was submitted to the gentleman, and we present it to our readers that they may determine for themselves whether unfair advantage had been taken of him or not. A committee of persons was to be mutually agreed upon, whose duty it was to designate some philosophical or metaphysical subject, to be discussed by our medium and Mr. Barber. This committee was to be composed of persons competent to judge of the question they propounded to them. Neither Mr. Barber nor the lady were to know what the subject was until they stood before the audience. If the reverend gentleman did not care to accept this, she would give him a month in which to prepare upon the question submitted, during which period of time she was to be kept in entire ignorance of the subject that she was to discuss with him, when the debate should take place. Strange to say, the reverend gentleman declined to accept this proposition, no doubt fearing that he would be worsted in the encounter, as he certainly would have been.

On this extended tour many ingenious arguments to account for the wealth of thought, that she was constantly pouring forth in her discourses, were advanced. One of the strangest we mention at this point—that her so-called trance or hypnotic condition brought her *en rapport* with the minds of eminent men, living in the body, from whom these marvelous thoughts were derived, although these eminent men might be living in cities thousands of miles from the point where the lectures were delivered. Some said it might be possible for her to come *en rapport* with eminent minds in the Spiritual world, but the theory that it should apply to the world of matter was the one most strenuously advocated. This is unconscious cerebration that beats the theory of Dr. Carpenter in every respect. Admit for a moment that it was true that the minds of these eminent men did give her her thoughts— by what law could these thoughts be transmitted across thousands of miles of space to her sensitized brain without some spiritual agent or medium coming in to carry the message to and fro. Our readers will see that this theory of the wiseacres proves too much, and cuts the ground out from under their own feet. It only shows how anxious the opponents of Spiritualism were to disprove the fact of Spirit communion.

The fame of our subject had by this time become national, and her services were greatly sought in every city of any size in the United

States. Many liberal Unitarian ministers opened their churches to her, and even requested her to occupy their pulpits. She was the marvel of the time, and was always greeted by crowded houses.

October, 1857, finds her *en route* for Boston, in the vicinity of which city she spent the next two months. During this time she spoke in Chelsea, Cambridgeport, Salem, New Bedford and Boston. At Cambridgeport her subject was given her by Prof. Felton, of Harvard University. He chose a Bible text from the Book of Ecclesiastes, 9th chapter, 10th verse: "Whatsoever thy hand findeth to do, do it with thy might, for there is no work, nor device, nor knowledge, nor wisdom in the grave whither thou goest." At the conclusion of the lecture Prof. Felton arose and, with deep emotion, spoke about as follows:

"It is well known that I have no confidence in the Spiritual idea—I have written against and talked against it. The discourse to which I have listened this evening is most truly a christian one, and sets forth in the most beautiful and sublime manner the teachings of our holy religion. I cannot recognize it as a fact that Webster will come through a medium and utter language such as I have heard attributed to him; I cannot believe that Isaac Newton would come through a medium and be unable to spell his name properly. If I were Isaac Newton I would come

through your organism," he continued earnestly.
"I would be happy to see you rid of this delusion, and see you going about the world demonstrating the beautiful doctrines you have advanced to-night."

Prof. Felton was much affected by the discourse
to which he had listened, and it made a deep and
lasting impression upon his mind.

The Newburyport "Herald," November 21,
1857, says: "The lady made no failure in anything she undertook, no hesitation in giving an
answer to any question upon any subject, and
these answers gave satisfaction to her interrogators. To say that she does it herself is to invest
her with understanding, information, qualifica-
tions, and taste possessed by no person on earth,
while it is obvious that she is not above ordinary
intellects, and her age precludes a possibility of
her being at all conversant with the topics that
come before her. Her language is perfect. All
that N. P. Willis says of her was perfectly true
here. She was watched by the best scholars in
town and they did not discover the misuse of a
single word. She claims that it is a Spiritual
power that assists her. If she is not right, by
what power is it? If we deny her affirmation we
feel bound to give some other explanation more
rational, and that explanation we have not.
The facts were as we have stated, and five hundred persons were witness thereto. But by what

influence these facts were produced, we leave each person to say for himself."

This testimony from a secular paper we consider of great moment, and it shows the attitude of minds outside the ranks of Spiritualists, towards the work that was being done by our subject.

In nearly every city of New England, visited by her, this same report was given by the secular papers, all of which gave full reports of her lectures.

At Lynn, Mass., in December, 1857, she was greeted by an audience composed largely of Catholics and ignorant Protestants. The committees that selected her questions, however, were composed of scholarly men, but they were intensely orthodox in their views, and they began by putting a series of questions to her in order that they might confound the guides who were to give the lecture of the evening. The first question was, "Will you please define the Pythagorean proposition?" The guides immediately asked the committee, "Which proposition do you mean—the Moral Code or the so-called Scientific Proposition?" The committee refused to answer, saying the guides ought to know what they meant. The guides took up the Moral Code of Pythagoras, as it was presumably the one the committee desired explained. She gave her usual explanation of the Pythagorean morals in a most

scholarly and eloquent manner, but the committee immediately arose and stated that they meant
the Scientific Code. *The guides immediately
stated that they were willing to give a lecture on
that subject if the committee would give them an
opportunity, but this they refused to do, much to
the delight of the rabble, who were intent on
breaking up the meeting. The committee seemed
upon persecuting our subject, so asked her,
''When will two parallel lines meet in space?''
and ''Could she give the diameter of a bucket
that was filled to the brim with water?'' Her
answers will probably be long remembered in
Lynn by the members of that committee and by
all Spiritualists. They were about as follows:
''Two parallel lines will meet in space when a
speaker can find intelligence for her interrogators
and interpret that intelligence to themselves,''
and, ''The diameter of a bucket of water is probably as great as the diameter of a cranial structure, destitute of the grey material denominated
' brain' by so-called scientists.'' She was equally
ready with her responses to any and all questions
propounded to her in all of the cities she visited
in New Englan

The demand for her services was so great in
New England that instead of remaining two or
three months as she at first purposed doing, she
remained in that section until August, 1858.
During this time she published a book contain-

ing her discourses, given through her organism, during the months passed in New England. This was issued from the press of Beale Marsh, 14 Bromfield street, Boston. in 1858. We commend this work to the attention of our readers, as it is especially valuable in connection with the life history of this gifted speaker.

From one of her lectures, delivered in Meionian Hall, Boston, June 13th, 1858, on the subject, "The Distinction between Truth and Fact," we quote:

"It is customary for man to speak of the truth from the position to which his mind has attained. In court a man swears to tell the truth, the whole truth and nothing but the truth, yet he only promises to tell the truth as he conceives it to be. You speak of the truths of religion. All that appears to you in the consecrated religious dogmas has no relevancy to religious truth. The Bible, as far as it is historically correct, is not a truth but a record of facts. There is no such thing in nature, in art, or in intellect as truth. Intellect is but fact, and mind is built upon the basis of cold facts. Art and science are not truths, only in so far as they speed the soul on in its attainments. So with architecture, it is a matter of beauty. There is no principle of truth in the statement that the earth is round. It is but a fact. Is there any evidence that any one law of science is perfect?

None at all. Facts, then, are but stepping-stones to truths. Creeds and dogmas ever remain the same—they never progress. They are not facts, consequently they are not truths, only man's expression of what he considers to be truth as regards religion. You cannot cling to favorite opinions or old-time institutions and arrive at truth. The greatness of truth is its simplicity. In the Spiritualism of today there is a large amount of facts and not enough of truth—many witness and acknowledge its facts yet deny its truths. You should not dwell upon the facts of the tippings and the raps always, but you should question the spirits what you may do to advance your soul toward truth."

These words, we opine, would apply to the Spiritualists of today as forcibly as they did to the Spiritualists of the year 1858. These sentences simply show her power as a speaker at that early age, and prove that there is a rich treasury of knowledge in her books, published during these earlier years.

Dr. A. B. Childs says of her, July 24th, 1858:

"The lady can address an audience of five thousand people with great ease, and the guides through her give an elaborate discourse upon any subject the audience may choose. There cannot well be a greater test of Spirit power than this."

In four years, commencing with the year 1854,

coming down to the present time, she has given over six hundred lectures.

It is not strange in view of the vast amount of work performed by her during these four years of active labor, that her health should fail her as it did during the summer of 1858. For some six or eight months she was in retirement, in the hands of kind friends who were endeavoring to nurse her back to health and strength. Her home during this period and for several years thereafter was with Mr. and Mrs. William A. Ludden, of Clinton Ave., Brooklyn, who ever took an earnest and loving interest in her and her work. She speaks of these friends at this time of trial and suffering with much feeling, and states that her kindest thoughts and soulful prayers have ever gone out to them for their sympathy and kind nursing during these long months of illness and consequent suffering. She was patient and bore her sufferings without one word of complaint, and endeared herself to all who knew her, by her serenity of spirit and her determination to rise above the pain that racked her slender frame. With the assistance of her kind Spirit friends, aided by the friends in mortal form, she recovered her health, and about the middle of January, 1859, was again ready for the public rostrum.

She reopened her public services in Clinton Hall, New York city. This hall is one of the largest in the metropolis, and standing-room was at a premium on this occasion, and on all subsequent occasions that she graced its platform. Her services in Clinton Hall continued through the Winter and Spring of 1859. She not only spoke twice on Sunday, but lectured Wednesday evening at the same place. Her meetings were attended by such able thinkers as Prof. J. J. Mapes, Horace Greeley, Henry Ward Beecher, Dr. E. H. Chapin, and other liberal clergymen, all of whom united in pronouncing her discourses to be almost miraculous in their production.

Her lecture of May 4th, 1859, is especially worthy of note. Her subject was "Facts and Fancies." This discourse has been published in full, and we simply call our readers' attention to it that they may procure it for themselves.

Space forbids our following in detail her several lectures, but we cannot refrain quoting from "Phœnix" (Prof. J. J. Mapes), in regard to the value of her lectures: "She renders the most abstruse points perfectly understandable to the most common auditor. In close analysis of words she is not surpassed, and her knowledge of natural law seems to be an intuition amounting almost to a certainty. Her high-toned moral character has at all times defied the tongue of calumny. In metaphysics she shows a degree of erudition hitherto unknown amongst the greatest scholars of the world."

During the Spring and Summer of 1859, she gave a series of ten lectures on the general sub-ject of the sciences and their philosophy. These lectures were reported in full for the "Banner of Light," and can be found in the files of that valuable paper of the year 1859. We call our readers' attention to the subjects treated by the speaker, in order that they may become acquainted with the thought of that far-off period, and understand for themselves that these subjects were formulated by such men as Prof. J. J. Mapes, Horace Greeley, Mr. Beecher and others. Her first subject was "Religion: Its Necessities and Effects;" the second, "The Applied Sciences: a Resume of Their Teachings;" third, "Religion of the Ancient Egyptians;" fourth, "Mental Philosophy;" fifth, "Religion of the Medes and Persians;" sixth, "The Primitive Elements of Chemistry;" seventh, "Origin, Progress and Effects of Mohamedanism;" eighth, "Geology;" ninth, "The Romish Church;" tenth, "Plants and Animals." This wide range of subjects indicates the versatility of gifts of the speaker, and shows that the higher guides, to whom we have referred, were correct in affirming that each one had his especial field of labor, and was able to give in his own way his thought to the people of earth, because of the perfect instrument upon which he had to play.

This valuable series of lectures was followed

by another of equal moment in Music Hall, Boston. Among the subjects treated during this course we notice the following: "Worship, and its Relation to the True Feelings of Religion;" again, "What Does Morality Mean?" "The History of Republics; Can their Rise and Fall be Traced to Moral and Religious Causes?" etc., etc. These were also reported in full for the Spiritual papers of the time.

In the early autumn of 1859 she made an extensive tour of the Northern New England States, lecturing in Bangor, Waterville, Augusta, Brunswick, Lewiston and Portland, Maine; Manchester, Concord and Nassau, N. H., where she was greeted with the same degree of enthusiasm she had aroused in New York, Brooklyn and Boston. She returned to her New York pastorate in November, 1859, resumed her labors in Clinton Hall. The people thronged this hall with such numbers that they could not obtain standing room, and her friends rented Hope Chapel, No. 720 Broadway, where larger numbers could be accommodated. It is said of her at this time that "she gave the veritable bread of heaven to the millions of earth. The fact cannot be disputed, and certainly admits of no disguise, that she carried the claims of Spiritualism home to the hearts and minds of multitudes who gave the subject no thought until they heard the music of her voice and were convinced of the super-

mortal origin of the ideas that took form in
words and burned on the lip, only to ignite the
elements of deeper feeling and higher thought in
all who waited on her gentle and persuasive
ministry." ("Banner of Light.") This quotation is from an editorial commenting upon the
change from Clinton Hall to Hope Chapel, New
York. Continuing, the editor of the "Banner"
says: "If this fair young preacher of a living
gospel is enshrined in the memories and affections of many people, it is because many have
been made to feel that the medium and her in-
variable inspirers have led them gently, and by
pleasant paths, towards the sources of light and
to the pure springs of a loving and living inspiration. She will continue her meetings in Hope
Chapel during the ensuing year."

During the greater portion of the year 1860
our subject was struggling with ill health, and
was unable to fill platform engagements for a
number of months. While she was in this forced
retirement it is safe to say that her powers as a
medium and speaker were greatly enhanced, and
that she came forth to the world better fitted to
discharge the onerous duties laid upon her by
her friends from both sides of life. Although
she was suffering from physical pain, she bore it
with an equanimity of spirit that presaged a
knowledge of the powers of her own soul that
enabled it to triumph over the ills of the body,

so she had no need to murmur against the fate
that had bound her in those chains. She was
sustained, no doubt, by the words of consolation from those higher guides, whose humble
servitor she had been for ten years, whose influence could not avert the disease that was the result of overwork on the mortal side of life. She
says at this period that "the ministry of pain is
always kind, because nature never calls upon us
to suffer more than we can endure." When pain
becomes too great to be borne some kind law
of nature has been provided by means of which
we become unconscious, totally oblivious of our
own suffering, and to the outside world as well.
In the midst of this sleep, or state of oblivion,
when the mind is unconscious, mortals often
lose their hold upon the golden chord of life and
set sail for

"That beautiful land we have never seen,
Where the feet of mortals have never been."

She occupied the platform in Hope Chapel as
long as her health would permit, and then as we
have stated was forced to go into retirement
until her health again warranted her in taking
the rostrum.

On Sunday, December 2nd, she again came
before the public in Dodworth's Hall. On this
occasion Christopher Cooker, a correspondent of
the Pall Mall Gazette, of London, England, was
present. In a letter to his journal he spoke of

the two lectures, to which he listened, in the most glowing terms, marveling at the beautiful language she used in her prayer, also at the scholarship and profundity of thought expressed in these lectures. He casually remarked that these trance lectures appeared to be immensely popular in America, inasmuch as the hall was well filled, notwithstanding the inclemency of the weather on both occasions. He also stated that only one trance speaker was then found in England.

On December 30th, 1860, the subject of her lecture was "Italy — its Past, Present and Future." This lecture excited widespread attention and was commented upon by the daily papers of New York, as well as by the Spiritualist papers in different sections of the country. The value of its thought was apparent to all, and much that was then said could be applied to the thought of our own times in a most helpful way. This lecture is published in the "Banner of Light," and can be found in the files of that most excellent journal for that year.

During the months of January and February, 1861, she continued to occupy the platform of Dodworth's Hall, and addressed the thousands who thronged to hear her upon any and all subjects that their curiosity or desire for information might lead them to wish to obtain through her.

Dr. Greer, now a distinguished exponent of

Spiritualism and an old-time friend of our subjects, speaks as follows of our philosophy and its
exponent, Mrs. Richmond:

Mr. H. D. BARRETT, Lily Dale, N. Y.

DEAR SIR AND BROTHER: I often recall with
pleasure the first Sunday in January, 1861, when
landing from Europe, in New York city, I had
scarcely more than put my foot on American soil,
when accosted at my hotel (the Stevens House)
by a stranger, asking if I had ever heard of the
wonders of Spiritualism. I replied that I had
come to this country, especially, to learn of its
movements and to investigate its claims, remark-
ing that much of my future in this country would
greatly depend upon my verdict of it, that if one-
half I had heard of it was true there would be
something in it for me to do, for that I had
wished to be somewhat connected with it. Then
said he ''Come with me to a Spiritual church
meeting, and I will introduce you, there, to the
pastor, (now Mrs. Cora L. V. Richmond), a celebrated trance speaker.''

I immediately acquiesced, and taking with me
my son Joseph, then a little lad in knicker-
bockers, I accompanied my new found friend to
a large and spacious hall, well filled with an intelligent audience of both sexes. I well recollect
my pleasure and surprise at seeing, on the rostrum, there, a woman—a bright young woman,
''divinely fair,'' in chaste attire, with clear cut

features and sweet blue eyes, radiant with beauty, purity and intelligence from a righteous indwelling soul, crowned by a rich profusion of pretty, blonde hair, falling from a perfect typical head, in graceful ringlets upon her shoulders, with contenance benign and voice of melody orating in sweetest tones of deep, religious fervor, on the love of the Infinite, the glories of the universe, and kingdom of the soul. And, oh! how the sublime thought and entrancing eloquence did uplift my soul and make my heart throb with sacred emotion and gratitude to the Spirit realm. Such exalted thought and charming oratory I had never heard before and such feminine loveliness, on a rostrum, I had never seen before. To possess such a lovely, fairy mortal—for her intellect and genius—I would have given a kingdom, or braved a world of dangers. Lost in wonder and admiration, I could only weep with tears of joy, and bless the stranger who had led me to this shrine of the New Dispensation, where, for the first time in my life, my ears were greeted with the voice of inspiration, direct from the world of spirits.

But, strange to say, my venerable guide, after introducing me to the pastor, immediately disappeared from the crowded hall and I never saw him more.

Thus did this remarkable woman first impress me—an ornament, a luminary and a power.

But the crowning remembrance of all was my
introduction to her after the service, when, at a
glance, she declared I had a mission in this country to perform, that I was destined for a long life
of spiritual work as a healer, and that my greatest compensation would be the favor of the
Divine. "Then," said she, "When you are old
and bent, with locks of white, this, your son,
will take your place. He will take up your work
where you leave off, and golden showers of reward will be heaped upon him."

These predictions are all now literally fulfilled
which illustrates well the power of prophecy in
those early days. For instance, I am now past
seventy, with thirty-three years before the public
as a healer; and, now, my son—a medical graduate—has taken up my work on lines where I
left off, some years ago, and already golden
showers have fallen upon him, as his real estate
possessions and financial ratings do show, and
so is prophecy fulfilled.

The name of Cora L. V. Richmond, famous
as a spirit medium, and exponent of the Spiritual philosophy, is known in every land where
the philosophy is cultivated.

In all the Spiritual centers of the civilized
world her genius has long been recognized. She
is acknowledged to be the leading Spiritual
orator in America. Her genius attracted the attention of the First Society of Spiritualists in

Chicago (the leading society), some eighteen years ago, when she was appointed its pastor. She is still its pastor, and is more revered by her people today then ever.

It is now some thirty years since first I chose her for my pastor in New York city; and, now, again, in Chicago, she is still my pastor; my wife, two grown daughters and myself being members of her society. ROBERT GREER.

Chicago, Ill., May 30th, 1894.

CHAPTER VII.

NEW YORK WORK. —(CONTINUED.)

IT was in the month of February, 1861, that
Spirit Andrew Jackson gave a lecture through
her upon the subject of "The Condition of the
Country." This lecture was published in pamphlet form, and was ready for distribution on
the 4th of March, 1861, at the time of the inauguration of Abraham Lincoln.

As our readers can well imagine, these winter
months of 1861-62 were full of stirring events.
Secession was in the air and the fires of patriot-
ism were being kindled in the breasts of the loyal
people of the North, upon the hills of old New
England, in the frozen regions of Minnesota, and
to the sunny clime of the Golden Gate, while
direful threatenings, ominous clouds of inky
blackness were coming up from the fair land of
the South. The subjects given our speaker bore
largely upon the questions of the day: "Hero
Worship"; "The Monroe Doctrine"; "Liberty";
"American Nobility"; "The Union," being
among the topics suggested, and showing the
trend of thought in the minds of her hearers dur-

ing those exciting days. She was then in her twenty-first year, and we cannot wonder that her audiences marvelled upon the fact that this young girl, frail and delicate as a lily, was able to speak upon these questions with greater power than the statesmen of the day, evincing a deeper insight into all questions of government, economics and sociology than these men, who had been a quarter of a century before the public, possessed. Such was the fact, however, and teachers in our academies and colleges, in all of the schools of the sciences, literally sat at her feet and were taught from the higher school, in the universities of the Spirit world. With almost unerring accuracy she foretold the coming conflict, named and located the places at which the leading battles of the Rebellion were to be fought, and told the people of the North that the conflict would not be settled in a few days or months, but that a long, cruel, bloody war was to result from the curse of slavery that was resting upon the American people. Some of the politicians who listened to her, being statesmen at heart, believed in her words, and would have followed the advice of the Spirit had they had the power to do so. The majority, however, scoffed, heeding the voice of the multitude, and went their way without having taken into their souls the awful meaning of this message from the

higher life. How literally these prophecies were
fulfilled, and how direful the consequences of
the war, can be found upon the pages of every
history of this great conflict between the states
of this Union. Two of her lectures are especially worthy of a few words of comment from
us in passing.

In speaking upon the subject, "The Union,"
she uttered some ringing words in behalf of the
maintenance of the supremacy of our National
Government, pleading that the Constitution be
amended so that slavery could be wiped out
forever, urging that that Constitution was the
sole guarantee of the prosperity and perpetuity
of our government. She said : "We do not
understand why any state should war against
the National Government, which has nursed it
into vigorous prosperity, any more than a child
should lift a parricidal hand against its natural
protector. If the slave oligarchy is to master
the Union, we might as well proclaim a mon-
archy at once, for under any species of aristocratic rule, our cherished principles of liberty
are lost forever. The secessionists seem to regard liberty first and union afterwards, but that
kind of liberty soon degenerates into savage ex-
cesses of rapine and murder. Liberty and Union,
'one and inseparable,' should be the motto of
all patriots."

Following this discourse came another of equal

value upon the subject of "Secession and its Consequences," in which, without referring to the question of slavery, *per se*, she showed the consequences of the establishment of two governments upon American soil, in the United States, whereas the one being wholly a non-manufacturing nation would soon come to depend upon the manufacturers of the North, and would ultimately become as much enslaved by the money power as the blacks were then enslaved by the planters of the South.

We may be pardoned for introducing these references to these lectures, at such length, in view of the fact of the importance of the subject which she was treating, and the times which called forth these thoughts from her guides.

It was during this course of lectures at Dodworth's Hall that Spirit Thomas Jefferson gave a lecture that attracted widespread attention through the lips of our subject. His topic was, "The Declaration of Independence," and was handled in her usually able manner, as we could well expect with such a strong soul as Jefferson's prompting her to speak. This series of lectures, from December, 1860, down late into the Summer of 1861, was a marked feature in New York life. The hall was crowded on every occasion, and the people instructed upon the live questions that were then agitating the public mind. Her services were in constant requisition in New

York and Brooklyn throughout this year, and with the opening of the new year, 1862, we find her again addressing crowded houses at Dodworth's Hall. The same wide range of subjects was given her as in the previous Winter. Her guides kept pace with, in truth led the thought of the times, and were always demanding forward steps on the part of the people. She spoke most eloquently upon the "Real and Imaginary Dangers of the Republic," in February, 1862, and gave a lecture that thrilled all hearts, upon the seemingly stereotyped subject, "The Crisis." This was at the time in the history of the war when paralysis seemed to have struck the army in the field, and the government at the Capital. A new departure of thought seemed to be necessary, and the guides came forward with some important advice in relation to the necessities of the times, "A higher ideal," said they, "is needed to enthuse the people. That ideal is the emancipation of the slaves." This same thought was being expressed to President Lincoln through the mediumship of Nettie Colburn in Washington. The many friends of the President, and even Members of Congress, visited certain mediums, from whom they received the same slogan cry, "Emancipation." We learn from good authority that our subject gave audience to many visiting statesmen in New York city, who were urged by the invisibles to take active steps toward the accomplishment of this much to be desired object. President Lincoln and his most intimate friends heard these messages gladly, and guided by their straightforward and righteous words he penned the immortal Emancipation Proclamation, we doubt not at the dictation of some arisen guide of our Republic. The guides of our subject were knowing to these interviews of President Lincoln with Miss Colburn, and through her would give messages of similar import that wended their way to the White House, to unite their influence with the words of Miss Colburn in urging forward this great reformatory measure.

Throughout the Winter and Spring months, and far into the Summer, we find her discoursing to the people upon social, religious, political, and reform measures in New York city. All of her lectures were received with the same degree of enthusiasm that had characterized the people in former years. The hall was thronged with eager listeners on every Sunday evening, and her rooms were visited daily, during each week, by those who sought instruction upon the different phases of human thought, from the standpoint of the advanced thinkers in the Spiritual realm. Her lecture of May 18, 1862, upon the subject of ''Mind, Spirit and Soul,'' must here receive especial attention, as the thought expressed in that lecture has a direct bearing upon the teachings that have been advanced by her in later years.

From this lecture we quote at length, and leave our readers to deduce their own conclusion therefrom. We shall endeavor to show when we come to apply the thought of this discourse to these later teachings, its direct connection therewith. From this lecture we quote as follows:

"That which we call mind is in its external and real sense but an effect, not a cause—signifying that conscious power of executive thought which belongs exclusively to the human brain, and which is a result of reasoning intelligence combined with matter. Mind, therefore, is that peculiar quality which proceeds from the human brain—the effect of the conjoined operation of forces in themselves specific, distinct, and the result of other combinations. When we speak of mind as a power, we mean, simply, that mind is the active product of causes superior to itself—a combination of material forces and mental or soul-life acting upon the brain, which produces, as its natural result, thought. Mind, then, is both the thinking power and the aggregate of thoughts. The term mind is wholly inadequate to express the idea of an immortal essence. The mind is all material; its relations are strictly mechanical; it belongs to matter, conceives of nothing else, and measures all things by a material standard. Ideas may be the results of a superior faculty, but the conclusions the mind draws from them are always material. In other words, Mind belongs to the body, and is that which conducts the human being to a conviction of immortality through the evidences afforded in this life, but it does not itself create or share that immortality.

"The term spirit is usually supposed to signify something immaterial, but to our conception it implies much more than this. We rank spirit as next to mind, and define it as that substance which is most closely allied to matter, but more ethereal in its nature than the perishable and changing elements of the bodily form. Spirit is that which causes the blood to course through the veins, which animates the eye and gives color to the cheek, which, in short, maintains the harmonious activity of the functions. Take away the spirit, and you have no form, no color, no life, no beauty. The spirit is that which causes life to circulate in the tender germ, and sends the sap upward from the root, through all the branches of the giant oak, which causes the powers of life to work in all forms of verdure and bloom. Spirit is that, which, living, is unconscious of life, and exists, therefore, without power of thought, but is pervaded, controlled and guided by that power of which we shall next speak. Mark the antithesis. Mind is the result of thoughts, spirit is pervading life; mind is distinctly consecutive, positive in its action; spirit, diffusive, general, and without definite form;

mind is material, dependent upon outward nature for its inception and growth, produces only outward results, cannot compare or reason, except of outward things, draws all its themes from material substances without which it possesses nothing. Spirit is the same wherever matter is, whether the latter be endowed with grossest or loftiest qualities, whether it take the form of an archangel or the humblest worm. We may call spirit, not *God*, but the breath of God. Spirit is that impalpable presence you perceive when no material form is near; the unseen power which unites the visible to the invisible; the mysterious chain which binds the finite to the infinite, and is the medium for the transmission of thoughts, the result of whose creation is mind.

"The soul is as clearly unlike the mind and spirit as a ray of sunshine is unlike the glittering icicle. The soul is perfection, consciousness, will. It is not like the mind which depends upon matter; it is not like the spirit which diffuses life through matter, but is the conscious power of all things combined, the essence and perfection of being. God is this soul, for this is a perfection, and perfection is God. As white, which seems no color, is a combination of all prismatic hues, so the soul is a perfect combination of all qualities, so that in it they are made one, and if there is anything which expresses at once all life, thought, knowledge, wisdom, that idea is the soul, and that is what makes it like God. It is the consummate combination of all being, of all insight, of all wisdom—such as your soul is, is God, and God is that soul within you. The soul is the pilot, guiding the frail bark of humanity, heedless, in its superior knowledge, of all the alarms of ignorance and credulity. Spirit may be changed and modified, may wear bright hues of goodness or be marred by outward conflict, but the soul through all but burns more brightly in its assured perfection. The soul cannot sin, no more than can God.

"We may summarize their peculiar relations thus: As mind is the result of matter and spirit; as soul animates the spirit; as the spirit pervades the body, and through this combination forms the mind, so the expression of that mind gave to the world all the ideas of the soul. Between the mind and soul there is ever open antagonism; they are sworn enemies. Atheists and materialists reason exclusively with the mind and ignore the soul. We should deal with the soul in its unimpaired vitality through the mediumship of the spirit as its agent, with the mind as their outward manifestations."

The first of July, 1862, in company with her brother, Mr. E. T. Scott, she made an extensive tour of the West. On this trip she gave a series of lectures at her old home, Cuba, N. Y., from which place she went to Cleveland, Ohio, where she spent three weeks, lecturing, on an average, four times per week. She visited Toledo, where, as well as in Cleveland, she was received with great enthusiasm by the people. From Toledo she went to Chicago, where, on the 13th of August, she gave a remarkable lecture under the influence of Spirit Stephen A. Douglas, upon the subject of the "Rebellion." The late Wilbur F. Story, then editor and proprietor of the Chicago Times, was deeply interested in the subject of this lecture, as were many other prominent citizens of Chicago. This lecture so impressed the many friends of the gifted Senator from Illinois, as having the internal evidence of the personality of Douglas, that it created a great deal of excitement among them. She was invited to return to that city, which she promised to do early in September. In Milwaukee, Wis., she was greeted with the same large audiences that everywhere welcomed her in the leading cities of the West. Here again, Spirit Douglas gave some of his trenchant thoughts upon the present crisis. Many who knew Senator Douglas personally, testified to their firm belief in his presence at that time, saying that they had no doubt that his was the mind that prompted the lady's utterances. Many favorable notices in the "Daily Wisconsin" and other papers in Milwaukee and other places in the State, commended these utterances in the highest terms. Upon her

return to Chicago, in September, she was again
controlled by Senator Douglas in such a positive
manner as to astound many of the skeptics present
on that occasion, who had been personal friends
of Mr. Douglas when in earth life, one person
in the audience asking a personal question in
broken English to which Mr. Douglas instantly
responded, recognizing the individual. This
led to a wide-spread discussion of the claims of
. Spiritualism among the citizens of Chicago, particularly in regard to the power of Spirit Douglas
to use the organism of our subject for the purpose
of expressing his thought. A committee composed of some of the leading citizens of Chicago
sent her the following letter, on the 17th of
September, 1862:

To CORA L. V. SCOTT:

DEAR MADAM:—We have heard with wonder
and amazement that our fellow-citizen, the late
Stephen A. Douglas, has purported to address
his fellow-townsmen. We do not know what
manner of phenomenon this is, but we would
like an opportunity of testing this wonderful
fact. Therefore, the undersigned invite you to
allow the people of Chicago to listen to an address by Stephen A. Douglas, and if it be he we
will have no difficulty in determining it. To
this end we have made arrangements for Kings-
bury Hall for that purpose, for Friday and Saturday evenings next, and trust you will consider

favorably this proposal from those who admire your gifts and have loved Mr. Douglas.

Your obedient servants,

JAMES CAMPBELL,	ROOT & CADY,
A. BARNUM,	J. C. HALL,
I. Y. MUNN,	W. SARHONG,
M. W. LEAVITT,	J. A. WEDGEWOOD,
R. A. B. MILLS,	D. E. MILNOR,
T. S. HOLMES,	E. H. PATTERSON.

To this she responded as follows, September 18th, 1862.

MESSRS. CAMPBELL, BARNUM, HALL, MUNN, ROOT & CADY, AND OTHERS:

The writer begs to acknowledge the receipt of your kind favor of September 17, in which you honor her with an invitation to appear before the people of Chicago, for the purpose of allowing them an opportunity to test the truth of the purported presence of the late Stephen A Douglas. Her greatest desire is to serve the truth. She will accept of your proposition, at the time and place mentioned in your letter. Allow me to thank you for the high appreciation which your courtesy expresses, and believe me, gentlemen,   Very truly yours,

CORA L. V. SCOTT.

A large audience greeted her on the occasion mentioned in the above correspondence, and the subject, "The Union Must and Shall be Preserved," Andrew Jackson's historical saying, was given her. Spirit Douglas' remarks were identical with those made in his speeches to the people previous to his decease, and the manner in which he replied to questions at the close of the address were truthful and very characteristic of the man. His friends identified the eminent statesman readily. The audience was well pleased with the lecture, as was attested by the frequent applause that greeted her.

One of the leading Chicago journals, commenting, editorially, upon the lecture speaks as follows: "The sentences are terse but vigorous, like Senator Douglas. The sentiments expressed were his throughout; the language, mannerisms and general appearance of the speaker were like him; but whether it was Senator Douglas or not, the public must decide for themselves. The sentiments were Union throughout and breathed a loyalty to the flag, with which we are well satisfied. No one could avoid being pleased with this lecture."

The letter from Henry Strong, from which this is taken, is too lengthy to be quoted in full, hence we have given this brief excerpt. Mr. Strong spoke enthusiastically of the lecture and was positive that the controlling intelligence was that of the Illinois statesman.

We are indebted to Henry Strong, a gallant Union soldier for the account of this lecture upon which our comments are based. This dis-

course made the people of Chicago more desirous than ever of investigating the claims of
Spiritualism yet further, and during the next few
weeks, the public mind was much occupied with
this important subject.

Our subject had started to return to her Eastern home, had lectured in Elkhart, Indiana;
Sturges and Coldwater, Michigan, and was giving
a series of lectures in Toledo, when she received
an urgent request from a number of prominent
Spiritualists and investigators in Chicago, to return to the city for the ensuing Winter.   She
accepted this invitation and remained in Chicago
until the following March.   Her return was
marked by an increased interest among all classes
of people in the subject of Spiritualism, which
interest was evinced by the crowded houses that
greeted her every Sunday.   The impressions
made by our subject this Winter in Chicago,
were so marked and left such an influence upon
the minds of her hearers as to cause them to desire her return to that place, for a permanent
residence among them.   This result, however, was
not accomplished until some fourteen years later,
as your readers will see for themselves later on.

In the Spring of 1863 she again visited Wisconsin, spoke in many of the leading cities of
that State, and visited her friends at her old
home at Lake Mills, where her mediumship was
first made known to her.

During the month of April she gave a number of addresses in the towns within a radius of a few hundred miles of Chicago, in the State of Illinois. The comments upon her visit to Geneseo are of such a nature as to warrant our copying the following from the Geneseo Republic, of April 15th, 1863:

"There was no ranting or bitterness, no attempt at lofty flights, striving to appear flowery and eloquent, but the eloquence of thought, uttered in language elevating the mind above its ordinary level. No description can do justice to the lectures, they were unspeakably beautiful, the language eloquent and pure; sentences perfect; thoughts grand and noble, and the manner of speaking was simple and quiet, but it was the simplicity of strength, the quietness of conscious power. Whence comes the power of this young, uneducated woman? How can she lecture with such ability, on such a variety of subjects, calling out crowded houses night after night, for weeks and months in succession. Only twenty-three years of age, has not been to school since eleven, writes nothing, reads but little and appears like an ordinary woman, but when she is influenced to speak in public, we have thoughts so profound and rich in language, so vigorous and appropriate as belong only to great talents and ripe culture."

May 1st, 1863, again finds our subject in Boston where she opened a series of lectures in Lyceum Hall. Of her return to the Hub, the "Banner of Light," says editorially:

"After an absence of four years this lady is again speaking to a Boston audience, with the same deep interest on the part of the public as before. During this four years' absence she has labored mostly in New York city. She has just returned from a most successful Western tour, where the desire to hear her was very great, her audiences always being as large as the capacity of the house would admit. Those who heard her years ago thought there could be no improvement in her elocution, but we notice a marked change in the tone of her voice. It is much stronger and clearer than it was and is most beautifully modulated. Her accents fall upon the ear with a clear, soft, musical sound that perfectly charms the auditors, while the plain, logical, philosophical argument she uses, rivets the attention till the last utterance dies away in her closing benediction."

Her second lecture of this series was given by Spirit Theodore Parker, whose subject was the "Future of America." This lecture led to much discussion upon the part of the friends and opponents of Spiritualism, in regard to the identity of Spirit Parker. Many who knew him intimately testified to their recognition of his personality in the gestures of the speaker, and style of language used. So powerful was the control that the tears coursed down the medium's cheeks, thereby indicating the deep feelings of emotion actuating Spirit Parker upon this, his first public address, given to his old friends in Boston since his ascension into spirit life.

An anonymous writer in William Lloyd Garrison's "Liberator," made a bitter attack upon our subject, claiming that the personality of Parker was not proven in the lecture purporting to come from him. This led the friends of Mr. Parker, who knew that he was interested in Spiritualism at the time of his transition, to come out in her defence. The testimonials as to the recognition of Parker's thought and personality are so numerous as to preclude their admission here, but the concensus of their opinions was that external as well as internal evidence proved the claim of the spirit to be strictly true.

At this point we may mention the fact that her contemporaries upon the Spiritualistic platform in New England, at this time, were such men as William Lloyd Garrison, Ralph Waldo Emerson, H. B. Storer, H. C. Wright, H. F. Gardner, Charles A. Hayden, now a noted Universalist minister, and such women as Lizzie Doten, Susie M. Johnson, Fannie Davis Smith, Mrs. A. M. Spence and many others.

Our Spiritualistic friends of the present gen-

eration may not be acquainted with the fact that
the gifted Emerson did not hesitate to attend
Spiritualistic meetings, nor to accept engagements upon our platform.   With these speakers
our subject took equal rank among the scholarly
minds in Boston, and held her position with
great ease.

It was during this engagement in Boston that
she gave a lecture upon the subject: "The
Soul; Its Origin and Destiny," which aroused
much thought in the minds of her hearers.   This
lecture has been published in one of the earlier
volumes of her discourse, hence its reproduction
is unnecessary.   Our readers can determine its
value from the following quotation from the
editorial columns of the "Banner of Light," in
the Summer of 1863: "She gave one of the
most lucid arguments in elucidation of the subject ever listened to.   We will not mar its beauties by any attempt to give a synopsis of it, for
it was so complete and connected that it would
be unfair to give it in parts."

She aroused such an interest among the people who flocked to hear her in the subject of
Spiritualism, that she was invited to spend
another month with this society.   She did so,
and gave them a series of eight addresses, covering the last two Sundays in June and the first
two in July.

May 31st found her at the home of the Ballous at Hopedale, where she was ever a welcome guest. It is well for us at this point to state that Adin Ballou from the very first accepted the fact that the controlling spirit was, of a verity, his son, and during his entire life he was the faithful friend and staunch supporter of our subject. His heart and home were ever open to her, and his good wife and daughter shared his feeling for Cora.

After a pleasant visit at the home of the Ballous, she returned to her Boston labors. At the close of her July engagement the managers of the Lyceum Hall Society, through its lecture committee, consisting of L. B. Wilson, Jacob Edson and Daniel Farrar, presented her with a testimonial indicative of the appreciation of the society and its officers, of the great good she had accomplished through her Boston labors. As this was given with practical unanimity, it shows the confidence the people felt in the unseen powers that were guiding our instrument.

Early in the Autumn of 1863 we find her at her old home in Western New York, where she gave a series of lectures in the town of Cuba. Both believers and unbelievers among the citizens of Cuba heard her with delight, for she was much loved by her old friends and neighbors in that place. Two pleasant months slipped quietly away from our subject as she tarried in her old home, during which time she regained her strength and gathered new courage to again go forth to do battle for her religion.

She returned to New York in November and filled one month's engagement at Clinton Hall, where she was warmly welcomed by her many admiring friends. The month of December was passed in Boston, where she was greeted with the same eclat with which she always had been received in the nation's literary center. She returned to her New York engagement where she spent the remainder of the Winter and the greater portion of the Summer, lecturing with great acceptance in New York city and Brooklyn. There was no diminution in the attendance at her meetings, and the people seemed to have as deep an interest in her inspired utterances as they had expressed during the eight previous years that she had ministered unto them.

In September, 1863, at the invitation of Dr. John Newcomer, she visited Meadville, Pa., and gave a series of lectures in Newcomer's Hall. These were the first public lectures on Spiritualism ever given in that city, so Dr. Newcomer says in a letter to the " Banner of Light," and the hall was packed on every occasion of her appearance. Here she met the Hon. A. B. Richmond for the first time, who was chosen by the audience to select the subject of her discourse, in company with other scholarly gentlemen, equally as able as the dis-

tinguished jurist.   As Mr. Richmond has made
this visit of our subject a matter of especial
reference in his splendid work, "What I Saw
at Cassadaga Lake," we take the liberty of
quoting our brother's words in full at this point,
relative to this lecture:

"Cora L. V. Scott came to our city.   The
public was notified that the young lady was
a 'trance speaker'; arrangements were made
for her to lecture at Library Hall, and it was
proposed that a learned professor of our college
and myself should be appointed a committee to
give her a test subject, *i. e.*, one that in her
normal condition she most probably would be
ignorant of.   It was arranged that the young
lady was to be invited to visit my museum, a
large private collection which I had made while
engaged in scientific studies and investigations,
as a pastime, and as a relief from the labors
of an arduous profession; should she call as was
intended, I was to engage her in conversation on
various scientific subjects, and then we were
to give her a question involving a knowledge
of that science which she appeared to be the
most ignorant of.   The afternoon preceding
the evening of the lecture she called, in company with a young lady and gentleman of my
acquaintance, who were no *particeps criminis*
in the conspiracy against her, and who knew
nothing of the object of her visit.

"When she called, I saw a very pretty young girl, apparently eighteen years of age. She was sprightly and intelligent, yet it soon became evident from her conversation that she was not learned in the sciences. She viewed my electrical and chemical apparatus with undisguised wonder ; the collection of shells, insects and birds excited her admiration, which she evinced in an almost childlike manner. When I saw her and conversed with her a short time, my heart relented at the severe ordeal we were preparing for her; and if I had been fifteen years younger, I would have thrown up my commission and resigned my position as a committeeman. But Science is no respecter of persons, and in her investigations no caste is recognized, no condition in life can claim immunity from the effect of her demonstrations.

"I accompanied the young ladies around the room until we came to a case of geological specimens. This she would have passed by with a casual glance. They evidently did not interest her ; therefore, there I paused. 'Ah, yes!' I thought; 'this is *terra incognita* to you. Young lady, you shall lecture this evening on geology.' I showed her specimens of *metamorphic rocks*, of *fossiliferous formations*, of *infusoria* in *bog-iron ore*, talked to her of *pliocene strata* and *plutonic rocks*, until she looked thoroughly bewildered and bored; but I kept on with my torture until, in the midst of one of my most learned essays, her wandering eyes caught sight of a beautiful little stuffed bird in a near-by case, when, with an exclamation in a delighted child-like voice: 'Oh, Lizzie! do just look at that dear little bird! Don't you wish you had it for your hat?' 'That will do,' thought I; 'you do not appear to understand what I have been talking about; you shall deliver to us a lecture this evening on one of the most abstruse theories of geology, and may the Spirits have mercy on you if your inspiration fails you, for you certainly know nothing of the subject yourself.'

"Evening came; the hall was filled with an intelligent, anxious, yet incredulous assembly. The young girl was seated on the rostrum, looking over the audience with a modest, innocent, and almost child-like expression of countenance, apparently wholly unconscious of the awful fate that awaited her. My friend, the professor, arose and read the question she was to discuss. It was so ponderous that I fancied it shook the building as he read it. The young girl looked bewildered for a moment, then modestly suggested that 'she feared the subject would not be interesting to a popular audience.' We informed her that it was given as a test of her inspiration. She closed her eyes resignedly, shivered a moment, and then appeared to become unconscious. A friend of the committee, who was a learned professor as well as a wit, whispered in our ear, ' See, your question has paralyzed her; no wonder! If the Philistines had met Sampson with that question, they would have killed *him*, and with a weapon very like the one he used so effectually against them.' A few moments more, and the young girl arose and stepped slowly forward to the front of the rostrum.

"A singular change had come over her face. She looked ten years older, her girlish expression was completely gone; her features seemed at first rigid and death-like, then they relaxed, and in a clear, melodious voice she commenced her lecture—and here my pen fails me. I cannot describe the beauty of her diction, or the deep and profound learning she manifested on a subject that in her normal condition she could have known but little about. For over an hour she held her audience spell-bound; a more profoundly learned and eloquent discourse I never heard before. It was very soon apparent to me that she could teach the committee many things in the science of geology unknown to them. She quoted from authors old and new who had written on the subject. Geological terms flowed from her lips like music from the strings of a harp. When she closed her lecture and took her seat, she appeared very much exhausted; her girlish expression of countenance returned; for a moment the audience remained silent, then an applause followed that shook the building to its foundation. Her lecture was an overwhelming success. The people looked at her innocent young face with astonishment. A savant in learning, dressed in silk and lace, with the face of a schoolgirl and the eloquence of a Cicero, had spoken as I had never heard man speak before.

"The next day I met the professor. 'Well,' said I, 'what did you think of that lecture?'

"'I'll tell you, Richmond,' said he, 'it was the most wonderful instance of mind reading I ever heard of.'

"'Mind reading!' I replied; 'what do you mean by that?'

"'Why,' said he, 'you know that if you place a magnetic needle on a stand away from any immediate influence, it will point north?'

"'Yes,' I remarked; 'I have observed that for some years, but what then?'

"'Why,' continued the professor, 'if you take a couple of magnetic bars of steel, and place them at unequal distances on the right and left of the needle, it will oscillate for a few moments, and then finally settle at the resultant point between the three forces operating on it, *i. e.*, the magnetism of the earth, the magnetic influence of the one bar on the right, and the one on the left. Well, it was so with the girl. Her lecture was but a reflex of your mind and mine operating on hers. She combined our ideas on the subject with what little *she* knew, and a very fine lecture was the result. But it was unconscious cerebration.'

"I felt flattered by this learned explanation. It was not the young girl after all who had lectured, but the professor and myself. I was willing to accept this explanation. The only trouble was how to divide the partnership properly between the professor and myself. This we were never able to do up to the time of his death, which occurred ten or fifteen years after. But I have always thought that that lecture of the professor's and mine was the greatest effort of our lives."

October found her at her old home, at Cuba, visiting her mother and other relatives in the home of her childhood. Of her visit to this place she has herself written (under the aid of Ouina), in a most beautiful poem, the thoughts that thronged her mind during these golden autumnal days.

BEYOND THE HILLS.

All hail, once again, my native hills ;
   I kiss your feet, ye pine-crowned kings !
A holy reverence my being thrills—
   Your loyal subject grateful homage brings.
My world in childhood was amid your forms ;
   The sunset glory was your royal crown ;
Majestic and unmoved ye bore all storms,
   And reigned in silence when the sun went down—
When the sun went down to an unknown valley,
   An unknown valley beyond the hills !

I dreamed golden dreams, oh, shining hills!
 I climbed to where the wild breezes play,.
Or wandered in joy by your gushing rills,
 To pluck the wood flowers in early May.
Then life was but a fleeting hour of bliss,
 And the busy world seemed a fairy dream;
I pressed to my lips false Fortune's kiss,
 And eagerly sought life's changeful stream,
Where the sun went down to an unknown valley,
 An unknown valley beyond the hills.

And I had fond friends, oh, silent hills,
 Who came each day to the cottage door,
And gathered around the warm wood fire,
 To tell strange legends of ancient lore—
Of the red man who trod the forest green,
 Who made the hills echo his loud war-cry,
While his nodding plume and his arrow keen,
 Went swift and sure when the blast swept by;
But they all are gone to an unknown valley,
 An unknown valley beyond the hills.

I weep on your bosoms, oh, solemn hills!
 I water your emerald robes with my tears;
I weep for the hours forever gone,
 For the hopes and friends of childhood's years.
The world, when tried, proved false and cold,
 And love was betrayed with poisonous breath;
Kind friends drank deep of Lethe's stream,
 And one by one slept cold in death—
For they all went down to an unknown valley,
 An unknown valley beyond the hills,

But ye have not changed, my native hills;
 Though friends prove false, ye still are true,
The pine trees sing their solemn praise,
 And the wild flower sips the evening dew;
Ye are robed still in royal green,
 And at eve ye wear a golden crown,

While the pale moon flashes a silvery sheen
  On your darkened brows when the sun goes down—
When the sun goes down to an unknown valley,
  An unknown valley beyond the hills.

I am calmer now, oh, soothing hills !
  And I worship another Higher King ;
To the spirit of endless Life and Hope
  To Nature's God my allegiance bring.
I bow my head to life's storm and pain,
  While onward I press o'er the stony ground,
For I feel that hope's flowers shall bloom again,
  And the loved and lost be once more found,
They will all be found in some pleasant valley,
  Some pleasant valley beyond the hills.

April, 1865.

In November, 1864, she began an engagement
in Boston at Lyceum Hall. People flocked to
hear her in the same large numbers that they had
always done upon her previous annual visits to
that place. In fact, she has ever been greeted
by large and enthusiastic audiences in the New
England capital ever since her first visit there,
nearly forty years ago. One of her lectures was
upon the subject, "The Reconstruction of the
Constitution." This lecture aroused a great deal
of thought on the part of the people who heard
it, and was taken up by the metropolitan press
and widely discussed by people of all denominations. Concerning it, the now venerable Luther
Colby, of "The Banner of Light," says: "We
do not overstate the case when we say that probably this subject has never been treated by any

statesman with more ability than on this occasion.
It was a clear and elaborate expression of the intent and meaning of the various parts of that
famous instrument, and worthy of the brains and
genius of Hamilton, with the wisdom he gained
in Spirit life. She pronounced it the most perfect constitution ever formed for a free people to
live under, with one exception, and that was the
clause in reference to persons he held to servi-
tude and labor."

So great was the popular demand for her services that she was re-engaged for December and
January immediately following.

During the Winter and Spring of 1865 she filled
engagements in New York city, and Meadville,
Pa., returning in May to Boston, where she spoke
in Melodeon Hall in behalf of the Sanitary Commission. She also supplied the platform at Lyceum Hall, giving two lectures, owing to the illness of Miss Lizzie Doten, who was then one of
the most popular and highly gifted lecturers in
the ranks of the Spiritualists of the United States.
Her Summer work was divided between New
York city and Chicago. In the latter city, despite
the hot July weather, she filled Metropolitan Hall
with large audiences to listen to her inspired utterances. She was invited to visit Camp Douglas
and speak to the veterans there who had just
returned from the war. It was on this occasion
that she delivered a lecture, entitled, "To the

Union Army," closing with a poem of exquisite
beauty, entitled, "Song of Welcome to the
Union Armies." This poem contains such lofty,
patriotic sentiments, and beautiful imagery of
thought, that we take the liberty of quoting it
at this point, believing that it will be of interest
and profit to our readers:

SONG OF WELCOME TO THE UNION ARMIES.

(Poem, "B. of L." July 29, 1865.)

Open wide the palace portals,
 Wreathe with the flowers the banquet hall;
Let lights gleam from every cottage,
 Hang fresh garlands on each wall;
  Roll the drum!
  Bugle sound!
Let the land with joy resound!
Soldiers, welcome home!

Who are these with fearless bearing,
 Battle-worn, yet brave and strong,
With their tattered banners waving,
 With their wild and joyous song?
  Never fought
  Braver men—
Force of gallant Sheridan!
Brave boys, welcome home!

Who are these like war-birds flocking,
 Filling street and public square,
Dashing, restless, brave, undaunted,
 Thronging, shouting everywhere?
  When we thought
  All was lost,
Down swept Sherman's winged host;
Warriors, welcome home.

Who compose these mighty columns,
 Marching proudly, rank and file,
With no stain upon their laurels,
 Wreathed in victory's bright smile?
  Bravest sons
   Of the free,
Led by Grant and Liberty!
 Veterans, welcome home!

Where the wild-rose blooms in beauty,
 On the distant woodland slope,
And the golden prairie lily
 Lifts its dew-filled chalice up,
  And the birds
  Sweetly sing,
All their wild notes to you fling;
 Welcome, welcome home.

Where the corn-fields stand like armies,
 With their plumes of gold and green,
Driving back pale-faced famine,
 In whose clutches ye have been—
  Fields of wheat,
  Waving grass,
All salute you, as you pass,
 Whispering, "Welcome home."

But, alas! all are not with you,
 Who went forth in strength one day;
Mothers vainly watch their coming;
 Wives can only weep and pray—
  Watch and wait
  For nevermore,
Through palace hall, or cottage door,
 Will they come welcome home.

One by one their names were written
 Upon Heaven's muster rolls;
Death, Time's great senior commander,
 Led them to the land of souls;

> From cold marches,
>   Bloody glens,
> From foul, loathsome prison dens,
>   Angels bore them home.
>
> Now they wear the shining armor
>   Of eternal, endless life,
> Truth is sword, and shield, and sabre,
>   Love has conquered every strife.
>   Ever true
>   Still they stand,
> Sentinels o'er their loved land,
>   In their shining home.
>
> Where the camp-fires of the heavens
>   Gleam above the clouds of earth,
> And where all souls are promoted,
>   By the standard of true worth;
>   Led by them,
>   Heaven sent,
> Your loved, martyred President!
> They are " welcome home!"

The latter part of the Summer and early Autumn was passed at the home of her mother, in North Cuba, where she gladly addressed the friends of her youth upon the topics of the day, and the subject proper of Spiritualism.

We find her filling the first regular engagement in the Nation's capital, Washington, D. C., in the month of November. This is the opening of a work whose importance commands especial mention in a chapter by itself, hence, we shall not dwell at any length upon this first visit, but refer readers to the able account of her Washington labors, from the pen of George A. Bacon, in a subsequent chapter.

She was a delegate to the Second National Convention held in Philadelphia late in the Autumn of 1865, in the proceedings of which she took a prominent part. This convention was presided over by the venerable John Pierpont, whose fame as a poet, Unitarian preacher and lecturer on Spiritualism is world wide. She opposed all attempts to define Spiritualism, and threw the weight of her influence against a limited organization, to be composed only of those who were willing to acknowledge the name "Spiritualist." She felt that any definition of Spiritualism, for the masses at large, would eventuate in a Spiritualistic creed later on in its history, or the commitment of the body as a whole to some established line of thought or hobby, advocated by extremists, either on the radical or conservative sides. She was a ready debater and presented her views with great clearness. Her opinions upon the subject of Spiritualism were deemed of so much importance as to lead to her appointment, by President Pierpont, as a member of the committee of fifteen, to prepare an address to the country. Of this committee the late able jurist, Judge A. G. W. Carter, of Ohio, was chairman. Many other prominent Spiritualists were on this committee, among whom we notice the names of Miss Lizzie Doten, the Hon. S. S. Jones, founder of the "Religio-Philosophical Journal," Prof. J. S.

Loveland, now of California, all of whom were considered leading lights in Spiritualism.

Late in June, 1866, she delivered a lecture in Boston, entitled "The Coming Conflict." This lecture produced an unusual sensation among all classes of people. She spoke ably upon the need of reform in governmental affairs, and stated many trenchant truths in regard to the outcome of reconstructionary efforts that were then being made. She arraigned the Catholic Church for its luke-warm loyalty to our flag, and told the people that the mysterious visits of certain ex-Union generals to the Pope of Rome meant more than appeared on the surface. One of these generals had commanded the grandest army the world ever saw for two years, until it dwindled away because of his inactivity, hoping thereby to play into the hands of the dis-unionists, until the loyal North called for his removal, while others high in authority had also, through their apathy, sought to betray the Union cause. She warned all people against listening to that subtle voice of conservativism that promised a base peace to all through a surrender of principles vital to the life of the republic. She favored placing the penitent leaders of the Southern Confederacy upon probation before restoring them to the full rights of citizenship, and spoke a few plain words in regard to Andrew Johnson's universal amnesty ideas. What she predicted in regard to the restoration of these men indiscriminately to citizenship was literally fulfilled in the terrorizing and ultimate deprivation of the blacks of their political rights, in the days of the K. K. K.'s in the different states of the South. She advocated the gospel of forgiveness, but thought the lines,

> "When the devil was sick,
> The devil a saint would be," etc.,

should be applied to our brethren of the South, in order to see if they would not make good use of their restored political privileges. This lecture we deem one of the most important and one of the most valuable of all lectures that have fallen from her lips. Its delivery marked a new departure in the political world, and was much discussed throughout the country. The influence of this lecture was widespread and caused many to pledge themselves anew to the cause of maintaining the new Constitution of the United States and their fealty to the flag as well.

We have been thus explicit in regard to these years from 1851 to 1865, inclusive, because of the youth of our subject, the large number of places visited by her, and the wide range of subjects treated in her scholarly lectures. Concerning these fourteen years of labor, several large volumes could be filled with valuable thoughts, couched in choicest language, if we were to enter into the minutiæ of detail. We have deemed it wise and expedient to follow her thus closely in order that our readers may see what an immense work the child, the maiden and the young woman could accomplish with the aid of her advanced helpers in spirit life. We must bear in mind that she was without scholastic training, and that these thoughts were imprinted upon her consciousness by some power outside of herself. In view of this fact, we cannot wonder that the universal verdict of the public was summed up in the one word—marvellous! Other youthful organisms have been touched in like manner since that time, and the results of their labors have received the same verdict, hence we do not point to our subject alone, as the only marvel that Spiritualism has presented to the world. We do hold this work to be of most material value to the history of Spiritualism, and an integral part of the same. Therefore, these years, lying nearly three decades behind us, are of interest to all because of the wonderful lessons of spirit power contained in them for all who will read the lives of these gifted workers, who have been developed to bless humanity by the Spirit Guardians, whose homes are in the "Morning-Land of Souls."

We now enter upon the consideration of the work in Washington, and the specific teachings of our subject, and details will be lost sight of in the larger subject of general effect of these thoughts or teachings upon the people of the world.

CHAPTER VIII.

WASHINGTON WORK.

OUR medium's work in Washington, D. C., opened in the Winter of 1865-66. Concerning this work we append, as the best account of its effect and general scope that we can find, an ably written chapter from the pen of George A. Bacon, Esq., who for more than thirty years has been a valued friend of our subject. Mr. Bacon's account is too valuable to be reduced by even one sentence, and its literary merit warrants its reproduction precisely as it was penned by him. While in Washington she made her home much of the time at Mr. Bacon's, who was well fitted to speak of her and her work in that place:

MR. H. D. BARRETT,

ESTEEMED FRIEND AND BROTHER:—You ask for my reminiscences of Mrs. Richmond's spiritual work at Washington during the troublous times of the War and of the reconstruction period. These are of such a character, growing out of the then existing conditions, as well as my personal relations to them, that from the very nature of the case I could not readily forget them. Not only do I retain a vivid memory of that epoch and the events as they occurred, but in addition to what an old farmer called his "good remember," I possess a bulky scrap-book which bears record of that history.

As President of the Spiritual Society at that time, it became my duty to engage the several speakers who addressed us, and, among others, I wrote to Cora Scott who was then in New York, a protege of Judge Edmunds.

This was in the Winter of 1865-66. Her advent on our platform was an event our little society felt to take some degree of pride in. The numbers of the audience became largely augmented, anticipating which we had taken a new and more commodious hall, while the character of the company was no less marked. New faces and older heads generally were in the majority. Men of note were to be seen at each lecture, manifesting unabated interest, while several became regular contributors in defraying the expenses of the meetings.

Her parlor receptions each week were among the notable events of the day, unique in character and phenomenal in versatility, while their intellectual scope and spiritual revelation filled her listeners with the most profound wonder. Never before had their counterpart been known to the many who were privileged to attend upon these gatherings. On one occasion, I remember, there were present sixteen public officials, senators, representatives, judges, doctors, *et. al.*, each of whom marvelled at the power and wisdom displayed in her responses to the ever varying questions, chiefly relating to national complications, which were submitted by the more prominent members of her distinguished company. For two hours at a time have I seen her seated in the center of a group of earnest and interested politicians and others, answering promptly, clearly and apparently satisfactorily, questions that involved a practical knowledge of finance, history, political economy, jurisprudence and the science of government; and it was no wonder that coming from one but just out of her teens, naturally filled all who thus heard her with profound surprise.

During these days, among those who seemed to be interested in these matters were such men as Senators Benj. Wade, of Ohio; Jacob Howard, of Michigan; Henry Wilson, of Massachusetts, afterwards Vice-President of the United States; General Banks, Judge Lawrence, George W. Julian, Hon. Mr. Beaman, and many others. As several of her public discourses, applicable to our government, partook of a prophetic character, all appeared anxious to learn explicitly, if possible, as to the future course of the country. The times were alarmingly problematical; every-

thing was in a state of transition; nothing was
certain.   Through the aid of French arms, Maxi-
milian was on the throne of the Montezumas, in
a country adjacent to our southern border; the
financial situation was at a supremely critical
stage; active operations in the field between the
North and South had but recently ceased and
the era of reconstruction was just on.   Never
was there a time in the history of the National
Government when the highest statesmanship was
so imperatively demanded, never a time when
temporary. makeshifts in legislation were so
readily adopted as a substitute for the perma-
nence in state-craft.   It is no secret that certain
efforts were made to incorporate into national
law some of the hints and suggestions received
from spiritual seances; as usual, however, short-
sighted policy was in the ascendant then as it is
today.   When will governments learn to progress through methods evolutionary rather than
revolutionary ?

Perhaps I could say nothing in this connection
more pertinent than to here insert a few extracts
from my notes made at the time and printed in
"The Banner of Light," thirty years ago.   Writing in November, 1865, I quote as follows:

"This month we have been and next month
we expect to be, favored by the presence of the
spiritually endowed Cora L. V. Scott, whose appearance in our city marks an era in the history

of the Spiritual movement in this part of our
country. Doubtless her fame had something to
do with calling out a large gathering on the occasion of her first lecture, but it does not account for the continuously increasing number of
her listeners. There must be something back of
and superior to her mere earthly name, as the
power behind the throne, to satisfactorily explain
this.

"Her being here at this time has created great
enthusiasm among her friends and kindled an unusual interest among those who heretofore never
deigned to speak of the subject, much less to
attend our meetings.

"As is customary elsewhere, so here, for the
morning services the controlling intelligence
choose their own subjects and at the close of the
lecture, answered questions relative to what has
been advanced by the speaker. Her ability to
triumphantly carry herself through this severe
ordeal, to the discomfiture of the carping critic,
thousands of readers, with thousands of others
who never read, well know, from their having
personally witnessed the fact. Yet, without
meretriciousness of any sort she has more than
sustained the high position that was accorded to
her in the beginning of her ministry."

Through misunderstanding, skepticism, reproach and calumny it is rationally impossible
for a naturally timid, true and innocent nature—

for she was but a child when she first encountered the public criticism—to so successfully ''face
a frowning world," and in spite of its accumulated
opposition from bigotry, prejudice, and malice,
to overcome it so as to receive its approval, and,
for a succession of years, to command its respect
and homage, without the possession of wonderful
gifts—even the vice-gerent of the angels.   For
graceful poise, dignified deportment, subdued,
distinct, yet thrilling enunciation, for beauty and
pertinency of expression, with heart and soul
eloquence, she has no superior if an equal in all
the land.

It has been repeatedly intimated in our hearing by the friendly Indian spirit, who in private
circles usually controls our sister, that the higher
intelligences would have something to say for the
special benefit of those who sit in the big council fires of the Nation—which if they are wise
they will considerately heed.   It is greatly to be
desired that our congressmen, for earth and
heaven know they need it, should have a favorable opportunity to learn politics from a standpoint entirely new to most of them; should have
political predictions presented, based upon such
internal and external evidence of their truthfulness as shall set them to thinking and acting in
a manner that means actual down-right business
—presented, too, with a power of authority, as
though of a verity it was being proclaimed by

the arisen ones of earth ! It is felt that the approaching congress is to be the most eventful one since the Continental Congress was convened, for it is to consider and decide issues which shall fully and peculiarly test the strength of republican institutions.

The political trimming, the coarse selfishness, the extreme partisanship, and unscrupulous methods which characterize the weak-kneed and crooked-backed politicians who throng our city with their baleful presence; the treason of words and acts not only to the government, but what is infinitely worse and saddest of all, to humanity and to God, which grows so rank in Washington atmosphere—too oft, alas ! nourished by executive care and patronage—must in the might and majesty of God be soon brought low, or else the whole body politic will ere long become so thoroughly poisoned by their political virus, that only by the most radical and heroic treatment will the patient's life be saved.

All signs portend that the government is on the eve of events which are again to "try men's souls," aye, and woman's too, perhaps, as never before. The rebellion for the present has been transferred from the battle-field to the plane of politics in the halls of congress.

Military genius is to be supplanted—let us hope—by the highest political wisdom. The sacredness of law is to be maintained—law based upon impartial justice.   Principles, not passion, must rule.

The times demand the exercise of the most practical and far reaching sagacity.   Not the interest of the few but the good of all must dominate, for only as the principles of equity prevail can we expect peace and prosperity, like twin angels, to dwell among us as a people !

I append a prophetic vision in verse, given by Miss Scott to a large and discriminating audience at the close of a characteristic and masterly Thanksgiving discourse, by Theodore Parker, in 1865.

A PROPHETIC VISION.

In a parlor, music haunted,
  Kindly faces beaming near,
  Kind hearts breathing words of cheer;
By the moonlight's waves enchanted—
  Bathed and folded in the moonlight,
  In the music and the moonlight,
    Sat we there.

Conversation and sweet stillness,
  Circling all our hearts around,
  Blending with the waves of sound—
Such a perfect rapt'rous fullness,
  Such a strange and perfect silence;
  Moonlight, music, and sweet silence
    Floating there.

Suddenly the parlor vanished,
  Moonlight, music—all were gone;
  And upon my spirit shone
Scenes and sights I thought were vanished,
  Of a strange prophetic vision—
  A thrilling and prophetic vision,
    Dawning there.

I.

I stood within the Nation's Capitol:
The Senate Chamber was the scene
Of deepest interest;—there to extol
The virtues of the Nation, were convened
The people's giant minds,
And every gallery was filled,
And every aisle was thronged,
And every heart was thrilled
By some deep theme debated there:—
The theme of justice to a people wronged!
When, lo! an angel clad in white,
With dazzling face of wondrous light,
With plumes of majesty and might,
Holding a sheathed sword with olive twined,
Bearing a manuscript, swept like the wind
Close to the Speaker's stand—
Even the highest seat the power could reach:—
Placing thereon the paper, did command
By silence more palpable than speech,
That officer to read. With voice subdued
And tremulous (the multitude meanwhile
Thrilled with a strange expectancy)—
And thoughts whose strange foreboding did beguile
Him from his task—yet thus he read:
"A voice from South Carolina—
A true memorial from man to man—
From a people long oppressed,
From a people sore distressed,
Long dishonored and betrayed;
Asking if the promise made,
Hailed by them with deepest ecstacy,
Of justice in accordance with God's plan
Shall be theirs?"
No voice was heard, save that of one whose form uprose
As if to grant the boon, when, lo! the angel sped
And every Senator bowed low his head,
In shame and fear.

II.

Again within that hall I stood,
  And multitudes were gathered there;
  The young and gay and fair—
And foolish, wise and good,
  And solemn faces there were seen,
  And each one with a thoughtful mien
    Listened attentively.
    The Nation's voices spoke,
    And in solemn debate
    Questioned they of the state
    Of those who had just broke
    Their fetters and were free—
When, lo! the angel clad in white,
With wondrous power and great might,
Again appeared, bearing the sword,
Sheathed and entwined as before,
Bearing again the written word—
Came to the Speaker's desk once more,
And bade him read, while, o'er and o'er
    That vast assemblage gathered there
    A thrill was visible, as if the air
Was filled with unseen wings.
    "Voice from man to man,
    Asking if heaven's plan,
    Shall be fulfilled on earth:—
    If honor and true worth
    Shall find their just reward?"
Alas! alas! it was so very hard
    To see that angel bow its shining head—
    To see the slow and measured tread
With which it stalked away—
While one uprose with swift regret,
As if to speak.   The angel soft did say,
Smiling on him so sweetly, "No, not yet."

III.

Once more within the Nation's Capitol
I stood; *this time* in that high Hall

Of Representatives from all the States;
Which august body evermore debates
The people's liberties, and rights, and powers;
More thronged and crowded than before,
Filled from its ceiling to the floor,
With anxious, earnest faces, longing eyes,
Watching the Nation's destinies.
    An armed guard was there,
        Stationed throughout the crowd,
    And near the outer door,
        Talking in voices loud,
    Were those who seek for power
        At the expense of right—
    Who in the darkest honr
        Of the Rebellion's night,
    Sought to o'erthrow the government
        With treason's serpent might;
When suddenly, more swift than before,
The crowned angel there appeared,
Rushing through the open door;
While the vast multitude, who feared,
Yet welcomed the strange visitant,
Sat awed, silent and expectant:
        " Another and a last appeal,
        To know if ye will still conceal
        The truth—and barter souls for power,
        While rank corruption doth devour
        Your manhood.—From the South,
        Speaking through paper's white-lipped mouth,
        We ask again, if man to man,
        Will grant the right of Heaven's plan?"
The Speaker ceased to read; a silent " No " was heard,
When, at the sound, as though a magic word
Were breathed, the Angel drew the sword,
Like Michael, the Archangel of the Lord;
Swept like the lightning, when afar
    It cleaves the cloud and strikes the giant tree,—
    So struck that lightning sword for Liberty!
Or, as the ocean by the tempest driven.

Wave after wave upon the rocks are riven;
   So swayed and broke that tide of human forms.
   Touched by the breath of the Avenger's storms.

IV.

          The scene was changed anew,
          And slowly to my view
          Appeared the shining, blooming land,
          Blessed by perrennial Summer's hand,
Two armies, rank and file, were thus arrayed
For battle.   A wronged and outraged race,
Who had so long waited and watched and prayed,
          Were now about to trace
          Their record on the page
          Of human liberty.
Their faces colored were, but in their eyes
Gleamed the true fires of Freedom's prophecies.
          The angel led them on,
          And myriads of those
          Who long with tongue and pen,
          Have plead the rights of men,
          In rank and file did close,
          Sustaining them in deed—
          Now in their hour of need,
          Fighting for Liberty.
Arrayed against them were the hosts
   Of *lawful* power—of tyrants and of fools,
   Who make the hearts of men but simple tools
To serve ambition;—and the horrid ghosts
   Of treason and theology were there.
The Nation's government had sold its soul
   Unto the Fiend of Power, whose mocking prayer
In waves of solemn blasphemy forever roll
   Through temples built by man!
And now those hosts, born of great wrongs,
With Church and State to make the strong,
          Came forth to crush humanity,
          And trail the flag of Liberty
             In dust and human gore.

Over the whole bright land,
O'er mountain, city, town,
Their ravages were spread;
And still the strong, true band
Of freedmen swept them down—
Until their leaders dead,
Their cause unjust and false,
Their hearts corrupt and sore—
They ceased to battle more.
And those who fought for Liberty and Truth,
And by the angel of Eternal Youth,
Beheld a newer government arise
Like that which governs all the skies,
And valleys teeming with rich grain,
And man, pure, free and glorified—
His truth and wisdom then applied,
While unto him was given:
Peace that was born of pain;
Liberty, child of Joy;
Love, with naught of alloy,
And Justice, born of heaven.

Subsequently she made Washington her home for several years, finally settling in Chicago, over a regularly organized society there, to which she has continued to spiritually minister to the present hour.

In February, 1882, she again visited Washington and lectured before the society; and again it became the duty of the writer to officiate at these meetings The following account of her services appeared from our pen in the issue of the "Banner of Light" of March 11th, 1882:

"During February our spiritual strength has been renewed by the ministrations through Mrs.

Cora L. V. Richmond. She has occupied the
desk twice a day every Sunday this month. On
each occasion, especially in the evening, has the
hall been handsomely filled, even when the
weather was unpleasant. It fell to the writer's
lot to invite Mrs. Richmond to this city to lecture
before the society here during the Winter of
1865–6. The impression made upon many who
then heard her for the first time, though most
profound, has but deepened with the added years.
The inexhaustible wealth and wondrous quality
of thought she has ever displayed has always
been a marvel to the skeptic as well as to the
believer. That her utterances seemingly grow
in earnestness and power, in depth and insight,
in height and breadth, is often asserted by those
who have for years followed her spiritual ministrations. Why should it not be, and why should
not those who have thus attended upon her inspirations also grow and be better able to appreciate the truths that flow from her lips. Her
forenoon remarks were based upon written subjects furnished by the audience—necessarily covering a wide range of topics,—while the subjects
of her evening lectures were left entirely with
her guides. At the close of the lectures questions germane to the subject were invited from
the audience, to which prompt and straightforward replies of great clearness and satisfaction
would invariably be given. I have a long list of

these questions, but as I failed at the time to make an abstract of the answers, from an engrossing interest in the responses, their enumeration here would serve no special purpose. The titles to her lectures were respectively: 'Spiritualism in Relation to Life,' 'Materialism *vs.* Spiritualism,' 'The Christ and the Anti-Christ of Today,' and 'The Spiritual Outlook in this Country for the Next Ten Years.' To say of these lectures that they were pre-eminently distinguished throughout by wonderful unity, consistency and harmony, revealing in melodious phrase the wisdom of her spiritual inspirers, appealing not only to the deepest intelligence, but to the intuitions and soul-nature of her listeners, awakening in them life and stimulating to earnest endeavor the outcome of highest and holiest thought germs born of the spirit and nurtured in mortal soil, is but to indicate the character of the lectures and the effect wrought upon her receptive hearers.

"Large posters throughout the city announced that on Friday evening, February 24th, at Lincoln Hall, a 'Message to the Nation' would be delivered through Mrs. Richmond by Spirit James A. Garfield. This brought out a large audience, many of whom, probably for the first time heard and saw in public the control of a medium by a disembodied spirit, and the novelty of it to them, as well as the nature of the discourse, must have awakened thoughts no less startling than profitable. Hon. Warren Chase happily introduced the speaker. The message in question could have proceeded only from a fruitful and comprehensive mind enriched by spiritual knowledge. After a graceful exordium in pictured speech, which recounted the sensations of the spirit in its introduction to the new life, the speaker proceeded to give a most wonderful address of a prophetic character to the nation. It related to national trials of great importance through which it must pass, of radical changes to be outwrought affecting the relation of the people to the executive, simplifying the methods of transacting government business, the permanent establishing of Peace Congresses for the adjudication of all vexed questions by arbitration, an increased appreciation of the sacredness of human life, the abolishment of the death penalty, the establishment by government of a moral department for criminals morally weak as well as mentally unsound, etc., all of which were predicted for the coming century.

" The exercises closed with an inspirational poem, subject, 'Sunshine and Shadow.'

" The present visit of Mrs. Richmond has been a happy and successful one. The great good it has done will long remain as a blessing with those who partook of its spiritual favors.

"At the close of her last lecture the following resolutions were unanimously passed:

"Wishing to express, as far as our words can do so the high and kindly appreciation in which we hold both the efforts of the angel-world and their fitting instrument who has so earnestly and successfully labored in our spiritual vineyard during the past month, it is, as the sense of this meeting, therefore:

"*Resolved,*—That while we are conscious that the meed of praise from human life cannot be the highest incentive to noble effort on the part of man, either embodied or arisen, we yet feel it a pleasant duty we owe to the lofty spiritual intelligences who have been our teachers on this and other occasions, through the efforts and instrumentality of Mrs. Richmond, to convey to them the earnest and sincere tribute of our thanks; and that we feel to congratulate the spiritual and material world (the latter especially), on the possession of an instrument so finely attuned as the medium through whom such teachings can come.

"*Resolved,* also, that we desire to express in the most sincere and emphatic manner, not only our thankful appreciation of the matter and manner of these lectures and other communications through the lips of Mrs. Richmond, but of our confidence in her as a true and faithful exponent of the theory of Spirit intercourse and control.

"*Resolved,* That while we part with regret

from her and the wise and interesting teachers from the other life associated with her, we yet feel she is more a messenger to humanity than to any small or particular section of it, and therefore bid her God-speed, and earnestly commend her as a most reliable medium for the presentation of the higher and more profitable phases illustrative of the teachings of the Spiritual philosophy."

The following beautiful poem was spoken impromptu at the close of one of her lectures, from a subject furnished by the audience.

OUR HOMES AND EMPLOYMENTS IN SPIRIT LIFE.

Home is not fashioned, even on the earth,
    Of pictured wall and tesselated floor;
Of sculptured forms, though rare in art their worth,
    Nor pillared halls, nor proud domes arching o'er.

Nor is home *here* ancestral pride and state,
    Nor names and images of human power;
Nor glorious presence of the high and great,
    Nor splendid blazonry of beauty's dower.

But home is love!   Where'er the loved ones dwell,
    Whether in cottage low or palace hall;
Affection and sweet memory weave their spell,
    And human love wins and reclaims you all.

The sailor-boy in visions of the night,
    Storm-tossed and weary, dreams of home afar;
The desert wanderer sees the beaming light
    Of home shine out like a resplendent star.

And world-worn, hardened by life's daily care,
    You turn to childhood's home—to early love
This moves, sustains, and guides you unaware,
    Where'er in life your weary footsteps move.

But *place* is naught; if the dear ones are gone,
    The home deserted like an empty nest,
You cannot call it home; you miss the tone,
    The form, the presence that once made it blest.

Within the Spirit-world your home is where
    Your loved abide—the innermost of love;
Life's morning holds them, and the ambient air
    Is filled with beauty where the Spirits move.

You make your heavenly homes of thoughts and deeds,
    Of loving work, of duties daily done;
The planting on the earth of heavenly seeds—
    These bear you golden fruit when life is won.

The pictured images of early youth,
    The aspirations here for human weal,
Become by toil, temples of living Truth,
    And these the Heavenly home will not conceal.

Ye build your habitations, not of clay
    But of the Spirit and its atmosphere;
And while the earthly home must fade away,
    The home of Spirit is an endless day.

The loved ones dead restored unto your arms,
    The hopes once perished blooming fully there
The fervent spirit that all being warms,
    Possessed, retained, abiding everywhere.

The occupation is for spirit state
    Whate'er the spirit has most need to do;
Planting the seeds of love—uprooting hate,
    And letting rays of splendor glimmer through.

Seeking for knowledge—Wisdom's high behest;
    Striving to find the secret source of things;
All laws, all science, and the soul's deep quest
    To find Truth's fountain—Love's exhaustless springs.

To minister to those who are in need;
    To find that light and spirit most requires.

To sow in earthly hearts the heavenly seed;
  To fan to flame the flickering altar fires.

 Home and employment, every lovely thing
   You do or are, these form your spirit's home;
 And these shall meet you, ever to you cling,
   _ When to the Spirit realm your thoughts shall come.

The foregoing complete statement from Mr. Bacon leaves but little to be written concerning the Washington work except to summarize its grand results.

Our medium was the close friend of Miss Nettie Colburn, now known as Nettie Colburn Maynard, whose able work, "Was Abraham Lincoln a Spiritualist?" attracted so much attention in the literary world some three years ago. It was at the funeral services of Mrs. Maynard where Mrs. Richmond, in fulfillment of the friendship of over thirty years and a long existing pledge, was called upon to officiate June 30, 1892, that she said that Mrs. Maynard has understated rather than over-stated the facts in that remarkable book concerning the interviews that President Lincoln had with the Spirit world, through Nettie Colburn.

Miss Colburn was repeatedly called to the White House and Mr. Lincoln often visited her at her rooms, where he would receive messages concerning the welfare of the Nation from those in the supernal world, whose statesmanship and knowledge of politics gave him a clear light by which to guide his own actions as the ruler of the nation. Distinguished jurists, United States senators, member of congress, and clergymen were among those who listened to Cora Scott's lectures at the nation's capital. As has been stated by our brother Bacon, Senator Howard, of Michigan; Senator Julian, of Indiana; Senator Benj. F. Wade, of Ohio; Gen. N. P. Banks, of Massachusetts; Senator Henry Wilson, afterward Vice-President, were regular visitors at her soirees on week evenings during her Washington pastorate. They were knowing to Mr. Lincoln's interest in Spiritualism, as were also Congressman Somes, from Maine; Col. Kase, of Philadelphia, and B. B. Hill of the same city. These gentlemen were all open and avowed Spiritualists at that time, but they have nearly all passed on to the higher life, with the exception of Senator Julian and the two last named—Col. Kase and Mr. Hill.

Mr. Lincoln was also personally acquainted with our subject, and enjoyed her discourses in company with these other distinguished gentlemen to whom we have referred. The committee on reconstruction from both Houses of Congress, of which Senator Howard was chairman, sometimes called upon our subject as often as twice each week for advice from the spirit side of life upon the reconstruction of the Southern States. · It was particularly to Senator Howard

that this advice was given and he ever listened
attentively and reverently, urging upon his col-
leagues the recommendations given from the
Spirit guides. The guides always gave to these
public men sound advice and some of the suggestions advanced by them were adopted by these
gentlemen in their reports to Congress; but, as
Brother Bacon says, short-sighted policy too
often governed the majority and the recommendations of the guides were not followed in their
entirety. Had they been, we have no doubt but
what the stupendous blunder made in the reconstruction of the Southern States would have been
avoided. The guides advised provisional measures at first, as controlling powers for the lately
rebellious States, opposed the granting of suffrage
to the freedmen, and urged the adoption of an
educational policy by means of which the blacks
could be shown the duties and responsibilities of
citizenship, which would have kept them free from
the designs of scheming politicians and unscrupulous men, whose victims they became later on.
The guides would have had the willingness of
the Southern people to accept the results of the
war demonstrated in other ways than by the in-
discriminate amnesty pardons and laws that were
given forth by President Johnson and the Nation's
Congress. They always plead for leniency in
the treatment of the conquered people, but urged
that their fidelity to the nation should be tested

before it was accepted as a fact by the lovers of the Union, who were in control of the government.

Mr. Lincoln was often the controlling spirit who gave these sound sentiments to the distinguished committee which was seeking light upon the vexatious problems with which they were wrestling. He was, in fact, one of the leading controls, as we have stated earlier in this work, during the six years of our subject's Washington pastorate. We learn from reliable sources that the Rev. Byron Sunderland, the distinguished Presbyterian pastor, was also a frequent visitor at her parlors. All of these gentlemen were personal friends of Mr. Lincoln and his personality was so marked during his control of the instrument that they had no hesitancy in pronouncing the sentiments they received to be Lincolnian throughout.

It is impossible for us to measure the full effect that the words of these guides had upon the teachers in the Congress of the Nation who sought communion with the statesmen in the higher life. It is safe to say, however, that many of the measures, outside of reconstruction, were tinctured with the ideas conveyed to our lawmakers through spiritual agency.

Her Washington pastorate, as we may call it, extended over a period of six years, from the Winter of 1865–6 to 1872, inclusive. Many ref-

erences to this work may be found in the files of
the "Banner of Light," and other Spiritual
papers for those years. Comments upon the effect
of this Washington work are almost unnecessary,
as our readers can readily see that they must have
reached nearly every section of the United States,
as her words were heard by the statesmen from
all parts of the Union; as well as by government
employes, representing also all of the Federal
States. It gave Spiritualism an impetus and a
standing in Washington heretofore unattained,
for our readers must remember that there were
gifted mediums then living in Washington, such
as Nettie Colburn and others of equal power,
who had attracted to the Spiritual meetings, warriors, statesmen, and jurists, such as Gen. Chrys-
ler, Major Chorpening, Gen. Longstreet, and
others whom we have named on these pages.
When the history of Spiritualism is written as a
finality, then will the full value of this work of
the spirit in Washington be made known to the
world. Now it stands recorded upon the pages
of the records in the archives of the Angel world,
where each mortal must stand face to face with
his or her own record and reap the reward, or
meet the consequences of the deeds wrought in
earth life.

The Congress of Spirits, in the halls of the In-
ter-National Legislature in the higher life, will
continue to send forth instructive thoughts to

teach the children of men in all the nations of the earth, and ultimately lead them all to a recognition of the religion of human brotherhood, which was the earnest purpose of the guides of our subject to introduce and carry forward through the work in Washington.

CHAPTER IX.

WORK IN ENGLAND: LONDON, THE PROVINCES AND SCOTLAND.

A S we have seen from the foregoing chapters, our subject's work had won fame that extended far beyond the confines of our beloved America to our brethren across the sea, and even far down in the southwestern continent, Australia, her writings and works were well known to the friends of the cause there. The English Spiritualists had long been desirous of securing our subject's able services in the interests of the propagandism of Spiritualism in the United Kingdom, and particularly urged her to visit them during the reconstruction period, and even at earlier dates in the history of her mediumship. She was unable to visit the Old World until the Spring of the year 1873, when, by the promptings of her guides who directed the change because of her health, and in response to the urgent appeals of many devoted friends of the cause throughout England, she acceded to their request and took leave of her native land for an indefinite period of time. This call marked a new epoch in the history of her work and, we might say, in the history of Spiritualism as well.

Perhaps we can imagine her emotions as she embarked upon the beautiful steamer that was to bear her three thousand miles from her home to work among strangers, who were yet her friends and were united to her by the ties that link souls together in this mortal expression. The deep blue of the majestic ocean, the soft sea breezes that played upon her brow, the flapping of the wings of the seagull, the white sails of the vessels that flitted past to and fro, all made a beautiful panoramic picture of some fairy scene, as she reflected upon what these things meant to her, while the steamer bore her yet farther away from those who knew her best and had been her constant companions through the earlier years of her life. She could almost fancy that she heard "the music of the spheres come pealing through the sky," as the poet says, as she listened to the soft sounds of the gentle breezes that played about the vessel, and the gentle murmuring of the waters as they laved the sides of the steamer. The phosphorescent lights that floated in the steamer's wake at night, the occasional glimpse of some fish as he sprang out of the water or arose for a breath of invigorating oxygen to carry with him to his home beneath the waves, constituted a picture and a prophecy showing that the old scenes had

changed and that the new were opening for her.
These things bore in upon her mind many pleasant reveries, many painful emotions, many
prayerful thoughts and utterances for strength
with which to meet the new duties upon which
she was entering. How strange are one's emotions upon an extended ocean voyage! Old
Neptune seemingly has sway, not only over the
vasty deep, but also over the minds of those
who brave his anger by breasting the storms that
he is supposed to send from over his kingdom,
through the magical music of his voice so low,
so melancholy, and yet so sublime—for the
voice of the ocean *is* sublime. It tells its story
to the smooth pebbles upon the beach, and the
white spray as it dashes up the sides of the
rocks, upon the promontories or cliffs along the
shore, speaks of some mighty power greater than
that which man exerts over the inanimate objects
of earth, telling of " Him from out whose hand
the centuries fall like grains of sand." Its song
is sublime; its music, like the threnodies of the
angels, steals softly across the subtle chords of
the soul and attunes them to hear the voices of
the muses that these Naiads express to us in the
wonderful symphonies and harmonies that are to
be found in the murmurings, the heavings, the
billowing of the savage sea.

But we must turn from these pictures. The
steamer rolled on and on, and carried our sub-

ject to her home across the sea. Queenstown
was reached, and the lights of the harbor of
Liverpool gleamed upon her, and she had reached
the soil of Great Britain.

· Here opened a ministry of such great import
to the Spiritualists of the world that we feel impelled to pause to contemplate the wonderful
work that was accomplished. The people whom
she met numbered among them some of the
most prominent of the titled and untitled nobility
of England, some of the gifted philanthropists
whose names are household words in both con-
tinents, among whom we may mention the noble
George Thompson, the anti-slavery agitator; his
enthusiastic daughter, Mrs. Noswortley; the gifted
John Bright, whose friendship for America in the
dark days of the rebellion has become a matter
of history; Rev. Stainton Moses ("M. A. Oxen");
William Oxley; Mrs. Strawbridge, one of nature's
true noblewomen; Mr. and Mrs. Tebb; Benj.
Coleman; N. Kilburn, and we must extend the
list to name that noble worker, the Countess of
Caithness, whose letter of appreciation appears
in a subsequent chapter in this work. Our subject bore with her letters of introduction from
one whose name is well known to the Spiritualists of America, the gifted Robert Owen, who
held many high positions under the United States
government, and whose services in behalf of
Spiritualism are now known wherever it has had

a hearing. Mr. Owen's interest in her and her work was such as to lead him to write, after an informal introduction, in the following appreciative manner:

"We have not among the women of America any more enlightened, or more judicious, or more eloquent exponent of the principles of what, in modern phrase, is termed Spiritualism than this lady, and I am sure that those who have thought deeply on the subject will be much gratified by making her acquaintance.

ROBERT DALE OWEN."

Mr. Owen's position in the literature of Spiritualism is too well established to need comment from us. His "Foofalls on the Boundary of Another World," will ever stand as a living monument to his memory, and indicates the power of his thought, the sincerity of his motives, and his devotion to the fundamental truths of Spiritualism. His services as a diplomat in foreign lands are recorded upon the pages of our nation's history, and show that, while he was a devotee at the shrine of a religion that was despised, and its adherents treated generally with contumely by the unthinking and the rabble, he commanded the respect of even the opponents of Spiritualism, and was made the recipient, at the hands of our nation's rulers, of one of the brightest positions in the diplomatic services of our country. He was well known in England to the lit-

erateurs and scholars, as well as to the statesmen
Bright and Thompson, to whom we have already
adverted.   Among the friends of Mr. Owen in
England to whom he referred our subject, are
the distinguished authors, William and Mary
Howitt, Professor Neuver, Mr. and Mrs. S. C.
Hall (authors), Benjamin Coleman, Mrs. D.
Morgan (author of the celebrated work, " From
Matter to Spirit "); Mrs. Drayson (a splendid
medium); William Wilkinson, barrister (former
editor of the London Spiritual Magazine); Dr.
Garth Wilkinson, his brother (also a distinguished
author); Mrs. Milner Gibson (whose husband
was a member of parliament and an earnest
Spiritualist); Mrs. Twort; Mrs. Cox ; Mr. and
Mrs. Henry D. Jenckyn (formerly Kate Fox);
Alfred Russell Wallace, the distinguished natur-
alist, and Professor William Crookes, F. R. S.,
and editor of a journal of science.   Professor
Wallace reviewed Mr. Owen's great work, " The
Debatable Land," in a London scientific journal
from the standpoint of an appreciative friend.
All of the above became warm friends of our
subject, and were instrumental in introducing
her to the Spiritualists of England.   Mr. Owen's
letter, in referring to these friends whose names
we have given above, is filled with the kindliest
thoughts and heartiest wishes for our subject's
success and restoration to health while in England.

After a private reception in the parlors of his spiritual institution, she was introduced to her first public audience by James Burns, located at 15 Southampton Row, London. He is one of the earliest Spiritualists in England, a most indefatigable worker, writer and thinker, through whom has come much of the success that our cause has attained in that country. Mr. Burns was also an early friend of Dr, J. M. Peebles, and other American mediums and speakers who visited England as representatives of the Spiritual philosophy. Mr. Burns is the able editor of " The Medium and Daybreak," in the columns of which verbatim reports of the discourses, or "orations" as our English friends name them, of our subject, were given during her stay in England. Mr. Burns has kindly placed the files of his paper during the years 1872 to 1875 inclusive, at our disposal, the perusal of which has enabled us to give our readers a consecutive and succinct account of our subject's work during her ministrations in England.

From the commencement of her work in St. George's Hall, London, to the close of her labors in Southport, England, the work of that period presents an uninterrupted line of success for the cause and for the teachings given through her lips. In public and private the utterances were listened to with most profound attention by many of the ablest minds of Great Britain. Of

that first meeting the London *Daily News*, after
noting her personal appearance, says:

"There was no nonsense in her mode of dealing with the question, and the use of the judicious letter of Mr. Owen in recommending her
to the British public could not be more aptly
applied." The article gave at some length a synopsis of the discourse.

The following is from the "London Standard":

"Judging from the densely crowded state of
the hall, and the large number it was necessary
to close the door upon, it was evident that there
was great excitement among the believers and
inquirers in this movement at the advent of the
new speaker, whose first appearance in England
was the occasion of this meeting.   *   *   *   No
one could question the great beauty of the word-
ing of the opening prayer nor the felicitous manner in which it was delivered. Another hymn,
and then the lady proceeded to her oration on
'Spiritualism as a Science and as a Religion.' It
may at once be said that her speech was delivered with great fluency and good elocution, her
language at times abounding with highly poetic
thoughts, and at others with effective practical
points.   *   *   *   On resuming her seat the fair
lecturer was greeted with loud cheers, and as a
sort of *encore* recited a poem descriptive of the
general illuminative powers of Spiritualism in

bringing human nature from its previous darkness and its assurance of the immortality of the
soul. The assemblage was composed mainly of
well dressed persons of mature age, the sexes
being fairly divided. The greatest attention was
paid thoughout the whole of the service."

The following extract is from another London daily, The Telegraph, I believe, of the same
date:

"Spiritualism at St. George's Hall. — Last
evening St. George's Hall was densely crowded
by ladies and gentlemen, assembled to hear an
oration on Spiritualism, delivered under spirit
influence, by an inspirational speaker from the
United States.

"The most prominent members of the London
Spiritualist world together with a number of
transatlantic supporters of the movement, occupied seats on the platform. * * * The
lady having been introduced, a hymn was sung
from the "Spiritual Lyre," and the lady then
delivered a preliminary prayer, the gist of which
was the universal praise offered up by all things,
animate and inanimate, to the Creator. After a
second hymn, the lady, who is of pleasing personal appearance and apparently of some five
and thirty years of age, began her oration, the
subject being, 'Spiritualism as a Science and
Spiritualism as a Religion.' By her first position she sought to establish the existence of

what she styles a 'super-science,' the formulæ of which have yet to be ascertained by strict investigation. This investigation the Spiritualists are anxious to have carried out by the scientists, arguing that feats accomplished by Spiritual aid which we are now apt to regard as the direct violation of the laws of nature are really due to the existence of higher, and, as yet, uninvestigated laws, not 'super-natural,' but 'super-material.' The direct action of disembodied spirits upon the human will may be regarded as analogous to that of the mesmerist upon his patient. As a religion Spiritualism is to be distinguished by its universality, embodying within its scope all differences of creeds and tending to universal brotherhood. To it the inspiration in all ages of prophets, seers and poets is to be set down. All creeds at all times have felt its influence, and it may be said to form the keystone of the arch between materialism and religion. * * *

"For upwards of an hour the lady poured forth an uninterrupted flow of language, without hesitating for a single instance, sentences of the most involved character and abounding in parentheses, being evolved without apparent effort, and every word fitting into its place as in a child's puzzle. Though somewhat devoid of elocutionary emphasis, her delivery was clear and telling, and her diction of a very high order. If, as stated, she is merely a mouthpiece of the Spirits, the condition of *belles lettres* in the Spiritual world is decidedly encouraging. If, on the other hand, her lecture is a mere effort of memory, its recital is a feat rarely excelled.   *   *   *

"Another hymn having been sung, the lady, still under the Spiritual influence, recited a short poem, with a somewhat Swinburnian ring, the last lines of it announcing that

> "Not with trumpets, nor splendor of gold,
> But hushed voices, the story is told—
> The bright day of truth it is come!"

*   *   * After a vote of thanks to the fair orator the assembly dispersed."

Many other extracts might be made from contemporaneous London and other papers, but they all bear the same testimony. In the provincial towns the papers contained column after column of reports, comments and discussion, editorial and correspondential, caused by her public utterances. Piles of excerpts from these papers are before us, but we can only choose, almost at random, a few to show the trend of thought awakened by her labors.

The Spiritualistic press kept earnest and enthusiastic records of her words in the provinces, as well as her seances in London, and, as said before, the "Medium and Daybreak" published most of her London orations verbatim.

During the Summer (after the close of the late London "season") and Autumn months of each year, we find our subject making a tour of the provinces, more particularly the northern counties of England and the cities of Edinburgh and Glasgow in Scotland. The center of these provincial labors was in Yorkshire and Lancashire, although most of the large towns north of London were visited, including Birmingham, Manchester, several towns in Derbyshire, Leeds (the home of Geo. Thompson and Mrs. Ford), Bradford, Rochdale (the home of the Brights), Oldham, Halifax, Liverpool, Darlington, York, Bishop-Auckland, Newcastle-on-Tyne, etc., etc.

At all of these places there was manifested a great desire, not unmingled with curiosity, of those who knew little of Spiritualism, to see and hear her. One woman in a small town in Lancashire walked ten or twelve miles to see "yon woman who talked with dead spirits."

Whenever the meetings were held in Rochdale, or, in fact, anywhere in that county, the family of John Bright were certain to be present—the great statesman himself also being one of the audience whenever relieved from his political labors.

The local papers made copious extracts from the discourses and gave extended notices of her appearance and work. These "North country folk" differ essentially from the more conventional, although none the less earnest people of the great metropolis. An intelligence and en-

thusiasm combined with hearty good will and an
instinctive desire for "fair play" make up the
qualities that distinguish the good people of
Yorkshire and Lancashire. It must also be remembered that the labors of such men as Richard
Cobden, Geo. Thompson and John Bright, in
opening up libraries, reading-rooms, and free
lectures had served to create a basis of appreciation of free thought and progressive ideas that
prepared the way for these ministrations. There
were always a few—or possibly only one—
staunch Spiritualists in these English towns who
prepared the way and invited our speaker to
visit them; around these occasions centered an
interest that can with difficulty be described. And
can be better estimated by mentioning among
scores of interesting incidents, a few that serve
to illustrate the effect of the work in the provinces.

It is needless to premise the account of these
interesting occurrences with the statement that
there was at many places a manifest opposition
aroused, both among the secularists and the
bigoted orthodox, but to their credit it is noted
that the Wesleyans as well as the church people
of the North were usually very liberal and toler-
ant, and the influence of the schools of thought
of John Stuart Mill and Robert Owen had prepared the more independent thinkers for the
work of the guides of our subject.

Mr. Thos. Kershaw, of Oldham, in a letter to a friend, relates that the Rev. Mr. Ashcroft had been lecturing all through Lancashire and Yorkshire against Spiritualism, asserting that the physical phenomena were all produced by fraud and trickery, and that the claim made by that "Woman from America" of being in a trance and of *not preparing her discourses beforehand* was entirely false.

Already a good impression had been made in Oldham and that vicinity by the discourses of our medium, and many feared that the statements of the "Rev." (?) gentleman would do harm to her subsequent work there. The sequel was most interesting. Other meetings by our subject followed closely upon those of the clerical calumniator. *The Co-operative Hall* was filled to the utmost capacity by an interested, indeed, an excited multitude. A minority were the friends of the fair lecturer. A majority were those who came to put to the test—especially the claim or pretense of impromptu speaking upon any subject chosen by the audience. Mr. Kershaw asked the medium if she was nervous in any way about the excitement. Her guides responded, "certainly not; let the audience have its own way absolutely in the selection of the subject." The chairman was instructed by the Spirit inspirers to say to the audience that in view of the recent false statements made concerning the preparation of these discourses by the lady, the audience could *select the subject* of the discourse in any manner decided upon by the majority of those present; either by committee chosen by the audience or by popular vote. A most unique method was decided upon! A little girl was found in the rear of the hall, who was placed in front of the audience with a hat in her hand. A committee of non-Spiritualists went through the audience and gathered up all the subjects that were written amounting to thirty or forty; these subjects were placed in the hat and thoroughly mixed. The little girl was then directed by the committee to draw a slip of paper from the hat which was to be the subject of the discourse. It is unnecessary to state that no Spiritualist went near either the little girl or the hat. The subject drawn was "The Trinity." For an hour the audience listened, more than a third of them standing, with breathless attention to the discourse. Then followed a pause and the little girl drew another subject upon which an improvised poem followed. When all was over, and the full meaning of the evidence dawned upon the people who were there, evidence of the genuineness of the claim that the discourse had not been prepared and committed to memory, aye deeper evidence to men who were before unconvinced of inspiration and the world beyond, there arose such a tumult of applause and such cheering as our medium had never experienced (even in the exciting days of New York and the conquest over the Tammany leader). It was a complete and overwhelming triumph for her and for the cause of Spiritualism. Mr. Ash--croft was never permitted by the irate populace to speak in that place again.

Another incident of a different nature comes to us from the little town of Yeadon, one of the manufacturing villages just out of Bradford.

Our subject was called there to speak by the only Spiritualist in the place, a Mr. Waugh, who in his sincere and humble way received and entertained the lecturer in his family. The Wesleyan Chapel had been secured for the occasion, for these simple folk had not yet been warned that Spiritualism was a dangerous heresy; besides they remembered that there were visiting spirits in the Wesley family in the early part of the century. The lectures were delivered before large audiences, a lay preacher of the chapel taking the chair. The subject of the discourse was chosen by a committee selected by the audience, and was: "What better means have the Angels in Heaven of knowing the will of God than mortals possess?" The lecture was listened to with most profound attention by the entire audience, and at its close the chairman said reverently: "If that is Spiritualism then all Wesleyans are bound to be Spiritualists." But the interest of this visit to that little town centers upon another incident so remarkable that we give it place, making our statement in synopsis from an account published in the "Medium and Daybreak," and from private letters to the friends of our subject.

A young man who was a plumber by trade had been much interested in reading the discourses given by our medium in London and the provincial towns, especially Bradford, so close to Yeadon, and was most eager to hear the lecturer from America. He knew of the invitation extended to her to visit Yeadon, and looked forward to the occasion with the greatest anticipations, although not a Spiritualist. About two weeks previous to the date announced for the lecture the young man injured his foot. It became painful and swollen, and his friends were afraid of blood poisoning, caused, they thought, from some of the mineral poisons used in his work. He could not wear a shoe, could not walk, and, to his great and bitter disappointment was unable to go to the lecture. He asked and obtained permission, however, to call at the neighbor's house where she was staying and "just look at her." He succeeded in accomplishing the few yards of travel, with the aid of a friend and a crutch and cane, but suffered acute pain all the time. The speaker was partaking of some slight refreshment, but at intervals conversed pleasantly with the young man and the few friends who were present. Suddenly he became very pale and said he felt a prickling sensation down his limb, and was afraid of paralysis. She reassured him, for she spiritually saw (as she afterward narrated) the spirit form of Dr. Rush bending over the young man, and she saw a Spiritual light envelop the injured foot and limb. At the time she only said, "Do not be afraid, you are not paralyzed." A few moments later when the young man arose to go he gave a start of amazement, refused the aid of his friend, rejected the cane and crutch, and said, "I am cured; I am cured!" He walked home beside his friend without assistance, hastening. When his wife met them at the door she looked horrified, saying: "Give over yer fooling; ye'll never be well." "Na! I'm not fooling," he replied; "yon woman has cured me." The next day he put on his shoe and went all about the village proclaiming his cure. At no time during this brief call was he nearer in bodily presence to our medium than ten or twelve feet; but the healing power manifested in her childhood had never departed and only waited the time and occasion to come forth at need. Many hearts were stirred, many lives were moved by this brief ministration in the little town of Yeadon, among the smoky hills and valleys near Bradford.

When the medium left in the carriage that came to convey her the people would draw it out of town, and but for her protestations would have thus drawn her in triumph to Bradford, a distance of nine miles.

The incidents in the provinces alone would fill volumes, to say nothing of the discourses which were ever listened to with most profound interest. Hundreds who came to scoff remained to pray.

During these summer tours she visited the beautiful and almost classical city of Edinburgh, Scotland, "The Athens of Great Britain," as it is properly named.

Her home there was always with Mr. and Mrs. J. Stuart Smith; the latter an artist of eminence and a most gifted medium in and for her own select circle. These friends have ever been true to the cause and to her. Into that circle our subject was received as teacher, leader and friend. And the communings and ministrations there will ever be cherished by the favored participants, including herself. There she met that truly inspired and venerable clergyman, John Pulsford, (afterward resident in London), who was never so happy and uplifted as when listening to her inspired utterances.

In Edinburgh there were very large public audiences. On one occasion many clergy of all denominations were present numbering about thirteen and a D. D.—Rev. MacDonald—in the chair.

As in the early days of our medium's public work in New York, the clergy came to "try the

spirits " and to endeavor to put them to flight, so
these clerical gentlemen vied with each other
in trying to puzzle or overthrow the arguments
of the "fair lecturer," for little did they apparently know the power with which they were cop-
ing.   When a very bright answer or brilliant
repartee met one of these questioners all the
others would join in the applause; and they each
had their turn.   After the clergy had chosen their
own subjects for the discourse and poem, after
they had exhausted their store of questions and
difficult propositions of theology the chairman
said, in substance: "I do not know what my
fellow clergy who are present this evening may
think, nor to what conclusion they will arrive
after this marvellous exhibition of intellectual
and Spiritual power, but my *self respect* prompts
me to accept the theory of inspiration as the only
feasible one in explaining the sources of knowledge of this lady, who could not have had access
to Universities and Colleges.   If she is not inspired what becomes of all our boasted scholarship and classical education ?"

The Edinburgh visits were most delightful to
our subject and to her friends.   While the historical and beautiful surroundings made many
a pretext for excursions and picnics, at which
times Ouina would often control her medium and
give rare poems appropriate to the scenery or
historical reminiscences of the places so visited:

"Arthur's Seat," "Holyrood Palace," in Edinburgh, and near there the ruins of "Hawthorn-
den," within whose caves and mysterious cells
Robert Bruce and his "merrie men" found shelter—all these we must pass for the most important record of this wonderful Spiritual work.

In Glasgow an equally intelligent, if not as
scholastic audiences greeted our subject. She
was warmly welcomed by Mr. Nesbitt, and by
that staunch, sturdy champion of our cause,
James Bowman (and his true hearted wife) and
many others. Here also she met that marvellous
medium James Duguid, through whose powers
direct paintings in oil (without human hands)
were given and through whose mediumship came
that remarkable book, "Hafiz, Prince of Persia."
The people of Scotland, more especially the
citizens of Glasgow, are much more enfranchised
in thought (notwithstanding the "Scotch Kirk"
—the descent of the Covenanters) than one
would believe. There is also a popular vein of
true Republican feeling and fraternity with
America. When Mr. Lincoln was assassinated,
our subject was informed there was as great evidence of mourning in Glasgow as in Boston and
New York. There the audiences gave way to
unbounded enthusiasm and permitted no carping
critics to disturb the speaker, although they
sometimes tried.

One is so tempted in wandering with our sub-

ject through the land of Bruce and Wallace to
go with her on those little excursions to Loch
Katrine and Loch Lomond, to visit the scenes
so vividly portrayed by that master of English
literature, Sir Walter Scott, (we doubt not one
of the scions of that family of Scotts from whom
our medium descended). One place of interest
we will name that she visited, "Cora Linn" (or
Cora Falls) on the River Clyde, from which her
name was derived, a great uncle having given
her this romantic name after reading about the
Roman maiden Cora who was killed while crossing the Linn or falls of the Clyde. This name
coupled with Victoria, given by another great
uncle makes her name truly emblematic.

One of the most popular clergymen of Scotland has ever been a faithful student of these
teachings from the time of the first visit of our
medium to Edinburgh, when she met him, to the
last visit in '85 and on to the present time.

It is impossible to give, however one may be
tempted to do so, the names of all the friends
who thronged around our medium in her wonderful work in Great Britain.

In Liverpool there was a literal "outpouring
of the Spirit" as well as of the people. She
was received at the home of Mrs. Louisa Thompson Nosworthy where during this and all subsequent visits to Liverpool she was welcomed with
open arms; and such was this lady's zeal that

she often declared if it were not for her family
she would travel with Mrs. Richmond and devote
her whole life to the work.   It was here that
Hon. George Thompson—broken in health from
long service as ambassador in India—renewed
his acquaintance with the work of our medium,
coming from Leeds to Liverpool or London
whenever his health permitted, to listen to the
addresses or enjoy the society of our subject and
her guides.

The work in Lancashire, including Liverpool,
was largely promoted by John Lamont, a sturdy
and zealous advocate of Spiritualism for many
years, and the late Mr. Fowler was instrumental
in procuring the services of our medium in
Liverpool at a later time.   Dr. William Hitchman (or Hycheman, as he afterwards spelled
his name), was chosen by the Liverpool friends
as their chairman, to present the speaker to the
audience.   Although a gentleman of considerable self appreciation, he was certainly educated,
talented and gifted in a great degree.   His fine
appearance (strikingly resembling, we are told,
the portraits of our Benjamin Franklin), and
ready command of language made his presence
as a presiding officer very acceptable.

It must be remembered that at that time our
medium was very frail in body, having but partially recovered from severe hemorrhages of the
lungs which were the result of a delicate consti-

tution and the severity of the climate in her
native home, yet with partial restoration her
labors were continued with unremitting zeal, and
the friends in Great Britain everywhere sought
to bring her every aid through sympathy and
tender care.   It was therefore with some anxiety
that Dr. Hitchman saw the immense concourse
of people that this fragile form had to meet.

Lord Nelson Hall and other places where the
meetings were held were taxed to their utmost
capacity to hear the guides of Mrs. Richmond,
sometimes hundreds were turned away unable
even to obtain standing room.   It was soon evident that the controls, aided by the efficient
chairman were masters of the situation.   Dr.
Hitchman told a friend, from whom we have the
words almost verbatim, that this lady convinced
him of Spirit control.   He called upon her at
the house of Mrs. Nosworthy, having an introduction from a friend.   He saw the mild, fragile
looking lady and thought her possibly the victim
of some nervous disease, but when she was entranced and answered his questions one after
another with knowledge, fearlessness and force
of logic as well as scientific statement, he became convinced that a mind beyond the mortal
power of this sensitive woman prompted her utterances.   '' I put her to the most crucial tests
of learning and logic at my command, and was
met in every instance by calm self-poise and

mastery of the subject." From that time forward the learned Doctor was her earnest friend and a true champion of the cause.

It was on one of these occasions of a crowded house in Liverpool that a questioner persisted in quibbling and asking the same question in a little different language, when on his declaring that he could not understand the lady's meaning, the controls said: "We did not promise to furnish *understanding*, only arguments."

On several occasions, both in Lancashire and Yorkshire, a secularist of some local fame had made his appearance at the meetings each time with new questions and subjects intended to annoy, perplex, or defeat the purposes of the meeting. The guides of our subject had answered all the interrogations and arguments in their usual concise and clear manner. On one occasion, the last that he ever attempted to annoy, he had recourse to theological questionings for the purpose of eliciting answers that would, perhaps, differ from the religious views of those present; when he had gone far enough the guides turned to the audience and said, "Friends, you perceive that this man, who has *no* religious views, seeks to place us in an unfavorable light before you by endeavoring to show that our views do not harmonize with yours!" Cries of "shame," "we've had enough of him," were heard, and the audiences refused to give him any further opportunity of questioning.

In Darlington great interest was awakened, our medium going there under the invitation of George and Thomas Hinde, who became deeply interested in the work from that time, and conducted meetings in all that portion of Yorkshire.

Andrew Cross, now a resident of Portland, Me., was largely instrumental in presenting our subject to the public of the north of England and of Scotland.   He has ever been a faithful advocate of free thought and speech, and a staunch friend of our medium and the cause.   The following is from his pen:

"Previous to the advent of Mrs. R. in England our shores had been visited by several mediums of note from the land of the Setting Sun. These had sufficed to arouse, on the one hand an intense interest in the subject, and on the other an inveterate hatred and opposition.   The great wave of Spiritual power, which had swept over and into the religion and science of America, had at last invaded Old England, and the sentinels from the outposts of the church rushed in with pale faces, whispering, ' They who have turned the world upside down have come hither also.' Miss Hardinge had come over, and landing in the South, passed like a flash to the North, and in one instance was likened to a ' Destroying Angel.' Dr. Peebles had spent some of his fire on his pilgrimage across the country; D. D. Home, Davenport Brothers, Dr. Slade and others had represented the more physical side, along with Mrs. Marshall of London, and when it was announced that the subject of this sketch had come, a frown more felt than seen passed over the face of the church. Science was startled, but the great Almighty People 'heard her gladly '— her advent in London, almost unheralded, was an instant success. The 'Medium and Daybreak,' issued weekly, was greedily read and passed around when it contained her discourses; and her name known only to a small circle in the Old Country soon became almost a 'household word' —it was a name that thrilled dead Spiritualism into life, and charmed from the stony and unloving church many of the warm hearts of her people.

''The ordinary press of the country which had as yet only sneered down from the towering cliffs of its self-conceit upon the movement, paused at the calm but eloquently uttered philosophy which fell from the lips of this lady, and gradually softening under her genial influence, their columns were soon re-opened, but this time not to curse but to praise her. Clearly the little 'leaven was leavening the whole lump.'

''This lady's London triumphs I am not quite so familiar with, as at that time I had not become personally acquainted with her, but I had a distinct intuition that through her pure inspiration and peerless eloquence, combined with her

matchless affability and demeanor, the bitterness
of the opposition to our ' New Gospel ' was to be
overcome, *and I was not mistaken.*"

"In the year 1874, when I was a resident of
Leeds, England, the subject of our remarks was
announced to speak in Halifax, York, and I
resolved to hear her; luckily I was in good time
and therefore had a good seat, for the place soon
became crowded. Prompt upon time the lady
appeared on the platform and took her seat;
her attire was simplicity itself—plain and tasteful,
and an entire absence of all unnecessary ornamen-
tation—the exquisite taste with which one or two
flowers were made to nestle amongst her light
brown hair, the ever bright smile on her lips,
the strange indefinable something that thrills
you when her eye falls on you—all unite in
producing such a favorable impression that many
of her audience are psychologised before she
rises to speak. After the preliminary services
on this occasion, at the suggestion of a medical
gentleman, the audience selected for subject of
lecture the following, 'One mode of operation
by which the optic nerve conveys its impressions
from the eye to the brain.' I took the liberty
of protesting against this subject, stating that
probably there was but one or two individuals
in the hall who could judge of her treatment of
it, and it would be unfair to risk the reputation
of both the medium and the cause in the hands

of those. It ought to be a subject of general
interest on which we could *all* judge, and that,
too, with a far greater likelihood of giving a
righteous verdict. At this point some one proposed ' Mediumship,' and on a vote that was
carried by a large majority. I confess I was
pleased that amongst so many strangers the
Spiritualists' vote had prevailed. But wait, a
much needed check was here put upon me, for
the medium—whose every motion on the rostrum is poetry—rose gracefully and asked if I
and those who voted with me, would favor her
by giving way on this occasion to the minority,
who she believed were honestly striving after
truth. Spiritualists choose your own subject at
next service and say if I may take that of the
minority this time, and a hearty *aye* was the answer from all parts of the room.

"The subject was taken and handled scientifically and yet popularly, and the M. D. referred
to expressed himself thoroughly satisfied and
much gratified at the result of what he considered a good test.

"Of course it was not long till calls came from
all quarters of the midland counties of England
— Leeds, Bradford, Liverpool, Manchester,
Huddersfield, Yeadon, Ilklee, Oakley, Batley,
Morley, Sowerby Bridge, etc. At nearly all of
these places I was present, and, indeed, at
many of them presided, and I can honestly de-

clare that her visits there were a series of brilliant triumphs, for, like the Roman emperor, she 'Came, Saw and Conquered.'

LEEDS.

"The Music Hall, Albion street, is the scene this time and as usual a crowded house. I was to preside. I cannot forget my feelings when I heard and conveyed the fact to Mrs. R. that Mr. Geo. Thompson, M. P. for Tower Hamlets, noted anti-slavery advocate, pronounced by Lord Brougham 'the greatest orator of the day,' was present. I found him and with her consent begged of him to take my position as president, with reluctance he did so, and I understand it was his last public appearance on earth.

"In his opening remarks he told how those streets had to be barricaded to regulate the crowds who came to hear him when last he spoke on that same platform, and, proceeding, freely acknowledged his sympathy with Spiritualism. Today he still fills an advanced position across the mystic river, and using ' Our Cora' still strives to spread a 'knowledge of the truth.'

YEADON.

"At Yeadon I expected to find another great success. I and a few friends went there on the Sunday morning and found that small Yorkshire town in great turmoil and when the time of meeting arrived and with it the carriage containing the medium, the police had to clear a long passage through the multitude to the door and after that much difficulty was experienced in making our way through the packed passages and across the platform to the front. It was interesting to notice how the charming magnetism of our medium lulled that great surging mass, swaying it from resistance to acquiescence until the souls of the people were so stirred that with one accord (even on the Sabbath) cheer after cheer resounded through Yeadon Town Hall. It was here that the midland people of England began to love our medium, for they found that she was equally a lady in the humble cottage of the laborer or at the table of the rich man, for *that* I and many others from the old county admire C. L. V. R.

BRADFORD.

"At Bradford, too, we had several meetings, all successful and enthusiastic. These were held in Temperance Hall. Well do I remember the difficulty we had at one of these to suppress and extinguish an excitable individual, but the calm, dignified and always pointed remarks of our subject soon restored order.

"Huddersfield, too, felt the force of her invasion. From there, however, I have not the particulars, as in some of the other cases. Liverpool, Manchester and Preston are large cities where also this voice was heard—not loud, but distinct, still proclaiming glad tidings and the way of life to the people.

SOWERBY BRIDGE.

"It was fitting that when this great truth had so moved the inhabitants of Sowerby Bridge, that *they* should be the *first* in England to *build* a temple of *their own*, and it was equally fitting that our great apostle from the West, should be invited to open the same and to break to the people the bread of life. The temple is still there sacred to the same cause. God grant it may long stand not only a monument to the Sowerby Bridge pioneers, but likewise to the early efforts there of our own C. L. V. R.

BATLEY.

"Oh! what a glorious Summer Sunday morn when we took carriage from Newlay to Leeds. The lark had left his nest on the ground and tapped his bill at the very gate of heaven, which opening awhile flooded the air with the music of the spheres; the sun shone brightly gilding all the scene and our medium felt it all, I *knew*, for she seemed *transfigured*. I shall never forget what I might call the psychic glory of that day. I happened to be president and I do believe that an overpleasing inspiration fell upon the medium and that thus I too was 'filled with the spirit.' Suffice it to say, that all Batley was carried away with her, and I have reason to *know* that

'seed fell upon good ground' and is now bringing forth good fruit.

"All subsequent visits were repetitions of the
first, but intensified. Mrs. R. was by this time
both well and widely known in *England*, but I was
anxious that she should be also known to my own
countrymen, the 'canny Scots.'

GLASGOW.

"So having arranged for a short series of lectures in Glasgow we set about securing a hall. We
applied for, then hired and signed for the 'Cor-
poration Rooms'; then had the city's walls properly decorated with large posters, announcing the
details; also posters were put out: '*She* is coming!' In a few days we followed with. 'Who is
coming?' Another lapse of a few days, and out
came, 'C. L. V. Richmond is coming!' After
all this was done we were coolly notified by proprietor of the building that we could not get the
hall *for that purpose*. We reasoned with him,
even threatened him, but to no purpose. 'You
have your remedy in law if you choose,' was all
he would say.

"We next made application to the janitor of
the City Hall, then the largest hall in Glasgow,
told him of our treatment in the other case,
warning him well of our unsavory reputation, etc.
He replied that he could let us have the hall for
those dates, and that we would receive no such

scurvy usage from them. So now we were happy.
We got slips printed altering place of meeting,
etc., and hired men to paste them over all the
posters. This done we were immediately notified that the Sunday meeting could not be held
in the City Hall, the City Fathers having declined
to allow it to be used for that purpose on the
'Lord's Day.' A delegation waited upon Chairman Miller, who, on receiving us, looked bewildered for a moment, then blurted out: 'Why
you seem respectable, intelligent looking people;
surely *you* are not Spiritualists?' We argued that
they let their hall to the Mormons, who advocated polygamy, teaching violation of the law.
We are law-abiding people, and you refuse it to
us. All he could say was that they had to draw
the line somewhere. The upshot was that we
had to postpone our Sunday meeting till Monday. The difficulties we encountered seemed to
have advertised us for on Monday eve the hall
was crowded with a most select and intelligent
audience of three thousand people.

"The 'Revs.,' 'Hons.,' and 'M. D's.' were well
represented and the proverbial pin might have
been heard drop when that vast assemblage of
upturned faces gazed with rapt and breathless
attention to the words of wisdom from another
world.

"At a still later date our medium repeated her
victories, but now all opposition has been over-

come, and in vanquishing prejudice against us in
England and Scotland, I feel bound to say that
our subject, the matchless inspirational medium,
the impassioned speaker and accomplished lady,
has done more than any other, and a great deal
more than her share."

Saltburn-by-the-Sea, Belper, Derbyshire, and
a score of other places, might be mentioned, each
bringing its record of golden words of promise,
hope and instruction, but space forbids.

One other incident: Near Leeds are some coal
mines, and our medium in company with a party
of friends descended into these pits, and taking
lights in their hands entered the small cabs or
"trams" provided for them and drawn by don-
keys. They passed more than a mile under-
ground, and when near the "quenchless fires" of
the pit the men were called together and received
an address and poem, they furnishing the subjects. It was a scene that never could be forgotten.

The work in Manchester was no less interesting.
Not only were the public audiences large and appreciative, but here she was a welcome guest at
the house of that staunch friend of Spiritualism
and mediums, Mr. Blackburn, who later befriended and sheltered Miss Florence Cook and
her mother, when the former was attacked by a
so-called investigator (?).

In Manchester she also met Mr. William Oxley,

whose scholarship and spiritual perception attracted him to the work of the guides of our subject; and here she was an honored guest and teacher in that little circle of choice souls who were chosen to receive ministrations of a high order through one of their own number. Mr. Oxley, being a thorough Oriental scholar, appreciated the discourses on Egypt and other kindred topics.

At Newcastle-on-Tyne the people were awakened to a very high degree of interest, and bitter opposition from bigots only served to heighten that interest. Here P. T. Barkas, Esq., presided and introduced the speaker whenever she appeared in Newcastle, and being somewhat of a scientist and litterateur, he certainly was qualified to judge of the quality of thoughts presented by our speaker as well as the language with which they were clothed.

Equally interesting was the work in Brighton— the fashionable, brilliant, cosmopolitan, sea-side metropolis of the southern coast of England. There is nothing provincial about Brighton, and we know that when a victory was won there it was but in a lesser London.

It was in the year 1874, during the height of one of her most successful engagements in London, that she made a flying visit to Brighton, only sixty miles distant. A young boy was seen in the midst of an audience of 1,500 or 2,000 peo-

ple, listening intently to the inspired words that
fell from her eloquent lips. This boy was Wil-
berforce Juvenal Colville. It was through the
seeming chance visit of his to this lecture that
discovered to Mr. Colville his own wonderful
psychic powers, of which he had been possessed
from childhood, but, up to that time, had never
been brought into use through a lack of fitting
opportunity. We feel that it would be wise on our
part to introduce here Mr. Colville's personal
reminiscences of this event, and of his subsequent relations to Mrs. Richmond, to whom he
has ever been a valued co-worker and appreciative friend, and a highly esteemed brother. We
present his account in full in order that our
readers may see for themselves what one great
worker can say of another:

" My first acquaintance with Mrs. Richmond
and her work in England dates from May 24,
1874. I was at that time a child under fourteen,
residing temporarily in Brighton, a world re-
nowned seaside city, in which there were many
influential Spiritualists; notably, Mr. Tiedman
Marteze, a wealthy, generous man, who was
always ready to devote means and effort to
spread the cause which lay nearest his heart.
Through the enterprise of this gentleman, assisted by several other earnest Spiritualists, Mrs.
Richmond was engaged to deliver a series of
inspirational discourses in the music room of the

Royal Pavilion, the Town Hall and other public
places where the seating capacity was in the
neighborhood of four hundred, and where a charge
for admission was made to defray expenses. These
gatherings were all very successful, and the local
press (usually very conservative), particularly the
'Examiner,' gave excellent reports of the lectures, and commented especially upon the marvel
of improvised poetry. It was in consequence of
this preparatory work that so large a gathering
(not less than 1,500 strong) assembled in the
largest hall in the city, when the doors were
thrown freely open to all comers on the memor-
'able evening when it was my good fortune to be
personally brought in contact with Mrs. Richmond and the Spiritual guides, who then, as now,
inspired her utterances.

"I shall never forget the placard announcing
the event, nor the eagerness with which I took
my place among the throng who gathered to
hear an entranced lady speak upon 'The Advantages of Spiritualism to the Present and
Future Life.' The services were conducted in a
stately and impressive manner. The grand organ pealed forth majestic harmonies as the
graceful speaker, announced by Mr. James Burns
(editor of the 'Medium and Daybreak,' London),
appeared upon the platform and took her seat
amid beautiful flowers, surrounded by a select
company of representative people, all interested

in the great theme announced for the speaker's discourse. From the very moment she arose and pronounced the invocation to the last word of the benediction, my interest was not only rapt, but I felt myself actually in the closest possible communion with the spirit guide who was using the fair lady on the platform as his instrument. I was mediumistic when a child under six, but for several years previous to 1874 I had lost consciousness of my infantile endowment, and never had the least expectation of developing a faculty of inspirational speech, as the phase of sensitiveness which appeared in early childhood was clairvoyance with no attempt in the direction of oratory. I have always believed, and believe still, that our aspirations have a good deal to do with affording necessary conditions for a pleasant, harmonious exercise of any gift we may possess; and in my case the desire on my part to be able to do a work similar to that being accomplished through Mrs. Richmond, who was positively irresistible from the instant she opened her lips to voice the sentiments of the power unseen by ordinary eyes. On that evening the clairvoyant faculty which had lain -·dormant in me for seven years re-awakened, and I saw distinctly the form of the spirit who was prompting the address, and, more than that, I felt a strong, clear current, an inspiring current of vitality, passing from his sphere to my brain.

I was seated about the middle of the large hall, fully fifty feet away from the platform, and there were hundreds of people in the intervening seats, but my own sensation was that of being alone with the lecturer, and so directly in vibrating accord with the source of her inspiration that even she seemed remote and indistinct compared with the forcible realization of the presence and action of the guide, which completely enthralled me. Quite unlike many sensitives who have 'sat for development,' I there and then, after leaving the hall and returning home, commenced the work with which I have been unremittingly engaged ever since, though it was between two and three years later when I was thrown out upon the world as a public lecturer, consecrated to the life work in which I have been conspicuously engaged since March 4, 1877, the date of my first thoroughly public appearance in the British metropolis. Returning home after listening to Mrs. Richmond's inspired utterances on the evening of Sunday, May 24, 1874, I convinced several skeptical persons, who doubted the possibility of such phenomenon, that I, an unpoetical and quite uneducated child, could, under some mysterious influence, which completely changed my voice and manner, answer abstruse questions and improvise verse on subjects presented offhand by my questioners. Whatever may have been the source of this singular mental phenomenon, its immediate cause was, beyond peradventure, the stimulus granted through ministrations of the remakable lady to whom I certainly owe the deepest debt of gratitude and esteem. During the Summer of 1874 I occasionally addressed small companies of invited guests in private residences; and I eagerly read Mrs. Richmond's public discourses, published at that time weekly in the 'Medium.'

"When October came, and the Brighton fashionable season commenced, Mrs. Richmond was again called to the platform in the same hall, and on Sunday, October 4, 11 and 18, 1874, it was my unspeakable privilege and delight to again listen to discourses the wonder and beauty of which I can never cease to remember with the keenest sense of gratitude. Though I often saw Mrs. Richmond in public, and felt quite at home with her guides, I did not meet her in any private way, and, though I should have regarded a personal introduction as a great honor and privilege, she always seemed to me so identified with a spiritual power external to her own personality, that I never regarded her in those days as a friend, but as a mysterious prophetess who lived in a world or circle of her own, revolving in an orbit distinct from the common pathways of mankind. Shortly after the dates I have mentioned my destiny carried me into strange places and experiences which need not be men-

tioned in this connection, and Mrs. Richmond,
after a tour through the English provinces and
a sojourn in London, returned in 1875 to America.
Though it was seldom that I could avail myself
of the privilege, as she and I were not often in
the same locality during 1875, I did occasionally
rejoice in the auspicious fate which granted me
another opportunity of drinking in the inspired
truth which flowed from the lips of the teacher
who was certainly in a very real sense the mother
of my own public ministry.   I heard from time
to time, during 1875–6, several distinguished
lecturers on the Spiritualistic rostrum, but,
though I was interested in what they said, not
one of them made the slightest individual impression upon me, nor did I feel any renewed
spiritual awakening in their presence.   As my
age was so very tender, and an aunt who was
my legal guardian objected to my appearing
before the public, my work, till the beginning
of 1877, was conducted privately; but it was
steadily and ceaselessly carried forward where-
ever and whenever opportunity permitted.   As
it was my mission to follow Mrs. Richmond
through the English provinces after she had departed for America, I was constantly brought in
direct contact with many people who owed their
first introduction to Spritualism to her inspired
and inspiring instrumentality.   I am convinced
that she was the one above all others to open

the eyes of multitudes to the larger light and
clearer knowledge of life here and hereafter,
which Spiritualism offers beyond all other systems of science, religion or philosophy. Not
only was Mrs. Richmond's diction so profound
that her ministrations won their way wherever
culture and profundity of thought could be appreciated, but the kindly sympathetic handlings
of the many subjects treated by her guides caused
many to accept a philosophy presented in love,
which they would have indignantly spurned had
it been offered in a spirit of iconoclasm. The
singular charm and versatility of Mrs. Richmond's
work in England can never be in any degree
adequately measured by the historian, unless the
recorder has traveled from the haunts of the
nobility to the quiet, unpretending dwellings of
the humblest of the working folk; then, when
the investigator has become convinced that Mrs.
Richmond has been equally appreciated at both
ends and all up and down the social ladder, some
faint estimate may be drawn of the amazing
scope of her work and the vastness of its influence.   W. J. COLVILLE."

We deem it wholly in keeping with the spirit
of our work to state that Mr. Colville has always
been in close sympathy with our subject in regard to the teachings that have come through
her organism. Since his coming to America
they have labored together upon many platforms,

and on scores of occasions, when impromptu poems were called for by the audiences, they have given alternate stanzas in perfect rhythm, sometimes alternate lines, with the same perfect expression of thought and poetic feeling. There is no more appreciative and unselfish worker in the ranks of Spiritualism than Mr. Colville. His psychical powers are marvelous, and have given forth to the world many wonderful demonstrations of the truths underlying mediumship. His teachings are of the highest order and conform, in the fullest possible degree, to those that have been uttered through Mrs. Richmond by her guides. Mr. Colville is a scholarly speaker, and his lectures are filled with sublime thoughts, always leading his hearers and readers to a consideration of the ideal in life from every possible standpoint. In painting his pictures, like Mrs. Richmond, the bright colors are always turned toward our view, so that the thoughts of men may deal with the brighter and happier themes of life rather than with the seeming shadow side.

In commenting upon an oration by our subject the Brighton, (Eng.,) "Daily News," of January 29th, 1874, says:

"She is about thirty years of age, of average stature, slender build, but extremely good figure. Her complexion is fair and the charms with which nature has endowed her are brightened by

the artistic simplicity with which she dresses.
She speaks deliberately, yet fluently, and however involved her sentences may be, she never
loses herself—a very rare thing with speakers
dealing with complex subjects. In clear, forcible and elegant language, the words always being well chosen, the speaker traced the history
of Spiritualism from its commencement to the
present time. * * * At the commencement
of her remarks the greater part of the audience
seemed to treat the whole affair as a joke; but
as she proceeded with her oration the demeanor
of her auditors changed in a most marked manner, and she was listened to with the most respectful attention, her felicitous language and
strong arguments producing a manifest impression, and evoking frequent applause."

From all quarters of the United Kingdom we
have received testimonials in regard to Mrs.
Richmond's work in that country. Some of
these letters are in point here, and can be introduced with profit to all. It was during our
subject's first visit to England that semi-public
discourses were first given with reference to
the wonderful soul teachings that have given
solace to so many hungering human hearts.
Reference is made to these teachings in the first
letter that we here introduce, from the pen of
Adelaide Slater, whose husband, Mr. Thomas
Slater, officiated as chairman on many occasions

when our subject appeared before London audiences in 1873-4-5. The following is Mrs. Slater's letter:

"12th March, 1894.

"N. KENSINGTON, LONDON, W.

"Amongst the varied experiences and associations into which I was thrown during the early days dating twenty years back of my investigation of modern Spiritualism, by far the most interesting was my personal acquaintance and friendship with Mrs. Cora L. V. Richmond. Her human endowment of mind, coupled with many womanly graces, made her during her sojourn in England a more than ordinarily charming companion. These, in addition to her higher gifts, made her ever welcome, not only in our quiet home, but wherever she went. We used to look forward with pleasure to her Saturday visits at our home, with the idea of inaugurating a "Spiritual Sisterhood," as a type of what might be under Spiritual culture. At the residence of one of that Sisterhood occurred, under the most indisputable conditions, the marvelous manifestation in full light of a quantity of waving lilies! Beneath that same roof, Sister Pearl's (Mrs. Strawbridge), than whom a more devoted Spiritualist could not be, commenced and were sustained a series of addresses entitled, ' The Higher Teachings.' Be it remembered I am recalling several years gone by, in which most

of the members have crossed the narrow boundary and gone up higher, for aught I know to
strengthen Spiritual bonds and help lift the veil
between matter and spirit. ' Cora's ' deeply
touching psychometric delineations are still fresh
in the memory of the few who survive; because,
in old England, there is not so much known in
public resorts of Spiritualism, does it follow that
its *cui bono* has become extinct, or that, through
the pressure of the scientific mind, it has flown
out of its old harmonies, and ceased to become
a helper in the ceaseless struggle for existence?

"Faithfully yours,

"ADELAIDE SLATER,

" 'Morning Star.' "

The next letter is from the pen of John C.
Ward. Mr. Ward is a valued friend of our
subject, and his letter, although written personally to her, is in point here, and we reproduce
his reminiscences of her work:

LONDON, Eng., August 10, 1894.

MY DEAR MRS. RICHMOND.

"I may mention at starting that, save Mr.
Lowenthal, whom I met at the Convention of the
London Spiritualists' Alliance, at the end of September, and, by the by, Mr. and Mrs. Burns, and
Mr. and Mrs. Tebb, all the old faces met at your
gatherings, have drifted away out of our ken,
from various causes, death and removal being

accountable for much of this. I remember hearing with great delight your first public delivery at St. George's Hall, which I attended with my wife. The position you took up, religious and spiritual and non-antagonistic to true science, was what I had for many years longed to see maintained. Your teaching made me feel at home. The whole seemed to tend in the direction of bringing about better understanding and mutual—I was going to say toleration, but perhaps love would be the better word, between all the children of the great Parent, and reverent and loving adoration of the latter, with due appreciation of the loving ministry of those on the other side. The essence, in fact, of that which I regarded, at that time, as the special province of practical Christianity to effect—judging from my own personal experience of it as, by the by, a Trinitarian (not in the materialistic sense, as so often misdescribed by speakers holding different views). Of your regular work at Cavendish Rooms I can only say that my wife attended the meetings and found them both delightful and profitable, my own avocation preventing me from doing more than occasionally being in "at the death." (By the by, I am not a sportsman; kindly excuse the expression.) Concerning your provincial work that season, the only thing I knew of it beyond reading of it in the "Medium" was that I had the pleasure to assist on the platform on one occasion, Sept. 2,

1875, at Newcastle, Mr. Barkas in the chair; and I think also at Derby or Belper, where we were both guests at Mr. Adshead's. You gave your farewell lecture at Doughty Hall on Sunday the 12th, and the following day you left for Liverpool.

"On the 17th of June, 1880, we met you at St. Pancras. You had a reception at Neuemeyer's Hall, July 1st, and lectured at St. James' Hall on several subsequent occasions. We next met you in April, 1884, at Euston. On the 2d of May you gave your first private lecture on the subject of 'Celestia,' which course was continued weekly until June 14th. In the course of these teachings were given of matter new to myself, and I believe most others, in *re* the history of the soul in past lives, etc., etc. The form in which the teaching was given seemed to allow of certain conflicting theological views of deep importance, being rationally harmonized. In *re*, the doctrine of the dual nature of the soul—embodiments of male and female—final reunion, etc., I was much amused when hearing Mrs. Besant's lecture on Theosophy, dealing with reincarnation, etc., to hear that lady say that 'Spiritualism denied the doctrine of reincarnation,' when, as a matter of fact, all that she had in her lecture been so ably laying down, besides some other things, was matter with which, through your instrumentality, at your private lectures, Mrs. Ward and myself were quite familiar. Mrs. Besant appears to have summed up Spiritualism under some such head as 'The gospel according to egotistic phenomenalists.'

"Much good resulted from your work in England, although no noise may have been made about it. Such good seed as you have sown has taken root and influenced lives which, in their turn, will influence others for good, I know.

Yours faithfully,

JOHN C. WARD."

It is but proper to say that Mr. and Mrs. Ward are among Mrs. Richmond's most valued friends. Mr. Ward is a musician of rare and almost inspired beauty of expression, talented, cultured, harmonious. At the time of which he writes he was organist in one of the most popular chapels in London, hence could not always be present at the meetings, yet when possible he was there; and we find that much of the musical harmony of these meetings held by our subject in and about London was due to Mr. and Mrs. and later the Miss Wards.

We cannot let the opportunity pass to introduce a few words from the pen of Emma Hardinge Britten, who has been a life long friend of our subject, and whose feelings toward her are evinced by the letter that we here subjoin. It is more than pleasant to show the world that our platform workers are able to work together for the good of our cause, without jealousy and envy:

DEAR MR. BARRETT.

"I am truly sorry that I cannot comply in full with your request for information concerning my dear friend, Mrs. Richmond's visits to England. I was with my husband abroad on every occasion when Mrs. Richmond was in England except one, her last visit here, when I happened to return from the Australian lands just as she was leaving this country. I managed to meet with her just one hour. We were truly glad to meet, for we had often lectured in the same towns, but never in any spirit of rivalry, as the world would call it. I think you could obtain much useful information from James Burns concerning Mrs. Richmond's work in England, as he was largely instrumental in introducing her to this country. She is a most talented lady, and one of my most esteemed friends, and I sincerely regret that I am not able to give you more concerning her work in England. With every good wish, I am,

Truly yours,

EMMA HARDINGE BRITTEN,

The Lindens, Humphrey Street Cheetham Hill, Manchester."

We have before us a pile of letters received by our subject while in England, and at the time of her departure, from Dr. Hitchman, L. L. D., Mrs. Louisa Thompson Nosworthy, Benjamin Coleman, S. C. Hall, Anna Maria Hall, William and Mary Howitt, Mr. and Mrs. Watts, Emma

Hardinge Britten (congratulating her on her success in England), Mrs. J. Stuart Smith, Mrs. Hamilton, J. N. Tiedman Marteze, W. Stainton Moses, M. A., Alex. Calder, Webster Glynes, Mr. and Mrs. H. D. Jenklen, Henry Pitman, Rev. Thos. Colley, Sir William Dunbar, Charlotte Sevier, M. Grove, Countess de Panama, Beatrice Nosworthy, James Burns, Mrs. A. Strawbridge, and scores of others, all full of kindly thoughts and good wishes for our subject's success in life, and expressive of their deep interest and affectionate regard for her personally, and for the guides, whose mouthpiece she is and has been for so many years These letters would be but reproductions of the splendid tributes that have gone before, hence we do not deem their publication in full necessary at this time.

While the public press of England generally were very generous in according lengthy reports of the "orations" of our subject in the various cities and towns of the British Isles—all the large daily newspapers of the places where she spoke giving from one to three column notices of her meetings on each occasion—there is very little that can be gleaned from them that would be of interest in this work; for they were very careful to make few or no comments, nor express any opinions, (more especially the papers of the large cities). They would give correct reports of the meetings, synopses of the "ora-

tions" and other proceedings, frequently verbatim reports of discourses, poems and answers
to questions.   We have made copies or extracts
of some of the expressions of the reporters or
writers in those secular newspapers which we
have inserted in this chapter.

In an account of one of her lectures at Bury,
England, the "Bury Times" of August 15, 1874,
says: "She is unlike many lady lecturers, having nothing of the masculine about her, either in
appearance or style of delivery, but is quiet and
ladylike.   She has nothing of the strong-minded
woman, which characterizes some of our American female cousins. Her voice is sweet and clear,
but somewhat low in pitch.   She spoke for perhaps three-quarters of an hour on the abstruse
subject, given in a very logical style, unusual
certainly to a lady, especially when totally unaware of the subject to be chosen, as she must in
this case have been.   The arguments she used
were necessarily somewhat abstruse, and we are
sure were not easy for the audience to follow.
We express no opinion as to the nature of the inspiration under which she spoke, but certainly
her style of treating the subject would not have
disgraced a professional lecturer after much preparation.   She was never at a loss for a word, and
spoke easily and confidently throughout in what
Spiritualists would call the trance state, but in
this instance with her eyes open."

At the close of a very exhaustive synopsis of one of the discourses of our subject at Oldham, the "Oldham Express," Aug. 24, 1874, says: "In eloquence and discriminating treatment of her spontaneous subject, the orations are unrivaled." The following are extracts from an article in the "North of England Advertiser" (published at Newcastle-on-Tyne), of July 25th, 1874, entitled "My Experiences of Modern Spiritualism," and signed R. W. After a bitter and violent attack of Spiritualism generally and J. J. Morse (a spiritualistic trance medium) especially, and scouting all the inspirational claims of our subject, he says:

* * * "The prayer with which she commences her performance is the most offensive part of it. With the lie upon her lips, she seeks to enthrall the holiest affections of her audience by an invocation to Deity, which is expressed in words of great solemnity and well fitted to bring into operation the emotional rather than the intellectual faculties of her hearers. If she has not been upon the stage, she has certainly been a close student of the dramatic art, and apart from the blasphemy of her pretentions, *she may be listened to with interest and enjoyment.* She possesses in a high degree that gift which especially makes the orator—self-possession and command of the knowledge and ideas of which she has possessed herself.

* * * * * *

"Contrasted with the stolid nonsense from the lips of pompous teachers, to which we are so often expected to listen, her orations were an *intellectual treat of the highest order.* She said many things eminently calculated to knock down the idols which society so persistently sets up to worship in place of 'the only living and true God;' but then it was impossible to forget that the whole was a piece of acting. * * * *" [The italics are ours.—ED.]

" The Newcastle Critic," after giving her portrait and a sketch of her public work, says:

"Her time after this was devoted to lecturing, and before she reached the age of thirty 3,000 public discourses had been delivered by her. That her discourses are eloquent, intelligent and clever, no one can deny, however much they may differ from the lady in their views. Her lectures are extraordinarily clever, no matter whether they are the result of spiritual inspiration or that inspiration which is common to thoughtful, intelligent minds. There is an eloquence which we deem natural to this lady; her articulation is clear and deliberate, her figure is commanding and graceful, and she possesses those qualities which are necessary to successful public speaking. Her knowledge is something marvellous, and that is shown by her ability in lecturing intelligently on any subject that may be chosen by the audience. This gifted lady

lectures in the Lecture Hall, Nelson St., on
Sunday, 29th inst.; Thursday, 31st inst., and
Wednesday and Thursday the 1st and 2d of September, and we warmly advise our readers, if they
have not heard her, to go and listen, and we
feel assured that they will be delighted by her
eloquence."

The "Glasgow Herald" in a long report says:
"She is a lady prepossessing in appearance, not
more remarkable for her intelligent looks than
happy in the abundance of flaxen hair. She
rose and prefaced her lecture by an exceedingly
beautiful prayer. In afterwards discoursing on
the question of man's immortality, she treated
the subject with undeniable ability, and spoke
with a dignified deliberation and fluency of
language which apparently impressed her hearers.
The address occupied over an hour, and the least
favorable criticism that can be made of it is
that, if nothing better it showed a wonderful
power of memory. Questions were invited at
the conclusion of the discourse, and a number of
gentlemen availed themselves of the opportunity.
The inquiries were very cleverly taken up and
handled by the 'medium.' She always prefaced
her replies, 'We answer;' and sometimes when
the questioner did not explain his meaning very
clearly, she emphatically, though always politely,
administered a gentle rebuke. In one case she
characterised 'the gentleman's question as a

paradox;' another time she told an interrogator
that he did not know his own question, and then
explained in refined language what he evidently
meant; while another questioner was coolly informed that if his facts were correct his argument would have been excellent, but as they
were not, the argument fell to the ground."

The "Glasgow Mail" of the same occasion
says: "Previous to commencing her oration,
she offered up a prayer, which by its singular
effectiveness of delivery, produced an obvious
impression on the somewhat miscellaneous audience. She then proceeded with her address,
which was listened to throughout with keen attention, the only interruptions being the applause
with which the audience marked its appreciation
of a vivid illustration or of a cleverly-worded
proposition. Her style is undoubtedly fitted to
'tell' on an audience. There is no wordiness in
her arguments, no vagueness in her propositions,
and without being in the least degree declama-
tory, her intonation and gesture have a wonderful effect in adding weight to her eloquence.
Add to these the advantages of elegance of person and careful and correct pronunciation, and
it will be allowed that, apart altogether from the
principles of which she is an exponent, the
critics who are bold enough to accept the task of
disputing her theories, have a difficult undertaking before them."

The following extracts are from tne 'Liverpool Courier," which commences by stating that "she has been lecturing before crowded audiences in London during the past six months."

"Although it might be assumed by the advertisements that the lady is an American, she spoke with an unmistakable Scotch accent. The lady has a fine presence and much grace of manner, a clear and somewhat impressive delivery. . . . Her illustrations and statements lead very skillfully to a justification of modern Spiritualism. . . . Afterwards the fair orator invited questions on the subject of her oration. . . . Many questions were asked by other individuals. They were chiefly of a theological character, and as the majority of them were intended not to elicit information, but to 'confuse' the speaker, it must be stated that she proved herself more than an equal for any or all of her questioners."

The "Liverpool Mercury" in its report of the same meeting says: "The lady was listened to with the most respectful attention while she was delivering her discourse. . . . She is a most charming lecturer, and even those who have the greatest repugnance to lady 'orators' must admit that her discourses are pleasant and intellectual in the extreme. She affects none of the manly peculiarities of make-up and language which are so offensively obtrusive in some lady philosophers. There was nothing in her appearance to proclaim

(as in some cases) as plainly as if it were printed,
'I am a strong-minded female.' She looks, no
doubt what she is—a bright, cheerful, intelligent,
well-read, liberally-educated lady, and, however
extreme her views may be, it is only fair to say
that she states them temperately, that her language is always well chosen, that she shows unbounded charity for those who differ from her,
and never expresses a sentiment or word that can
offend the moral susceptibilities of the most sensitive. She is described as 'of New York,' but it
was surmised from her accent that she was not
unacquainted with Edinburgh. (At that time she
had never been in Edinburgh.—Ed.) She is certainly well acquainted with Scottish theology, and
dealt most trenchantly with what was called the
'hard doctrines of Calvinism.' Light-haired,
blue-eyed, and bright complexioned, dressed with
rare taste, as she stepped upon the platform she
looked more like a lively Scottish lady about to
proceed to an evening party than a lady polemic.
She spoke in a trance state, and for upwards of
an hour discoursed—sometimes philosophically,
sometimes poetically—upon the subject of her
lecture."

The "Liverpool Mercury," July 1st, 1874,
after a lively report headed, "Extraordinary
Scene at a Spiritualistic Meeting," in which the
reporter gives a description of the crowded house,
of the animated scene during the asking and an-

swering of questions, when some fifteen or twenty persons tried to speak at once, and a laughable reference to one of whom the reporter says:

"An excited gentleman in the body of the hall shouted out, 'Will the lady tell me the horigin of hevil hinfluences?' our speaker replied, 'The origin of what?' when the gentleman dropping his aspirates, said, 'The origin of evil.' The answer was, 'The principal origin of all evil, I should say, is ignorance.' 'He's sorry he spoke,' cried out another voice."

After describing an exciting scene in selecting a subject for a poem, the reporter says: " The subject was 'Temptation,' and the poem, if impromptu, was a wonderful production. The feet and rhythm were perfect, several of the lines were of rare poetic beauty and if it was composed on the spur of the moment almost justified the remark made by a gentleman in the hall that, 'she left Tennyson nowhere.'"

In the report of one of the English papers we found the following expression of opinion from the kindly disposed reporter.

"To pass a candid opinion it is really to be deplored that this gifted lady ascribes her orations to spirit influence, as she really possesses abilities which she may reasonably be proud of."

The following extract, showing George Thompson's acquaintance with the medium, is from one of the daily papers of Leeds:

" Last night, as before, a committee of six gentlemen nominated by the audience retired into the ante-room to select a subject for Mrs. Cora, and during their absence Mr. G. Thompson, well-known throughout the country for his anti-slavery advocacy, delivered a short address, and expressed his belief in Spiritualism and the communion of spirits with human beings. He had for years known the lady lecturer, and he had ever listened to her intellectual and argumentative orations with pleasure. The committee having returned, the following subjects were read out from the chair: 'The Physical Basis of Life,' 'The Physical Forces—the Laws of Material Change,' 'The Exact Figure of the Earth,' 'Natural Crystals and their Composition,' 'Astronomy,' and 'Atoms and Molecules.' The audience having decided in favor of 'Physical Forces,' Mrs. Cora advanced to the front, and after having offered up a prayer, she at once plunged into the consideration of the abstruse question of her lecture. For upwards of an hour she continued to speak on this difficult subject, with a fluency and flow of language which greatly astonished her audience. Mr. Jefferson afterwards addressed himself 'to the spirit' on various important points which he alleged had not been touched upon, to which quick replies, delivered in the same intelligent manner, were given."

The work of our subject was borne forward in London and in the provinces and by those whom Mr. Burns' efforts had aroused. The reports of her meetings in the Spiritualistic press, particularly the full accounts and verbatim reports in the Medium and Daybreak caused everywhere an awakening of interest, a new inflowing of inspiration over all parts of the United Kingdom. No place into which her labors extended was so remote that reporters and correspondents did not find them out and send full or condensed reports of the meetings. We have given in the few preceding pages an account of her work from the secular press, from those entirely outside of the works of Spiritualism; there will follow in this chapter accounts from those most familiar with the work and in sympathy with the medium.

Under the head of appreciation, etc., the Medium and Daybreak of Jan. 2, 1874, has several letters from which we quote the following :

"I have read her lectures as reported in the Medium with inexpressible pleasure. They have opened to my mind new and enlarged views of God, of nature, of man, and of man's destiny; greatly increased light on biblical subjects has dawned upon me; my enjoyment of the present is more real and prospects of the future brighter. I have new thoughts, new feelings, new aspirations. I now enjoy the consciousness that in an

ever-present God I live, move and have my being.
My faith in divine things has abundantly increased, being no longer the result of early training and dogmatic teaching, but because it now
goes hand-in-hand with plain common sense and
sound logical reasoning, having, indeed, become
'the substance of things hoped for, the evidence
of things not seen.' I love the Great Architect
of the universe, I adore Him, I trust in Him, I
enjoy Him as I had never done before, and in
my own experience realize the fact that man—
that mere atom in God's universe—is one with
the Infinite Creator. My case, I have no doubt,
is far from being singular as one of the successful results of her inspirational addresses; and I
think some substantial recognition of the value of
that estimable lady's services in the cause of truth
should forthwith be presented to her." Then follow generous suggestions covering a "purse," etc.
The letter is signed "A Freemason."

The following extract is from another letter to
the "Medium and Daybreak," of the same date,
and speaks of the writer's attendance at the
lecture in St. George's Hall, Dec. 29th, '73 (a
few days before): "I listened with deep interest
. . . and I was confirmed in the opinion previously formed that this medium is not only of no
ordinary character, but one whom nature has
eminently qualified for the transmission of high
moral and Spiritual truths, not by means of em-

phatic declamation and offensive dogmatisms, but
by feminine refinement of manner, purity of logic,
and eloquence of pathos, that at once reach and
satisfy both head and heart.   In expressing this
opinion I am fully sensible that I but echo the
sentiments of thousands, some of whom have not
only known her in her public life, but, who, like
my wife and myself, have had the pleasure of her
further acquaintance as an honored guest at home.
That so valuable an acquisition to the cause of
Spiritualism (in England), as this gifted lady,
should remain in this vast center of civilization,
where the field in which to sow its divine sentiments and exalted truths is, perhaps, the broadest posssible, is a common desire on the part of
English Spiritualists." Then follows suggestions
and a most generous offer financially, as a fund
to be used "as a remuneration for her lectures,
or to aid her in case of illness—a contingency
quite possible owing to her delicate state of health
. . ." This is signed, Geo. N. Strawbridge.

It is noted that the home of Mr. and Mrs.
Strawbridge was one of the first whose hospital-
ity was extended to our medium, and that it became really her place of residence where she
could be in constant companionship with Mrs.
Strawbridge (the "Sister Pearl" of these words),
and that it continued to be one of her *homes*
until she left the mother country.

After the first course of lectures inaugurated

and carried forward so ably by Mr. Burns in
Royal Music Hall, the work in London was
taken up by a committee formed for the purpose, and we find our medium in the West End
of London, every Sunday, varying her one regular Sunday service with an added lecture in
afternoon or evening or on week days in the
suburbs, Eltham, Dalston, "Eyrie Arms." The
following were named as a committee for the
proposed new course: Dr. Gully, M. D., Chairman ; N. F. Dawe, Esq., Portman Chambers,
Portman Square, W.; J. T. Hoskins, Esq., 5
Connaught Square, W.; T. H. Noyes, Jr , Esq.,
"United University Club," Suffolk Street, Pall
Mall, S. W.; Mr. Thomas Slater, 136 Euston
Road, N. W.; Mrs. Honywood, 52 Warwick
Square, S. W., Treasurer; Webster Glynes, Esq.,
4 Gray's Inn Square, W. C., Hon. Secretary,
and were supported by an eminent and influential list of subscribers.

It is but just to say that Mr. Burns had
labored most arduously in inaugurating the
series of lectures in the Royal Music Hall, and
that he had done so at a great sacrifice of
time and means.   This committee was the outgrowth of his efforts and the increasing desire
to hear the guides of our subject.   Mr. Burns
most heartily and generously co-operated with
the new movement, and the new season was
inaugurated at Cleveland Hall.

One feature noted by us in this compilation is that at each of the lectures of the series, on "Spiritual Cosmology" given in the Cavendish Rooms during the Winter and Spring of 1874-5, there was a different presiding officer. It was found upon further examination that those who presided were among the most earnest and noted Spiritualists in London and the provinces, who frequently made the journey to London to participate in these meetings, the committee of arrangements having invited these gentlemen severally to be the Chair on one of the Sunday evenings.

At the close of the series when the subject was, "The Harmony and Divinity of All Religions," it was expected that Dr. Hitchman, of Liverpool, would occupy the chair, but he being unable to be present in person, sent an introductory address, which was read by Alexander Calder, Esq., who was called to the chair in the absence of Dr. Hitchman. From this beautiful, although necessarily brief, address we make the following excerpts of eloquent appreciation of our subject:

" . . . It may be said, therefore, with truth and justice, that the medium of mediums who this day closes her third course of lectures in our metropolis does so with the most blessed encouragement that could possibly befall our common humanity, namely, the faith founded upon facts, and tested by the touchstone of science, or an

experimental knowledge of nature, whether called
Spiritual, mental, or physical, that leaves not a
tear behind, save that of comfort and joy.

> "Through the circles high and holy,
>   Of an everlasting change,
>   Now more swiftly, now more slowly,
>   Form must pass and function range.
>   Nothing in the world can perish,
>   Death is life, and life is death;
>   All we love and all we cherish
>   Die to breathe a nobler breath.

"Lay that truth in lavender of the sweetest, in
the choicest portion of your soul's paradise, since,
I doubt not, it is revered as one of the highest
and most majestic amongst the immortal guides
of this cosmopolitan medium, our gifted sister;
and I pray that the peace of God may dwell with
all Spiritualists richly, in thought, word, and deed,
as our angel-guides make the desert of materialism to blossom and flourish like the rose."

The work in England at this time may be
summarized as follows:

1. Public addresses treating of general Spiritualistic and other topics of interest always followed by an improvization of poetry. Addresses
and poems usually on subjects chosen by the
audience and covering the entire range of human
thought. Of these there must have been in London and the provinces two hundred.

2. Addresses to semi-public or select audiences
including the series entitled *Spiritual Cosmology*

in three parts.   In this series there were twelve
on *Dynamics*; six on *Statics*, and six on *Individual Experiences* in *Spiritual States.*   The discourses on dynamics relate to the powers of the
Spirit over and its limitations by organic matter,
especially to health and disease.   Those on
Statics relate to the Absolute, to Deity, the Soul,
Angelic states; expressions of the Soul in successive human lives (more fully treated by us in the
next chapter), Messiahs, etc., in fact, the entire
outline of the Soul teachings.   The third series
relates to particular experiences of individuals in
Spiritual states (beyond earth life), and are very
graphic pictures of personal experiences and
characteristics.

These discourses were given for a thoughtful
and interested class to which others were admitted by special ticket making an audience of
about two hundred.   They certainly epitomized
the words of the guides up to that time.

3. Work in private circles and homes—un-
classified and not of a nature to be measured or
stated, but into which work the name poems or
poetic readings, by Ouina, and the conversations
and answers to questions by Mr. Ballou, entered
as the concentral part (if we may coin a word).
In the social circles that gathered round our
medium it was often a part of an evening's entertainment to invite a few friends to dinner and
after withdrawal to the drawing room invite the

controls of our medium who gave poems, brief
addresses and answers to questions. Everywhere
—whether in the humble abodes at the East End
or the aristocratic mansions of the West End, or
the residences of the so-called "middle classes,"
there was the same cordial welcome, the same
earnest longing for the "Bread of Life."

4. The particular work in the Spiritual Sisterhood. This small circle was formed of a few
devoted friends who rallied round our medium
and some or all of whom accompanied her into
her public work. A circle called together by
loving sympathy for her and appreciation of the
work. But for their tender care and true
womanly aid, the health of our subject was such
that she could not have gone forward with the
work without much greater suffering.

It was to this circle that an especial line of
teaching was given through our medium from the
Spirit side of life—coming from spirits of women
eminent for their gifts, or great in the lowliness
of their lives.

This series of sacred meetings was held at the
home of Mrs. Strawbridge (named "Pearl" by
Ouina), and it was to that circle of Sisters
who had so lovingly grouped themselves around
our subject to aid and strengthen her for her
public work that the crown of lilies was shown
at its closing meeting. Following is an admirable account of this incident and the occasion

of it, with the one or two other similar occurrences during that memorable period; it is essentially that written by Mrs. A. C. Burke, one
of the circle of ladies who attended the ministrations of our subject and witnessed the manifestation on the occasions referred to by her.

Her account is entitled :

"AMONG THE LILIES."

She states that having received the permission
of the guides of our subject to publish an account
of these manifestations she obtained from a lady
friend who was with the medium on the occasion
of the first appearances of the lilies the statement
that on the first of February of this year (1875)
the lady had retired to her bed-room leaving the
medium alone in the drawing-room. After some
short space of time the friend perceived the
medium advancing from the adjoining room (the
drawing-room), and her first thought was to arise
and assist her to undress—as she was quite feeble;
but perceiving that the medium was entranced
she paused, and on looking more closely she observed a large white lily resting upon the medium's
head. She noticed that her countenance had assumed an exceedingly angelic expression; while
at the same time she repeated in most solemn
accents some passages of Scripture from the
chapter that had engaged her attention. The

whole atmosphere of the room, even in the gas-
light, seemed to be charged with a spiritual aura
so perfect that the friend was enabled to perceive clouds of white light resembling a veil in
front of the medium's face and about her head.
A similar manifestation took place on the 8th of
February in the presence of the same lady friend.
Again on the 12th and 14th of the same month
and on the 7th, 14th and 28th of March, three
other friends being present.   One of these friends
informed the narrator that there was distinctly
seen three kinds of lilies, and thus describes what
occurred :

"On returning from the lectures, (which were
always earlier in London than in America.—ED.)
we were in the habit of conversing together for
the remainder of the evening. 'Ouina,' one of
the guides of the medium, usually assumed control and joined in our discussions.   On the
particular occasions when the lilies were produced, 'Ouina' was succeeded by a very solemn
influence.   The medium's voice became deep and
grave; a peculiar atmosphere seemed to surround
us; we felt awed, and there was a great stillness.

"The medium would rise from her seat, and
with slow and measured steps enter her bed-room,
closing the door.   After an interval of about ten
minutes, the door would open ajar, and the lamp
ordered to be lowered, so that the room was
nearly half-darkened.   The medium would then

slowly enter, standing a few minutes at the door to show the lilies in her hair, and then proceed to her place and deliver to each of us a short and solemn address. She would then slowly return to the door, and after again standing still before us, would retire into her room.

"In about ten minutes she would come back in her normal condition, expressing surprise at having found herself alone without a light.

"The lilies were each time clearly visible; I could distinguish the leaves and petals. We were allowed to approach to the distance of one yard.

"On the first occasion the flowers appeared like small water-lilies placed in the hair, rather on the left side; the second time the flowers were more numerous, and appeared to consist of an eucharist lily in front and of water-lilies behind. The third time we saw, besides the lilies, a bright, fine-pointed star-shaped flower, which glistened as though of silvery hue.

"On the fourth occasion the flowers almost formed a complete wreath, commencing on the left side, and passing round the back of the head to the right. There was no star, but I observed a large white Easter lily on the right side.

"April 19, 1875.   "WEBSTER GLYNES."

The narrator (Mrs. Burke) then proceeds to relate that on Sunday evening, April 4th, she was one of a circle of friends in front of the platform at

Cavendish Rooms. She says: "From the fact of the medium being some minutes late in ascending the platform, and knowing the weak state in which she had been for some weeks previously, an anxious feeling prevailed, lest illness should be the cause of the delay, which anxiety, however, was somewhat relieved when she reached the head of the stairs leading from the room into which she usually retires for a short time previous to her lectures. Her appearance at that moment will, I think, never be forgotten by any of those who were present.

"The beautifully spiritual expression of her countenance, the dignity of her bearing, and the soul-stirring sentiments which, ere she breathed a single word, seemed to lend grace to every movement, and blend with the peculiar atmosphere with which she was surrounded; all this, together with the surpassing beauty of the materialized lilies in her hair, presented such a picture, and made such an impression on my mind, that it can never be effaced, and I cannot but think that it must have affected nearly all who saw it in a similar manner.

"The number of the lilies on this occasion, if I mistake not, was three. They were fully open, and accompanied by one that was either nearly closed or in bud. This time, however, they displayed the peculiarity of white stamens and anthers, instead of the gold-colored ones which

usually distinguish the white garden or Madonna
lily. Though much struck by their peculiarity,
I was not aware, until I was informed after the
lecture by Mr. George Hinde, who was chairman
on the occasion, that they were materialized during the few minutes that we were kept waiting
for the lecturer.

"Mr. Hinde also informed me that when he
descended the stairs to conduct the medium to
the platform, the atmosphere of the room, and
that in which her whole person seemed to be enveloped, produced such an effect upon him that
he almost fainted, and could with difficulty lead
her to her seat. Though not gifted with fully-
developed spiritual sight, I could perceive a transparent atmosphere surrounding her the whole
evening, and once I saw the shadowy form of a
spirit head near her right shoulder.

"From Mrs. Strawbridge (the friend with
whom the medium is staying) I learned that the
lilies on this particular occasion became gradually
dematerialized on their way home from the lecture in the carriage. . . .

"But, sir, though I am aware that I am occupying much of your space, I have still another
beautiful lily-manifestation to record, and as it
would seem that each one that I have mentioned
is more lovely than the last, so, in accordance
with this law of harmony, do we now reach the
loveliest of all.

"On Friday, the 16th instant, I joined a highly-privileged circle of friends, who had assembled around the medium, at the house of Mrs. Strawbridge, 84 Redcliffe Gardens, West Brompton, where we were permitted to behold a manifestation surpassing in spiritual sublimity all that I have ever witnessed, and which, as I recall it, fills me with an indescribable feeling of awe. Ouina assumed control, and conversed with us in her usual sweet manner for some time, at length desired that the room should be darkened, but not to a greater amount than would occur at this time of year by the lowering of Venetian blinds.

"Attached to Mrs. Strawbridge's drawing-room, which is separated by crimson curtains, is a small music-room.

" This little music-room was made somewhat darker than the drawing-room, and into it, after placing each of the sitters in front of the curtain the medium withdrew.

" Before doing so, however, she emptied her pockets, and insisted (still under control) that every article of wearing apparel should be thoroughly examined, even to her 'moccasins,' as ' Ouina ' styled her foot-gear.   The office of examiners fell upon Mrs. Tebb and Miss Dixon, and these two ladies also made a thorough investigation of the room and all that it contained. The only entrance to both rooms was locked, and Miss Euphenia Dixon put the key into her

pocket. These preliminaries having been satisfactorily gone through, the controlling spirit ob-
serving that though such precautions were quite
unnecessary as far as those present were concerned, yet as an account of this manifestation
might be published, it was better that these ex-
aminations should be gone through. We were
requested to sing, and 'Hand in Hand with
Angels' and I believe another short hymn were
gone through, at the close of which the curtains
slowly opened, and though indeed, the bodily
form of the medium stood before us, I verily believe, but for the dress she wore, we should have
found it difficult to recognize her. Her features
had assumed that look of heavenly inspiration
which can only be imagined by recalling the pictures of Dante's Beatrice, and the resemblance
was rendered complete by the wreath by which
her head was adorned, except that in the present
instance the garland was composed of pure white
Madonna lilies, instead of laurel, as in the case
of Beatrice. Yet this wreath of lilies had been
materialized in about, I should say, the space of
from three to five minutes. It was formed of
the white blossoms of the virgin lily; some fully
open, others only partially so, and those that
were the most fully blown were at the back of
the head, diminishing in size as they met in a
point a little above the forehead. I believe they
were twelve in number.

"Whilst under the influence she breathed forth one of the most spiritual and beautiful poems I have ever heard or read; the words seemed to fall from her lips like silver-dew from the pure fount of heaven. Her tone, manner, and expression, and even her attitude on this occasion, together with the exquisite beauty of the lilies, are things that can never be effaced from the memories of those who were so privileged as to behold them.

*   *   *   *   *

"I must here also remark that the transparent glistening, the sparkling whiteness of the flowers, struck me very forcibly; they looked as if they had that moment been brought in from some lovely partierre, and we all know that natural white garden lilies are not to be had at any price at this season of the year. On this occasion the anthers displayed the bright golden pollen which characterises the Madonna lily, and which actually seemed to move before our eyes. I should have mentioned that, on this occasion when the medium, under the control of 'Ouina' entered the music-room she observed that we were now to witness something that we should never have an opportunity of witnessing again, and, indeed, I believe, we never shall, until we reach that land where the lilies never fade.

"After the termination of the poem, the curtains were again closed, and in less than two minutes (indeed, I might say, in less than one minute), and while we all remained in solemn, silent awe, overpowered, as it were, by what we had seen, ' Ouina '—who had again resumed control—said, in rather a low tone, 'You may come to her now,' whereupon we all followed into the music-room, only to find the medium in her normal condition—greatly surprised at seeing herself reclining on a sofa in a partially-darkened room, instead of the well-lighted, cheerful drawing-room, in which she was sitting when she first passed into the trance state.

" During the whole of this wonderful manifestation the atmosphere of the room (in spite of the large fire) was so chilly that some of those present were obliged to throw their wraps around them, while all around the person of the medium there was a cloudy appearance occasionally visible; and I have no doubt that had the room been more completely darkened, she would have stood revealed in a white transparent mist."

The narrator then went on to say that it was not to be inferred from the appearance of these lilies on these several occasions that the guides intended to use their medium for physical manifestations. These lilies came as an accompaniment of the especial work then being performed.

This record of the manifestation of the lilies was attested by the signatures of several of the ladies present including Mrs. Tebb and Mrs.

Strawbridge, and by the three gentlemen who witnessed them in private as well as at the Cavendish rooms.

We cannot refrain from mentioning here a work for woman in which our subject took part and which resulted in a discourse on "Spiritualism and its Work for Woman," at Doughty Hall.

Mr. Burns refers to this meeting as being called "for the purpose of hearing an address on the somewhat complicated question of the 'Social Evil.'"

It was really to aid a lady of benevolence, whom the spirits named "The White Messenger" in her noble efforts for the rescue of the "unfortunate." Our subject readily consented to give the address and was introduced by Mrs. Burke, who took the chair for the meeting:

LADIES AND GENTLEMEN:—I feel that it would be altogether an act of supererogation on my part were I to say anything by way of introducing to you our highly gifted sister.   *   *   *
The many beautiful lectures to which it has been our good fortune to listen—beautiful alike in their eloquence and teaching—have won for her, I am sure you will agree with me in saying most deservedly so, a world-wide reputation, which cannot fail to leave its stamp upon the present generation, and not upon this only, but upon the present century.

Interested as this lady is, and her guides, in everything tending to the enlightenment and elevation of humanity, especially that portion of it hitherto regarded as the feebler one (and for which, happily, a more appreciative day is dawning), she has kindly consented, under the influence of her guides, to deliver a lecture upon the subject set forth in our handbill in aid of the funds at the present moment so urgently required for this movement.

Of this address by the guides of our subject, Mr. Burns says:

"All who listened to (or will peruse attentively) the beautiful address by the guides, cannot fail to see how they go at once to the root of the matter. If the glaring evils of social life are to be removed, there must first be a reformation, nay, a complete revolution in the false sentiments, thoughts and ideas now too prevalent upon social questions, a revolution which must have for its watchwords Justice and Purity.

"The meeting was well attended, the woman element being in great force, and a very earnest spirit characterized the proceedings throughout. It was, indeed, almost exclusively woman's work from beginning to end. Women organized the meeting, women advertised it and sold the tickets, women attended to all the business matters connected with it, women received money at the doors, women gracefully handed visitors to

their seats, women sang and also played the piano
and harmonium, a woman occupied the chair,
and a woman lectured.   It is, in truth, woman's
work; and we feel persuaded that if women
would largely and earnestly join in this excellent
sphere of labor, taking the views enunciated by
the lecturer as the basis of their efforts, both in
attacking the erroneous and artificial opinions of
society on the subject, and in practically saving
grace it would be a step in the right direction."

We give entire the closing paragraph and
poem:

"When St. Agnes, in the place where she was
sent to be destroyed, invoked heaven to send its
maledictions upon her declaimer, and his eyes
were made blind, it was but a token of that spiritual blindness that comes to every man who forgets that the young woman whom he would de-
fame is the daughter of some mother, the sister
of some brother, the child of God—and he is
made passion-blind only to be disenthralled by
the same gentle hand that he would ruin.   If it
be said that temptation first came to the world
by woman, be it also said that the same hand
has shown the way out of temptation.   The
Madonna of the Romish Church—the ideal typical Christian woman, the zeal and fervor of the
sainted souls that in the cloister waft their
prayers to heaven, are surely enough to bring
about this reform.   All who seek with hearts

attuned to heaven, and eyes and spirits turned
upward to find the remedy, may find it in these
words: 'Blessed are the pure in heart, for they
shall see God.'

"The name which the spirits gave to the
kind lady who has undertaken this work is 'The
White Messenger.' We therefore dedicate this .
poem to her.

POEM—IMPROVISED BY 'OUINA.'

I.

" I saw a pale girl standing outside the city,
 Wandering alone the whole weary way;
For her was no voice and no eye filled with pity,
 But only despair through the livelong day.

" She bore no flowers, though by the wayside she lingers,
 She ever bore but a thorn in her heart,
The lilies of life had all drooped in her fingers,
 And the cares nevermore would depart.

" Then I saw a white dove flying straight from the heaven
 And it bore a sweet message of peace,
As down by the wayside she lay all unshriven,
 And the dove was her spirit's release.

" Away, far above all the earth and its sorrow,
 I saw her upborne on its wings;
And they who passed by, with a sneer, on the morrow,
 Scorning ever such lowliest things,
Scorned also her name and her memory forever;
 But an angel of light there she sings.

II.

" I saw in the halls of the thick-peopled city
 A man, sitting in pride and in state,
But he had no heart full of shame or of pity,
 And only the world called him great.

'' And offerings came each day to his door,
    He was pledged to the people as high, and the poor
    Looked up to his face with its cold, stern decree,
    But there was no token: then what do I see?
    A shaft straight from heaven sent down to his heart.
                    And he died
                    In his pride;
    Such a soul to depart!
    And his name it was mentioned with many a word
    Of praise and regret, and where'er it was heard,
    The loud-tolling bell proclaimed that a soul
    Had gone out to the region of God's great control.

III.

'' And there, face to face, the pale girl and he met,
        Where bend angels in silence around,
    '   She, a lily within her white hand, tear wet,
        And he bowing low to the ground,
    Grovelling there, as if in God's great endless city
        There was no mercy for him to be found,
    And no eye full of sorrow or pity.

'' But she, with never a word of reproach,
        Breathed an offering of prayer unto heaven,
    That for all the great wrong which on earth he had done
        His spirit might there be forgiven—

'' Not forgiven at first, nor with one breath alone,
        But only by constant well-doing;
    His spirit still strives, and, uplifting his heart,
        His soul for forgiveness still wooing.

'' 'Go thou,' saith the Master, 'and undo the wrong,
        Make clean all the pathway before you,
    Tear away from your heart the cold pride that was strong:
        Kneel down, and of heaven implore you
    The gift of its grace.   But for this gentle soul,
        For her there is light and gladness,
    Her's alone was the burden on earth, whose control
        Is usurped, and she beareth no sadness.

IV.

" The white dove descends to the earth once again
    With quivering light on its pinions;
It searches the hearts and spirits of men,
  ' Searches all of their pride and dominions,
And wherever a wrong is it sendeth a flame
    Through the dark, of great fire from heaven;
And wherever a victim, there breatheth the Name
    Full of peace, whereby sin is forgiven.

" The White Dove through its Messenger ever doth preach
    To the innermost spirit's recesses,
 ' Whatsoever on earth you seek for or reach,
    That in heaven your spirit possesses.' "

The full summary of that work is left for the reader to gather from the written and spoken words, and the heart beats that they convey, when in September, 1875, our subject was about to take her departure for her own native land. It is from these tributes, public and private, brought by those who had shared her labors and received her ministrations that the true estimate can be made, emanating as they did from the hearts of those to whom our medium and her guides had become most endeared.

The following is from the pen of friends who were with her a month on the eastern coast of England, and, indeed, for a much longer period was she a guest at their home in Darlington:

REMINISCENCES OF SALTBURN

By Mr. and Mrs. G. R. Hinde:

"The most eventful year of our lives has just been brought to a close at the retired and beau-

tiful watering-place, Saltburn-by-the-Sea. Sunday evening, July 19, 1874, found us there with
our greatly-beloved friend and sister.   *   *   *
This fact necessarily brought us into almost daily
communion with the illustrious hosts of spiritual
beings who have anointed her to be their mouthpiece, discoursing sweetest melody to the world
of mortals.   They have watched over her, guiding her powers from earliest infancy for special
and particular work.   She possesses an organism
peculiarly adapted for expressing (normally as
well as abnormally) the lofty attributes of the
soul that has been tried by the fires of affliction,
and left without a speck of earthly dross to mar
its innate loveliness and purity.   Thus she has
become the fitting vehicle for the transmission of
loftiest thought and divinest revelation to the
world; and we are in all truth and justice impelled to give our humble, and it may be feeble,
testimony to the world of Spiritual minds regarding the qualities that we have recognized in the
short space of one year's intimate family communion with that sweet and exalted mind.   Fully
conscious of the inadequacy of language to express the intrinsic value of even one quality of
the human soul, we need scarcely say that such
a close tie as that of brother and sister fully sustained for twelve long months might be deemed
sufficient to reveal to each member of a family
maintaining it the separate and particular foibles

of every one of the family group.   If you would
fully know persons, live in the same house with
them, and you cannot remain long in suspense.
*   *   While she finds it absolutely necessary at
times to assume an apparent dignity of character in order to keep off a certain class of mortals
who, like our little family of children, are ever
open-mouthed, ready to consume every atom of
vitality that parent can give, without yielding any
adequate return—nay, leading one to exclaim,
'You will kill ma with kindness; let her have a
little repose to get strong again before you again
approach with your demands.'   Oft have we
known her to suffer tortures unexpressed rather
than suffer a cloud to hang on the faces of visitors
or friends present whose capacity to receive was
greater than hers to give.   This is the cause which
imperatively demands for her much retirement in
private life, which retirement should never be invaded save when it is known to be desirable to
her, or in response to an invitation given by her.
This is necessitated by the importance of the public work which she has been chosen to perform,
and to which she makes everything subservient,
and, in fact, a more loving and perfect obedience
to the wish and will of her illustrious spirit-guides
may not have been attained by any mortal medium, for seemingly (and I believe in reality) the
relation she sustains is similar, though in a higher
sense, to that occupied by the child who is fully

persuaded of the wisdom and goodness of its
parent to unerringly guide it toward that which is
best and most conducive to its present and future
well-being; and this springs from an intuitive
perception of the more complete and perfect
state and wisdom possessed by those who guide
her destiny.

" The precious golden link which ever unites us
to her, being of the spirit utterly, far exceeds in
strength any other that can possibly exist, and
there are many other golden links forged by the
spirit of love uniting our dear sister to many others,
who will be as glad to read these humble breath-
ings as we are to pen them, among whom are
they who have, step by step, with the eye of their
spirits, traced the wonderful—nay, marvellous—
career of this sweetly-dispositioned and richly-
endowed medium, while she has been unremittingly laboring among the Spiritualists and others
of this country. We, who have watched the
course of events in the realm of mind and spirit,
must be full well aware that with the advent of
this illustrious medium among us there came a
great Spiritual wave that could not fail to palpa-
bly affect every mind which was more or less
finely attuned to the harmonies of Spiritual life.

" Opposing powers and influences there undoubtedly have been (as necessarily there must) to
illustrate the power of bigotry, envy, and the
host of other phases of spiritual darkness; but

such has been the greatness of the light that has come and the revelations that have been made, that all those have fallen back, glad, as it were, to hide their diminished heads and retire to their native obscurity, while the light still shines on— a light which will be a beacon to many a soul, seeing that it stands pre-eminently in a lofty position, and will there serve the purpose for which it shines. They whose souls are near maturity will not fail to recognize it and behold its mighty import; and as for others, the centuries to come are laden with the power of recognition to them, which, when it comes, will be the expression of the ripening of their spiritual powers upon earth or in spirit life. The higher expressions of truth can be of no import to minds not able to perceive them, therefore argument avails nothing to convince a mind that such and such is true. Let all minds have free course to express the truth as it comes to them, and not be wounded wilfully for so doing, because it may differ from the conception of others as to what is truth. We have observed a most commendable line of action in the conduct of our brother Burns, which must be obvious to all, in that while unhesitatingly denying any allegiance to the doctrine of re-incarnation, he has righteously, in the fulfillment of his impartial position as editor of a public spiritual paper, given to the world a course of lectures that plainly lay down and teach the

expression of truth. For this he will ever have
our best thanks, and the thanks of all who by
intuition are able to perceive in this truth the
key to unlock the many mysteries of mortal existence inexplicable by any other philosophy.
There is much light yet to be thrown on the subject, but its central truth cannot reach the soul
by the methods of reason, argument, or scientific
demonstration, since these are but the outward
expressions of something within. The truth itself must come first to the innermost and then
express itself outwardly, and when it can do this,
owing to the removal of all outward impedi-
ments, it will speak in no uncertain sound,
though all may not understand its meaning. I
do, however, think that free expression of opinion should be invited and received where an important truth is involved, though nothing can be
gained by contending parties in an argument.
Contention should be discountenanced, ' not free
expression.' But I have wandered from my subject.

"A Sunday meeting in a sequestered stop
hidden among the dense foliage of the woods at
Saltburn, so wild that they might be called a forest. This spot was reached by winding paths
through the underwood, and had been carefully
selected by her friends residing near, who were
well acquainted with the locality. It was a most
lovely evening, and a delightful spot, situated far

up a deep gorge, piercing inland from the sea-
shore. On either side of this gorge were steep and
lofty hill-sides, studded with the giant trees of this
wild forest. By a steep and winding path we
entered a natural arena covered with grass and
bramble bushes. Nature all around was silent,
save the twittering of a bird or the subdued
music of the brook near by as it danced in its
channel away down to the sea. The burning
sun was descending in the West, the tops of the
trees were yet tinged with his golden beams; in
the shade beneath them (where we were in circle
seated), it was cool and refreshing. A solemn
and imposing calm reigned around, our dear medium occupying a place at the foot of a stately
oak; and thus were we seated awaiting the kin-
dling of the ancient fire of the spirit, which has
never ceased to burn since the earth began. In
subdued melody we sang, 'Hand in Hand with
Angels,' and as the last notes died away, the
spirit of inspiration fell upon our sister. Slowly
she arose and uttered a thrilling prayer, after
which she spoke to this effect: 'There is a
world of spirit all around you which responds to
the vibrations of your melodies of song and
thought. There is a world of spirit all around
you whose beautiful processes are hidden from
your dull sense. Could you see with the eye of
the spirit, you would behold in the innermost
structure of the trunks, branches, and leaves of

those forest trees all around, the living channels and tubes through which the tiny, many-colored, and luminous globules of life are careering in haste to reach their appointed places, the whole forming streams of vitality to sustain and upbuild the entire structure of each forest tree. You would perceive this process going on in the blades of grass beneath you and the tiny shrubs all round. Living, moving, dancing, in varied hues and tints, are the particles of spirit in all the forms and structures which nature has builded up around us. You can behold at a glance the external, perishable garb of nature, but just that portion which is hidden from your sight, and all that portion which you cannot behold, is the world of spirit, open and revealed to the admiring gaze of those who have put off the garb of mortality. Shall I tell you how this world of spirit, impalpable to your senses, is builded up, and of what it is composed ? Amid all the processes and ceaseless changes which material forms and substances undergo, there are some particles thrown off which are too refined to be again caught up and utilized by any new growth or form of nature; so your thoughts form an impalpable atmosphere in the realm above and around you, and are by the laws of spirit amenable and obedient to the potent power of will; and when will is guided and directed by knowledge it can construct out of this forms of beauty and grandeur to you inconceivable. The magnificent temples and gorgeous scenery of the spirit-world, reared and sustained by its advanced peoples, are thus fashioned; hence you will perceive that the habitation or abode of each individual spirit must necessarily partake of the perfections or imperfections of its builder, since all must help to build their own surroundings. If the thought of the individual is pure and beautiful, his or her surroundings will be the same, seeing that the substance of the spirit-world in any locality takes the conformation and appearance of the thoughts of its inhabitants; the converse also holds good.

There is, however, a tendency, which is universal in all nature to throw off all that is imperfect, retaining the perfect only; hence, in obedience to this law, the imperfections of all spirits contracted in earthly life are eventually thrown off or outgrown, subsequently the structures of material nature are shaped according to their position, being acted upon by the direction of the sun's rays falling upon them. These rays, however, do not in any way similarly affect the structures of the spiritual world, seeing that its substances are too refined, and are therefore in a sense impervious to its piercing rays—aye, even impervious to the action of the glittering sword, of the lightning's flash, or the subtle particles of light which in the photographic processes record the delicate form of the materialized spirit, and are, in fact, affected by no material force whatever, known to us as such.   You are all children worshipping in your own way in the temple of your Father, God.   Strive to let that worship be perfect.   As the mother would warn her boy from the adverse influences and surroundings of the crowded city, so would the angels seek to point out to you the influence of numbers in worship, for wherever there are numbers of worshipers, there are found the influences of pride, and pomp, and earthly display.   Would you worship the Great Spirit in truth?   Then the most congenial place will be found in the retirement of the wood, the mountain-top, or the isolated abode in the still twilight hour, where thought responds to thought, love to love, and life to life.'

"After the above address, 'Ouina' came, the most lovable of all spirits whom we know, and who has two sides to her character, one that of an Indian maid, which she fully sustains alternately with that of a poetess endowed with lofty thought and purpose.   She now came in the former character, and said she had just arrived in her white canoe of pearl garnished with myrtle, and drawn by snowy white swans.   In this canoe she had brought with her a number of papooses (children), some of whom belonged to the friends present.   At this stage anxious ones put questions to her, and held her in conversa-

tion some time, apparently with immense satisfaction and pleasure, after which she said she
would now commence to distribute to each one
present some flower, gem, or other gift which,
in her Spiritual basket, she had brought for that
purpose; whereupon she gradually assumed her
lofty appearance and character, and, advancing
gracefully toward each, extending an arm till the
tips of the delicate fingers gently rested upon
each head, she then uttered to each a separate
poem, the express language of which was typical
of the Spiritual quality of that person to whom it
was addressed. About twenty-five were given.
This account but faintly describes what occurred; it was good to be there. Glowing, intense, and perfect were the utterances of our
beloved medium, such as we rarely, if ever,
have experienced in public with her, sublime as
we have there heard them. One regret lingers,
in that we cannot do justice to the occasion. It
was like entering the vestibule of heaven, and
leaves an impression that time can never efface."

Mr. W. P. Adshead, of Belper, Derbyshire, writing a little later to the "Medium and Daybreak" of
the work of our subject in that place says among
other things: "Of the lectures I am happy to say
the results are most gratifying. She delivered
two most excellent addresses, which were listened
to by large and intelligent audiences, the great
majority of whom appeared to be in perfect sym-

pathy with what was advanced. The subject for
the second lecture was chosen by the audience,
as were also subjects for two impromptu poems,
which were given after the addresses. * * *

"I do not think that I exaggerate when I say
that even those listening to the orations who
were not prepared to endorse the theories or receive the facts of Spiritualism were nevertheless
greatly impressed with the elevation of thought,
purity of sentiment, and beauty of language, of
which the addresses in question were such distinguished examples. * * *

"It is pleasant to record that all the friends
here, without exception, most lovingly and with
a hearty good will, worked to make the visit a
success, while on both occasions we were honored with the presence of a large number of
Spiritualists from Nottingham, Derby, Ripley,
and other places, whose advent reminded one of
the early days of Methodism, when a journey of
fifteen or twenty miles formed no barrier to the
communion of kindred spirits. * * *"

Mr. Adshead records a painful surprise when
our medium—ever obedient to the behests of
those whose wisdom guided their work—came
down stairs one morning and said:

"I have to go back to America, I must leave
England in about three weeks. My guides came
to me during the night, and said, 'After deliberation we have decided that instead of spending

the winter in Cornwall it will be best for you to
spend it in California.' This is their decision,
and I always act accordingly.' In proof, she
sat down and wrote a number of letters to
friends, making, as far as she then could, the
necessary arrangements for her journey.

"The departure from our shores of the richly-
gifted medium will be a loss we may not hope to
supply. As an exponent of the Spiritual philosophy she is without her equal amongst us. To
thousands she has been a messenger, bringing
glad tidings, carrying the light of immortality
into darkened homes, and the joy of spirit-com-
munion into saddened hearts.

"The announcement of her departure is, however, relieved and tempered by the fact that in
connection with the decision of her guides came
the intimation that at no distant date she might return to England, better fitted, let us hope, physically, to carry on the work she has so well begun."

Mr. Adshead further says:

"When I read Mr. and Mrs. Hinde's interesting account of their sojourn with our sister at
Saltburn-by-the-Sea, and the pleasant times
made for them there by the beautiful spirit
'Ouina,' I certainly wished that I had been one
of the privileged few, little deeming it possible
that a similar foretaste of heaven could come to
us amid our less perfect surroundings. But it
was even so.

"On Wednesday evening we met at tea, at the house of my brother in Derby, several friends. ' Ouina ' came into the mouth of ' Water Lily,' (' Ouina's' name for her medium), and in her own inimitable style chatted with us for about twenty minutes. She then requested us to draw back from the table and form a circle round the room, saying, 'Water Lily' would lay her hand on the head of each sitter, and give to him or her their spiritual name, and three or four verses of poetry as nearly as possible descriptive of their character. This was done, that in the case of our excellent sister Mrs. Hitchcock, of Nottingham, a well developed trance-medium, to whom was given the name of ' Spiritual Lyre,' being in my opinion exceedingly appropriate and beautiful. In all there were about thirty verses of poetry spoken without the slightest hesitation in about fifteen minutes.

"Words are almost inadequate to describe the nature and extent of the blessing which at such a time comes to the soul which is fitted to receive it. It was good to be there. How good? Who can tell, so that the telling of it shall create in others the desire to breathe the atmosphere which comes to us from Summerland!

"On Friday morning a clergyman from a neighboring parish, who was present at the first lecture, drove up to my house. He said he called

to tell me how very much pleased he was with
the address, and to express his regret that he
could not possibly be with us on the second
night. He said he had read a number of her
orations, but it was an additional privilege
and a rare treat to hear one delivered by the
medium herself. He thought he had never
heard anything more beautiful or truly eloquent.

* * * * * * * *

"There were also present members of churches,
who, on theological grounds, have hitherto
deemed it their duty to try and nip the heresy
in the bud. Let us hope that Spiritualism was
made to appear to them that which it really is,
the solvent of the hitherto unsoluble—the recon-
ciler of the hitherto irreconcilable; an angel, who,
taking by the hand the man with, and the man
without, a creed, and, standing with them amid
the decay of material forms, flashes his light
across the realm of change on to the shores of
the higher life, saying unto each, 'He that
soweth to the flesh shall of the flesh reap cor-
ruption, but he that soweth to the spirit, shall
of the spirit reap life everlasting.'

"Be this as it may, I think there can be no
doubt but that a truer charity, a higher type of
spiritual thought and speech, and a diviner ap-
prehension of the obligations of men to each
other and to God, will in time to come be noted
as the distinct results of those orations."

THE FAREWELL IN LONDON.

The farewell meeting in London to which the friends of our subject were hastily summoned, was such an outpouring of love as seldom has greeted mortal before. This meeting occurred Sunday evening, Sept. 12, 1875, at Doughty Hall.

Dr. Hallock (a veteran Spiritualist from America, one who had known our medium ever since her advent as the girl apostle of Spiritualism) led her to the platform; and as was fitting in view of all he had done to promote the work of the guides in Great Britain, Mr. James Burns, by request of the medium, occupied the chair; and Mr. J. C. Ward presided at the harmonium—"a most essential element in the impressive service." We would like to give the service entire, from Invocation to Benediction, but want of space forbids. So we give some fragmentary extracts from Mr. Burns' introductory remarks:

"My Dear Friends:—The appearance of this meeting indicates that it is no ordinary occasion. I know of no other circumstance than that which has this evening called us together that would have attracted such an overflowing assembly at so short a notice. It is just two years ago since the lady, whom we are to listen to for the last time for, it may be for years and it may be for ever, commenced her work in England, which was begun at St. George's Hall, London, September 21, 1873.

"It is indeed a wonder that she found the means of gaining a hearing, or had physical strength to address the public. At the preliminary meeting there was only one humble individual, supported by a gentleman under spirit-influence, Mr. Thomas Slater, who thought that a work could be accomplished through her agency in London. This small minority, in the face of the opposite opinion of an influential meeting, commenced arrangements which led to an achievement for Spiritualism such as has not been seen in connection with the movement of Spiritualism, in this or any other country, in so brief a time.

"In the early days of my work in Spiritualism I saw a book with a youthful countenance beautifully depicted therein as a frontispiece, and I said to myself, Shall I ever see that sweet face; shall I ever listen to the voice that gave utterance to these discourses? Just over two years ago the answer came in the affirmative; and I had the honor of introducing her to her first English audience. And thus it is that you also have seen and heard her. Nor have her utterances fallen alone upon your ears and hearts. Through the printed reports of them they are known all over the world as well as they are in London.

"What has thus been done in these two years, eternity alone can disclose. Though I have been breasting the storm all the time, and doing as best I could the task assigned me, yet I can form no sufficient estimate of the grandeur of the work that has been accomplished. I am, however, thankful that I have been an instrument in promoting a cause capable of bestowing such blessings upon mankind. Of the immediate occasion which has brought us together this evening, I cannot express myself adequately. You will best realize what ought to be said in the unutterable emotions which occupy your own breasts."

The guides of the medium then proceeded to deliver their farewell address at London before her departure to Liverpool, from whence she was to sail for America.

After the discourse Mr. Burns made a valedictory address from which we extract the following:

"MY DEAR FRIENDS: — We cannot let this occasion close without a few further remarks. Had this been a week-night meeting, instead of a religious service, I should have suggested that certain gentlemen should have been appointed to have spoken to a formal resolution; but that might detract from the sacredness of the love we bear our sister here.

"It were a work of supererogation for us to hope and wish that our inspired sister may be well and do well, for, in truth, she is not in our keeping. Her work is more wisely planned than we can aspire to; she is watched over by more kindly souls than we possess. We know that those who are chosen to do the work of the spirit-world on earth—grand and beautiful as in itself it is—often suffer the most of all human beings. There is in their case a more severe crucifixion of the flesh and painful crises of experience than ordinarily fall to the lot of humanity.

"We must now bow to the necessity which calls her away, but we live in the hope that she will visit us again. With the number of applications for her services before her, may I say that she has pledged herself to return to fulfil the prayer of these requests? That this removal from among us has been decided in the spirit-world for some time I have no doubt.

"In submitting to the bereavement which has already saddened so many hearts here and throughout the British Islands, and will yet sadden many others as the news reaches distant places, what is our duty? We need not express our requests to those higher powers who know better than we do ourselves. All we have to do is to manifest—silently, it may be, in our own bosoms—our love and esteem. Our love and sympathy will follow her wherever she goes, and aid her in all she has to do. It is the only tribute which soul can render to soul; all require it, and it profiteth the giver as well as the recipient. This tribute I sincerely, and in your name, extend to her to whom we are all so deeply attached, and may the chain become the stronger the farther the links thereof are extended."

Dr. Hallock and others of the audience rose and expressed their sorrow at parting with her, and extended her their blessings and God speed.

Mr. Enmore Jones rose and said that he was a member of the Church of England, that he could not concur in all that had been given through the lips of our medium, "yet we recognize ghost-life, and I think we ought to thank our American ghosts for giving us their wisdom. It is Sunday night, yet I suggest that we calmly, thoughtfully rise, and by that act show our affection to our ghost friends who have done so much for us."

Heartily responding to this suggestion the whole audience rose, and calmly stood in solemn silence for a few moments. It was an impressive scene. The homage of earth was rendered to celestial outpourings.

The guides of our subject, in tendering their thanks to the audience and those who had spoken, responded to Mr. Jones as follows:

"Our friend, Mr. Enmore Jones, we also thank. And to all whose hearts are in sympathy with his words we give you in return the greeting, not of the ghostly land, but of the spirit land, which is more than ghost, namely, a ghost that is alive."

Mr. Ward, with great effect and touching pathos, sang an appropriate benediction—''Peace be with you." At the conclusion of which, amidst a thrilling silence, Ouina gave the parting poem.

Only one or two private receptions to say farewell to our gifted sister could be arranged for in the limited time at her disposal before the sailing of the steamer that was to bear her hence. Of these the Medium and Daybreak says:

''The brief time intervening between the announcement of her withdrawal from our midst and her actual departure from London—and from England, only allowed of one or two such social gatherings as could be rapidly extemporized among her more immediate friends, many of whom at this season are scattered abroad in pursuit of health or pleasure." The writer of the article was present at one of these *reunions* in the West End, and after giving the names of some of those who were present says:

''Centered, as all thoughts were, on the lady whose many inspired drawing-room utterances have been treasured up in the hearts of her admirers, a response quickly came from her spirit-guides, who one after another took control for a few parting words. Space will not permit these to be given *in extenso;* we therefore extract such as afford encouragement, and have a practical and useful bearing.

" 'Adin A. Ballou ' observed that the cause of
Spiritualism in this country had never in the
opinion of the spirits, been in such a favorable attitude as at present. The influx of spiritual power in all directions places the cause
today in as good a position as its warmest
advocates could desire. He had noted to
what an increased extent the immortality of
the soul had been recognized in this country;
also that the great fact of man's spiritual existence was being rapidly withdrawn from the
region of doubt and of hope into that of certainty and knowledge. Herein was cause for
congratulation and rejoicing.

"Addressing Dr. Hallock, an old worker from
America, the control remarked that there was
a vein of practicality in his mind eminently
suited to the English people, for they look for
facts more than theories. The Spiritual experience of thirty years of a mind like his adds
weight to his stated facts. A sphere of usefulness was predicted for the Doctor, equal to that
of any who have come across the water, the
English people being ready to receive ideas,
opinions and truths growing out of experience
and based on reason.

"In answer to a question from Dr. Main,
whether the organization of the English people
did not present a better spiritual basis than elsewhere, the control remarked that there was a

general ripe-mindedness toward the cause among Spiritualists here; and that, although there were divisions, the signs were most hopeful and there was no great danger of progressive truth becoming crystallized. They (the spirits) could see that Spiritualism is creeping into every stage of life and knocking at every door; and it would be more readily received here than in America, because the people are less hampered with an all-absorbing daily occupation, and thus the minds of the many are more liberated for the investigation of truth. Nevertheless there is need of a revolutionary work to be done here, to rightly adjust the religious, political, and social life of the country, to blot out the hard and fast lines of demarcation, setting class against class, and to refound society on a spiritual basis.

"One source of hope was the sincere spirit of inquiry they had observed among the clergy. Quietly the Church is becoming imbued with the spirit of Spiritualism, and a new form of thought is growing up among the leaders of religious opinion. This is particularly conspicuous among the Wesleyans."

"Dr. Rush" next took control. His affinity with two of the world's prominent healers—Dr. Main and Dr. Hallock—also with Mr. Linton as promoting the healing movement, drew him at once to the subject of healing, on which Dr. Rush uttered thoughts full of potency and mean-

ing, most deserving the attentive study of all interested therein.   He observed that the primary
basis of the true healer is that his sympathy
shall extend to all the infirmities of his patients,
and that he should have the power to administer
mental healing to accomplish the physical good,
for the physical state often depended upon the
mental.   The wise physician is he who looks to
the soul.   He therefore commended for serious
consideration the course pursued by his friend
Dr. Main—viz., to prove the spirit, and find
what is needful there.   He ('Dr. Rush') was engaged in searching out the hidden laws of sympathy in the human mind which undermined the
body; and he perceived that thereby the process
of healing was already begun.   That being his
province, he did not devote much time to what is
called Spiritual teaching; the truth is, Spiritual
teaching and healing are the same thing.   The
teacher gives the philosophy—the healer the palpable demonstration."

Much more was spoken on the subject of Spiritual teaching and true healing, and the evening
closed with an appropriate "baptism of poetry"
from Ouina, who bestowed "name poems" upon
those present who had not previously received
them.   A general excursion of Spiritualists from
all parts of England took place to be present at
the final discourse and reception at Southport on
Tuesday, the 21st of September.

Words are inadequate to express our feelings in looking over the published accounts of that farewell, and more particularly of the personal letters, fluttering like flocks of doves to bid her *bon voyage* and speedy return; letters laden with the incense of grateful and uplifted hearts, and bathed with tears of regret for her departure, we can say nothing; too sacred to meet the public eye they would form a rare volume in themselves.

For the following account of the farewell reception tendered her at the Queen's Hotel, Southport, England, Sept. 21, 1875, we have drawn largely from the report published in the Southport Daily "News," and West Lancashire "Chronicle" of Sept. 22, 1875.

"Her personal friends from all parts of the United Kingdom had assembled to bid her goodbye; the late Geo. Thompson, M. P., although at that time in very feeble health, coming all the way from Leeds to take part in this final reception to our subject on her first visit to Albion's shores. Dr. William Hitchman, of Liverpool, opening the proceedings, said: "He regretted her departure from them as akin to a national loss. Under these circumstances it became them as brothers and sisters to present some testimonials of their regard for one who merited more than they could possibly perform, for her incalculable services on behalf of one of the noblest and most stupendous truths ever bestowed upon mankind. He could not say how deeply they regretted the cause of their assembling there that afternoon so far as the loss of their dear sister was concerned. Independently of the great good she had done, he knew many acts of kindness that appealed to the philanthropy of the human heart that were performed by her, but were never destined to meet the public eye. These and many more interesting traits in her noble character he could relate were it not supererogation and an act of impertinence to allude to them in her presence. She was so well known to those present, and not only to them, but to all Europe; nay, not in the United States alone, but throughout the civilized world. She seemed as though a halo of glory had been shed around her from another world; she came like an angel of light from those heights, going from glory to glory. Her merits belong to few of God's children. Every philosopher and Spiritualist would recognize in her departure the loss of a gem; she would shine in his soul as a spark emanating from the Great White Throne."

Mr. Webster Glynes, of London, entirely concurred with Dr. Hitchman's remarks, as to her services and their regret at her departure from among them. The London Spiritualists, who had so many opportunities of hearing her, and deriving benefit from her admirable addresses,

felt that it was a great loss to have her taken
from them so suddenly and unexpectedly.

Mr. George Thompson, the great anti-slavery
advocate, lately M. P. for the Tower Hamlets,
stated that twelve years ago he had the pleasure
of hearing the lady in Boston, having previously
heard of her name and fame. Perhaps they
would now take his testimony as to her eloquence.
He had lived for sixteen years in constant, eager
and vigilant watchfulness of the gifts of public
men, especially their elocutionary gifts. He
had mingled with them in his own country, and
he had mingled with them in other countries; he
had heard public speakers of all kinds, from the
rough and unpolished eloquence of the peasant
to the highest senatorial efforts, as well as all
that were included in the practice of the bar and
other bodies; and, therefore, they might believe
that he was competent to form comparisons and
to come to a judgment upon public speaking.
Probably the lady would remember the occasion
on which he was drawn to hear her. An eminent man in America had recently died, and had
been buried during the week that was followed
by the Sunday on which he heard her speak.
That man's name was Edward Everett. At the
time he died he was classed as the second man
as a public speaker over the whole of the United
States; there was one man who took precedence
of him, and who was then living—Daniel Web-

ster—after him Edward Everett by common consent was the chief public speaker in the highly cultivated State of Massachusetts. Edward Everett had died and had been laid down on Thursday, and the lady here was announced to speak in the hall where he (Mr. Thompson) heard her. Her subject that night was (he did not give it *in ipsima verba*) the judgment of the spiritual world on Edward Everett. For one hour he sat between two ladies hearing her, and both of the ladies who were distinguished for their intelligence, asked him what he thought of the lecture. He gave them his judgment at the moment, and he gave it now as his long matured judgment; that if six of the most highly-gifted minds in England had united with six similarly-gifted minds in America and had applied their combined intellects for six months in arranging a lecture that would be faultless they could not have produced the one given by the lady.

He was sad, because they must soon say they had her no more among them in the body. In her they had an extraordinary spectacle—a wonderful philanthropist. He did not know how to account for the strange want of interest that scientific men took in a spectacle like that; and they were shut up to believe that that sublime philosophy and those beautiful discourses they were privileged to hear, from time to time, were extravagances given by some power extraneous to her. Take it as they would, he maintained that she was the most extraordinary woman in England at that hour. Since he heard her in America he had kept an account of her progress. She had come to England, and after two years of incessant labor, in weakness and weariness of body, her treasure being in earthen vessels, she had to leave them —he hoped for her own good. He believed she had been wisely advised, and he hoped she would be long spared to this country. In every good wish that could be expressed for her there or elsewhere he most heartily and fervently joined for the sake of what came to them through her. She was a great mystery to him; he could not understand, he could not comprehend, or grasp the mediumship; but he was content to live in the hope that he would know it bye and bye. He also bore testimony to the gentleness, sweetness, and amiableness of her manner; she was most loved by those who knew her best, at those firesides where her company was cherished. He joined in every good wish regarding her.

Mr. John Lamont, of Liverpool, explained that they were indebted to Mr. Benjamin Coleman for having prepared the address to be presented to her. He endorsed the remarks of Mr. Thompson with regard to the medium, who endeared herself to all with whom she associated; that was a peculiar trait of her character."

Dr. Hitchman then, in behalf of the Spiritualists of England, presented her with the following testimonial, the original of which is beautifully illuminated:

"On the eve of your departure for your native home we, the undersigned members of a committee representing the majority of the Spiritualists of the United Kingdom, desire to convey their high admiration of your gentle, amiable, and highly intellectual qualities — qualities which we are assured have endeared you to all who have the privilege of meeting you in close social relationship.

"We beg to express to you and to the spirit-band who, under God's providence, has guided and directed your movements in the country, and to that happy, faithful spirit, 'Ouina' who inspires the beautiful poetry which flows so gracefully from your lips, our best thanks for the great services you have all rendered to the cause we have so much at heart.

"Recognizing the fact that, in the absence of all educational advantages from your childhood to the present time, you have been able for many years past to deliver an impromptu discourse in an eloquent and strictly logical manner on any subject presented to you by a promiscuous audience, we think that no greater proof could be given to a skeptical world that your thoughts are inspired from a higher source, and so we believe them to be.

"At a time when Spiritualism has been placed under a passing cloud by some of its advocates, your mission, and the gifts which you command and wield so wisely, stand out in bright relief, and satisfy us that our creed, freed from all charlatanry and fanaticism, teaches a grand and ennobling truth.

"We beg, dear madam, on behalf of those we represent, to hand with this illuminated address a few articles of usefulness which we hope you will do us the honor to accept as a slight testimonial of our love and respect.

"In bidding you farewell, we sincerely trust that your health may be thorougly re-established, and that you may be impelled ere long to revisit our shores, and in that hope we venture to assure you that you leave behind you for a time a multitude of friends who will gladly welcome your return to renew your most useful labors among them.

"We sign our names on behalf of the general body of Spiritualists of the United Kingdom—

CHARLES BLACKBURN,	ALGERNON JOY,
JAMES BOWMAN,	EMILY KISLINGBURY,
ANNA C. BURKE,	J. LAMONT,
JAMES BURNS,	JOHN MACKAY,
ALEXANDER CALDER,	J. N. T. MARTHEZE,
BENJAMIN COLEMAN,	HAY NISBET,
HENRY COLLEN,	E. L. S. NOSWORTHY,
ELLEN COLLEN,	MARY PEARSON,

SOPHIA J. CREIGHTON, SARAH PEARSON,
EMILY COMBES, JOHN PRIEST,
ANDREW CROSS, THOMAS SLATER,
ELISABETH DICKSON, ADELAIDE M. SLATER,
EUPHEMIA DICKSON, GEO. N. STRAWBRIDGE,
MARK FOOKS, ANN STRAWBRDGE,
WEBSTER GLYNES, WILLIAM TEBB,
J. HARE, MARY E. TEBB,
WM. HITCHMAN, M.D., GEORGE THOMPSON,
G. R. HINDE, JAMES WASON,
THOMAS P. HINDE.

Among those present on that interesting occasion were: Mrs. Strawbridge, London; Mrs. Nosworthy, Mrs. Casson, Mrs. Lamont, and Miss Hamilton, Liverpool; Miss Bennett, Birkenhead; Mrs. Lewes and Mrs. Raby, Bury; Mrs. Vernon, Uttoxeter; the Misses Culpan, Miss Longbotham, and Mrs. Spencer, Halifax; Mrs. Houghton, Southport, and several other ladies; Mr. George Thompson, late M. P. for the Tower Hamlets; Mr. W. Glynes, London; Dr. Hitchman, Mr. Robert Cusson, Mr. Davies, Messrs. A. Lamont and J. Lamont, Liverpool; Mr. Kershaw, Oldham; Mr. Fenton, Dewsbury; Mr. J. N. T. Martheze and Mr. Snow, Brighton; Mr. James Culpan and Mr. John Longbotham, Halifax; Mr. Griffiths, Southport.

Accompanying this testimonial which, in its handsome frame, occupies an honored place in

Mrs. Richmond's home, were several articles of "use and beauty," none of which was more prized than a photographic album containing the "shadows" of many of her English friends, faces through which the soul shines revealing the true spirits within.

From only a few of the letters sent her can we venture to even make a quotation or extract, but these from the venerable philanthropist George Thompson—who fulfilled his promise to be present at her farewell meeting at Southport—will not be deemed inappropriate.

In a letter to his daughter (Mrs. Nosworthy), whose guest our medium was, he expressed his sadness that she was about to leave England.

"Say to her," he said, "on my behalf, all that is kind and affectionate. Assure her of my deepest respect and of my best wishes for her happiness and the success of her contemplated visit to the far distant shores of the Pacific. It is not impossible that I may arrive in Liverpool on Monday or Tuesday."

Under the date of September 18, 1875, he writes as follows:

"My Dear Friend:—I will try hard to grasp your hand, and look upon your face once again—once again. May God and good angels watch over, defend and bless you, and, if it may be, bring you to our shores again.—George Thompson to Cora."

This letter is followed by one dated:

"LEEDS, ENGLAND,

"Monday evening, Sept. 20, 1875.

"MY DEAR FRIEND:—I am deeply grateful for your kind letter received this morning. To-morrow, if well enough, I shall leave by the 10:40 train which gets to Liverpool at 1:30, and drive at once to Richmond Terrace. I find I can write no more, but that I am

"Yours affectionately,

"GEORGE THOMPSON."

In this letter he enclosed a stanza indicative of his high appreciation and regard for our subject:

"Farewell! If ever fondest prayer
For others' weal awarded on high,
Mine shall not all be spent on air,
But wave that name beyond the sky.'

It must not be forgotten that Mr. Thompson at this time was well advanced in years, yet his mind was as clear as ever, and his deep interest in spiritual truths is evinced by the letters we have quoted above, as well as by the fact that he was a constant attendant upon her lectures whenever his health permitted.

CHAPTER X.

IT was in the month of April, 1880 (our subject had then been ministering to her congregation in Chicago constantly for the period of four years), that the subject of this work and her husband gave a reception at their residence, 38 Ogden Avenue, Chicago, to two gentlemen, Mr. Emmet Densmore and Clint Rondebush, of New York (who had been firm believers in and followers of her guides, and had always contributed largely of their means for the furtherance of her public work), as they were passing through Chicago on their way to Colorado. On this occasion all the officers and representative members of the First Society of Spiritualists of Chicago were present. After a most delightful hour or so of social enjoyment, interspersed with music by the wonderfully inspired musician, Ellen McAllister, and her sister (who accompanied Ellen's selections on the piano with the harp), during which time it seemed to our subject and her husband that the company present acted unusually constrained; they looked signifi-

cantly at one another as though they were knowing to something, and all seemed waiting ex-
pectantly as though they anticipated a startling
denouement. And it came! when Dr. Bushnell,
President of the First Society of Spiritualists, to
the unmitigated surprise of Cora and her husband, announced to her that the society, in col-
lusion with some of her personal friends elsewhere, including the two gentlemen whom we
have named, had made all the arrangements for
giving her a six months' vacation and sending
her and her husband to England; that she might
—in response to numerous petitions and appeals
from that country—continue her work there. At
the conclusion of his remarks he handed to her
husband passage tickets to London on a steamer
sailing June 5th, and a purse of money sufficient
to defray their expenses there and back.

Our subject's surprise was so great that (as is
the privilege of all fair women) she would have
fainted had not Ouina taken possession of her,
and graciously thanked all interested for such a
generous and unselfish manifestation of their appreciation of the work of the guides of the medium. Ouina also assured them that, while she
was cognizant of their plans, the medium was
wholly unaware of and unprepared for what was
coming, until "Live Oak's" (Dr. Bushnell) announcement.

About the first of June they left Chicago, visiting Boston, New York, and Philadelphia, where she had largely attended meetings and receptions. On the fifth of June they sailed, this being her second voyage, for England. "Rocked in the cradle of the deep" she had a much needed and welcome rest from all work for a few days. To her the ocean suggests the bosom of eternity, and there she rests as never upon the land; and all too soon the Irish coast springs into view, and she realizes that there are anxious hearts waiting to welcome her again to England's shores.

As the ship with its precious freight enters the Mersey, about nine o'clock in the evening, a tender comes alongside bringing her faithful friend and admirer, Mrs. Nosworthy, the first to welcome her back to the scenes of her very successful labors. She accompanied Mrs. Nosworthy to her home at Blundill Sands, near Liverpool, where she had a few days' quiet rest before commencing her labors at London.

On the evening previous to her departure for London a reception was tendered her by the Spiritualists of Liverpool, an account of which was published in the "Medium and Daybreak," of London, June 25, 1880, from which we extract the following:

"After a quiet time of three days at Mrs. Nosworthy's retreat by the sea, she and her husband were entertained by a representative few of the Spiritualists of Liverpool, at a *soiree* given in the

Camden Hotel drawing-room. Mrs. Dickinson-
Cheever, the eminent healer from America, Mr.
John Lamont, Mr. Shepherd, Mr. and Mrs.
Wharmby, Mr. R. Glendinning of Birkdale, Southport, Mr. Bean (late editor of the 'Liverpool
Albion'), Mr. Duke, Mr. Casson, and many other
ladies and gentlemen, Spiritualists and outsiders,
were collected at hardly a few days' warning, to
give the eminent medium a warm welcome; and
a hearty one it was. Mrs. Wharmby presented
a bouquet of beautiful flowers, Miss Edith
Thompson and Mrs. Nock did their part in discoursing sweet strains from Beethoven and Men-
delssohn at the piano; tea and coffee were gracefully presided over by the lady of the hotel herself; and at 8 p. m. the chair was taken by Mrs.
Nosworthy—this by request of Mrs. Richmond's
guides, otherwise Mrs. Nosworthy would greatly
have preferred giving the post to Mr. Lamont.
Mrs. Nosworthy said:

" 'LADIES AND GENTLEMEN:—You are all, if
not most of you, Spiritualists, therefore I need
scarcely introduce to you the lady we are assembled to welcome to our shores on this happy occasion.

" 'Most of us have heard her speak under the
influence of her lofty and noble guides, and if any
there be who have not had that pleasure, they
have doubtless read some of the sublime discourses which have fallen from her inspired lips.

Well, here she is once more amongst us, and I feel that she is sent on a special and great mission; she comes not of her own volition, but by direction _purely_ of the mighty powers who are gathering in stronger force around the instrument most peculiarly adapted to reproduce on the earth-plane the lessons which the Spirit-world alone can give us. She comes with teachings which I sincerely trust we may each in our individual capacity as human beings, be able to appropriate, each to our special needs, and which each society may also find good to make it more broad, free, catholic, harmonious, charitable, Christlike. She comes to bring the spirit of love and peace which should brood over every household of Spiritualists, and over every society. Nearer; she comes to invite us all to throw aside the _self_ (which is also in many of us, too much considered and too much loved) and live more in the spirit of Him who knew no thought of self. Why do we ever have a jar in our houses; in our societies? It is because the self in some is thought more of than the promotion of the general welfare of the whole community. Alas! that we should have received so many grand teachings, so frequent admonition, and yet that we remain very much on the same low level, and so far beneath the great model of the Spiritual man. Alas! that each one is ever, even in this great work, more intent on self-glorification than on _its_ advancement.

" 'I will not overwhelm the gifted medium with fulsome flattery, as is customary on these occasions; nor to her let the glory be given, but to the great Father who gave her an organization so admirably attuned to beauty of thought, word, deed, that the spirits of His angels,the *just* made *perfect*, might be brought near to us by her. But for myself I may say, that I welcome her with open arms, she is my dear sister in the spirit, and that draws her, if possible, nearer than the bond of consanguinity in the flesh. I am thankful for her, and in such a small way as is at my command I shall try to show it.'

"Mr. John Lamont then rose and made a short and most admirable speech."

Our subject, the recipient of this public welcome, on rising betrayed deep emotion, and after a few words by the controlling spirit, tears welled from the medium's eyes, and for a moment she was overcome. Her hand was extended to grasp that of her friend in the chair (who was scarcely less affected), and the spirit controlling thus saluted his daughter—for the control was that of " George Thompson," as was announced at conclusion of his short address.

[I wish to state here that the spirit of George Thompson had departed from its earthly tenement shortly after our subject's former visit to England.—ED.]

The next day our subject left Liverpool for

London. Her arrival at the metropolis is thus chronicled in the "Medium and Daybreak":

"A large party of ladies and gentlemen were in waiting at St. Pancras station when the train from Liverpool arrived on Tuesday afternoon, bearing with it Mr. and Mrs. Richmond. There were present Mrs. Strawbridge, Mrs. Gilham, Mrs. McKellar, Mr. and Mrs. Cowper, Mr. Slater, Mr. Burns, Mr. and Mrs. Towns, Mrs. Swindin, Mr. and Mrs. Yeates, Mr. and Mrs. Ward, Mr. Lowenthal, etc., etc. When the train stopped at the platform, Mrs. Strawbridge, Mr. Slater, and Mr. Burns were the first to greet the visitors, and it may be noted that these gentlemen were instrumental in bringing Mrs. Richmond first before the London public; and had it not been for their action, we might never have heard her voice in this country, and the whole course of her work would have been different. What a change in Mrs. Richmond between then and now. When she attended her reception at the Spiritual Institution in 1873, which led to the meetings at St. George's Hall, she was so weak and emaciated that she could with difficulty walk upstairs. Now she is plump and vigorous, and apparently in excellent health.

"The party remained on the platform a considerable time expressing words of welcome and congratulation, which were kindly reciprocated. Mr. Herbst, as the secretary of the Goswell Hall meeting of Spiritualists, presented an address of welcome. Accompanied by Mrs. Strawbridge, the visitors then drove away, and the London friends returned to their several avocations.

On the second day after her arrival in London she was tendered a public welcome to her sphere of work in Spiritualism, at Neumeyer Hall, Bloomsbury Mansions, the following account of which is taken from the " Medium and Day-break":

"Mr. W. Stainton-Moses, M. A., presided, in his well-known, refined, and genial manner. He explained the purport of the gathering by stating that it was a meeting of friends to welcome Mrs. Richmond on her present visit to London. The time had been short and the attendance spontaneous and without public request, or a much larger audience would have assembled. Mrs. Richmond was no stranger to them, hence she needed no introduction at his hands. Her truly eloquent words and valuable Spiritual teachings, which terminated amongst them five years ago, would not be forgotten. She came again amongst London Spiritualists as a most welcome guest. It was but just to state that her work had been appreciated in all places where her voice had been heard or her utterances read, but that appreciation was not least in London. Since she left this country she had been working with great energy and success with the First Society of Spiritualists of Chicago. Mr. F. F. Cook, whose name was so favorably known by many in this country, had been kind enough to write respecting her work in Chicago. He was sorry that the state of his health and heavy pressure of work should prevent him from devoting his energies as he could wish to providing suitable means in London to render her valuable instruction available for public use. She was a representative medium, and brought with her words of greeting to English Spiritualists from their brethren in Chicago, which he, as chairman of that meeting, had the honor to receive on behalf of his countrymen, and which he would now read:

"To THE SPIRITUALISTS OF ENGLAND—GREETING: It is with mingled feelings of sadness and pleasure that we comply with the wish of the spirit-guides of Mrs. Cora L. V. Richmond, our beloved medium, to grant her leave of absence for a brief sojourn in your midst. If we part from her reluctantly, even for the short period of a few months, it is because she is to us the embodiment of our highest ideals; if the sadness of this separation is softened, it is due to the conviction that what is our loss will be your gain— and in this brotherhood of one faith, personal predilections should ever give way to the general weal.

" We are aware that Mrs. Richmond comes among you not wholly a stranger. The memories

of a former visit we doubt not are still fresh in
your minds, and the good-will and many kind-
nesses then shown to her will not fail of repetition on this occasion, as the instrument most
harmoniously attuned to voice the inspiration of
this day and hour; and hence we rest with content in the assurance that she leaves one company of warm-hearted and devoted friends only
to pass into the midst of another equally zealous
and true.

"During the better part of five years that Mrs.
Richmond has ministered to the First Society of
Spiritualists of Chicago she has been to us and
all within the wide circle of her influence—an
influence extended not only by the spiritual but
the secular press—what the beacon light is to
the storm-tossed mariner.

"Outside this society Spiritualism has been a
prey to bitter dissensions; within there has been
peace, and unspeakable cause for thanksgiving.
All about us the waves of discord have beaten
the shores of time with relentless fury; within
this refuge there has been a placid sea—concord,
forbearance, and a joy that can come only where
the spirit is manifest in the fulness of its power
and beneficence.

"If we, who are no more deserving than others
have been thus showered with blessings, it has
been solely due to the presence among us of our
beloved 'Water Lily,' and the benign influence

manifested through her by the wise and good, to whom she ever accords implicit obedience. The work she was given to do she has done unquestioningly. The light of her illumined countenance has been to us what the Star of Bethlehem was to the shepherds and magi of old.

"Her words, uttered with the power of the spirit, have brought strength and consolation to thousands whose lot otherwise would have been despair, and with one accord the true and faithful of this land now look to her for guidance and counsel, as the foundation of highest inspiration. This is our message to you.

"For the First Society of Spiritualists, Chicago,

"L. BUSHNELL, President.

"COLLINS EATON, Secretary."

" Mr. Stainton-Moses concluded his speech with a very hearty expression of thanks on behalf of English Spiritualists to the First Society of Chicago for their fraternal and cheering message. He hoped the same measure of success would attend the ministrations of Mrs. Richmond in this country as had followed her course in the Western Continent. To her he extended a most cordial and hearty welcome from the meeting, and he trusted she would have strength to perform the great amount of work she would without doubt be called upon to undertake.

"The chairman called upon Mr. J. Burns, as one who had seen something of her work, to make some remarks on what had taken place in the past.

"Mr. Burns said he had been ahead of most present in welcoming Mrs. Richmond, whom he met, accompanied by other friends, at the railway station on her arrival. He much regretted that his work in London prevented him from meeting her at Liverpool. From his earliest knowledge of the literature of Spiritualism he had been related sympathetically to Mrs. Richmond. In that volume of her early orations an engraving appeared of a fair young face, with upturned eyes, and light, graceful ringlets; and a dozen years in advance of the event he felt that he should some day meet the original. He asked: Have men lived and been acquainted in some other state before they took their present bodies, and do recollections of former friendships sometimes burst through the shell of flesh giving rise to these recollections and anticipations of personal acquaintance; or do we in sleep pass to another country where we enact different characters from those of our waking moments, and there become acquainted with those who are widely separated from us, and the link thus formed is partially recognized in day-dreams, and ultimately draws such persons together? Be that as it may, he had always desired to participate in their visitor's spiritual work, and it was an unexpected joy to him, when, seven years ago, he was informed that the lady was actually in London, and would visit him in a few days.

" 'The first reception and welcome at the Spiritual institution was by no means such a promising meeting as the one he now addressed. The attendance was limited, and only two persons were in favor of a public work for Mrs. Richmond. One of that minority was himself; the other Mr. Slater, under spirit-influence. That minority soon gathered strength, became the majority, and Mrs. Richmond's first meetings in St. George's Hall were the grandest demonstrations of the kind ever seen in connection with the movement in this country. The advertising was not expensive nor extensive, but it was effectual in cramming St. George's Hall with most enthusiastic and respectable audiences — not Spiritualists. After all the seats were full, the speaker said he took £6 at the side door, in about as many minutes, in half-crowns, from ladies and gentlemen, who gladly paid that sum for the privilege of being squeezed in anywhere. The press were invited, and they responded in a body, and on Monday morning in the daily papers Spiritualism stood as high as any other topic of the day. The critiques were most laudatory and respectful. Had the journals been spiritual organs they could not have been more faithful exponents of spiritual facts. Thus Mrs. Richmond occupied an historical position in the cause in London, and he was heartily glad to see her amongst them again, and apparently in a far better condition for hard work. There were much better prospects for work in the cause now than then. There was possibly not that vacant curiosity now, but there was greater intelligent appreciation of spiritual teaching, and she had only to be properly placed before the public to do more good work now than at any time in the past. That meeting should not only be a formal welcome, but a genuine invitation to participate in the work of Spiritualism, and she could not well do so unless her friends took the initiative. The inspiration should not be all on one side. Spiritualists should hold themselves in preparation to be inspired to get up meetings, and Mrs. Richmond would be inspired to address them. Whatever was done, he would be glad in his capacity of newsman to co-operate with any plan that would render her presence among them of use and benefit to the cause."

Our subject then rose and addressed the company as follows: "Mr. Chairman, sisters, brothers, and fellow-workers all." The control then proceeded to thank the meeting on behalf of the medium for the cordial friendship manifested in that meeting. It was much more significant than a mere memory of past friendship; it was a greeting of spirit unto spirit — a soul greeting from the audience to the medium's spirit-band.

It was through the admonition of her guides that she had visited this country, and without any knowledge on her part of the nature of the work she would have to perform on her arrival. They in the spirit-world were united in their methods, whatever divergences of thought, word, or action might exist in the outside sphere of man's mind. With man there might be many opinions entertained on spiritual manifestation and philosophy, but where they dwelt it was unity — one heaven, though the stars differed from one another in glory. Every medium is as valuable as every other in demonstrating the existence of the spirit-world. It is not all oratory, it is not all scientific demonstration, though these may be required as necessary parts of the work. Spiritualism is the theme of humanity, and is related to the life of everyone, declaring to the king as to the beggar the immortality of that life.

"The control then alluded to Mrs. Richmond's former visit to London, and thanked the friends who so steadily co-operated on that occasion. The medium was now strong to bear in her hand the banner of truth, as the audience might give it to her to bear. The spirits had made no statement of the nature of the work to be performed in their midst. For a brief season they (the guides) would work in any and every capacity that they might be called upon to fulfil. To the individual 'Ouina' would present the flower of spiritual consolation, as opportunity offered, and if other work was needed it would be unfolded in due course. The control thanked the meeting for the welcome extended to the medium, and commented at some length on the battle between materialism and man's spirit, but that the victory was sure, and that the dawning of a better day was at hand.

"After a song by Mr. Ward, Mrs. Richmond was again controlled, and when she had uttered a few words it was evident that the control was 'George Thompson.'

"The control commenced by alluding to his having been freed from the debility of age by the change which separated him from his body. Since that time he had tried several mediums in England, to see if through them he could again speak to the world of the work of his life—freedom. The spirit-band controlling the medium he then spoke through had permitted him to address audiences in America. Mrs. Richmond had come to this country because of the control's earnest desire for her to do so—first, because of his family, with whom he desired to communicate, and secondly, to the nation at large he wished to speak, and advocate those principles of liberty so dear to him—liberty to live, to honestly procure daily bread, to be free. He could remain in no heaven and fail to speak to man that one other word which the soul longs to hear. As the humblest amongst immortals he now came into the midst of mankind to claim his destiny of immortality, and for the benefits he had derived as a spirit from the knowledge of Spiritualism which he obtained in earth-life he warmly thanked all who had labored for the cause of Spiritualism. He still clung to the only one of his daughters who knows of this truth.

"Mrs. Nosworthy, the lady alluded to, was on the platform, and was deeply affected by the words of the spirit, of whom she has had many evidences that he is indeed the one who on earth she called father. At the conclusion of the control the spirit gave the name 'George Thompson.'

"The chairman expressing a hope that they might have a poem from 'Ouina,' accordingly a characteristic poem was given. The sentiment expressed therein was that the spirit had no speech, no grand music, no bits of written paper to present, but the love that welled up in the heart, and that she freely tendered to the true friends amongst whom she was glad to speak again. That going away she remembered, and they also would remember, that she said it would be a few short moons before 'Water Lily' (the medium's spirit name) would be brought back again. On the fulfilment of that parting prophecy she now congratulated them on the evening of welcome. Then she alluded

to those who had meanwhile left the mortal
form, but who were in reality still nearer than
those in the body. She greeted well-known
voices and faces, and assured her hearers that in
the world to which in a few short years all would
go, there would be no painful partings, but the
fruitage of seed sown on earth would remain a
permanent enjoyment. That pure love-light
which irradiated her home in the spirit-land she
would present to them as a gift in acknowledgment of their welcome.

"Mr. J. J. Morse said Mrs. Richmond would be
everywhere well received by the Spiritualists of
this country. He was glad to see her so strong
in body and able to do the work required. He
proposed that the chairman be empowered by
the meeting to reply to the address received
from the Spiritualists of Chicago.

"This proposition was seconded by Miss
Georgina Houghton, and carried, when the meeting closed with many friendly greetings."

After a number of private receptions of welcome our subject commenced her public work in
London, for that season, at Goswell Hall, Sunday evening, July 11th.

We will preface a short notice of this initial
discourse by a notice clipped from the "Medium
and Daybreak" of July 9th, 1880.

"On Mrs. Richmond's arrival at St Pancras
station from Liverpool, amongst the London

friends who were in waiting to welcome her was
a deputation from the congregation of Spiritualists meeting at Goswell Hall, who presented her
with an address of welcome, inviting her to her
' former field of labor ' on their platform, where
she would be surrounded by old friends. It will
be remembered that Mrs. Richmond's farewell
meeting when she left London was at Doughty
Hall, and as the Doughty Hall congregation now
meet at Goswell Hall, her acceptance of the invitation to give her first oration there complies
literally with the phrase used in the address presented to her on her arrival.

"The committee of that congregation desire us
to express their grateful feelings that she has
given them the first work which she will perform
for the cause, and the more so that in the kind
letter announcing her intention she has desired
that the whole proceeds be retained for the support of the meetings."

By a singular coincidence, which seemed to
lend appropriateness to the occasion, Judge P.
P. Good, of Plainfield, New Jersey, U. S. A.—
an old acquaintance of the medium—who was
making a tour of Europe, happened to be in
London at that time, and hearing that our subject was to speak that evening had come to list-
en to her. On being introduced to the officers
of the Society they prevailed upon him to preside at the meeting.

In introducing the speaker he said he had
been acquainted with her for upwards of twenty
years, and he considered the privilege of being
there and introducing her to the present assemblage was more than worth coming all the way
from America for, and that when he left the New
World some months ago, he little knew what
honor was in store for him.   They would now
listen to one of Truth's great teachers.

The guides commenced the address by saying:
"It will be five years next month since we addressed a public audience in England.   There
are many persons present who were there on that
occasion—many familiar faces, many hearts that
throbbed in earnest sympathy with the work of
ministration carried forward by us through this
instrument. To-day we give you greeting; to-day
we again summon you as Spiritualists to the solemn councils of the spirits."

The following Friday evening our subject commenced a series of discourses at St. James Hall,
Regent Street, a place and locality hitherto unin-
vaded by the Spiritualists; and grave doubts were
expressed by our London friends as to their success.   But their fears proved groundless.   The
subjects of those discourses (they were reported
verbatim and published in the Spiritual and other
papers), which were very successful, attracting
widespread notice and praise, were, "Body and
Spirit," "Is this a New Dispensation of Truth to

the World?" "Life in Other Worlds as Revealed by Spiritualism," and "The Future of the Earth —Material and Spiritual." At the close of the first discourse of the series Rev. Sir William Dunbar, Bart., who occupied a place on the platform, rose, and in making some commendatory remarks, said: "I certainly have been very much edified by the address to which I have listened this evening and, but that the rules of my church forbid, I would ask the lady to address a congregation from my pulpit." The want of space forbids our giving any press notices of these meetings. Suffice to say that the influence of those meetings seemed to dedicate the place to the gathering of Spiritualists, for afterwards the "London Spiritualist Alliance" (a reorganization of the "British National Association of Spiritualists") held their quarterly *soirees* there.

About August 10th our subject left London for a tour through the "provinces," but during her brief season in London—about six weeks—she gave fifteen or sixteen public discourses, and attended a score of private receptions.

Before following our subject further, we would like to insert here a short extract from an article, giving an account of her arrival and reception in London, published in the "Herald of Progress," which says: "In the resolutions of the Chicago Spiritualist Society, recommending her to English Spiritualists, occur the words, *'our beloved me-*

dium.' I wonder when the English mediums will be so regarded and esteemed and such feelings will be entertained towards them. * * *"

The following is taken from a letter by Mrs. Wm. Tebb to the "Medium and Daybreak" after our subject had left London:

"Early in August and shortly before Mrs. Richmond went North, we were sitting in seance when the spirit of her guide and my old friend 'Adin Augustus Ballou' came to give messages to his father and mother, and my husband. Your readers will recollect that this spirit was the first to control Mrs. Richmond for her public work, and that he has ever since taken charge of our mediumship.

"When Mrs. Richmond awoke we told her what had been given and she said that for some days she had felt that on her return to the United States she must make it convenient to pay the venerable Adin Ballou and his wife a visit. She had not seen them for years, and she thought it only right to give them an opportunity of speaking with their son once more. I sent the messages to Mr. Adin Ballou, and only on the night of the concert at Neumeyer Hall I received a letter dated from Hopedale, Massachusetts, November 1st, in which he said how glad he should be to meet and converse freely with Mrs. Richmond, and he adds, 'My wife and I have always read the public discourses of which she has been the mouthpiece and which have been printed, with great satisfaction as decidedly the best, purest and most Christlike of all that have been reported in the prolific Spiritual press, and of these none have seemed to us more really elevating and practical than those which have been discoursed by our spirit son.' "

Although of recent date, November, 1894, we will here insert, as the most appropriate place, the following letter from Mrs. William Tebb (whom Ouina named "Amethyst"), although formerly living in London, now of Rede Hall, Surrey, England. She writes:

"More than forty years ago I made the acquaintance of Mrs. Richmond, then a little girl of about ten years of age, in the village of Hopedale, Mass. She had arrived with her parents on a visit to the distinguished social reformer, the Rev. Adin Ballou and his wife who had their home there, and it must have been during that visit that she first saw their son, Adin Augustus Ballou, who has been so long her chief spirit control. He was living at Bridgewater, a town in the same state, for scholastic purposes ; but he always spent his holidays at home.

"I can recall her arrival one wintry day. The coach which used to run between the village and the depot at Milford brought her with her parents to Mr. Ballou's door, and from an upper window of a house on the same street, I noted the descent of the passengers.

"Shortly afterward Cora appeared in the village school, where her bright face and pleasant manner at once attracted friends. There was, however, nothing in her appearance to indicate the wonderful gift of mediumship with which she afterwards proved to be so richly endowed.

"Our ways in life separated after that winter and we never met again until her first visit to London in 1873. She had come to this country with the hope of regaining her health, which had been for some time in an unsatisfactory state, and also to speak, as opportunity offered, under spirit guidance.

"I recollect her first discourse here, given under the inspiration of Adin Augustus Ballou. Knowing, as I had known, something of his noble life and expectations during his all too short earthly career, it was to me a revelation of how the spirit in the use of another organism may continue the education of his own powers, and at the same time assist in developing the gifts of the medium.

"Cora had come under his influence very early in her psychological experiences, and as he himself was under the constant training of the higher intelligences, she came to be, what she has ever since continued, a remarkable example of a mind illumined by spirit power, with the ability to impart to others in speech the knowledge so acquired.

"During this first visit to London as well as on her three subsequent visits, Cora arranged for a private weekly class, in addition to her public weekly ministrations. The public lectures were reported and read by many outside the audiences gathered in one or other of the larger halls of the metropolis.

"Having been one of those privileged to attend the private classes, I may say that I regard the teaching there given of the highest importance. Some of this has seen the light in her published works; notably in 'The Soul in Human Embodiments.'

"To add to what is here indicated will be to repeat what has been better said elsewhere. Those who have attended the ministrations of Mrs. Richmond, either in the Old World or the New, will not easily forget the profound impression produced upon her audiences. Her teachings, as the Rev. Adin Ballou once wrote to us, are more in conformity with those of the Great Master than any similar utterances with which he was acquainted, and in this opinion my husband and I fully concur."

The private letter to Mrs. Richmond accompanying this breathes the most affectionate interest in all that pertains to her and her work.

This interest, manifested by occasional correspondence, has continued unabated ever since our subject's first visit to England.

On leaving London she accompanied her very dear friend Mrs. Strawbridge to Buxton, where she remained about ten days, resting and visiting places of interest in the neighborhood. At the request of the Unitarian clergyman there she gave two discourses at Buxton.

From her delightful sojourn at Buxton she went to Manchester, where she was most enthusiastically received by a delegation of Spiritualists, headed by Wm. Oxley, Esq. The next day, Sunday, she gave two discourses there, of which Mrs. Nosworthy (George Thompson's daughter) wrote:

"The subject in the afternoon was 'The New and Old Dispensations,' and in the evening, 'The Needs of the Time and Who Shall Supply Them.' The poem in the evening was on ' John Bright,' which was heartily received, as were also the orations. Many old veterans were recognized as being present, the staunch representatives of the cause from far and near being in attendance.

"There are those, I regret to say, who, never having met George Thompson in *propria persona* till death of the body was near, have questioned the identity of the spirit now speaking through Mrs. Richmond in his name. On what grounds such pseudo-Spiritualists presume to base their doubts I know not, but a murmur having reached my ears only this last week, that a *late* Spiritualist has said my father's 'utterances on earth were infinitely more eloquent than anything which has been given, presuming to come from him on the other side,' I now assert, as one who since childhood has had the *best* opportunities of becoming familiar with George Thompson, that his simple style of rhetoric consisted *not* in the piling up of a mass of unnecessary words, strung together for display, and selected, more with a view to dazzle the hearer than to enlighten him, but in the exquisite delivery of the plainest *unaffected* English.

"It has been said of my father, that 'you could not gain any acquaintance with his powers by reading his utterances.' *No*, to be appreciated fully, he required to be *heard;* and when heard, it was *not* the mere words which moved his auditors, but the deep pathos, and intense earnestness of his fervent delivery which touched all hearts, and roused the most callous. Mrs. Lydia Maria Child wrote of him:

> I've heard thee when thy powerful words
>   Were like the cataract's roar;
> Or like the ocean's mighty waves
>   Resounding on the shore.
>
> I've heard thee in the hour of prayer
>   When dangers were around;
> Thy voice was like the royal harp
>   That breathed a charmed sound.

"The poem, which has been many times printed in America, winds up with these words, which fully express that which I wish to convey of my father as an orator:

> Still great and good in every change,
> Magnificent and mild,
> As if a seraph's godlike power
> Dwelt in a LITTLE CHILD.

"As I sat by my dear sister, Mrs. Richmond, on Sunday last, at Manchester, in front of the fine, sympathetic audience who greeted her, my heart was full of thankfulness, for not only did I feel the people in front stirred as of old by the words of their countryman encouraging them to make ready their hearts and minds for the 'Angel of the New Dispensation,' but I felt that my father had led me to the place in which I then sat.   Mrs. Richmond, speaking under his control, uses his actions, takes his attitudes, and deals, as he did, with questions on which I am assured she has no acquaintance, *i.e.*, the recent legislation of this country, both at home and in our colonies. Of legislative reforms, and of the dates thereof in England, she has no knowledge, much less has she been able to follow all the various complications of the British rule and military power in India.   Under the control of 'George Thompson' she discourses glibly of these, and with his expressions and statistical confirmations.

" I have no hesitation in saying that the fund

of information on these points then betrayed is
not in her store of mere earthly historical records;
she has not, to my knowledge, spoken even under
control in the peculiar manner in which she now
speaks of India, and our recent tactics with regard to that country.

"As one who was present at the evening meeting at the Athenæum of Manchester on Sunday
last, I testify with a thankful heart to the success, in a spiritual point of view, of her visit.
A splendid audience filled the hall, who listened
with rapt attention to the long, eloquent, and
impassioned discourse of my honored father. An
outburst of applause, suppressed by a sense of
probable unfitness for the solemnity of the occasion, followed the announcement of his name.
A deep sense of devotional fervor pervaded the
meeting, which I have rarely felt. Tears were
in many eyes of the crowd of faces upturned to
the speaker's. Oh! that I had power to reproduce some of the words which caused those tears,
and also drew approving, but suppressed utterances of assent, from hearts deeply touched in
the audience immediately around us, many of
whom where on the platform. I also was deeply
moved, and therefore—passing by the long historical review which was panoramically brought
before us of mighty kingdoms extending their
love of power and riches at the expense of others
poorer and weaker, and one after another falling

from that power by the very force they had employed—I can only record the lesson drawn from the review. The Angel of the New Dispensation will take up his abode with us when this lesson shall be learned and *practiced;* that *only* the principle of LOVE can ever be true and lasting *power.* Everything taken by force shall be lost, everything won by *love* shall be kept. Men may rob us of the means to live in the body, may traduce and malign our names, but can never take from us our spiritual inheritance, which we shall win both here and in the better state when the Angel of the New Dispensation has full sway and dominion in our lives and hearts. The spirit announced that angel as near, and bid each one present to prepare the way by an individual purification, and it seemed to me that the echo from all hearts was an Amen.

"An enthusiastic vote of thanks was accorded to Mrs. Richmond and her husband for coming to Manchester."

Space will not permit us to notice the work in detail throughout the provinces. This tour lasted about six weeks during which time she visited the following places, giving from one to six public discourses in each, and attending private receptions: Gateshead, Newcastle-on-Tyne, Bishop Auckland, Edinburgh, Glasgow, Macclesfied, Liverpool, Nottingham, Halifax, Sowerby Bridge, Sheffield, and other provincial towns.

As a specimen of the effect of her work on this tour we will take at random an extract from the secular press. Here is the first one we lay our hands on. It is from a lengthy notice in the Nottingham Journal, September 30, 1880:

" There was a crowded audience, and it was announced that the lady would speak on any subject the audience selected. Seven or eight topics were suggested, and eventually the vote was in favor of the following: 'Is Spiritualism in Accordance with the Christian Doctrine?' Without a moment's hesitation she rose and spoke for about three-quarters of an hour with the greatest possible fluency, beginning by saying that in order to answer that question it would be necessary to know what Spiritualism is."

October saw her again in London. On Sunday evening, October 3rd, she commenced a course of six Sunday evening discourses at Neumeyer Hall, Bloomsbury Mansions, and also gave a number of public discourses at the Goswell Hall meetings. In addition to the public discourses she gave instructions to a private class on "The Soul in Human Embodiments."

While, in recounting the work of our subject, the greater stress is laid upon, and the most said of its public manifestations, the most potent and lasting part is accomplished at the private receptions and meetings; unto fully as many of such our medium ministered as in public gatherings while in London.

On Saturday evening, November 13, 1880,
there was another assemblage of Spiritualists
and friends of our medium, at Neumeyer Hall, to
say farewell, instead of welcome; the following
account of which we take from the "Medium
and Daybreak :"

"On Saturday evening, November 13th, Mr.
and Mrs. Richmond were entertained at a farewell concert at Neumeyer Hall, Bloomsbury Mansions, prior to their departure for America. It
was a pleasant and wholly harmonious meeting;
and the programme which has appeared in these
columns was, under the direction of Mr. J. C.
Ward, presented in a truly attractive and enjoyable manner.

"It is not necessary that we dilate upon the
merits of each item or the efforts of the perform-
ers; these friends are well known, and sustained their reputation in a way which gratified
all. The Misses Ward, though young in years,
are old friends to entertainments of this kind,
and are each year received with that special expression of favor which has always been accorded
them. Mr. E. Tietkens is a vocalist of a superior order and high culture. He renders his music
with an expression which is more than artistic —
it is inspirational. His mission appears to be to
sing, and the more mankind hear such strains the
better will it be for them. Miss Ada Earee was
apparently a stranger to most of her auditors, but

she won herself steadily into their favor, receiving a perfect ovation in her last song ' The Kerry Dance.' Miss Kathleen Hunt sang very pleasingly; the more she is known the better will she be appreciated. Mr. Ward's performances on the English concertina are always looked forward to with interest, and on the occasion in question they evoked a full measure of applause.

"At the close of the first part, Webster Glynes Esq., took the chair and introduced an interlude of a very pleasing character in the following appropriate speech:

" The first part of to-night's entertainment has gone by, and this is, I think, a fitting opportunity for carrying out the chief object with which we have been assembled, namely to give a few words of farewell to Mr. and Mrs. Richmond, who will leave England at the beginning of next week. This is not the first time Mrs. Richmond has been with us. She was here a few years ago, and enchanted us with her eloquent instructions concerning the principles of Spiritualism, leaving in our hearts a lasting remembrance of her teachings, and earnest desire to hear more of them. Mrs. Richmond is permanently settled in Chicago but our kindred Spiritualist brethren there have taken steps by which she has been enabled to pay a short visit to us. Her stay has not been a prolonged one, and our regret at losing her is deep and sincere, though

tinged with the hope and trust that after her return she may find time to again come amidst us
(hear, hear), when the beautiful and benign
lessons we have heard from her will have taken
deep root, and she will perceive with joy that the
seeds she has planted have brought forth abundantly. In saying farewell to our medium we
must not forget to send our hearty thanks to our
brethren in Chicago for the kindness they have
done us in sparing her to come and say a few
words to us. Let our gratitude to them serve to
unite us; let us join hands together as Spiritualists and think of them as they think of us. Still
more are our hearty thanks due to the band of
spirits who control our gifted medium. Let us
show our gratitude by laying to heart the lessons
they have taught us, and by an earnest endeavor
to fully justify the steps that they have taken.
(Cheers).

"What mighty things have been accomplished
by Spiritualism, and what a privilege is it to be
Spiritualists? Spiritualism has broken the bands
which religion, as it crystallizes into form and
loses its fluent spirit, weaves about us. It en-
larges our vista. Not one life, not one world
only, have we to look forward to. Age after age
will unroll, bringing us, let us hope, nearer to
perfection, but eternity will still be ours to live
and to work. Not until we have lived many
lives can we join the angelic spheres, but we may

hope ever to progress toward perfection. Spiritualism, too, though it cannot reveal to our finite minds a true idea of the Almighty Being, who created the worlds, bids us worship Him with reverence, and encourages us to hope that we may ever progress in our knowledge of Him, ever learning how to worship Him. Spiritualism teaches also our duty to man—to despise no one, to pity and succor the weak, and never to be proud with our attainments. Let us then, as Spiritualists, be hopeful as looking forward to a glorious future; patient, as knowing that pain and suffering are ministering angels; reverent and humble, as feeling how feeble has been the measure of our attainment and how wide is the circle of God's love and wisdom.

"Our hearts are full of sincere feelings of gratitude and devotion, and well aware are we that these are the best gifts love can offer; but friends, although Mr. and Mrs. Richmond will not treasure aught we can bestow so greatly as our love and esteem, several of us have thought it well to hand to them a more substantial proof of our regard, and I hold in my hand a purse which I beg them to accept as a sincere mark of our love and devotion. Let us wish them a hearty farewell and a safe return to our friends in Chicago, and let us part with them in the hope that we shall have them yet again with us."

Mr. Glynes here handed Mrs. Richmond a purse of money.

Our subject, under control, responded to Mr. Glynes' speech, thanking them for their manifestation of appreciation, and bidding them goodbye for the medium in a few well chosen and beautiful words.

W. Tebb, Esq., rose in his place in the stalls, and delivered an eloquent address which left a deep and fitting impression:

"It is now twenty-two years ago since I had the pleasure of hearing Mrs. Richmond for the first time. That was in the city of New York. There was a large assemblage of intelligent people; there were, I remember, doctors of divinity and doctors of medicine; there were cultured lawyers and there were clever querists generally; and, at the close of the address, so interesting, so eloquent, so full of noble thoughts, Mrs. Richmond asked any member of the audience to submit to her questions. If I remember rightly, Dr. Sawyer, an able preacher of the Universalist Church, was present, and he submitted one question after another, each one seemingly more difficult than the one which had preceded it, with the intention of puzzling the lecturer; after that Professor Mapes, or some other scientific man, asked questions bearing upon his own special studies, and he in turn was followed by one or more able lawyers, and well do I remember the applause which greeted the ready and singularly pertinent responses. At that time it seemed to be marvelous; it was something quite inexplicable, and the New York papers were filled with the reports, giving both the questions and the answers. Mrs. Richmond since that time has devoted herself to the service of Spiritualism, and to the advocacy of those views and principles which we most value; but we must all feel that it is no slight sacrifice for Mrs. Richmond and her husband at the beginning of winter to travel a thousand miles by land and three thousand miles by water to deliver a message. Those of you who have attended the meetings here and elsewhere on Sundays, and the lectures and addresses which have been given on Saturdays must have esteemed it a privilege. I have not often been present myself, but from those who have been, I have gathered how full of noble ideas, of high and exalted truths, of incentives to earnest endeavor after a higher and better life they have been. There has been nothing narrow or intolerant; there has been no denunciation against those who disbelieve; no terrors of the law, but a sweet reasonableness after the manner of the Great Teacher. While listening to the music this evening my thoughts passed away to a scene which I saw some months ago. I no longer heard the music, I no longer saw the people, but my thoughts were carried away to the mountains of Bavaria. I was again in a village in that district, and I was a witness of the Ober Ammergau

Passion Play, and of all the beautiful scenes in that marvelous drama, so vividly represented, I think there was nothing more touching, nothing that excited deeper emotion or stronger interest than the parting of Jesus from his friends and disciples. It was a most pathetic scene. But it was that 'touch of nature that makes the whole world kin,' for these feelings of emotion, excited by the near separation of teacher and the taught, are not confined to Ober Ammergau, or to Bethany, but are exhibited in London, and they are present with us to-night. (Applause.) I must not say more, but I am sure that the fitting words of our Chairman are responded to by every heart here present.

"We feel that Mrs. Richmond's teaching has been good for us, and we echo Mr. Glynes' wish that she may be with us again. She carries with her our affection, our best wishes, our benediction."

The usual votes of thanks having been passed, the friends gathered round Mr. and Mrs. Richmond and gave them a hearty shake of the hand, and many expressions of good will and regret at their departure.

The following Monday, although it was very cold and a black-fog was settling over London, there was a large concourse of people at the railway station to see her off. Bidding them good-bye, she, accompanied by a delegation of her

London friends (who were going to see her safely aboard the steamship), took the train for Liverpool. It was a cold wintry day; a snow storm accompanying the train all the way, and the "warming pans" had to be renewed at every stop. When the train reached Liverpool there was a large delegation of Liverpool Spiritualists, headed by John Lamont, to receive her at the station. Mr. Lamont said; just before the train arrived he had seen, clairvoyantly, a majestic Indian nearly seven feet high, who came up to him (Mr. Lamont) and pointed, with an expression of pride, to a medal — a token of appreciation from the United States government of some service performed by him — which was suspended from his (the Indian's neck). He took Mr. Lamont's hand and pointed toward the incoming train. Mr. Lamont knew intuitively that this was one of the medium's accompanying spirits, and that he meant she was there, in the train. Mr. Lamont immediately, after greeting our subject, related the above incident. She recognized the spirit as "Omwah" her healing influence, who in earth life was a Cheyenne "medicine man," and who had been presented by the United States government with a medal bearing the likeness of Abraham Lincoln, and of which he was justly proud. The most interesting part of this incident is, that it was a confirmation of what "Ouina" had told the group of friends, who had accompanied her medium from London, at a little gathering in that city a few nights before, viz.: "That Omwah always accompanied the medium when she was traveling; when she was going by train, he was always astride the 'fire-buffalo.'"

That evening she had a farewell reception at Liverpool; data of which we have not at hand.

The next day Tuesday, November 16th, accompanied to the steamer by a large number of friends from all parts of England, she sailed for America, on the White Star steamship Baltic, due at New York, Thursday, November 25th.

Much to our subject's delight—for she is a good sailor—the voyage was a very tempestuous one, on account of which the steamer's time across the ocean was considerably extended. Our subject was advertised to speak at Masonic Temple, New York, Sunday morning, November 28th. Thursday there were no tidings of the ship. Friday passed, still no tidings; her New York friends began to get anxious. Saturday passed, no tidings; her friends were hopeless; the large audience that would assemble to welcome and hear her would be disappointed. (She all the time was in blissful ignorance of the arrangements that had been made for her). Early Sunday morning the glad tidings came that the 'Baltic was off Sandy Hook.' As soon as the boat arrived at her pier, Cora's friends told her of the arrangements made for her to speak at the Masonic Temple. She immediately sprang (just as she stepped off the ship, without any other preparation) into a waiting carriage, and drove to the place of meeting, arriving there just in time to fulfill the public announcement to the letter.

About the middle of April, 1884, Mrs. Richmond again sailed for England. The Spiritualists of London stood aghast, when they learned that her friends there had engaged Kensington Town Hall, in the aristocratic neighborhood of Kensington, for her to give a course of Sunday evening discourses in, saying, it is altogether too fine a place for Spiritualistic meetings to be successful there. That they were mistaken the subsequent portion of this chapter will show.

On her arrival at Liverpool Mrs. Nosworthy was again the first one to clasp her hands and welcome her to England. After spending the night at Mrs. Nosworthy's, Blundill Sands, near Liverpool, she went immediately to London.

The following is taken from an account of her arrival and reception in London, which was published in the "Medium and Daybreak":

"Mr. and Mrs. Richmond landed in Liverpool on Monday, and having announced the fact by telegraph to a friend in London, a considerable party awaited their arrival at Euston Station, on Tuesday afternoon,

"The travellers looked exceedingly well, and

were in good spirits. Mrs. Richmond is in excellent health, and has been so for some time. Her appearance presents a striking contrast to her condition in September, 1873, when we first made her acquaintance. During her subsequent course of lectures in London, she was sometimes so ill as to be unable to sit up, yet when literally carried to the platform, remarkable discourses were given through her, as reported in this paper at the time. Now physical conditions are altogether of a favorable kind, which is a source of gratification to all friends, and, no doubt, a more effective basis for spiritual work.

"It was, strictly speaking, 'news' to read in last week's paper that Mrs. Richmond was expected in London in a few days, and that in less than a week a reception would be given her at the Town Hall, Kensington. As a kind and well-tried friend of the cause said to us privately at the reception, 'It is the most daring flight the Spiritualists have taken in the propagation of the cause!' Of all places in the metropolitan district, Kensington, The Old Court Suburb, as residents delight to call it, is the most exclusive in its tendencies. Being the site of a Royal Palace, the ancient distinctiveness of the locality has not been obliterated as yet by the huge democracy of the great city, which, in its approaches towards Kensington, appropriates the name to every new region of residences that

springs up around it; so that now we have not
only Kensington, but a vast variety of Kensing-
tons, with their distinctive prefix or affix. The
official centre of all this vast area is Kensington
Town Hall, situated in the High Street, not far
from the Palace, and it is one of those elegant
civic mansions that have sprung up of late years
in London and elsewhere ; each new erection
being destined, apparently, to outstrip all its
predecessors.

"On this new ground, with short notice, and
without any apparent organic machinery, it would
be a source of anxiety to see whether there could
be a response worthy of the occasion. The
result was, indeed, more than could be expected.
There is a series of halls at Kensington, and the
reception took place in the large room, a beautiful apartment, capable of seating four hundred
or five hundred persons. It was well filled by as
fine a representative selection of London Spiritualists as has been seen for a long time. How
they all got to know it is a mystery, but it is evident that Mrs. Richmond holds out attractions
that secure a successful gathering with the least
possible chance of success attending it.

"Being held on the eve of publication, our
representative could not leave his duties at the
office till the proceedings were more than half
over. The large and influential gathering was
the first gratifying surprise. There were to be

seen all the well-known faces, and, in addition,
many who appeared to be strangers to such
scenes. The friends of Mrs. Richmond, visible
and invisible, had been at work. There was a
spirit of harmony and unity, which all seemed to
perceive and enjoy. M. A. (Oxon), so well-
known and justly respected in the movement
throughout the world, most appropriately filled
the chair. We much regret that we missed hearing his opening speech, as also the inspirational
address of Mrs. Richmond. The foremost
orators of the movement took part in an appropriate manner, and all they said was received
with a running fire of applause from the audience,
who were disposed to cheer everything.

"We heard some of the remarks of Mr. J. J.
Morse, who in his congratulations suggested that
this would not be the last visit of Mr. and Mrs.
Richmond to London. He earnestly urged the
meeting to work as one man for the success of
the series of discourses to be delivered in that hall
by Mrs. Richmond as had been announced.

"Mr. Colville's speech was singularly felicitous
in that his inspirers claimed the lady to whose
honor that meeting was held, as the cause through
which their instrument had been developed as a
medium and called into the field of Spiritual
work. A mighty work indeed has been added to
what Mrs. Richmond has herself achieved, in the
calling of this other powerful speaker into the field.

"But why need we repeat words of speakers which the heart of every one present or absent will be able to supply in their own fashion. It is not the mere letter of the remarks, but the spirit of the occasion, that chiefly lingers on the mind after the scenes have passed away from view.

" 'Ouina's' pretty voice was heard through her medium soliciting a subject for an inspirational poem. Several were proposed from the audience, and 'Welcome' gained the vote. On this most suitable of themes, Mrs. Richmond, under control, delivered a stately poem, which was received with great enthusiasm."

" M. A. (Oxon's) "—Rev. Stainton Moses— address of welcome and Mrs. Richmond's response were published in "Light," from which we take the first paragraph of " M. A. (Oxon's) " speech:

"LADIES AND GENTLEMEN:—I think I shall best interpret your wishes if, in speaking from the chair, I offer a very cordial welcome to Mrs. Richmond, who has come so far from across the ocean to offer us the instruction and enlightenment she is enabled to afford. To many of us she has come as an old friend. It is not the first time I have had the honor of presiding at her receptions, and she will receive the welcome that an old friend deserves. And again, she comes, not merely as a friend who has been with us

before, but as a medium, a vehicle of instruction
— spiritual instruction — that is to us always
welcome, and we know that the welcome we
afford to her in that capacity will be infinitely
more prized and valued than any other welcome."

The musical programme was as follows: Vocal-
ists: Miss Katherine Poyntz, Mr. Ernest A. Tietkens, Mr. John C. Ward.   Pianoforte: Miss Amy
Chidley. Concertinas: Mr. John C. Ward (treble),
Mr. E. Chidley, Jun. (treble and bass), Miss Amy
Chidley (baritone), Mr. C. F. Compton (baritone
and bass).   Programme of music: Overture,
pianoforte and concertinas, "Mirella" (Gounod);
song, "The Streamlet" (Killiwoda), Mr. John
C. Ward; song, "Truant Love" (Cowen), Miss
Katherine Poyntz; song, "The Last Watch"
(Pinsuti), Mr. Ernest A. Tietkens; quartettes,
concertinas, (*a*) Adagio in B flat (Haydn), (*b*)
Minuet and trio (Boccherini); quartette, con-
certinas (Haydn); song, "Sunshine and Rain"
(Blumenthal), Mr. John C. Ward; aria, "Gurdi-
cesti" (Lotti), Miss Katherine Poyntz; song,
"Come into the garden, Maud" (Balfe), Mr.
Ernest A. Tietkens; overture, pianoforte, and
concertinas (Gurlitt).   Conductor, Mr. John C.
Ward.

In conclusion of its account of the reception
the "Medium and Daybreak" says:

"Now that the reception has been such a
marked success, it is to be hoped that the Sunday

services, to commence at the same place on May
11, will be even more popular. There is no district in or around London in which reside more
Spiritualists than that of which Kensington Town
Hall is the center. It is eminently residential in
its character, and that is of the highest class. It
is really the London West End. Our West
London friends have been severely exercised
over the matter of local Sunday services. Now
their loftiest ambition ought to be satisfied in
that respect, and we hope they will use every
effort to crowd the spacious hall every Sunday
evening, while Mrs. Richmond can make it convenient to minister therein."

The public work, continuing at Kensington
Town Hall to June 22d, was an unqualified success. We would like to make extracts in regard
to the same from the public press, but we are
reminded that this chapter is being too much
extended. However all those discourses were
reported verbatim and published in the "Medium
and Daybreak" and "Light." Besides the especial work at Kensington, there were a number of
public discourses given at various halls in the
metropolis. She was also the recipient of
numerous private receptions, at some of which
W. J. Colville (who was then in London) was
present and participated in the exercises. She
also gave instructions on "The Soul" to a private
class while there. The following few lines are

extracted from an account of the last Sunday evening meeting at Kensington in the "Medium and Daybreak":

"At the close of Mrs. Richmond's discourse on Sunday evening, in the Town Hall, Kensington, the chairman made a few feeling remarks about that occasion being the last one, for the present, when a London audience would have the opportunity of listening to the guides of Mrs. Richmond; but he made no doubt if they by their lives gave evidence that the seed had taken root, and brought forth fruit, the guides would again bring Mrs. Richmond to minister in London. The audience — which crowded the room in every part — responded to this sentiment fully. Mrs. Richmond's controls answered this expression of appreciation and affection, by a few fevent remarks."

After a farewell reception, June 23d, similar to the preceding one recorded in her English work, she left London for Nottingham, where she has a large circle of friends. There she spent two weeks, giving a series of public discourses, and ministering in private ways. From Nottingham she made a tour of the cities in the north of England, including Birmingham, Sheffield, Halifax, Sowerby Bridge, Manchester and Liverpool, speaking once or more in each of the places she visited. It being necessary for her to be with her congregation at Chicago in Septem-

ber she could remain in England no longer. So
about the middle of August many of her friends
from different parts of England gathered at Liverpool to again say good-bye, and see her sail on
the steamship "Alaska" for America, and in
September she was again ministering to her congregation at Chicago.

The next spring, the first day of May, 1885,
she again left Chicago for England. Her mission being to complete the work so successfully
began at the Kensington Town Hall, Kensington, London.

As before, her old time friend Mrs. Nosworthy,
though much impaired in health, (she has since
departed to the spirit side of life), was the first
one to greet her as she stepped from the deck of
the "City of Rome."

Her work there this time was almost a repetition of the year before. She immediately went
to London, where she had a public reception.
She commenced a series of Sunday evening meetings at Kensington Town Hall, May 17th, which
were continued for eight Sundays. When she
again went North for a brief tour of the provinces. During this visit to London she also gave
a series of private discourses at the "Lincoln
Inn Fields Hotel," Lincoln Inn Fields, in the
heart of London. She also gave public discourses
in various parts of the city, besides attending
numerous private receptions. The work at Ken-

sington having proven so successful, her London friends prevailed upon her guides to promise to bring her back to London and give them another series of discourses before returning to America. Her tour of the provinces embraced Newcastle-on-Tyne, North Shields, and most of the principle cities of Lancashire and Yorkshire. Our space will not permit our mentioning incidents, connected with each place visited, that bring pleasant recollections to our subject. But two of her visits on this trip, one of one week with Mrs. Ford at Adel Grange, Leeds, where she gave five or six public discourses, and one at Holly Mount House, Nottingham, of two weeks, are fruitful of many pleasant memories.

The latter part of September she is back in London again, where she finishes her public work in England with a course of four Sunday. evening discourses, at the Assembly Rooms, Kensington, the Town Hall being otherwise engaged. As before, her last successful month in London, was fully occupied in public and private ministrations. Her last public discourse in England was delivered at the Assembly Rooms, Kensington, Sunday evening, Oct. 18th, 1885. The hall was crowded and it was a perfect ovation. Had her English friends then known that it would be so long before they would see her again, now nine years, it is doubtful that they would have consented to let her go. Within ten years

she had been there four times, and they had
grown to expect her every few years.   It may be
that her work in England is finished.   However
in contemplating what she has accomplished
there; the seed sown, and the harvest already
wrought in individual lives, one is amazed at its
vastness.   Few will ever realize what it has been
to England.   On the twentieth of October many
of her friends gathered at Liverpool to say good
bye as she sailed away.   For the last time ?

CHAPTER XI.

CALIFORNIA WORK.

UPON the completion of her English labors,
in 1875, she returned to America to go to
California, to enter upon an important engagement in the city of San Francisco. She paused,
however, to make a brief visit to friends in New
York, took a flying trip to Boston and to Hopedale, to see her venerable friends, Adin and Mrs.
Ballou, stopped at her native home, Cuba, N.
Y., and other places along the route where friends
and relatives came thronging to welcome her
home. In nearly all of these places there were
lectures and receptions. She spoke one month
(November) in Chicago in the church corner of
Washington and Green streets, special arrangements for which were made by a committee of
gentlemen. These discourses attracted a great
of notice from the secular press. "The Chicago
Times" had them reported verbatim and published
them entire. The meetings were such an unqualified success that the committee engaged her
to return the following Spring and speak for their
society for an indefinite time. During that

month she found time to make an all too hurried visit to Lake Mills, Wisconsin, the scene of her earliest spiritual work as a healer and teacher.

Few of the circle of friends who gathered around our subject at that early date remained; a quarter of a century had passed, and Time and Change with relentless hands had borne away most of those whom she knew in her childhood days.

She received many invitations to speak on the way, but accepted only such as would be most convenient, and enable her to visit an only brother, E. T. Scott, (whose letter appears in the first chapter, and who now resides in Hume, N. Y.) who lived in Missouri. One invitation accepted was from the Mercantile Library Association of Denver, and the meetings there were a great success. Christmas found her still on her way, but early in January, 1876, we find her in San Francisco.

Great preparation had been made to receive her, and during her stay she was entertained at the Palace Hotel, while the meetings were attended by large and most intelligent audiences in this truly cosmopolitan city.

Chief among those who arranged for this course of lectures, and one which followed (in March we think of the same season), was the venerable R. A. Robinson, a staunch and devoted Spiritualist, and Mr. George Hinde (who with his family had preceded our subject to the Pacific Coast where they took up their residence).

This was her first visit to the Golden Gate, where her teachings fell into soil ready to receive them. They quickly took root, sent up green shoots that promised a rich harvest when the time of reaping should come, at the hands of those reapers who would then be garnering the grain in the fields of labor seeded by her guides. This visit of 1875 was followed by two other engagements in California, chiefly in San Francisco.

The winter of 1882–83 was unusually severe, and our subject contracted a hard cold, which settled upon her lungs, so her guides thought it advisable for her to seek a more genial climate. Consequently about the 1st of February, 1883, when the mercury was ranging twenty degrees below zero at Chicago, she took a southern route for California. Mr. C. M. Plumb, of San Francisco, being apprised of her coming, had made arrangements for her to give a series of public discourses there.

It seems to be a part of Mrs. Richmond's mission (unconsciously) to dedicate localities and buildings to Spiritualistic work. Mr. Plumb had engaged Metropolitan Temple, as fine an auditorium as there was in San Francisco at that time. Since her services there, continuing for eight months, it has been used constantly for Spiritualistic meetings. Arrangements were first made for her to minister there for two months; but at the expiration of that time there was such an irresistible demand for the work to continue, that further arrangements were made for six months longer. The interest in the meetings was unabated. We have never known continuous Spiritual meetings to be so well sustained in attendance and financially as were those meetings at the Metropolitan Temple, San Francisco. At the conclusion of the extended time, after the final discourse, the guides bade the vast audience good-bye. It was as though a bomb had burst in their midst; for an instant there was a deep hush. Then a gentleman sprang to his feet, saying: "It cannot be! it cannot be! Why, we haven't any of us supposed but that these meetings would go right on; we are none of us prepared to have you go. Have be been remiss in anything? Have we lacked appreciation? If so, we will strive to be more appreciative. Have we been remiss financially? If so, we will double our subscriptions. Anything, but you must not go." Another gentleman, an old man, said: "I am wholly unprepared for this; can you not stay with us longer? If you go I shall feel that the light has gone out from my life forever." And many others spoke in similar strains, and most every member of the audience was in tears. It was one of the most sorrowful occasions the writer ever participated in. One present said:

"This must be something like the parting of the disciples with Jesus." The guides said their work there for the present was finished; being finished (no outward consideration could make it otherwise) they must go.

The letters from our California correspondents will finish the story.

An able account of her·work in the year 1883, from the pen of the gifted author, Mr. C. M. Plumb, is at hand, which we here give in full as the best expression possible relative to that important epoch, and a subjoined account from Mrs. John A. Wilson:

"Mr. H. D. Barrett:

"Dear Sir:—The request to contribute some personal reminiscences of Mrs. Richmond's public career, reaches me when, unfortunately, the prostration from severe illness seems to preclude a compliance. But as silence may seem to imply indifference, I cannot withhold an attempt, however feeble, to supply what should have been in clear and perfect lines.

" Approaching the close of this earthly experience, I feel most keenly the joy of having apprehended the truths which found expression through our most gifted and beloved sister. I am well aware that all forms of belief afford to the believer the gratifying assurance that 'Here is the Truth.' Not all, however, have this crowning excellence, that not one cherished faith of the world is excluded, and all are supplemented. That no claim of obligation to accept is enforced, and no penalty urged against denial. If the teachings of Mrs. Richmond's Spiritual guides are indeed true, there are abundant reasons why all do not perceive them at the same time. Hence differences of opinion afford no ground for disquietude, and so-called charity for such differences is no virtue, but a profound obligation.

"Truth is its own vindicator, in its own good time, and all grades of belief, like all phases of human action, are but tokens of difference in age or experience; the child is not at fault for immaturity, nor is there merit in grey hairs. Until my vision was opened to perceive these spiritual truths, I had no knowledge of the real meaning of charity, of the true cheerfulness of hope, the perfect assurance of destiny and design. Whatever in the scheme of things once appeared inconsistent, now seems but as a broken or fragmentary view—accident, but the distortion incident to imperfect observation of what is symmetrical and complete.

"The true measure of any Spiritual movement is not the number it apparently reaches, but the depth of the impression made, the height to which those, coming within its reach, are lifted, and the permanency of the influence exerted.

"Judged by these standards, the special visit

of Mrs. Richmond to San Francisco in 1883, and
again in 1884—as indeed her whole public career
—was most memorable.   It certainly proved the
dawn of a new era to some of the many who
were so fortunate as to come within the ministrations of her guides.

"The occasion was in many ways opportune.
The people of this distant, yet closely allied city,
are exceptionally free, unrestrained by either
social or traditional timidities from giving heed
to new propositions.   Soil wherein Thos. Starr
King successfully labored, and where the memory
of his life was so sacredly cherished, is not un-
fitted to support a new Spiritual growth.   The
preliminary work had been faithfully done, and
the vacancy of Metropolitan Temple opened a
large and attractive auditorium to her occupancy.

"More than curiosity, genuine interest attracted the crowds which filled the temple, and
later bespoke the thoughtful attendance upon the
private classes for the lessons upon the Soul in
Human Embodiments.   More than satisfaction
marked the feeling in many minds at the close.

"Here, as elsewhere, Mrs. Richmond's audiences embraced three classes.   First, and perhaps most numerous, those who were charmed
by the faultless diction, and who listened satisfied, scarcely either seeking or finding any special
good for Spiritual longings as yet unawakened.
A second number were gratified recipients of an

inspired message full of consolation and hope. Separate and distinct from these were a smaller number, drawn by fine but powerful lines of Spiritual attraction, to whom the word they heard with the outer ear, possessed an 'inner sense.' To these the Spiritual heavens seemed opened. At times they felt the presence of some mighty, far-advanced Spiritual teacher, and the very air vibrated with the tense, sympathetic, uplifting power of his word. Few words of appreciation were spoken; but the deep drawn breath, the light in the eye, the peace within, told the story of the meeting of kindred, and the recognition of truth.

"The public and private ministrations in San Francisco and vicinity were marked by these qualities, so far at least as some of the auditors were concerned. It would not be easy, even were it necessary, to put into words the value to these souls of the sacred teachings there received. Earth's problems seemed no longer vague or difficult; earth's life-lines ceased to be dark and painful; the words 'penalty' and 'punishment' disappeared, and instead, they read—'appointment,' 'opportunity.' Content and satisfaction beamed from out tear-dimmed eyes, and glorified pain-racked frames! There is no language to measure the value of a Spiritual truth to one prepared to receive it.   C. M. PLUMB.

San Francisco, Cal., June 7, 1894."

One writer in California says: "My mind is filled with vague pictures of so much that might and should be said, not only touching the outward facts of Mrs. Richmond's unrivalled career yet more relating to the sublime truths which have found expression through her inspired lips. If my brain and hand could convey the half of what is in my heart respecting that transcendant system of Spiritual truths, for which we are indebted to Mrs. Richmond and her guides, material for a whole volume would be supplied. All other teachings fade into insignificance and seem like shadowy questionings beside these luminous and satisfying assurances."

This chapter would be incomplete were we to omit a letter from one who feels that Mrs. Richmond has been to her more than a friend, pastor or teacher, since her advent into this present expression of her soul life. This friend is a resident of California, and her thoughts will be of interest at this point to all who may peruse these pages:

"MR. H. D. BARRETT,

"DEAR SIR AND BROTHER:—I was but a small lass of four years when I was first 'found' by Mrs. Richmond. Seeing me in her audience, she inquired: 'Who is that little golden haired girl?' And recognizing a soul kinship, she made the acquaintance of my people. I have been much with Mrs. Richmond since; one year continuously, when she was more than a mother to me, and have had many opportunities of seeing the perfect and beauteous womanhood, of which she is a model, as well as the results of the grand teachings which have come into the world through her lovely and ever willing instrumentality.

"I will relate some personal reminiscences of interest, knowing them to be types of thousands all over the land, and knowing that others will tell of the forty years of constant labor day and night, two lectures each Sunday with receptions, calls, weddings, funerals, and numerous other things each week, which would be more than ten women of ordinary strength ought to do, but which Mrs. Richmond, sustained and strengthened by the power of the angel band controlling her, seems to do with perfect ease. To show the wonders of this power, I remember when I was still a little child, Mrs. Richmond had a very severe illness at our house in New York city, being in bed for weeks, and much of the time too weak to feed herself. While in this state she lectured frequently, besides Sundays, I believe, each week, at Jersey City or Brooklyn. When the hour arrived that she should be put in readiness for the journey, Ouina would take control and take her up; my mother, her only nurse and attendant, would dress her; together they would go by carriage to the hall; she would stand before the audience and deliver a lecture of the usual length. She would then be taken to the carriage and home again, the control never leaving her until she was lain safely in her bed, where she would remain as helpless almost as an infant, until the next lecture time arrived.

"Is it any wonder that I grew up with the firm conviction that nothing is impossible with the guides? When I was in my eighth year, I was sick with the chills and fever. After having doctored and dosed for two successive summers, I became so weak I could not hold a small orange in my hand. Here Dr. Rush, through Mrs. Richmond took charge of me, all medicines were stopped, a careful diet prescribed, and I was put to sleep every day just before the usual time for the chills to come on. I never had another chill, began steadily to improve and have never had an illness since. Is it at all surprising that I have little faith in Materia Medica, but believe implicity in the great knowledge and healing power of the Spirit?

"Early in the year 1883, Mr. and Mrs. Richmond were called to San Francisco upon a six months' ministration. The Metropolitan Temple was hired for the Sunday discourses, it being one of the finest churches in the city at that time; there were two discourses each Sunday. The immense building, holding three thousand people, was generously filled for almost every discourse, the evening one being particularly well attended, and the meetings were a great success, both financially and spiritually.

"Many friends of Mrs. Richmond, both old and new(for she had been in California before), rallied around her, and there was scarcely an afternoon or evening in the week when she was not engaged, receiving calls, going to receptions, attending dinners, luncheons, etc. There was also a large class formed for instructions on the Soul, and there were the Wednesday and Saturday evening 'hour of prayer' meetings, which most of those permitted to enter them still observe. When the six months had expired, all were desirous of engaging Mrs. Richmond for a protracted stay, but owing to the urgent calls from Chicago, the guides could consent to only two months' longer stay, making eight months in all, at the end of which time a generous purse of something near three hundred dollars was most willingly subscribed by her many admirers and friends, and presented at a special farewell reception, given in the parlors of the Temple.

"The guides, in their usual beautiful language, and as only the guides can, thanked the people in behalf of their medium, and her noble companion, and for themselves, after which the throng, which filled the parlors (really a fair sized hall) bade Mr. and Mrs. Richmond a reluctant farewell and a hearty God-speed.

"Many and joyous are the effects of the

'Teachings on the Soul.' I knew two young girls, both of most melancholy dispositions; neither could see anything to live for; the world was filled with care and sorrow; want, injustice and wrong were everywhere; what was the use of it all, and why did God allow such things to exist? I was with these girls when they sat under the direct instructions of Mrs. Richmond's guides, and heard the beautiful 'Teachings on the Soul.' What a change came to both! The world seemed like a new and joyous place, for was there not an explanation for every wrong and injustice, a reason and a good purpose for every sorrow and affliction, and for each and every soul, no matter how seemingly lost in material darkness, God's great care and love eternally brooding above and about, lighting the way to final peace, joy and love. For the great sorrows of life there is help in these teachings; for every affliction there is comfort; but more than these (for in the great trials of life each soul is given added strength to bear the added burden) there is the light of spirit which lifts us above the thousand little worries and frictions of daily living, which so tries the souls of mortals on earth. More than *all* there is ever present before each that high standard of right and true living, which, if held to, even to the best of our ability, brings us where we shall not be 'weighed in the balance and be found wanting.'

"To illustrate: I knew a follower of Mrs. Richmond's teachings, who was a victim of legal thieves, who tried to steal a large property by process of law. Being himself interested, he was placed in charge of the case by the owners. The thieves took the property by force and held it with guns. 'They ought to be shot down, like the dogs they are!' etc., etc., came from all sides. But the follower of the Teachings said: 'No; all the property in the world is not worth the sacrifice of one human life.' 'Don't you think,' said one young man, 'that if that was all you had in the world, and the bread and butter for your wife and children depended upon it, that you would forcibly wrest it from them?' The reply was, 'No; I would not.' 'Well,' said the young man, 'I cannot understand that. When a man takes your living, he takes your life; and it seems to me *right*, and a man's *duty*, to defend his life and property against everything.' One year later this young man had, through his own mediumship, received undeniable evidences of spirit presence and return, and went to his friend for help and explanation. He was after a time given Mrs. Richmond's book on the Soul, the principles of which he readily accepted. Not long after, when a discussion arose in his presence about one man shooting another for interfering with his property, this same young man remarked: 'Well, I would rather be shot than kill another!'

I heard a gentleman in San Francisco tell Mrs. Richmond, when bidding her good-bye, that he held her second only to Christ, but I believe she is second to none. I would not wish to detract in the least from the veneration in which Christ is held; but do not the divine truths given through Mrs. Richmond include all of Christ's teachings and much more beside? Is not this the next step in the progress of the world? It most certainly is. Not only is she ordained truly of God, but her life is a living embodiment of the truths which are spoken through her lips. So pervaded is she by this light that her very presence is an inspiration to a better and a nobler living, and the very air about her seems filled with the loving ministrations of angels. May the all-wise and loving Father grant as many years yet of earth life in which we may be led and strengthened here by this, His angel messenger of light.

"I am fraternally yours,

"MRS. JOHN A. WILSON."

In the fall of 1884, she again visited San Francisco to give a course of four Sunday discourses at Irving Hall, perform a wedding service, an ordination service, and to minister privately to those who needed her.

We have read with much feeling many personal letters to our subject from friends in California, expressing the same high appreciation of her and her work during her four visits to that

city. On one occasion a young lady and gentleman, who had received their first Spiritual light
through her inspired teachings, sent for her to
come especially from Chicago to San Francisco
(or Oakland) to perform the ceremony of marriage. From this devoted couple words of sincerest affection come to their beloved "Water
Lily," at frequent intervals in her Chicago home.
These letters should be read to be appreciated,
and we regret our inability to give them all a
place in this volume. Mrs. John A. Wilson
whose account of our medium's work immediately precedes this is the lady referred to.

Our good brother Plumb has referred to her
engagement in Metropolitan Temple. This was
the place where she labored most successfully
during this extended visit to San Francisco. The
subjects upon which the guides discoursed covered the same wide range of thought that had
been their wont to express in Europe and in the
Eastern States. They there saw an additional
phase presented by the liberal thinkers of California. The atmosphere of that state seems to
be particularly adapted to the highest expression of inspirational thought, and the people
were seemingly given to transcendental and
Spiritual philosophy. Therefore, many of the
themes suggested by her listeners were upon
topics of this nature. Her audiences numbered
the best elements in San Francisco society, the

ripest scholars and profoundest thinkers in all the
schools of that section.   Many of the Unitarian
Church members, and even clergymen, were in
attendance upon her classes which here began
to be an important feature of her work in America.   The thoughts of Dr. Rush, upon the subject of psychopathy became known to the people
and were eagerly listened to by those seeking instruction through our subject.   The soul teachings by the higher guides created a profound
sensation in the minds of her pupils, and led
them to a clear perception of the Spiritual truths
they were seeking to convey to the world.   The
people hailed with delight these classes and
filled her parlors on the various evenings of each
week that she devoted to them.

The work of our subject in California marks a
new era of thought in her American labors,
and her visits to the Pacific Coast will ever be
remembered by the people who listened to her
on those occasions with feelings of gratitude and
pleasure.   They were not only instructed but
comforted, and many thereby enabled to recon-
cile their unhappy lots in life with a resignation
of spirit that showed them that life has bright
spots, even among the shadows, and that the
humblest duty when discharged conscientiously
could be made a stepping-stone to Spiritual unfoldment, if that duty were ever so menial in its
outward form of expression.   It takes a philos-

opher to say with W. C. Gannett, "Blessed be Drudgery," and no one but a Spiritual philosopher can utter that sentiment in sincerity and truth, and practically apply the same by a life of hopeful service to those dependent upon them. This happy result is attained, or is attainable, through a thorough comprehension of the uplifting teachings through the organism of our subject upon the soul.

The last visit of our subject to the Pacific Coast was in the last of November and during December, 1884. From the longing friends waiting there the letters, replete with affection, continually ask, "When may we look upon your face again and hear those blessed teachings?"

CHAPTER XII.

WE now come to the Chicago pastorate of our subject that has extended over a period of nineteen years, or a trifle less than half of her entire public work. Our readers will see, from the subjoined history, from the graceful pens of several of her most intimate friends in Chicago, that her work in that city has been measureless in its effects upon her hearers. She has been the friend, teacher, and counsellor of parents and children alike, and has been the means of giving them the bread of heaven to sustain them in all their material undertakings, as well as to open up the grand Spiritual vistas of the soul world to their mortal sight.

As we have seen in the chapter preceding this, in the autumn of 1875 on her way from England to California, she remained one month in Chicago, to give a course of Sunday discourses; this was the beginning of her long pastorate in that city, for it was then that arrangements were made for her to return the following Spring and resume her work there the first of April, which led to her settlement as pastor of the First Society of Spiritualists of that city, which pastorate has remained unbroken to the present time.

We have already given an account of her labors in that city in the time of the war, when Stephen A. Douglas, and other gifted statesmen, spoke to the people through her organism on the issues of the war. This was in reality, the commencement of her work in that place, for the impression made at that time was indelibly stamped upon the minds of the substantial Spiritualists of Chicago, who were desirous of continuing their investigations first hand, in the psychic field that had been presented to their view by the advanced ideas of the guides of our subject. This fact clearly proves that the thoughts presented by them are enduring, and exert an influence that is felt for years after their words fall into the minds of those who listen to them. Thought is said to be ephemeral and transitory, and lost to the world as soon as uttered. We can see that the thoughts of the guides, based upon Spiritual truths, are as enduring as eternity. Therefore, Spiritual thoughts or truths refute the old time arguments, and prove that thought is far more real than any material substance. Anything that gives instruction to the spirit always emanates from some higher power, hence to aid in the unfoldment, in expressions of human souls, is the highest work any mortal can be called upon to

perform.   Our subject's teachings had penetrated
so deeply into the minds of her Chicago friends
as to lead them to a clearer perception of this
truth in regard to the power of thought.   They
naturally wished to go forward, hence, with the
assistance of the guides, constrained her to remain with them for a time.

Here we feel impelled to state a fact most
palpable in connection with this call to Chicago.
The western metropolis represented the center
of thought of the mighty West, in the social
and business worlds.   People were engaged in
various occupations in a material sense, and the
bustling activity of Western life caused them to
forget the Spiritual side of their natures.   To
counteract the material tendencies of the times,
a strong Spiritual power was needed there, and
an instrument, through whom it could manifest
itself readily, had to be selected for that purpose.
The choice of the higher powers in spirit life fell
upon our subject.   She obeyed the call, and has
proved herself ever to be a veritable pillar of
strength in the defense of pure Spiritual principles.   When assailed by materialism on the one
side and pseudo-Spiritualism on the other, her
voice has rung out in clarion tones, the call to
halt, to those forces that were battling against
the right.   When Skeptics, Agnostics and Ethical Culturists have attempted to disprove the
facts underlying Spiritual phenomena and phi-

losophy, she has led them, by the persuasive
power of eloquence and clearest logic, to the ac-
ceptation of the truth.   When people were for-
getful of their higher Spiritual selves in a mad
scramble for wealth, she has gently admonished
them that they were not living for time, but for
eternity, and advised them to seek the upward
path.   When political tyranny trampled upon
principles of liberty, she has remonstrated, in
firm tones, and appealed to the people to deal
justly by their fellows.

In such a city as Chicago, the metropolis of the
Western world, such a teacher was needed as
had the power to do these things under the leadership of the advanced teachers in the higher
life.   Therefore, Chicago became the center
upon which was focussed the thoughts of these
leaders in spirit life, so that a healing influence
could radiate therefrom to bless the nations of
the earth with its power.   It has done so, and
the effect of the Chicago work can never be fully
estimated or appreciated.   When accounts are
settled in the higher realms, then can the potency
of these teachings in this bustling, throbbing,
sorrowing, yet majestic city of the West, be made
known.

The story of the Chicago pastorate of our subject is full of interest to us all.   It is best known
to the Chicago Spiritualists, hence it belongs to
them to write its history.   We, therefore, lay

aside our pen to make room for the sketches that
have been written by her impartial friends and
co-workers in the Society to which she has so
long ministered.

The following is from the pen of one who was
president of that society for eighteen years, Dr.
Lewis Bushnell, whose too brief, yet loving and
sincere tribute will be read with great interest as
epitomizing the results of her work in Chicago:

"H. D. BARRETT, ESQ.

"DEAR SIR AND BROTHER:—Your letter of
September 19th came duly to hand and got
pushed aside, and I forgot all about it until it
again came to light yesterday. I beg pardon for
the neglect. You ask my impression of Mrs.
Richmond as a platform worker. It is my opinion that the guides through her have done more
to instruct Spiritualists into a higher line of thought
and life than any other platform worker that I
know, and those who have known most of her
work and its effects, are those who prize her
work the highest.

"I think she has given fully 1,400 Sunday
discourses, besides giving a great number of
lectures before classes and other audiences, in
this city. She has visited England three times,
and San Francisco two or three times, New
York, Boston, Washington and other cities,
besides camp meetings, etc., many times during the eighteen years she has been the pastor

of the First Society of Spiritualists in this city; and all of those visits have been by special request, and previous engagements.

"During her labors with us, I have never known her to be one minute behind time. I had almost forgotten to say that for the last twelve or fourteen years she has attended the Thursday evening meetings of the 'Ladies' Union,' formerly, and the 'Band of Harmony' (during several years past), almost as regularly as the Sunday services, while living in this city, and since removing to Rogers Park (now included in this city). In addition to the before mentioned work, she has attended (for the purpose of officiating) many funerals and weddings and was always invited and generally attended all social gatherings of our people, such as birthday parties and wedding anniversaries, etc., etc.   "Very truly yours,

"L. BUSHNELL."

Upon her return to her society, after having been absent any length of time on her visits to other places—referred to in Dr. Bushnell's letter —she was always received with open arms and rejoicing; the members of the Society usually arranging a public reception, frequently very pleasantly surprising her. As an illustration of the receptions she receives from her Society, we will here give an account of one of many similar occasions:

On the first day of January, 1880, she left Chicago for a two months' ministration at Boston—speaking in Parker Memorial Hall to crowded houses. Upon her return to Chicago, the first of March, she and her companion were met upon the arrival of the train at the depot, by W. W. Chandler, a devoted member of the Society, who said to our subject that he had taken the liberty of getting a carriage and coming to meet them, and, if they had no objection, he would ride home with them. After they were seated in the carriage, he said the trustees of the Society were having a business meeting at the church, and were anxious to confer with the guides, and, if the medium was not too tired, they would drive around that way and let the trustees have the benefit of the guides' wisdom. Without the faintest idea in the minds of our subject and her companion that they were to see aught but the trustees of the Society, they were driven to the door of the vestry, where they expected to meet the trustees. The only light to be seen about the building was in the vestry.

They entered; there was not a sound, and no one present. Mr. Chandler surmised, "that they must have got through and gone home." Just then the voice of Dr. Bushnell was heard at the top of the flight of stairs, leading to the chancel, saying: "The trustees are up here." So up the stairs they went, thinking "what an idea for the trustees to go up-stairs." The moment our subject stepped into the chancel the lights were turned on, the massive organ pealed forth, "Home, Sweet Home," and, what a sight!—the auditorium was full of people. There were all the familiar and beloved faces of her congregation. If it had not been for the sustaining power of her guides she would have fainted, as it was she staggered at the sight. There was a storm of applause, and the travelers took the seats in front that had been reserved for them.

Then President Bushnell called upon Mr. Frederick F. Cook, who delivered the following address of welcome:

"MR. AND MRS. RICHMOND:

"It is the desire of the friends here assembled that I should, in their behalf, express to you the pleasure we all feel in having you once again among us.

"I accept it as a rare privilege to do this. You need but look on the happy, radiant faces that surround you, to feel assured that this welcome comes from the heart, and that words but faintly express what is conveyed to you in subtler manner.

"OUR WELL-BELOVED MEDIUM: We parted with you reluctantly two months ago, that others might benefit. We should probably have played a selfish part and peremptorily bid you stay, could we have known without this experience

how very much we should miss you, and how impossible it is to fill your place in our affections
and esteem. Though we thought we knew your
worth before, I am certain now we were mistaken. It was necessary that you should stand
in distant perspective, in order to estimate the
magnitude of your spiritual influence, and realize
how much you are to us.

"The tie that binds us is not of summer roses,
born to blight under the first touch of frost. It
is of hardier growth. It was born of trials, and
its quality is as enduring as that eternity which
you so beautifully typify.

"As we look over the years you have been permitted to minister to us, we note great changes,
and both inward and outward growth. The benefits bestowed have been inestimable, but may
we not indulge the pleasing thought that we have
also been of help to you?

"We remember you four years ago, an invalid,
with barely strength enough to mount the platform. We see you to-day a picture of blooming
health.

"If you have strengthened us from the Spiritual side, may we not cherish the sentiment that
our good will, the more than kindly feelings we
entertain for you, have contributed somewhat to
strengthen you from the earthly side?

"While you have advanced year by year in the
refinements of mediumship, you have as steadily

grown into our affections and esteem, and we hold you to-day the most precious gift the spirit world has yet bestowed on mortals. [Applause.] It is no more than due that I should say this on behalf of your people. It is no more than due that the world should be told in what estimation those who know you best, both as medium and woman, hold you.

"Your relations to us during the past four years have been virtually those of pastor. To fill this place successfully toward a congregation so heterogeneous as any Spiritualistic community at this stage necessarily must be, calls for consummate tact and a patience and forbearance that could only be the fruit of a native kindliness of heart. To say that you have succeeded in filling this office with credit to yourself and profit to us, is a meed of praise that but half expresses your dessert.

"We have gathered here with hearts full of thanksgiving that you are returned to us. It was not enough that words should greet you, that eyes should speak to you, as only the eyes of loving friends can speak, but even sympathetic nature has been pressed into service to assist in the expression of good will, and as none is more susceptible than yourself to the silent language of flowers, let these tributes lend their beauty and fragrance to the chorus of heart and tongue and eye, in bidding you welcome.

"But I must not forget that while we extend our greeting to the visible, there is also an invisible expression of the spirit world that claims a word of recognition.

"If there is a goodly company present in the body, I doubt not that a vaster invisible audience is in sympathy above and around us, for what can more strongly bind the spirit world to us than a just and tender appreciation of their chosen instruments !

"With you, Mrs. Richmond, are intimately associated the names of many of the great departed.

"To think of you is equivalent to recalling names revered by all mankind. Whatever the world may say, and even in the face of cavilers in our own ranks, we, who have for years listened to the utterances of your various controls, who know how wisely we have been led, step by step, from darkness to light, who are cognizant of the wonderful power that in hours of trial was manifested in behalf of this society and for the support and comfort of its medium, consider ourselves fully justified in believing that the spirits of the departed who select you as their instrument, are none other than they purport to be. It is a wondrous galaxy! I will not mention here the names of those who come to us from mystic ages, or even the classic age of Greece and Rome. But what a company is this almost of our own time and generation!

Very Sincerely Your Friend
Cora L. V. Richmond

"What names more revered than those of Angelo, Swedenborg, Franklin, Channing, Parker, Mapes and, though, perhaps, less known to fame, but none the less honored by us, that 'amiable, youthful spirit, Adin Augustus Ballou!'

"But there is one nearer and dearer than all. Who is this that has ever a pleasant word and bright smile for the sorrowing children of earth?

"Whose canoe comes to us laden with beautiful flowers of sentiment and poesy? Who with her magic wand, banishes the 'cobwebs' from 'think-boxes' and makes 'ezzery-body' happy? Who this strange compound of maturity and childishness, of dignity and simplicity, of gravity and drollery, of wisdom and nonsense?

"Whose wit so ready, whose sarcasm so keen, whose mirth so contagious, whose sympathy so beautiful, as it shines through the face of her 'Water Lily?' Ouina! [Applause.] Thrice welcome Ouina!

"Tell us not that this name, so dear to our hearts, stands for a myth! If Ouina is not, then are we not, and chaos is come again.

"If the names I have mentioned are realities to us, if we seem to know them as we know persons still in the flesh, it is because we know you, Mrs. Richmond. You are, as it were, the glass through which we see another and a better world. Yours is the voice that conveys to us the thoughts born in spheres celestial. We could not, if we would, separate you from the beautiful and the good that have gone before, and so we gladly include them in our greeting, and give you and them, one and all, an earnest, heartfelt welcome." [Renewed applause.]

Many others present had to say a few words of welcome.

Mrs. Richmond rose and attempted to express her thanks and appreciation, but, her feelings overcoming her, she burst into tears, when Ouina came to her relief.

At the conclusion of that part of the exercises, A. J. Hoffman, master of ceremonies, led our subject and her companion, followed by all of the assemblage that could be accommodated, to the lecture room below, where tables were spread for four hundred people (the service being kindly loaned by the Palmer House Hotel), who sat down to a sumptuous repast, some of whom, as soon as they were through, making room for others.

A band of stringed instruments, hidden within a bower of roses, discoursed soft music during the supper.

After supper, toasts and responses were in order, Mr. Hoffman opening the exercises with the following:

"LADIES AND GENTLEMEN:—The poet has truly said—

"We take no note of time, save from its loss."

"We mortals, in our imperfect vision and understanding, fail to comprehend or appreciate our truest joys till we either temporarily or eternally lose them.

" 'Water Lily's' return bears to us all the fragrance and joy we give to the Spring flowers. While we have welcomed and said farewell to the young man (W. J. Colville) whose organism so well attests the presence of a control beautiful in poetry and sublime in its profundity, how tenderly we welcome back our old and tried friend; how sacred to us seems the pure face and self-abnegated heart; how the vicissitudes of her young life in her ministry sparkle like gems, polished through work! How the mantle of the tender, sympathetic, beautiful Ouina falls over us like gossamer love! How like the rock of Plymouth we feel the dignified presence of Adin Augustus, whose nature, enshrined in the purest friendship, lifts us up into higher life! How that almost deific gradation that seems to reach the infinite, of which he is the mouth and throat, dazzles us by its stairway of intellectual and spiritual thought! In view of these great gifts that have been accorded to us, our first toast is to the bodily health of Mrs. Cora L. V. Richmond. May she live till she has filled the mission heaven has seen fit to impose upon her, and rest in perfect peace in that beautiful home well earned by this mortal conflict of error.

"Our second toast is to the noble man who stands by her side, a tower of strength and a staff when weary by the toil of her earthly pilgrimage." [Applause].

Mr. F. F. Cook happily responded to the toast, "The Spiritual Outlook."

Dr. Bushnell, in response to the toast, "The Ladies' Union," paid a high compliment to that organization.

Mr. T. S. Mitchell was called upon for a response to the toast, " Our Mothers," and referred to the subject in touching and appropriate language.

Z. T. Griffen responded to the toast, "The Red, White and Blue," giving the significance of the colors.

A M. Griffen responded to the toast, "The Spiritual Press."

B. T. Young spoke to the toast, " Our Spiritual Ambassadors, and their Mission to Us," urging faith in media.

J. Williams treated the company to a poetic improvisation upon the rather enigmatic subject, "The Enigma of the Circle; or, the Key that unlocks the Elephant's Trunk."

Mr. Slocum made a fitting speech in response to the subject, "Home."

G. W. Salter thought something ought to be done for "The Young People of the First Society of Spiritualists," since they were soon to take the place of the older ones.

Charles Bushnell spoke briefly to the subject, "Our Spiritual Guides."

W. T. Jones, in response to the toast, "The Progressive Lyceum," briefly sketched its history, and eulogized its usefulness.

A. M. Lewis thought he had rather *be* than *not be* in the majority of cases. His response was to the question, "To be or not to be."

Ouina gave an appropriate response to the toast, "The Medium and her companion."

Mr. H. C. Moore made a few remarks referring to a lecture once delivered by Mrs. Richmond, which he thought had furnished the best argument for immortality he had ever heard. Mr. Moore offered the following toast, "Woman, 'Heaven's last, best Gift to man.'"

"That man should properly estimate the value of that gift, she had been made the chosen medium between the spirit world and him. Let us then treat her with tender veneration and honor, and even stand ready, as brothers of sisters, and sons of mothers, not only to extend to her all rights we ourselves enjoy, but to shelter and protect her, as far as lies in our ability, from the storms and adversity of this life."

The auditorium and supper room were most beautifully decorated with abundance of flowers. We are unable to learn the full committee of arrangements, but we believe that Mr. A. J. Hoffman was general superintendent, Mrs. Hoffman superintendent of decorations, and Mr. John A. Wilson superintendent of music.

The toasts and responses being concluded, a number of the people retired to the church auditorium, and further remarks were made, mainly by the controlling spirits of mediums, among whom were Ski (Mrs. Simpson's control), Rosa (Mrs. Suydam's control), and Niconee (Mrs. De Wolf's control). Mr. Simpson, also, spoke briefly. After which, the friends dispersed, feeling that the occasion had been one of great enjoyment and benefit to all, and that the bond which linked them to the spirit world, through the ministration of Mrs. Richmond, had been strengthened beyond the possibility of severance.

We are indebted for much of the data of our account of the above reception to the "Spiritual Record" of March 13, 1880.

Our next letter is from the facile pen of Mrs. Fred Ashton, daughter of Dr. Lewis Bushnell, who has been a friend of our subject ever since the commencement of her ministrations in Chicago in 1876, and who, therefore, can speak of her from the standpoint of true appreciation and sincere affection. We give her letter intact, as follows:

"H. D. BARRETT, ESQ.

"DEAR SIR:—It is with the greatest diffidence, as well as pleasure, that I attempt on behalf of myself and husband, now in spirit life, to give a brief estimate of the invaluable work of the guides of Mrs. Richmond, during their ministrations in Chicago, and to bear testimony of the love and gratitude, which ever fills our lives toward them and their willing instrument, whom we dearly love and esteem for herself alone.

"Could the work be measured by its effect upon one life alone, it would be beyond compare, and when we know that many, many more have felt its influence and are now living in its light and spreading the truth in various ways and in many parts of the world, we send forth praises unto the Divine for the Truth which has been unfolded unto ready and waiting hearts by the ministrations.

"Nineteen years ago Mrs. Richmond came to Chicago. After a brief engagement in another portion of the city, and a season spent in California, she began to speak for the First Society of Spiritualists. From that time she has been our regular minister, although each year she has spent a few months away from us, so that from England to our own California the sustaining influence has been poured forth.

"Gradually the guides led us from the knowledge of facts and phenomena of Spiritualism to its philosophy, broadening and deepening our thought, spreading charity and tolerance, teaching that it is better to build a firm, beautiful edi-

fice of truth from individual lives, to unfold the
religion of *Love*, and *never* to attempt to assail
or destroy other systems of thought by unkind
attacks, or even by too great an attempt to ex-
pose error. To build and live the religion of
Love, of individual responsibility and of self-abnegation, was the sole thought for a time, until
at last we became prepared for the larger thought
of the Inner Teachings—I refer to the teachings
on the Soul. At first they were presented only
in private classes, and I well remember their effects upon myself, a young girl, with happiest
home life, and every path made radiant with
love. I felt and said: 'I feel now ready for life,
and would not shrink from life's responsibility,
even in its hours of trial and seeming injustice.'
The problems of life were solved, and I could
look about with no less sympathy for friends and
acquaintances, whose paths were thorny and
hard to travel, but with none of the bitterness of
doubt and questioning of the justice of God, which
had heretofore oppressed me.

"That glorious blessing descended upon me
then, and with reverent joy I welcomed each
added truth. It has never left me, and when the
sacred step of marriage was taken, with one who
also felt this benediction, life began its true
meaning. Parental love was also given to us,
and still the ever brooding presence of the Truth,
with its solemn duties remained with us, and the

ministrations of the guides grew more and more dear. At last the time came when the realm of spirit claimed one of us. Did the ministration fail us? Ah, no! Ever stronger and deeper the knowledge of the 'Soul' in its relation to the divine and the human, uplifted and sustained so that praises beyond expression were struggling for utterance.

"Even daily life, with its petty care and strivings, is made sacred, and not long can anything cloud the spirit which has received the Inner Teachings. Now these lessons have been received and prized by many, many others, and have also been published, so that all who are ready may receive, and there is ever growing interest as the questions from week to week testify. Yet other and still deeper truths have also been given to the world, through this same instrument, and if the first lessons could so fill life's duties with joy for one human spirit, may it not be that this experience is but one of many others? Indeed the members of our society all feel that same strength and uplifting power. We are all striving for Truth, striving to live unselfishly, striving to find only the good in all, striving to recognize the one divine principle in all religions, and striving to be worthy of the great light and blessing which the guides, through Mrs. Richmond, have so fully given to us.

'There are many other features of her work

here, but the Teachings of the 'Soul' are the chiefest.

"Many are led toward the truth by the weekly meetings of the Band of Harmony, which have been always held in some name. When Mrs. Richmond is present, questions are answered, Ouina converses, always with the theme of love to crown all subjects, many name poems are given, indicative of individual lives. These last are highly prized, and we often know one another almost entirely by the names Ouina has given us, and thus the public work is supplemented in these meetings which are also public in their invitation, but partake of the charm of private and social intercourse.

"The guides have always been the staunch and earnest friends of mediums and mediumship in all its phases, and have been ever ready to defend them when attacked with persecution, malicious or otherwise, and it must be said that in all their work, they have found ready co-workers in their pupils and friends, the First Society of Spiritualists, and they now extend the benefits of their ministrations to more than ever before.

" May the blessings of the Divine and His ministering angels allow us for many more years to enjoy the teaching, through Mrs. Richmond.

Fraternally yours,

MRS. FRED. ASHTON.

' Star-Flower,' and ' Bird of Paradise.' "

(Names given Mr. and Mrs. Ashton by Ouina.)

We now call our readers' attention to an interesting account of one feature of Mrs. Richmond's work in Chicago in regard to her defense of phenomenal mediumship. This involves the controversy with the late editor of the R. P. Journal, and will be of deep interest to all Spiritualists who believe that mediums have rights that the world should respect.

The writer of the letter (associated with his brother Z. T. Griffin) regularly attended the meetings and for many years reported them for the Chicago Times, Spiritual Record, (published under the auspices of Mrs. Richmond's society by A. M. and Z. T. Griffin), and other journals. He is a valuable contributor to literary journals like The Forum and others. Therefore we take pleasure in introducing at this point a most interesting letter from the pen of Mr. A. M. Griffin, No. 164 La Salle St., Chicago:

"Mr. H. D. BARRETT.

"DEAR SIR AND BROTHER:—I regret that I have not more time to devote to the preparation of an account of Mrs. Richmond's work in Chicago, but it seems impossible for me to snatch it from pressing business matters, therefore I send yon such data as occur to me hastily.

"I first met Mrs. Richmond in Chicago in the winter of 1875. She was on her way from the East to California, and stopped off in Chicago to give a course of lectures in Snow's Academy,

North Green and Halsted streets, which attracted widespread attention, not only among Spiritualists, but among the liberal public generally. She returned from California the next season, and continued her lectures for the First Society in various halls of the city until the Third Unitarian Church, corner Monroe and Laflin street, was secured for her, where she had large and appreciative audiences, of course carrying on her adjunctive work, such as Sunday School, receptions, parlor lectures on Psychopathy, the Soul, etc.

"It was during this period, *i. e.*, the winter of 1878, that the Religio Philosophical Journal made a bold and aggressive attack upon phenomenal mediums, especially singling out Messrs. Bastian and Taylor, who had been giving seances for several years under the auspices of S. S. Jones (then deceased), the former proprietor of the Religio Philosophical Journal. The charges of fraud and deception were so pointed and explicit that many of those who previously had confidence in the integrity of the mediums, were inclined to admit that they might have been mistaken and deceived. The new editor of the Religio Philosophical Journal, who had made great professions of fealty to the cause of Spiritualism, and of devotion to Mrs. Richmond, had come to enjoy, in a greater or less degree, the confidence and esteem of the Spiritualists of Chicago. At his instigation, after having attacked the mediums in his paper, some of the leading members of the First Society of Spiritualists were led to believe that an investigation of the genuineness of the manifestations given through Bastian and Taylor ought to be made. A committee of Spiritualists, therefore, called upon these gentlemen and stated that, in view of the charges, they thought it would be advisable, in order to put themselves right before the public, for them to give a series of strictly test seances; which proposition was, of course, indignantly rejected; although each member of the committee was invited as an individual, if he had any doubts, to attend the seances, and to form a judgment of his own as to the character of the manifestations. In short, there was some division—quite sharp—among the members of the First Society on this question, when Mrs. Richmond, in a spirited address, took up the defense of phenomenal mediumship, and in her powerful and convincing way, satisfied her hearers of the injustice of the mode of procedure proposed by the editor of the Religio Philosophical Journal. As I remember, she argued that the phenomena, being produced by departed spirits, it was for *them* to select and dictate conditions, and not the province of the recipients to prescribe them; that each individual must be his own judge as to the value and genuineness of the manifestations. Of course I cannot give anything like a full and satisfactory account of this discourse. The .impression left on my mind is that it was a complete exposition of the proper manner of investigating Spiritual phenomena, and a complete justification of the usual conditions under which mediums give their demonstrations. Upon the delivery of this address, the editor of the journal in question turned his guns upon Mrs. Richmond personally; this solidified her friends, who passed resolutions endorsing her course, when they, in turn, were attacked and ridiculed from the same source. The effect of these proceedings was perceptibly largely beneficial in strengthening Mrs. Richmond's hand and those of the First Society, as well as greatly encouraging to mediums of all kinds.

"About this time, the editor of the Chicago Times, Wilbur F. Storey, who had for some time been interested in Spiritualism, gave orders to the management of his paper that Spiritualism should receive the same treatment that was accorded other religious denominations, and he published Mrs. Richmond's lectures in full for several months. This was also a means of attracting a great deal of attention from various quarters. Mrs. Richmond was invited to speak before the Philosophical Society, of Chicago, and there produced an impression which, no doubt, had a lasting effect, although, of course, some criticism was offered.

"The lectures of Mrs. Richmond, almost from the starting of her work in Chicago, have been published in one form or another. At first, they appeared in weekly pamphlets, the expense of which was paid by sale at the hall, and sub- scriptions; then in the winter of 1879, a paper called 'Spiritual Record' was started for the ex- press purpose of publishing her lectures, and miscellaneous matters connected with her work. This publication continued something over a year. Soon after this, as you are aware, Mr. Richmond started the 'Weekly Discourse.'

"Mrs. Richmond's receptions and parlor lectures I always regarded as valuable as any other part of her work. Here, there was afforded an op- portunity to investigate Spiritual philosophy in a manner scarcely to be accorded anywhere else. The meetings were always well attended, and great satisfaction expressed by all.

"I wish I could give you a fuller account, and if I had time to refer to the papers of those days, I could do so: but I am exceedingly busy, which, of course, is an old excuse, but certainly a fact in my case.

"Trusting these few suggestions may be of some value to you in your work, I remain,

Truly yours,

A. M. GRIFFIN."

October 18, 1894."

This chapter would be like the play of Hamlet with Hamlet left out had we failed to receive a letter from Mrs. Richmond's devoted friend, John A. Wilson. It was Mr. Wilson's wedding that called Mrs. Richmond to California on a certain occasion, and he is therefore qualified to speak appreciatively of her and her work. The following is his letter:

"BENTON, CAL., Oct. 14, 1894.

"H. D. BARRETT, Pres. N. S. A.,

Washington, D. C.

"DEAR SIR:—Having learned from various sources that you are compiling and editing an account of Mrs. Cora L. V. Richmond's life work, I herewith send a few notes which may be of interest to your many readers.

" 'Seek and ye shall find; knock and it shall be opened unto you.' Wishing to know something of Spiritualism, one evening in January, 1877, I wended my way to Mrs. Richmond's home on Park Ave., Chicago, an utter stranger to Spiritualism and to Spiritualists, to attend one of Ouina's receptions. Being a stranger, I was in some doubt as to whether a welcome would be accorded to me. Much to my surprise and pleasure, Mr. Richmond received me cordially, and ushered me into their parlors filled with eager listeners to Ouina's conversations and readings or poems. Although it was not till many weeks afterwards that I would admit even to myself that I was convinced that Spiritualism was true, yet on that first evening I was more than

half convinced, and convinced in an unusual
way.

"Ouina gave many character poems and names
displaying wonderful psychological power. That
the delineations of character were correctly given
was evinced by the comments of those sitting
near me. When I sat before the medium for my
poem, I felt something invisible touching my
face and head. The poem itself was excellent.
I had always heard that Spiritualism was a delusion and a fraud, and had taken for granted the
statement as true, just as some people take their
religion; but here was something too beautiful,
too earnest and too ennobling not to bear the impress of truth upon it.

"Mr. Richmond made a strong and favorable
impression upon me. He seemed so well balanced,
honest, earnest and sincere, that it would be
impossible for him to engage in a work of deception (and years of close friendship have only
served to confirm and strengthen that impression). I said to myself: 'If Mr. Richmond is
a true man, and I think he is, then is Spiritualism true, because his position entitles him to
knowledge on the subject.' It is my firm conviction that Sapphire (Mr. Richmond) forms a
very important factor in Water Lily's (Mrs. Richmond's) work. Had it not been for him, she
would have left mortal life years ago. There
was no other link than this love strong enough to

nold her here. He considered it his mission to
be her protector, and nobly has he performed
that mission, defending her at all times against
the shafts of malice and envy and other unpleasant things. He also fully comprehends and
enters into the spirit of the guide's work; and
thus is the peer of any man, as she is the peer of
any woman.

"The work of the guides has always been in
advance of the people, as it necessarily should
be if the people are to learn, and for that reason
some have considered it transcendental or vague
and illusive. Frequent calls for something practical were made years ago, by those who did not
fully comprehend the scope or sweeping nature
of the reforms to be accomplished through this
work. In response to these demands, discourses
were delivered upon such topics as 'A Practical
Application of the Golden Rule,' 'A Practical
Application of the 'Sermon on the Mount,' and
others of like nature which were published in the
Spiritual Record. If the lessons of those grand
discourses had been followed by all who might
have read them, the world would now be spared
the disgraceful spectacle of starvation in a land
of plenty. Would not that have been something
practical ?

"Mrs. Richmond's life has been full of love,
yet not altogether a pathway of roses. A certain editor, in order to cast discredit upon her

mediumship and to show that her messages did not come from the spirit-world, once asserted that her wonderful store of knowledge, which was indisputable, was acquired by *psychological absorption* while passing through a well stocked library. This statement becomes comical from its absurdity. Mrs. Richmond never acquired her knowledge from books, even by reading, for books do not contain it. And, furthermore, she has no books of any consequence, and even if she had, her time is too much occupied with her work to read them. Of the latter facts I am aware, because it was my fortunate privilege to live in the home of Mr. and Mrs. Richmond for a considerable time. I was laughingly called 'Ouina's boarder,' because it was by her wish I became a member of the family.

"As an instance of Sapphire's protecting care of his companion, although not successful in this particular case excepting in spirit, I recall an occasion when an unwarranted attack was made upon her by a certain so-called spiritualistic publication. Sapphire received the paper, but kept it to himself to save his wife the pain of reading anything so disagreeable. A friend of the family, however, who was less thoughtful and considerate than Sapphire, brought the paper to the house, and showed the article in question to Mrs. Richmond. She read it quietly, and apparently without feeling the poisonous shafts, but she afterwards said that it seemed as though she had been pierced by a thousand needles. Mrs. Richmond has suffered more than martyrdom, because martyrdom ends with death, and can come but once, but these things made their appearance many times.

"These events took place in 1878 and 1879, which was a stormy period for mediums. Mrs. Richmond's guides have ever been staunch friends of mediums, because, without them, communication with the spirit-world would speedily cease. Yet, even among Spiritualists during the time to which I refer, many were found ready to take the popular side against them whenever doubts from doubtful sources were cast upon their mediumship. But the guides took a firm stand against those who were trying to force their claims against the claims of mediums, which meant that these instruments with their divinely bestowed gifts must submit to the authority and dictation of certain self appointed censors. As no restrictions could be placed upon the utterances of the guides through Mrs. Richmond by these enemies of Spiritualism, an effort was made by them to capture the Society, The First Society of Spiritualists of Chicago, which supported and endorsed her ministrations. And they very nearly succeeded, had it not been for the real strong-kneed supporters, who staunchly upheld at all points the teachings and the attitude of the guides in defense of other mediums. One of these defenders, who is now on the other side, was named by Ouina 'Silver Crown' Collins Eaton. (How he would like to help to compile a history of 'Water Lily's' life!)

* * * * * * *

"Sometimes when it seemed to her friends that all this work and excitement was too much for her frail earthly form, Ouina said, 'If the people do not want her here, we can take her to the other side,' but the people did want her, as they more and more realized. We all need her presence and the ministrations of the guides; for spiritual food, in some manner given, is as essential for man's life upon earth as food for the body.

"Among the many good works of Mrs. Richmond, one (of almost paramount importance) has been to aid in rescuing the fair name of religion from the misconception of bigotry and orthodoxy.

"The people of the Western States have felt the influence of her words of truth. In 1881 she visited the great mining camp of Leadville, Colorado, where she spoke two evenings in the Methodist church to large and appreciative audiences. Questions pertaining to spiritual subjects were answered in the usual manner by the guides. There were two Baptist ministers in the congregation, one of whom asked many questions, and

also expounded a few ideas of his own, all with
the evident intention of confounding Mr. Ballou
(Mrs. Richmond's control), but the audience
plainly showed that it thought the minister was
greatly overmatched, and some of his good Christian brethren twitted him of it after the services
were over. Many men before and since then
have found that Mr. Ballou could hold his ground
in argument against any of them. The conduct
of the other minister stood out in strange contrast with that of his brother. He said not a
word until the last question was answered. Then
he arose and said impressively, that he had par-
taken with great relish of the rare intellectual
and spiritual feast, and he had intended to call
on the lady the next day and tell her so; but
while he was enjoying it, he felt that if he went
home without acknowledging before all those
people the blessing he had received, he would
wrong his own better nature; therefore he wished
to be allowed to express his gratitude and appreciation, and to say he 'firmly believed the lady
was inspired by God.'

"After the meetings at the church, that well
known singer, Asa Hutchinson, was so filled
with the spirit of the occasion that he engaged
the Tabor Opera House for another meeting.
He managed everything himself, and surprised
some of his friends by distributing hand-bills advertising a lecture on 'Spiritualism.' Mr. Hutch-

inson, being a veteran in the business, knew how to successfully manage the external part of the program. The result was, the opera house was crowded to overflowing. The chairman of the meeting, if I remember rightly, was another Baptist minister, not one of the two already mentioned. It is needless to say the speaker was well received. If only a small part of that audience felt the quickening power of the spirit, how far reaching must now be the influence of only that one discourse.

"A few weeks ago, while on a business trip to a small out of the way town in the mountains, a friend asked me to call upon some Spiritualists residing there, who were strangers to him. I was glad to call simply because they were Spiritualists. Our conversation naturally drifted toward Spiritualism and its mediums, and of course to Mrs. Richmond. When we found that we were all her ardent admirers, a bond of friendship was struck at once.

"This incident illustrates two things, which I have frequently noticed; first, that the friends of Mrs. Richmond and Spiritualism are to be found all over the Western country; second, that the friends of Mrs. Richmond are friends of each other.

"A pebble cast into the water causes a ripple which extends to the furthermost shore. In similar manner does the word of truth extend

its influence for good through the hearts and
lives of all people.

"A young man living here, who knew nothing
about Spiritualism, whose sole information or
lack of it consisted of the usual misrepresenta-
tions of the daily press, believed that it was mix-
ture of deception and delusion. But a revelation came to him in the form of a personal
Spiritual manifestation, which was so completely
at variance with all his previous conceptions of
Spiritual existence, that he was greatly worried
and sorely perplexed. In an agitated frame of
mind he came to me, knowing that I was a Spiritualist, for an explanation of his trouble (?) I
gladly imparted to him a general idea of the lessons of the Great Teacher, with explanations
suited to his particular case. He became so
filled with the new light, that he wanted to bring
every one else into it. A class was soon formed
to study the published lessons on, 'THE SOUL IN
HUMAN EMBODIMENTS.' The results of the effort
have been quite satisfactory, but are undoubtedly
unequal to the results which would be effected by
a direct ministration of the guides through their
chosen instrument. Nevertheless, this is an example of the widespread and beneficent results
of Mrs. Richmond's labors. If the material rays
of light from a planet or the sun can traverse
millions of miles of space, how far may not the
Spiritual rays of light from our Great Teacher

extend to the souls of men? No man knoweth; God alone can tell.

"Fraternally yours,
"JOHN A. WILSON."

It may be mentioned here that Mr. Wilson was at one time a very active and efficient worker in the Society over which Mrs. Richmond is pastor, and in connection with other younger members of the committee (including Mr. Fred Ashton) helped to extend the work of the Society and the guides in many ways. Collins Eaton, to whom he refers, was for many years the secretary of the Society, and *always*, from first to last (and now in Spirit life), a most devoted friend to our medium and the work of the guides.

The next letter—or rather account of her work in Chicago—is from the present gifted secretary of the Society of which our subject is pastor. Mrs. C. Catlin, who, although comparatively new to the sublime truths of Spiritualism (having been "converted" to them as she herself confessed by the discourses of the guides through Mrs. Richmond), nevertheless was manifestly ready for the new light and brings great zeal and devotion to the work and the medium. Her account has been hastily compiled from the records of the Society and from conversation with its members as well as from personal observation since she became a member.

"Prof. H. D. Barrett, Lily Dale, N. Y.

"Dear Sir:—It gives me pleasure to contribute to your life-work of Mrs. Richmond my recollections of her wonderful work in the city of Chicago, and to testify to my appreciation of what that work has been to me. Therefore, I submit the following to your consideration:

"In the year 1876 this wonderful instrument was led by her guides to accept a brief engagement in Chicago. As a matter of course, the events of her young life, her early call to the ministry, and the wonderful work of her budding womanhood, had preceded her. The people flocked aronnd her, anxious to hear this new truth, presented as it was with such eloquence and force from this brilliant woman. Some years previous to this, a Society had been formed under the name of 'The First Society of Spiritualists of Chicago' for the propagation of these truths, and advancement of the cause of Spiritualism. Naturally, the fame of this remarkable medium had reached them, and at the close of the above engagement, led by the unseen intelligences, they extended an invitation for a short engagement as speaker for this Society.

"At this time she was frail in body and delicate in health, [the high altitude in the journey across from California, and the severe spring weather having caused a return of the hemorrhages.—Ed.], often leaving her couch for the rostrum, and the rostrum for the couch, and in this perhaps could be seen one of the most wonderful demonstrations of spirit power; for, supported by that mighty force that has ever been around and about her, the disabilities of the physical were overcome, and at these times some of the grandest utterances have fallen from her lips. Often have the people listened in fear and trembling lest the frail thread should be broken, her work here finished, and this grand life lost to the world.

"Sheltered by her husband's watchful care, guarded by his tender love, and that of his family, with every shadow carefully concealed, surrounded only by that which was loving and beautiful, the frail bark, escaped from the breakers of its early years, rested peacefully in this haven of rest. As was to be expected, the physical responded to this gentle wooing, and health rapidly reasserted itself.

"By this time the temporary engagement with the First Society had expired, but not so their love, for this frail and gentle creature had won the hearts of her people, and laid the foundation for that devotion which is only strengthened with time, and will last through all eternity. The result was a call to become pastor of the Society for one year. With this portion of the history we may pause for a moment to pay a tribute of love to the name of Dr. Lewis Bushnell, who at this time became president of the Society, and whose honored name must have its place in this work, for the next eighteen years, not only as president, but as a zealous co-worker with the guides, the devoted friend of the medium, and the untiring burden bearer of the association.

"The call was accepted by Mrs. Richmond, and her guides entered upon the work which was to give so much to the world, and lead to such great results. From the first her people yielded themselves to the influence of the wise and loving guides, and under their influence with her ever faithful control, Ouina, she at once became teacher, friend and guide. The meetings were successful and soon outgrew the place of meeting, Grows Hall or Opera House on Madison street, and in September, 1878, the Society moved into the Third Unitarian Church, corner of Laflin and Monroe streets. The success that had been hers from the first followed her here, and, with increased facilities and happier surroundings, the results, as might be expected, were more extended in scope, and more palpable in results. Large congregations flocked to hear her, and drank deeply from this fountain of inspiration. In the following year she received 'an all life call' from the society, which was lovingly accepted, reserving, however the right of responding to the call of her guides to work in other places for a certain time each year. In June, 1880, the members of the Society lovingly sent her to England at their own expense to minister to the Spiritual hunger of those in that country who could be fed only by her inspiration and who longed for her return. She was away on that mission seven months. The Society suspended its meetings during her absence, resuming again upon her return, this time in Music Hall building, State street. It was at about this time that the wonderful Bible interpretations of her guides were given, attracting so many thinking people, and making this a time ever to be remembered as a season of joy and exultation.

"The guides announced their intention of transferring their ministration to San Francisco. Owing to the severity of the winters several attacks of hemorrhage of the lungs had now left her in such a critical condition physically that, in yielding to the needs of the hour, and bidding her a sad farewell, but few dared to hope for her return, and the meetings were again suspended. A happy surprise was however in store for them, for beneath the balmy skies, and amidst the flowers and fruits of that sunnier clime, once more she recovered, and in the following October returned to her charge. An enthusiastic welcome awaited her, and the meetings were gladly resumed.

"Seven months later, she again visited Eng-

land for a brief season of ministration there, returning in the early autumn. In December of
the same year she went to San Francisco, for a
month's ministration there, returning to her Chicago charge again the first of January. After
ministering to her Society four months, she again
visited England, and was absent from Chicago
the balance of the year. So deeply had she become entrenched in the affections of her people
that not for a moment during these different
periods of absence did they contemplate a successor, preferring to wait until she returned to
resume the work.

"From that time the ministrations have continued without any extended break. She had
now been for all those years the chosen pastor
of the Society, loved by her people with a love
unspeakable. Year by year she had become more
closely interwoven with the family life, for, as
the teacher and friend of the parent, she had
seen the children ripen into manhood and womanhood. In many cases it had been hers to give
the nuptial benediction to these, and again to
bless the offspring at the baptismal font, so that
even the children have arisen to call her blessed.
But perhaps it has been when trial has darkened
the household, and the angel of sadness has
brooded over those she loved, that she has been
nearer and dearer to her people. Then it has
been that loving words of comfort have been

tenderly spoken, and, under their gentle influence, hearts crushed and broken were enabled to triumph over sorrow, and sing the sweet song of victory. Naturally buoyant and witty, quick at repartee, grasping at a moment any situation, and equal to any emergency, she became from the first the central sun, around which all times of rejoicing revolved, and at these times the dignified preacher was lost in the happy spirit, flitting here and there, like a sunbeam of love.

"These social results, however, were but the reflection of that wonderful work which has scattered its beams of joy and peace broadcast to the world. As was to be expected in these early days of Spiritualism, the Society, over which she was called to preside, was even then but upon the threshold of these grand truths, largely finding its comfort in facts and phenomena. Gradually, however, from the 'milk for babes,' she led them on to the more sustaining power of the philosophy, broadening and deepening the minds and souls of her people, preaching charity and tolerance, teaching as the better inheritance to build a firm edifice of truth from individual lives, to unfold the religion of love, of individual responsibility and of self-abnegation; and then upward and onward, as minds were prepared, she gently led them on to the larger thought, to the higher teachings, the lessons of the soul, and whilst, of course, these important truths per-

meate all the ministrations of the guides, these
lessons have been principally given in private
classes to those whose Spiritual unfoldment has
enabled them to climb these loftier heights, and
to these they have indeed been as the Mount of
Transfiguration, a lifting of the veil, and an entering into the Holy of the Holies, a blessed
communion face to face with the unseen powers.
It is needless to say, the control at such a time
is of the loftiest and most Spiritual character,
imparting to all a sense of exaltation and of joy,
an uplifting of soul experienced at no other
meeting. The writer well remembers the first of
these classes attended. The consciousness of
the presence, the lifting out of self into a higher
realm, the shrinking even from the greeting of friends, lest the spell should be broken
and the soul brought back again to the
conditions of time and sense, for so palpable was
the Spiritual surroundings, that the medium herself was as one transfigured; all of earth seemed
to have been removed, and by many she was
seen to stand as in a halo of light. So impressed were all with this, that, as she left the
room, still under the 'Teachers' control, they
instinctively drew back, as though shrinking
from bringing her into contact with material
things. It is at such times that one catches a
fleeting glimpse of that wonderful inspiration
that encircles her. In these teachings, life's true

lessons have been learned, souls have been fitted to meet trial and responsibility, leaving no room for doubt or bitterness, no place in which to question the justice of God, for in this blessed light the soul rises from the conflict, happier, stronger in spirit, and more ready for life, with all that it signifies.

"These classes have been held at intervals during the twenty years of her ministry here. Page by page this wonderful inspiration has been given to the world, each one containing new revelations, unsealing the hidden depths, and making manifest the mysteries of the ages, until now they comprise a complete series of lessons in soul teachings:

1. The Soul in Human Embodiments.
2. The Work of the Angels on Earth.
3. The Angels of Other Planets.
4. Messianic Cycles—The Messiahs.
5. The Book of the Madonnas.
6. Creative Angels.

And who can tell but in that new dispensation toward which we are tending, these wonderful revelations may form a part of the sacred writings! Certain it is, they are as far in advance of the growth of to-day as was the teaching of the Nazarene in the days of old.

"But her work has not been confined to these lines alone; all topics having for their object the good of humanity, whether Spiritual, moral or

political, have been dealt with by a master hand
and, whilst there has always been an absence of
all unkind attacks upon those who differ, there
has ever been a firm stand for principle and an
unswerving declaration for the right. Especially
has this been the case in all matters bearing upon
suffering humanity. The tyranny of mammon
and monopoly receive no mercy at her hands;
the helpless and downtrodden have ever been
subjects for the ministration of sympathy and
love, and perhaps she is never more eloquent
than when pleading the rights of these. In a
world so little prepared for this, such a line of
teaching can hardly claim to be popular, and
times have not been wanting when she has stood
almost alone in the support of her principles. No
better illustration of this can be found than in the
year 1887, memorable for the judicial murder of
five men, for the crime of expressing that which
is rapidly becoming the question of the hour.
Hers was the voice that proclaimed the wrong,
and even against the prejudices of many of her
people, she openly espoused the cause of those
unfortunate men—not indeed in the sense of rebellion to the law, but in their right to liberty of
conscience and of speech—and in the face of
public opinion, unflinching, fought the battle for
the right   Under the inspiration of her guides,
she was led to go to Springfield, personally to
intercede for the lives of these men and, not

wishing to lead her people where they were not willing to follow, she handed in her resignation to the Society, determined to go alone, rather than stultify her sense of right. But, true to the love they bore her, confident in the wisdom of the intelligence behind her, the resignation was unanimously rejected and, accompanied by her faithful companion in life, she went forth, strong in her sense of justice and of right, to plead the cause of humanity. The execution of the following November may point to the failure of her mission, but the ever growing sentiment of the day proves the righteousness of her cause, and the time will come when Cora L. V. Richmond will stand before the world as a heroine in the cause of political freedom as well as Spiritual truth. One especial feature of her work has been the absence of phenomena (except indeed that in her wonderful gifts she herself must be accepted as one of the greatest manifestations of this); but, although this phase of Spiritualism finds no place upon her Sunday platform, she has ever been a firm advocate for its truth, and the firmest of friends to her co-workers in the cause, the phenomenal mediums. Few who know anything of Spiritualism, but will recall the noble, self-sacrificing stand she took against the persecution of one of these by the late editor of the 'Religio Philosophical Journal,' who was at that time a member of her Society, and one of her

most appreciative hearers, and whilst, if we follow the teachings and the example she has so
nobly set us, we shall not cherish a memory of
the wrong, yet we cannot forget the arrows of
abuse and calumny, yes, even of slander, which
it was hers to meet. Perhaps never did the
beauty of her character make itself more apparent as, strong in the consciousness of her own
integrity and the righteousness of her cause, supported by that mighty power from the unseen
world, unfalteringly she stood her ground, and
in the majesty of silence met the venomed shafts,
restraining by her calm, quiet dignity the righteous indignation of her people.

"In the early days of her work, like all similar societies, this one had its 'Ladies' Aid,' or,
as it was called, 'The Union,' meeting at the different homes, ostensibly for social intercourse
and philanthropic work, but really to enjoy the
sweet ministrations of the gentle Ouina, for here
was the special realm in which she could come
more closely in touch with her friends and many
are the precious memories that cluster around
these happy gatherings. From the character of
the meetings, however, these of course were confined to the ladies of the congregation. But as
time went on, a wide sphere of usefulness
seemed to suggest itself, and eventually the
'Union' merged itself into the 'Band of Harmony,' a meeting held every Thursday evening

for the dropping 'of this gentle rain from heaven,' at which the phenomena of Spiritualism could also find a home, and Lodge Hall, 'The Little Upper Room,' became consecrated by the happy memories of meetings with the loved ones gone before.

"Here Ouina again reigned supreme, standing as a connecting link between earth and heaven, drawing all hearts to her by the cords of love, bestowing in her own inimitable manner the precious name poems so eagerly sought and so highly prized by all. In these the gift of psychometry as well as prophecy was made manifest to a remarkable degree, the name given usually suggesting the Spiritual character of the recipient. So highly were these prized, that many, especially of the older members, are known to each other exclusively by these.

"Nor must we forget that wonderful gift of unknown tongues, often manifested at the 'Band of Harmony,' and their interpretation. With the interpreter in their midst, it was not to be wondered at that this phase of mediumship developed in the Society, many of the people being controlled by these spirits, some of them so ancient that their very language has passed beyond the memory of man, and yet each and all of these are interpreted by Ouina. As may be expected, the phase has called forth no small amount of doubt and criticism both from Spirit-

ualists and skeptics, but there have been times
when the proof has been so perfectly given, that
all doubt had to succumb.   One of the many instances of this may perhaps be recorded here.   A
gentleman, who had made the languages of Indian tribes his special study, was at the meeting
one evening, when one of the mediums gave a
short poem from an Indian control.   The gentleman was mystified but not convinced.   He arose
in the meeting and asked for a test in the 'sign
language' used by a certain tribe of Indians, with
which he was perfectly familiar.   Ouina, in her
reply, said there was another spirit then present
who could converse in that language. 'Water Lily'
(Mrs. Richmond) herself was then controlled by
'Omwah,' her own Indian guide, and gave an
address in the silent language called for.   At the
close of the address and interpretation, the
gentleman arose from his seat, declared the language perfect, the test satisfactory, and himself
a convert.

"But perhaps that which has endeared the
'Band of Harmony' to most hearts has been the
precious gems of thought which seem always to
come at the right time, and bring the needed
strength or comfort, and few there are who have
been constant attendants at these meetings but
cherish them in their hearts as an open doorway
to heaven.   This gathering was at first small in
numbers, but year by year it has grown and de-

veloped until, 'The Little Upper Room' outgrown, larger quarters had to be secured, and
Orpheus Hall, Schiller Theatre, is now its home.
Large and commodious as it is, it is filled with
an audience second to none in intelligence and
thought, eager for some drop of this heavenly
dew to fall into their hearts. The 'Band of
Harmony is rapidly becoming a centre from
which is radiated on every side the pure white
light of truth.

"No record of her work in Chicago would be
complete without some notice of the Sunday
School. When she first became pastor of the
Society, like most Societies of its time, it had
its 'Children's Progressive Lyceum', of which it
was justly proud, and many are the loving memories still retained by those who belonged as
children to this. With that ever progressive cry
of upward and onward, so characteristic of the
guides, this Society was gently led out of these
more general exercises to the adoption of a
system of teaching that would bring the children
in touch with Spiritual truth. Ouina has had
special control of the Sunday School (for who
could do it so lovingly as she?), and one of the remarkable features of this has been the clear perception the little ones have of the true business of
life here, and beyond. Often their replies to
questions may well astonish older and wiser
heads. Here, as everywhere, Ouina has been the

beloved of all hearts, and no greater treat can
be held out to the children than a visit to Water
Lily's (Mrs. Richmond's) home.

"Thus far we have but touched upon her more
public work, or that particularly in connection
with the Society; but that which perhaps has had
even a wider scope, and has done more to mould
the thought of the world, has been the various
publications issued by her and scattered broadcast through the land. Of the value of these no
possible estimate can be formed. The results
must be seen in the ever increasing demand for
light and knowledge. For some years the discourses were regularly published weekly by Mr.
Richmond, and had a wide circulation, but after
nearly six years that work had to be discontinued.
Happily, however, some thousands of these are
still in existence, and the time is even now that
these are amongst the choicest literature of the
day. The work on the Soul Teachings demands
more than a passing mention. Year by year it
is making for itself a place in hearts and lives,
and no library up to date is complete without
this wonderful production.

"But now we come to one of those happy
times, so many in number, but of which so little
has been said, when out of the abundance of her
people's love they gather around her in seasons
of social joy. It was in the year 1890 that the
approach of her 50th birthday called forth not a

national recognition only, but a clasping of both hemispheres in laying at her feet a tribute of love. Naturally the place of celebration of that event was at her home amongst her own people in Chicago. A brilliant ovation was given her, and a magnificent birthday gift; a gift, however, which but feebly expressed the appreciation of her great work, and the love that has ever encircled her, as attested by the many letters received by Mr. W. W. Chandler, from all parts of the world, expressive of appreciation and love for her, which he presented to Mrs. Richmond with the gift.

"Mr. Chandler was the active spirit of that occasion. He wrote (one hundred at least) personal letters to the friends of Mrs. Richmond in all parts of the world, apprising them of the fact that she was going to have a 50th birthday jubilee, that they might be represented in some way if not present in person. Mr. Chandler was brought to the light of Spiritualism through her ministrations a few months prior to her connection with the First Society, and he has been a most devoted friend ever since.

[But for the feeble state of his health—he has been confined to his bed much of the time for the last two years—he would have been chosen as the one best fitted to write the Chicago chapter of her life work.—ED.]

"One especial feature of the work has been the

prophetic sermon at the beginning of each year. This is eagerly looked forward to, and always attracts large audiences, and so perfectly have the predictions of the past been fulfilled, that the people have long since ceased to question.

"Amongst the most remarkable of these were those of 1878 and 1879, relative to the Perehelion in the year 1881. And of more recent date, those of 1890, '91, '92, '93, of events that should take place in '94; these have been upon us to the very letter, and only await the death of the Czar of Russia to give absolute fulfillment to the entire prophecy. [An event which has now been fulfilled.—ED.]

"To form an estimate of the value of the work of this grand life, attuned as it is to every vibration of the spirit, is not in the power of mortal. Something, however, of its results may be seen in the ever growing interest felt in these subjects, and the ever increasing veneration in which she is held. So strongly has this made itself felt, that at the close of last season the Society determined to extend their borders and place her amidst surroundings more in keeping with her own great gifts, and the grandeur of the cause. For this purpose they decided upon Hooley's Theatre as their future home, and here, on Sunday, September 16th, she commenced the nineteenth year of her pastorate. Only those who know the place she holds in the hearts of her

people can understand the joy and gratitude they
felt, as they saw that graceful form surrounded
by the beautiful floral offerings, tributes of a
people's love; that sweet face radiant with the
pure light of the spirit, and listened to that gentle voice, as, with that wonderful eloquence, and
perfect diction, so characteristic of the guides,
she placed at their feet the Spiritual sheaves
gathered as the harvest of years of sowing; and
then at that vast array of upturned faces, gleaming with the light of intelligence and joy, hang-
ing upon every word as it fell from the gentle
speaker's lips, could but feel that here was more
than the realization of a people's hope, more
than a successful issue to a people's work.   It
was the evidence of the silent workings of that
mighty power, the angel of truth, and the fulfillment of the promise: ' Cast thy bread upon the
waters and it shall return to thee after many
days.'   "Sincerely thine,
                    "MRS. C. CATLIN."

Mrs. Catlin's account is a complete summary
of the public work in Chicago, yet, as truth is
many sided, we must present the personal views
of that work from the standpoints of other members of the Society, most of whom are her most
intimate friends.

The following is from the pen of our subject's
honored co-worker, Mrs. Orvis, ordained by the
First Society, Mrs. Richmond's guides perform-

ing the service. She has sometimes facetiously styled herself the assistant pastor or curate, having filled Mrs. Richmond's place on the platform a number of times when the latter was too ill to speak, at funerals, and always at the Band of Harmony, when Mrs. R. is absent, and Mrs. Orvis is able to be there.

"DEAR FRIEND, THE READER:

"It is with greatest pleasure that I add my testimony with others regarding my knowledge of the work of Mrs. Richmond and her guides. Words are inadequate to express all their teachings and association, covering the past eleven years, have been to me; but the work as a whole, discourses given through her organism and published while she was yet a child; others delivered before the society here; ministrations in public and in more private ways, and especially in the inner lessons of the private classes, has impressed me with the wonderful mission and purpose within it all, that perhaps not many have understood. It is more than to teach the philosophy of Spiritualism as commonly received; it is more than to teach even the wonderful life of Soul in its individual relations.

"It is the announcing to this age, the opening to this cycle of the special dispensation belonging thereto, from those wonderful celestial angels who are the protectors and directors of a dispensation. These teachings harmonize and unify

all Truth, past and present, as well as to fore-
shadow that which the future has in store for the
world. They show the *reasons* for life in all its
infinite variety of manifestation; banishing its
deepest shadows by the light of knowledge; giving hope instead of fear and despair by the same
divine light; explaining what all theological
teachers have either ignorantly or wilfully relegated to the realm of mystery, and placing in
the hand of every child of earth who is ready
and willing to receive it, a veritable 'Staff of
Life' that will guide, sustain and cheer the
weary traveller through all the journey.

"When the now unpublished and incomplete
works of her guides shall be given to the world,
as I most sincerely hope they may be at an early
day, they will show to those who have eyes to
see, and surely to others in years to come, the
light of the New Dispensation, the announcement
of a new 'Joy to the World,' the grandest, noblest, most complete statement of the Light 'that
lighteth every man that cometh into the world,'
that humanity has yet received.

"MRS. ANNA ORVIS."

And this from the pen of one who has been a
member of the Society ever since our subject was
in charge:

"In looking over the period since Mrs. Richmond commenced her ministrations in Chicago,
it is clear that the value and amount of the work

accomplished cannot be fully measured or estimated. It is obvious, however, that her coming
marked an epoch in the lives of many who were
waiting—perhaps unaware—for this gospel, and
her work as a result has, during the years which
have since elapsed, borne abundant fruit. How
many hearts, beset by fears and tossed by doubt,
how many souls borne down by a still heavier
burden of grief or guilt, have been comforted or
strengthened and brought into a renewed life by
her inspired words—numbers are today ready to
testify.

"Spiritualism has first its message of good
news for those who have hitherto looked in vain
for some satisfying proof of immortality. It has
brought the one emphatic, decisive declaration,
'there is no death,' and brings the proof—is itself the proof. This makes the message glorious
—because to our faith has been added knowledge.

"This announcement through phenomena,
however precious as it is and bringing comfort to
so many sorrowing and bereaved ones, bears
somewhat the relation of body to that spiritual
philosophy which is the Soul of Spiritualism, and
which has been given to us with such clearness
and such convincing power by this willing instrument for nearly twenty years. Never condescend-
ing to extravagance or sensationalism, always
aiming at the correction of the evils of the present

time and drawing lessons from the current events
of the hour, never sparing the stern rebuke for all
forms of selfishness found in this lower life—it
places above and beyond all creeds the law of
love as taught by the Christ, and the golden rule
as the only rational basis of human action. It
teaches that within the bitter cup of human suffering is concealed the germ of a higher and
nobler life—that suffering, and what we call sin
will pass away together—and that by the mighty
transforming power of the spirit will all souls
reach perfection.

'That one far off divine event
Towards which the whole creation moves.'

"H. T. L."

Mr. E. F. Slocum was a member of the First
Society when our subject was invited to become
its pastor. For a number of years during her
ministry he served as secretary of the Society; he
is at the present time its vice-president. He expresses all possible appreciation in the following
few words:

"CHICAGO, Dec. 1, 1894.
"MR. H. D. BARRETT, ESQ.,
"DEAR SIR:—With great pleasure I hear you
are about to publish the life work of Mrs. Cora
L. V. Richmond. I have attended her minis-
trations for the past eighteen years constantly.
Words fail me to express my appreciation of the

wonderful gifts of this lady as an exponent of the Spiritual philosophy.

"I am very truly yours,

"E. F. SLOCUM."

Here we append a brief but soulful letter from the pen of Mr. A. J. Hoffman, of Chicago, one of the most devoted workers and occult students in our ranks. He, too, through the ministrations of our subject, has been led to the higher light, and speaks with deep feeling in private conversation with us of his appreciation of Mrs. Richmond's great work. His letter is as follows:

"H. D. BARRETT,

"DEAR FRIEND AND BROTHER: — The greatest test on the planet to me is Ouina, Ballou and the higher guides. The revelations, after a migratory search for fifteen years in the cults that make this decade the awakening of the centuries, make me know that I have reached the end of my mental and Spiritual possibility in this embodiment in the statement of the guides, and I am conscious in my soul that no further Spiritual altitude is possible till I reach, by concept and vanquishment, the statement of the guides The tender, sweet ministrations of Ouina come to me like a ray from the home of my sainted mother; the intellectual culmination I find in Ballou; the Nemesis of error, the Hermes of my theology. the seven pointed sword that heals while he wounds, and the luminous flashes of light, like the vision of a new sun, that come to us from the sphere of those who must be nameless to the world are, like the oases in the sand, spots for rest, prophetic of the open door. I could add much more, but words fail to express that inner feeling which is mine in regard to this work that you are about to place before the world, I hope in its truest and highest light. Ouina says: 'Those who are faithful to the work are sustained.' Let us accept that statement as a truism in regard to all who have come to an understanding of the wonderful soul lessons that we have received. Indeed we know that it is true of this instrument, Mrs. Richmond, who has given us these advanced teachings. Fraternally yours,

"A. J. HOFFMAN."

We take great pleasure in introducing at this point a letter from Mr. F. E. Ormsby, who, for some time, was secretary of Mrs. Richmond's Society in Chicago. As his letter covers a field not traversed by any other writer, we deem it of great interest to our readers, and reproduce it intact for their consideration:

"No. 60 WABASH AVENUE,
Chicago, Sept. 22, 1894.

"MY DEAR FRIEND BARRETT:—It is with pleasure that I respond to your request for me to add a few words to your work in behalf of Mrs. Cora L. V. Richmond, and that you may know first

where I stood concerning the philosophy of
Spiritualism, when I first heard Mrs. Richmond,
I will say: I was born in the atmosphere of
Spiritualism and never heard much of anything
else in my early childhood, and for twenty years
past have experienced its phenomena in many
of its phases in my own home and was quite
well versed in the work, when about seven years
ago, we came to Chicago, and for the first time
heard this gifted medium speak. Having read
many of her sermons, I was, of course, familiar
with the language, which, in its simplicity and
beauty, had always appealed to me very forcibly,
so I felt at home at once after she began to
speak. Now, as to impressions and conclusions
after having been socially connected with the
Society, and, also, having been brought more
closely into contact with Mrs. Richmond's work.
As an officer of the First Association, of which she
has been the 'head light' for nearly a score of
years, I will say this: In my opinion, no historian or biographical writer can truthfully present
the history of Spiritualism to the world without
Mrs. Cora L. V. Richmond as the leading light
of the movement during the past forty years.
This conclusion is not the result of an intimate
acquaintance with Mrs. Richmond, through which
I have found her to be a dignified, conscientious,
and charitable woman, and a hard worker in the
cause so dear to her, but rather from the manner

in which her work has been carried on all these years. What I mean by this is, that her work in Spiritualistic line seems to be on a much higher plane than is usual with the majority of teachers. Her co-workers from the spirit side of life have realized the need of something uncontaminated with 'light phenomena,' such as have held the term Spiritualism up to ridicule ever since its first advent. I do not mean to say that phenomena have no place in the world, but that they have a place distinctively their own, and should be held there. In my opinion, the very fact that no phenomena have ever been allowed in connection with the sermons delivered by Mrs. Richmond, has been the Rock of Ages on which her work has ever stood and is to-day an example to the Spiritualistic workers which they will do well to consider. I might say that this one fact alone made me a member of the First Society of Spiritualists of Chicago. The philosophy of Spiritualism, of which Mrs. Richmond has ever been one of the leading exponents, is what needs to be more fully elucidated in public places, while the usual phenomenal work should be relegated to private circles.

"I have heard many speakers, some very good, indeed with oratorical ability, perhaps, beyond that of Mrs. Richmond, but as an inspirational teacher she certainly leads the van. Her work has been more for the world at large, and it is

almost impossible to find a township in the land
which does not contain one or more admirers of
her utterances. Her residence and labors in Chicago, familiar to a large number of people, has
been a wonderful leverage in holding Spiritualism
to the front in the face of opposition and prejudice of Church and State, as well as the more
potent influence of the unscrupulous pretenders
and fraudulent practitioners within our own
ranks. Her work at the National Convention
in Chicago, held October, 1893, was evidence of
her influence and power in the Spiritualistic
field. The trials and tribulations which one must
bear, who thus takes a stand before the world,
are never compensated in this life, and it is well
that they are not; for such a debt can never be
paid to Mrs. Richmond. The obligation of Spiritualists to this gifted and devoted leader is one that
they can never discharge in full upon this planet.

"Brother Barrett, I have given you my views
in a hurried manner, and trust that they may be
of service to you in your noble work of reward-
ing Mrs. Richmond, while she is still with us,
with an accurate sketch of her public career and
life work. You have my sincerest wishes for the
success of the undertaking.

"I am, most sincerely yours,
                              "F. E. ORMSBY."

And this from another wanderer led back to
the Father's mansion through the ministrations

of our subject at Chicago. Dr. J. E. DeWolf is
the president of the Society to which she has
ministered so long. At the last annual meeting
of the Society he was unanimously elected to fill
the chair so long and ably occupied by its late
president, the much beloved brother, Dr. Lewis
Bushnell. Living so far from where the meetings were formerly held, Dr. De Wolf was not a
regular attendant, but for years every stormy
Sunday night Dr. De Wolf and his wife were certain to be in attendance at the meetings, having
to drive about nine miles and back.

" 'If a man die shall he live again?' is the
soul's query when burdens press heavily, as it was
when Job battled with mortal life; as it was when
Paul said, 'add to your faith knowledge'; as it is
with many souls to-day, as they stand at the
graves of their loved ones and ask that ever recurring question, 'Whence? whither?'

"How the soul rejoices when the scientist discovers one of nature's secrets; when the physi-
cist recognizes the potency of forces, like that of
electricity awaiting our service in yet unknown
ways; when the astronomer perceives an undiscovered planet in our solar system; when we reflect that the earth is not the only care of the Infinite, and that our journey from the cradle to
the grave may be but one link in an endless
chain of life. Must these yearnings and questionings, which sometimes assert themselves often

in the young child as well as with the gray-
headed sire, receive but one answer, and in one
word, Faith? I ask in the name of the millions
of burdened hearts in the world, in the name of
the soul's sovereignty, can we not hear from the
numberless church spires, pointing skyward, the
echo—only faith?

"The moving generations hear and obey the
command—Forward! Held by the scenes and
experiences along life's pathway, but few comparatively have risen from the ranks and demanded the best answer the world can give to
the question, 'to what goal do we march?'

"There have been some in all ages who have
thus interrogated the past and the present. To
these destiny has turned an additional leaf, and
on its page is written 'Peace on earth, good will
to man.' Life beyond the grave is a certainty.
O death where is thy sting, O grave where is thy
victory! Faith, move forward and let knowledge take thy place. The veil between this life
and the next no longer conceals entirely the
future. Hope to the heart that weeps. Lift up
your heads, O ye down trodden ones of earth,
for the angels are often at thy feet. But hold!
What avenues lead to this knowledge? What
pulpit recognizes ministering spirits as inspiring
it? What minister opens his mouth and waits
for God to fill it, without first carefully preparing
his sermon? Are there any inspirational mes-

sages given from God, angels, or ministering
spirits, to man?   Are any moved upon by the
spirit, to-day, as when they spoke in divers
tongues?   Do any speak in foreign tongues now,
while others interpret? Yes.   God has not illumined with electricity man's pathway across the
earth, and then left him to grope his way in darkness as he nears the 'many mansions.'

"The door between the two worlds, or states,
is now ajar; the clergy stand with their backs to
it; the scientists are trying to pick the lock,
while the angels have already lifted the latch and
are opening wide the portals.

"It was at Chicago the finger of destiny
pointed the purpose of the world's exposition,
and there the progress of man was realized.   It
was in this same city by the lake that the world's
congress of religions was held, and where humanity learned for the first time that the spirit of religion is the same, regardless of the dress it may
wear.   Ah! and again did it fall to this young
metropolis to hold within her precincts, now
nearly a score of years, one of the most distinguished inspirational speakers this century has
known.   Her messages, when she is entranced,
are among the wonders of the world.   Her life
is but little less than a miracle.   In her personal
appearance she is modest, refined and queenly.
In her company one feels the presence of a great
person, and the halo of Spiritual gifts seem to

encircle her.   She was given to the world for a
greater purpose, and that pupose is being fulfilled.

"It is a man, Mr. Edison, who has lighted the
pathway of mortals across the earth; it is a
woman, Mrs. Cora L. V. Richmond, who has illumined the so-called dark valley and shadow of
death.   She has tunneled the mountains of materialism, and spanned the ever-varying streams
of the theological dogmas.   She has opened the
channels of inspiration into many lives, and the
Spiritual gifts of which Paul wrote to the Corinthians are now being possessed and enjoyed by
many happy hearts.   How like a mountain
stream in the desert has come this flow of modern inspiration through chosen media of the angelic world, irrigating the fallow theological
ground and giving fresh growth to the exegesis
of the school of divinity.

"How these newly ramifying rivulets of spirit
thought, as they course over the earth, refresh
the lilies of the valley and the forget-me-nots—
the weak and lowly ones on life's arid planes.
On the crowned heads of the old world, as on
the uncrowned of the new, fall the benedictions
of this most gifted woman. Through her guides,
what to many was a leap in the darkness, has
become an enchanted pathway; the yoke of
earthly environment has become easy, and the
burden of mortal existence has been lightened.

"What has this instrument of the spirit realm accomplished in Chicago? Ask of the angels; if you do not find an answer in the vibrating air. Listen to the forest leaves as they whisper to each other messages of love. Catch the scintillating vibrations of human gratitude as they swell the harmonies of the celestial spheres. Open thine eyes, if thou hast Spiritual vision, and behold a temple in our midst more glorious than that of Solomon, because it is builded, not of gold or precious stones, but of the golden offering of the spirit; and upon its altars are we taught to bring the incense of a pure life, and at its shrine may we ever meet her who has asked so little and given so much.

"J. E. DeWolf."

Many letters of like import could be added in testimony of the appreciation of our subject's work in Chicago, but such testimony would be merely cumulative, and out of keeping with the spirit of this work. What we have given is from those who are best able to judge of the value of that work, from the standpoint of knowledge of the facts they have related. We deem this of greater moment than redundancy of testimonies bearing upon the same point. The full measure of this long service in behalf of the cause in the city of Chicago cannot be immediately taken. Years must pass before the fruitage of that work can be found upon the branches of the tree of life of the individuals who have been enabled to come to a full understanding of what her message from the skies to the world really means to the race. We can approximately estimate its worth, and see that it has been a power for good in that great city, the Queen of the West, upon the shores of Lake Michigan. It furnishes a theme for careful study, and commends itself to the earnest consideration of thinking men and women in every quarter of the globe.

This work in Chicago is phenomenal in the fact that a Spiritualistic minister should be retained so long in one place to minister year after year to the same congregation, for the reason that a Spiritualistic congregation differs from other religious congregations. They have no creed nor doctrines that can be rehearsed Sunday after Sunday; no formal prayers and forms of service that are continually repeated; they must have something new, and if they fail to get it they call for another minister or teacher. During all of Mrs. Richmond's work in Chicago and elsewhere, every prayer differs from every other prayer; the same with the discourse, funeral sermons, wedding services and poems. The guides of Mrs. Richmond on a few occasions have, by request, reproduced some of their own poems very nearly the same as the original. The Rev. Dr. Thomas, commenting upon her work, said to an acquaintance of our subject, that he believed it to be beyond the capability of any mortal brain unaided by supernatural power. The Rev. Robert Collyer, speaking of one of her published discourses, said he believed it to be divine inspiration.

Chicago can well be proud of its gifted citizen, this leader of reform and advanced teacher of religion, Mrs. Cora L. V. Richmond.

CHAPTER XIII.

CAMP-MEETING WORK.

WE must now notice an important feature in the propagandism of modern Spiritualism—a feature distinctively American in character, having no parallel in the history of Spiritualism in any other country on the globe. We refer to the camp-meetings, or summer assemblies, that are now so popular in all sections of the United States.

There are about thirty-five well established camps in different sections of the country, all of which are well attended every season, and which form veritable Spiritual meccas toward which the Spiritualist pilgrim turns his face at least once each year, as he journeys on through life. These camp-meetings were not originated by the Spiritualists alone, for other denominations had held them for many years before Spiritualism was ever known, and the influence of these older denominations casts its shadow over the converts to Spiritualism in after years.

Early in the history of this movement, picnics were held by various societies in different

(504)

cities, in some shady grove adjacent to its borders, where they would have music, short addresses, and, occasionally, a few tests. After a time these picnics were extended to two or three days, sometimes even longer. In central New York, in the early fifties, several of these grove meetings were held, also in western Pennsylvania, and in many other sections of the country as well. Some of these grove meetings were held annually for several seasons, then a lack of interest on the part of the leaders or the removal of the most prominent workers, either to Spirit life or to some other section of the earth plane, would cause a lack of interest, and the speedy disintegration of the camps would follow.

One of these societies, however, organized in the year 1855, has continued to hold its meetings down to the present time, and is now a strong local organization in Erie county, New York, bearing the significant title of ''Friends of Human Progress,'' with its headquarters at the village of North Collins, N. Y. Contemporaneous meetings were established near Rochester and Waverly, none of which, however, are now in existence, and the history is lost to the Spiritualistic public. Throughout Massachusetts, and we may say throughout northern New England as well, many of these picnics were held each season. Dr. H. F. Gardner, Dr. A. H. Richardson and other leading lights in Spiritualism were the prime movers in organizing these picnic movements, but no attempt was made to establish camp-meetings proper until after the war. The Methodists, Adventists, and even the Universalists had been in the habit of holding open-air meetings for three or four days at a time, and the first named body—the Methodists—held camp-meetings continuing over a period of two or three weeks. The Spiritualists, by mutual consent, seemed to fall in with the precedent established by these denominations and held meetings of their own, with varying degrees of success, as we have already shown in the references made to the societies that have lived for a short time and then gone out of existence forever.

The camp-meetings, proper, have now become an integral part of the movement in the United States, and no history of Spiritualism can ever be written that does not give to the camp-meetings their full meed of credit, for the work accomplished by them in carrying the light of the new philosophy to thousands of minds who would not otherwise hear it mentioned. At many of these camps, our readers well know, thousands upon thousands of dollars have been expended in cottages and public buildings, in which the lectures, lecturer's seances and entertainments of all kinds are given; also in adorning the grounds with flowers and shrubbery that add to the natural beauty of the scenery that the God of Nature has so beautifully painted upon the canvas wrought by its own hand. The larger camps have fine hotels, with all modern appurtenances, boarding houses, groceries, and all modern conveniences for the comfort of the visitors. The American people, after experiencing the rigor of a Northern Winter, and the extreme heat of early Summer are glad to escape from their city homes for a few weeks' rest beneath the umbrageous trees and leafy bowers at the several camps.

The first Spiritualist camp-meeting in the United States, consequently the first in the world, was held at Malden, Mass., on the 30th of August, 1866. The committee calling this meeting was composed of P. Clark, M. D.; G. W. Bacon; J. S. Hoppin; C. C. York, M. D.; G. W. Vaugh; L. Moody; Dr. U. Clark and E. E. Thompson.

The first meeting was called to order at 10:30 in the morning with an attendance of more than three hundred people. Before evening closed in on that same day upwards of a thousand people were present. This camp was continued for three seasons only, when, owing to the organization of similar associations in different sections, the people were attracted elsewhere and the Malden camp was in consequence abandoned. The second camp-meeting was established at Harwich, Cape Cod, Mass., in 1867, but the first meeting was not held until the Summer of 1868. This camp-meeting has continued in existence ever since

that time and is now one of the ancient land-
marks in the history of Spiritualism.

We have already spoken of the society known
as "Friends of Human Progress," at North Collins, which was organized on a permanent basis
in the early Summer of 1855. It was then, as
its name indicated, a Society for promoting
human progress, chiefly in the direction of the
abolition of slavery. Woman's right to suffrage
was also advocated; and as Spiritualism was
the next step in human progress it became distinctively a Spiritualistic meeting. The meetings
were held in Hemlock Hall, a building whose
appearance can be imagined from the euphoni-
ous name it bears. Our subject, Mrs. Richmond, was one of the first speakers to enter
this hall. Her associates were such men and
women as Henry C. Wright, A. J. Davis, Mary
F. Davis, Fred. Douglas, Wm. Denton, Elizabeth L. Watson, Susan B. Anthony, Geo. W.
Taylor and Lyman C. Howe. Mrs. Richmond
has been employed occasionally, from year to
year since the early meetings by this sturdy band
of Progressive Thinkers in those days when the
subject of freedom was being agitated in all sections of the Union. When the Society was compelled to abandon Hemlock Hall, after twenty-
seven years of faithful service there, it purchased
several acres of land in another section of the
town, in 1883. The Society was then legally in-

corporated, and Mrs. Richmond was invited to give the dedicatory address and poem, and the guides requested to give the name to the commodious building erected upon the new grounds. The poem was one of the best that has ever fallen from the lips of our subject, and the name selected by the guides for the place of meeting was the "Forest Temple." Those who have visited this picturesque spot will observe that the building is most appropriately named.

Her appearance at the North Collins meetings was always the signal for a goodly attendance of people. In the early fifties she was always an attractive feature in the program of speakers. The interest in her and her work has been continued during the years that have passed since her first appearance there. Of the lectures given by her from the North Collins platform, all her contemporaries speak in the highest terms of praise. "She has done a great deal to spread the light of Spiritualism in Western New York," says her friend and co-worker, Lyman C. Howe; "as a child speaker she was deemed a phenomenon, and awakened an interest in the minds of hundreds who otherwise would never have taken any notice whatsoever of a Spiritualist lecturer. The effect of her teachings upon the general public cannot be estimated in words." The friends at North Collins also spoke in high terms of praise of her labors in behalf of their Society during past years.

Many attempts were made to organize camp-meetings in New England and elsewhere soon after the Malden camp proved such a great success, but many of these efforts were unavailing. Walden Pond, which has been immortalized by the pen of the gifted H. D. Thoreau, was the place where a camp-meeting was held two or three seasons, late in the sixties or early in the seventies. These meetings were conducted by Messrs. Richardson and Dodge, but after a time Dr. Gardner and Dr. Richardson moved this camp to Silver Lake, in Plympton, Mass. These meetings were very popular for a time, but were abandoned at the organization of the camp at Lake Pleasant, Mass.

Lake Pleasant was organized in 1874, and has grown to be one of the leading camps in the United States. In 1890 it is stated that over five hundred cottages had been erected at this place. Our subject was among the early speakers called to address the large audiences that assembled at Lake Pleasant. Audiences numbering ten, fifteen and twenty thousand people have been known to assemble here.

It was on one of these occasions, when there was given by her guides a discourse upon the significant and soul-stirring theme: "*To your tents, O Israel!*" of which a synopsis was given in the

"Banner of Light," by the gifted "G. A. B."
Spiritualists were summoned from their worldly
cares, the unceasing service that all, seemingly,
must render to mammon, to worship in the Temple of Nature, and there through the Spirit find
Nature's God.   The discourses given at these
places were always full of the themes needed for
the day and hour, as well as pervaded by those
truths that endure forever.

  She occupied the platform at Lake Pleasant
each summer for a number of years, her last appearance at that place being in the year 1882.
Her appearance upon the platform was always
gladly welcomed by a large number of admiring
friends, and her audiences as large as any that
greeted the several speakers at that place.   It is
impossible to state how her hearers received the
advanced teachings that came through her organism as each soul must answer that question for
itself.

  It is safe to say, however, that the people
received as much light from her as they did irom
any other speaker upon the platform, and that
the record of her work, imperfectly kept at best
on earth, will be revealed in all its splendor and
grand effectiveness, when the Spirit World has
opened to our vision, when we will see and know
each other as we really are.

  Of her work at Onset, one of the great camps
of the United States, its honored president, our

esteemed brother and co-worker, Dr. H. B. Storer
writes as follows:

"H. D. BARRETT,

"MY VALUED FRIEND AND BROTHER:—Your
letter of inquiry, concerning the work of our esteemed sister, Mrs. Cora L. V. Richmond, at
Onset Camp, was forwarded to me from Onset,
and reached me yesterday.

"I regret to say that I have no data by which
I can ascertain just how often Mrs. Richmond
has spoken at Onset since the camp-meeting was
founded. I am quite sure that it would have
been *every* year if *her* other engagements would
have permitted; for no one is more highly appreciated, or whose discourses are considered more
instructive and morally elevating than those which
fall from her lips.

"As to the literary quality and scholarly value
of these discourses, we have to remember that
her inspirations traverse the entire field of human
relationships; their philosophy intuitive and un-
assailable; their scientific arguments based upon
the nature of things, seen in their right relations;
their spirit worshipful and devout; while the diction of her utterances combine the most perfect
grace with the strength and volume of the most
significant language.

"It was my happy fortune to meet her upon
the public platform in the city of Buffalo, N. Y.,
in the year 1855, when she was but fifteen years

of age. The impression made upon my mind at
that time of the transcendent wisdom and beauty
and power of her inspirations has only been deepened and confirmed by my experiences of them
in subsequent years. Religion and Science, twin
angels in the realm of mind, move on together in
the harmony of her discourse. Eternal principles and the application of them to the exigen-
cies of present time, and the course of events in
the history of mankind, all come forth from this
fountain of inspiration, as the questioning minds
of her hearers are prepared to receive the truth.

"We value truth according to our conscious
needs of it, and since her appearance as a chosen
instrument for Spiritual teaching, the impromptu
questions pertaining to all phases of progress and
reform, coming up from tens of thousands of
earnest enquirers, have been answered with the
ease and conscious possession of power worthy
of the highest wisdom.

"I am glad that to you has been committed
the honorable task of compiling her life work;
for you will do it with the spirit and understanding necessary to put into comprehensible form,
something of the mighty work which Mrs. Richmond and her guides have been doing for nearly
forty years."

Our subject has visited Queen City Park but
once during this history, as we will see from the
following letter from the able president of the

Queen City Park Association, Dr. E. A. Smith, who says: "Mrs. Richmond has only given five lectures at our canp, having visited us but one season since Queen City was established. Her lectures gave eminent satisfaction to all who heard them. We should have her here every year were it not for the great expense of having her come such a long distance as it is from Chicago to this point."

In 1883 a Spiritualist camp-meeting was organized under the laws of the state of Tennessee, upon Lookout Mountain. The name of this association was given through Mr. George P. Colby, of Lake Helen, Florida, under the control of his famous guide Seneca, who gave the name of *Lookout Mountain Camp-Meeting Association*.

The first meeting under its charter was held in 1884. To Lookout Camp we find that our subject was called on three successive seasons, where she was, as ever, the center of attraction.

It was in the Summers of 1888, '89, '90 that she visited that most picturesque spot. During those seasons Mr. Paul R. Albert was president, and Mr. Seeman, his brother-in-law, treasurer of the association. Those two gentlemen with their families contributed much to make her visits at that Southern camp among the most enjoyable of her life. From the first she felt as though they were old and cherished friends, and we have no doubt that is the testimony of all true mediums who have come in contact with them. If we had been able to have reached them we would have called upon them to give our readers their impressions of Mrs. Richmond's work among them and her work at that place. The well-known Spiritualist who is now president of Lookout Camp, Jerry Robinson, writes as follows:

"H. D. BARRETT,

"DEAR SIR AND BROTHER:—I take great pleasure in saying—to the goodness of Mrs. Cora L. V. Richmond—she kindly gave her services for three years to our camp-meeting, out of her desire to assist us and a wish to serve the cause. She was appreciated by every one, especially by those who were desirous of learning something of the philosophy of life here and hereafter. I look upon her as one of the leading lights of the cause of Spiritualism. She spoke or lectured from four to eight times a week during the month of each year that she was engaged by us, She was teaching all the time, either on or off the rostrum, class work being included. I hope we may some day have her again with us.

"Fraternally,

"JERRY ROBINSON."

Her audiences at Lookout Mountain were among the largest that assembled at that place, and her hearers went away with a feeling that

they had been instructed by the words she
uttered. She dealt with questions the people
could understand and in which they were interested. One characteristic of her work may well
be noticed here. She has never been an icono-
clast in the sense of being a destroyer alone.
Whatever she has undertaken to destroy she has
done in a kindly manner and has always had
something better to offer in its place. This
teaching was peculiarly adapted to the people
who assembled at Lookout Mountain, as the
earnest words of Mr. Robinson indicate.

Copious extracts might be made from the secular press of Chattanooga, Tennessee, of her
work at this camp, but space forbids, and our
readers already know the universal testimony of
the press as to the scholarship and logic and sublime ethics of these discourses.

A religious camp-meeting association was
established at Frazer's Grove, near Vicksburg,
Michigan, in 1883. To this camp our subject
was called each season following the organization
of the same. Here she received the same appreciative attention that has been hers at other
camps where she has labored since the inauguration of the camp-meeting movement in the United
States. Vicksburg has none of the attractions
possessed by Lookout Mountain, Lake Pleasant,
Onset or Cassadaga, yet as a local camp-meeting
it has been largely attended and the best of

talent has appeared upon its platforms, Mrs. A.
M. Gladding, Lyman C. Howe, and Mrs. R. S.
Lillie being among the contemporary speakers
with our subject. Her repeated calls to this
place is indicative of her popularity with the
people and proves that the good people of Vicks
burg camp are highly progressive in their views,
and that they feel she is one of the leading exponents of the philosophy their camp represents.

She has also visited Maple Dell Camp, in
Ohio, during the past few years, where she has
received a warm welcome from the good people
assembled to listen to the uplifting truths of
Spiritualism. This camp is under the able management of D. M. King, an old-time worker in
our cause. Her lectures here were attended by
more than the average audiences and the teachings given from that rostrum were eagerly received
by all who listened to them.

Another large camp has been established at
Lake Brady, Ohio, where three annual meetings
have been held since its legal incorporation.
Captain B. F. Lee is the able president, assisted by a most efficient Board of Directors, of
which Mr. Stoeffel is the hard-working secretary.
Mrs. Richmond opened the camp and has been
given a prominent place upon the rostrum at
Lake Brady each of these three seasons. The
audience at this camp varies upon the various
days of the week. The Sunday audiences are

always large, receptive to truth, and possessed of a sincere desire to learn of Spiritualism. Our subject has always received a warm welcome at this place, and her audiences have been among the largest assembled there. In company with Mr. W. J. Colville, she was employed for the closing week of 1894, lecturing alternate days with him. The closing lecture was given through her organism to an audience of several thousand. From some of the regular attendants at Lake Brady, we learn that the teachings of the guides were eagerly sought by many who wished to learn something definite concerning the views of our subject upon the destiny of the human soul. Our informant also states that hundreds of friendships for Mrs. Richmond were formed at each of these three visits and that her return is eagerly looked for by them at many coming conclaves of the Lake Brady Association.

Wherever Spiritualism has a hearing there are people who have read or heard her lectures, and would feel grieved if her name were to be omitted from the program of the leading camps of the country.

About twenty-five years ago the Spiritualists in the vicinity of Laona, New York, began to hold picnics at Alden's Grove, on Cassadaga Lake, near what is now known as Lily Dale. These picnics lasted only a day or two each year for a number of years, but they were the origin of what is now known as the June meeting, or three days' picnic, held early in June of each season. We have not been able to find any record that our subject was in attendance upon these picnics, although we know that she spoke at Laona and Fredonia early in her ministry, and that she was frequently at her mother's home at North Cuba, N. Y., while these picnics were being held, hence, it is highly probable that she may have attended some of them.

In 1877 Dr. J. F. Carter was impressed to go to some of his friends and interest them in arranging for a camp-meeting in Alden's Grove. He was successful in his undertaking and was joined by many earnest workers through whose instrumentality the first camp-meeting assembled on the 11th of September, 1877, in Alden's Grove. Many eminent speakers were in attendance and were greeted by large audiences. Meetings were held annually at this place until 1880, when a new association was formed known as the *Cassadaga Lake Free Association*, now so widely known as Cassadaga Camp. The dedication of the new ground took place June 15th, 1880. Mrs. Richmond was first employed at Cassadaga Camp in 1881. Her next appearance was in 1887, during the same season that the Hon. A. Gaston was elected president of the camp. She has been one of the leading attractions upon that platform since the year last

named. Mrs. M. H. Skidmore considers Mrs.
Richmond to be one of the best speakers upon
the Spiritualist platform, and that the program
of Cassadaga would be sadly incomplete without
her name upon its list. Of her teachings Mrs.
Skidmore also speaks with much feeling, saying
that she considers them of the most advanced
order, and that they have come in at a time when
they were most needed, that their effect will be
to lead the thought of the people to the consideration of higher aspects of the philosophy
and religion of Spiritualism. "She ably eluci-
dates the profoundest themes," Mrs. Skidmore
says, "and opens up new fields of thought to all
those who listen to her words." Mrs. Skidmore,
let it be known, stands in the same relation to
Spiritualism in Chautauqua County, N. Y., as
Susan B. Anthony does to the suffrage movement in the state of New York.

Mr. T. J. Skidmore, ex-president of the Cassadaga Lake Free Association, speaks in equal
terms of appreciation of the work that Mrs. Richmond has performed at Cassadaga.

Her remarkable poem, at the dedication
of the Skidmore Cottage, in 1890, when the
beautiful names, "Bonnie Castle Avelon," were
applied to the Skidmore home, is feelingly mentioned by both Mr. and Mrs. Skidmore in connection with her work at Cassadaga. One of the
lines of this poem reads, "Avelon, Avelon, the

home of the blest." The muse was certainly in
the spirit of poesy on that occasion, as our readers can see from the reference to the home of the
philanthropic Skidmores as the "home of the
blest."

Hon. A. Gaston, present president of this
camp, says: "Mrs. Richmond has been the means
of drawing many people here in spite of the fact
that many differ from her upon certain lines of
thought. Her work has been of the very highest
order, and she ranks among the best of our speakers. She has been the means of giving a great
deal of instruction to our people, and is considered by all who know her to be a tower of
strength to the platform of Cassadaga."

Her classes have been a distinctive feature of
her work at many of the camps that she has
visited each year since the inauguration of the
camp-meeting work. To these classes we have
already alluded in our reference to her work in
England, California and Chicago, relating as they
do to Psychopathy and to the Soul in Human Embodiments. Some of the pupils who entered her
class room with feelings of doubt and utter skepticism in regard to her philosophy and theoretical reasoning, have become thoroughly convinced
of the truth of the same through the irresistible
logic and practical explanations she has brought
to bear upon the subject she was elucidating.

It is not too much to say here, that these

classes have formed a most important part of
her work at all of the camp-meetings visited by
her. Her pupils became her most enthusiastic
friends, and remain devoted to her and to her
teachings after having once become convinced
that the guides are right in the positions they
take upon these lofty themes. The letters that
have been received from these grateful friends
who have been led to a higher perception of what
they felt to be the truth through this class work,
and through reading her lectures and books upon
the same line of thought, would fill a volume
many times the size of this, and all would be of
great interest to the reading public. Space forbids their reproduction here, and only our word
in regard to the same can be given.

From all camps visited by our subject since
the camp-meeting work became a distinctive feature of Spiritualistic propagandism, come reports
similar to those we have mentioned above. All
regularly organized camp-meetings would be only
too glad to have her upon their platforms if her
services could be obtained, but as her time is
constantly employed by her home Society, in
Chicago, it is not possible for her to visit more
than three or four camps each season.

It is said that friendship is the brightest flower
that blooms in this cold world of ours, and the
friendships that are born of the soul must be the
brightest and sweetest flowers that bloom in the

celestial gardens in the world of souls; therefore, these friendships, born of the blending of the two worlds, seem to unite heart to heart and soul to soul, the material with the Spiritual, in a never-ending chain of love and sympathy, that moves around and around as the never-ending cycles of time flit away, carrying those thus united to supremer heights, to a broader view of the yet grander truths, still unrevealed in that soul world, which our gifted medium is endeavoring to make real and tangible to the children of men.

The influence of these camp-meetings cannot be estimated. From the rocky hills of New England, upon whose brows the pine trees whisper together in the summer breezes; or upon the western slopes of the Coast Range, in the Golden State; or upon the banks of the softly murmuring rivers in the forests of Oregon or Washington; or down upon the shining sands of the Gulf of Mexico; or upon lofty Lookout; in shady Parkland; in lovely Cassadaga; in smiling Lake Pleasant; or upon the hills overlooking the waters of glorious Onset, where old ocean rolls in his never ending waves upon the beach,—the voice of the spirit is surely making its way down into the hearts of the people who throng these sylvan retreats to hear what that world of souls has to offer to the soul-sick child of man.

Here in these various places the loftiest thought that Spiritualism has to give to the world finds

utterance; here speakers so touched by a high and
holy inspiration from off the very altars of truth
builded in the supernal world; here thousands
who never have attended a Spiritualist meeting,
or listened to even the tiniest rap upon the table,
are found. Many of these come to scoff, but,
like the man mentioned by the writer of old,
have remained to pray. These camp-meetings,
through the speakers and mediums who have
been employed upon their platforms, have been
the means of shedding the light and truth of
Spiritualism abroad in the land. Their effects
upon the religious, social, intellectual and moral
lives of the people can never be told in song or
story—they must be measured by the better
lives, by the nobler deeds, by the purer thoughts,
and by the higher conceptions of right and duty
that these thousands of people express in their
actions, in their daily walks of life, and by the
purer and nobler humanity that succeeds the
present generation, whose leading minds are now
in control of, or managing these splendid camps.
Of those who have taught and wrought earnestly in these fields of labor, we find our subject
among the foremost. She does not feel that her
work has been a center around which all others
must revolve; she has simply been one with the
reformers and teachers who have endeavored to
bring in a better condition of things for suffering
humanity. That she has been able to do this is

evinced by the multitude of facts that we have recorded upon these pages; by the coming to-gether from great distances of those who have listened to her voice in early years, or who have read the later teachings of the guides; by the expressions of divine sympathy and heartfelt love given forth by them. Now, that many of these friends of our subject are going down toward life's Western horizon, they are looking with eager eyes over the Western mountains whose tops are being painted vermillion and gold by the setting sun, as he is about to glide down into the darkness of the River of Death to rise on that bright shore where the enfranchised souls will bid us each a glad good-morning.

CHAPTER XIV.

LITERARY WORK.

It is not alone as a public speaker that our subject has become known to the thinking people of America and Europe, but also through her pen, by which she has reached thousands of human hearts in the uplifting influences pertaining to her published discourses, poems, and philosophical and scientific works. She entered the field of literature at an early age, being in her eighteenth year only when she published the first volume of her discourses, containing twenty of her first lectures in New York City. This volume has been succeeded by several subsequent ones, comprising about the same number of lectures each. They have been issued at various times during her ministry, when the subjects of the lectures and the thoughts expressed in them were deemed of greatest moment to the reading public.

Of the literary merit of these various works our readers can well judge through the excerpts we have made from her lectures, and those we shall make from her other works in connection with this line of thought. In presenting her discourses to the public, it is impossible for a reporter to give more than a record of the ideas advanced, clothed in the speaker's language, while the impressions conveyed through the gestures, voice and peculiar expressions of the countenance are all lost. The value of the thought, however, expressed in these several books is not lost by being put into cold tpye.

The oratorical embellishments, like a forest that has lost some of its leaves, are wanting; but our readers well know that it is the relation of a writer's thought to his language that makes a book valuable to him through his ability to apply it to his life and to his own expressions of thought. In order to do this one must familiarize himself with the style and spirit of the author. The discourses of our subject, as we have stated repeatedly, cover such a wide range of subjects as to constitute a continued series of progressive or upward steps for the reader. Each lecture is a story in itself, and opens the mental vision to a wider view in the intellectual fields of thought than ever before presented. She has blended in these published lectures religion and science in a way that leads one to the comprehension of higher truths underlying these two departments of human knowledge and aspiration, as we may say, so that there will be in the minds of all who follow her inspired pages a realization of the fact that Modern Spiritualism has come to the world to be at once a science, philosophy and religion. Her philosophical and metaphysical lectures present the most advanced thoughts upon the different subjects relating to the cosmos, and the deductions made from scientific experiments, possible for any mind to grasp under the limitations of mortal life.

The first volume of her lectures was published early in the year 1858, and comprises the discourses that were stenographically reported during portions of the previous year. Her lecture on the gyroscope, to which we have already alluded, will hereafter appear in full, so that our readers may have an opportunity of judging for themselves in regard to this most famous of her philosophical lectures. One volume of her discourses that is worthy of especial note, not only for the value of the thoughts expressed in the lectures, but also from a literary point of view, is the one entitled, ''The Sciences and their Philosophy,'' given in Dodworth's Hall, New York, in 1859. This book shows that the guides were versed in all the sciences, the history of the Christian religion, ancient history, moral and mental philosophy, and all of the applied sciences. The literary style of this volume is terse and vigorous, abounding in rare epigrams, which make the reader think upon the subjects presented to his vision on the pages he is perusing.

Verbosity and tergiversation of thought are

wanting in all of her works, only in so far as appropriate adjectives and the advancement from one stage to another in elucidating a subject to her readers, are absolutely needed. Neither can she be accused of being tautological in her writings; she makes her statements clear and distinct, expresses them in positive terms, and goes straight toward the point she wishes to make. The aim of the guides prompting her is to make each step an upward one, and to cause the reader to think for himself upon the points advanced in her works. This statement is true of all the volumes of her discourses that have been published since 1857, and it is doubly true of "Psychopathy" and "The Soul in Human Embodiments," published more recently.

In 1871, her famous poem, "Hesperia," was given to the world. This poem, a book of 235 pages, dedicated to the future Republic, attracted the attention of the scholars, litterateurs and statesmen of the nation, at the time of its appearance. The theme of this work is one in which all American citizens would naturally feel an interest, and from the introduction to Hesperia, we quote a brief description of the subject of the work.

"Astræa, the genius of liberty and justice, seeks a dwelling place upon the earth. Persecuted and driven from land to land, she follows the evening star and finds at last a beautiful kingdom in the

Western world; this becomes her home and the birthplace of her beloved daughter Hesperia.

"Erotion, the genius of love and fidelity, the husband of Astræa and father to Hesperia, after many wanderings in search, at last joins the objects of his love and care. Reunited they preside over this new land and seek to preserve it for their child's inheritance. They are recognized and cherished by a small band of devoted followers, who summon them to their councils in the city of Fraternia.

"At first liberty and love prevail, but Astræa discovers the presence of a serpent who breathes on her a subtle poison, and she (with Erotion) is slain.

"Llamia, the serpent of policy, then controls and takes in charge the beautiful child Hesperia; seeking to unite her in marriage to her foul son Slavery—who must be nameless evermore; but Hesperia is warned by the genius of nature, Calios, who, in the guise of a poet and magician, holds sway even over Llamia. When Hesperia beholds him she recognizes her soul's counterpart, and is prepared, by his words and love, to resist all the evil machinations of Llamia and her son.

"Llamia, however, holds temporary power over the form of Hesperia, and succeeds in throwing a spell around the maiden which she vainly imagines will prove fatal; the love of her parents and of Calios rouses her spirit, and with them she withdraws into the world of souls, where, for a time, she beholds the scenes enacted under the influence of Llamia. She witnesses in Athenia and Crescentia deeds of horror and the tortures inflicted upon the oppressed. Calios sings to her in plaintive songs of these down-trodden ones, lures her by the voices of nature, and in interludes of love and truth seeks to win her back to her earthly kingdom.

"Long years does Llamia hold sway and at last wakens the voice of war; when Astræa, not dead, but only withdrawn for a space, turns the sword of Llamia upon her son.

"Through long suffering is Hesperia made strong and pure. She listens to the voice of Nature's children and their tortures cease; slavery and war are known no more. Astræa and Erotion are again the attendant and abiding souls of this fair land; they witness with rapture and benedictions the union of Calios and Hesperia, who rule with undivided sway over the most lovely empire of the earth."

The induction to this poem, as she calls it, consists of forty-two triple lined stanzas of exquisite beauty and power. The Genius of Liberty and Justice she likens to a beautiful woman, who stands upon a high rock, looking out over the sea, musing over her failure to find a home in other lands, but with a feeling of hope in her heart that America will prove a land of safety, as well as of refuge, for her persecuted children. This beautiful woman spoke, and her voice "Filled all the vibrant air with harmonies," telling how the Orient and the Crescent had ceased to hold any place in their land for Freedom, and that in the islands of Greece, and in Italy she could dwell no longer, but must find a home far beyond the Pillars of Hercules. Then, closing with these beautiful words, almost prophetic of what is soon to be realized all over the earth:

"Europe shall feel my breath, ere while she hates
And loathes me and my children, but she waits
Until slow tyranny unlocks the gates.

Let Cross and Crescent bar the doors of pearl,
Let emerald waters all their wild waves hurl
Hope doth her banner brightly now unfurl."

She then turned and looked toward the West, and chose the fairest land beneath the skies for her dwelling place. This was our own loved native land. She claimed it from sea to sea as the home of the spirit of Liberty. The poet tells the story in the following triplet:

"Sandaled with plumes of thought, her spirit sent
Its living form across the continent,—
A thousand leagues on its great purpose bent."

After having brought all the land under sway, her daughter Hesperia, or the Spirit of Love, was born. Her story is one that tells us how the Indian tribes were subdued and exterminated one by one, and how Slavery was at last overcome, after causing much agony to the gentle mother Astræa or Freedom, and the daughter Hesperia.

The second portion, or the prelude to Book First, is entitled "Astræa," and shows us that the painter's skill, the sculptor's art, the poet's song, the architect's lofty conceptions, the sweet breath of music and the instruments of harmony are all transitory, fleeting in their natures, so far as their expressions on earth are concerned, but

> "Those high immortal minds, —
> Masters of harmony,
> Masters of poetry
> Masters of line and form,
> Masters of masonry,
> Each clasp their hands with all
> And climb the three-fold height
> Of that art pyramid
> That reaches up to Heaven."

and then, with a most wonderful word painting, shows us that Nature and Art are one, as souls are one with God:

> "Matter reveals God's form,
> As truth reveals his soul."

Our author's references to music are most beautiful, one of the refrains being, "The anthems of the sea still sound exultingly." So beautiful is the reference to the pine trees that

we reproduce it as it came from the master mind,
in these words:

"Broad peans from the pines,—
The matchless, murmuring pines,
The writhing, wailing pines,
The sighing, sobbing pines,
The music haunted pines,
We weep for melody like yours."

Her reference to Mozart, Haydn, Beethoven,
the grand oratories of all musicians of all lands
are most beautiful. We can almost hear the
sobbing, sighing pines, making melancholy music
as the winds of winter sweep through their
branches, the voice of the sky lark, and of the
sweet warblers of the forests, together with the
sweet song of the nightingale, are heard in spirit
as we read the poet's words. We can see the
hand of a royal architect erecting earth's mighty
pillars, a royal painter marking all the forms of
life with coloring, and making all the world to
glow with rare combinations of colors, like the
beautiful rainbow arch of heaven; the sweet
flowers unfolding their petals to greet the sun as
it rises o'er the earth, expressing a thought of far
greater potency than any ever given forth by
mortal mind. The sacred lotus and the water
lilies are indices of the uplifting of the thoughts
of man to this mighty power that has expressed
these perfect thoughts in the rare colors of earth
and sky, these rare symphonies of music in the
voices of the birds, and the moaning of the trees,

or in the forms of the flowers that have come to
bless the children of men.

> "So every perfect thought
> Enfolds us like a robe
> Becomes a part of all,
> That we ourselves become
> And paves the starry way
> To our eternal home."

We cannot enter into the consideration of the
thought expressed in the dialogue between Erotion and Astræa, but we find there some of the
sublimest thoughts expressed in blank verse that
it has ever been our privilege to read. The love
that Astræa had for Hesperia is most beautifully
told, but it would mar the rare beauty of the
poem to give even a brief extract here. The
poem itself must be read and studied in order to
understand its matchless beauty.

Astræa is one day watching the eagles pushing their young fledglings out of the nest, to have
them try their wings in flight, the mother bird
watches them that she may dive down beneath
them to catch the falling birds upon her back
lest they shall be dashed to pieces upon the
earth below. She applies this to the children of
men, saying:

> " So doth the Infinite with us,
> Pushing us forth from His eternal nest
> That we may learn to fly alone, His love
> Meanwhile extending far beneath
> To save us if we fall."

In speaking to her husband, Erotion, concerning Hesperia, Astræa utters some words that
are worthy of the consideration of all thinking
people.   We quote this at length in order that
our readers may see what the guides of Mrs.
Richmond have taught upon this all important
question of woman's emancipation, and have
been teaching during her whole ministry:

> '' Well I know
> To whom more than all others she will be
> A blessing and a guiding star of love.
> Woman—who, held as any chattel slave
> By other slaves, the monarchs of the world,
> Whose simple duty is to please their sense,
> Or while away an idle hour at best;
> Or who, in Europe sits upon a throne
> Of social power and plays the mocking-bird
> For some fool's pleasure, lending her rare powers
> To idle mimicry and glittering show.
> Woman—who sits with motionless white lips,
> But dares not sing the song that rises there;
> Though genius kindled and eloquent,
> She crowds it back to break upon her heart.
> Woman, who, loveless and unloved, becomes
> The sneer and jest of every idler's tongue,
> Because, perchance, she dares to walk alone
> The narrow paths of life, rather than bear
> The loathsome bonds of an unholy tie
> Which her soul cannot sanction; for a dream
> Has ever burned within her heart—a pure
> A lofty, bright ideal—and its flame
> Makes there a vestal altar unto God.
> Woman, who, at the worst goes madly forth
> From some harsh parent's roof, like a blind moth
> Allured by the false glare of pleasure's flame,

Or falser promises of a dark soul;
But who within her heart loathes things impure,
And only seeks for love and sympathy;
Woman, who, at the best, must watch and pray,
Keeping the vestal fires forever bright,
In battlemented tower and guarded wall,
Lest some rude breath of calumny and scorn
Shall mar the altar's spotless purity—
But who, if some bright being sudden came,
Endowed with heaven inspired eloquence,
To break the chains and gyves that bind her thus,
Open the gates of cruel circumstance
To the bright angel opportunity,
Would uplift heart and hands in purest joy
And thankfulness, and trusting, follow her
To those pure heights only attained by those
Who choose the martyr's glorious fiery doom,
Rather than bear the galling, gilded chains
Which unrequited love and labor forge
To bind in fetters the fair queens of earth."

To these splendid pictures of Astræa in regard
to Hesperia and what she hopes she will accomplish for women, Erotion replies with deep feeling. He commends this splendid dream, and
fearlessly rebukes parents for being petty tyrants
in their homes. Corporeal punishment is shown
up in all its horrors to the reader, and a strong
plea is made for the rule of love in every home.
Erotion then proceeds to discuss the marriage
question in a philosophical vein, and shows that
many parents are wedded only by the law of the
land, not by the law of the soul. Of true marriage, or union of souls, he speaks most eloquently, and says that from the union of souls

the saviors, martyrs, rarest poets, and grandest
intellects have sprung:

> " Who gives unto his age a thought complete
> Hath been the offspring of marriage as pure
> As that which gave a Jesus to the world."

All saviors and other high souls, who have
blessed mankind are twin born. "Perfect lives
become the full expression of Heaven's harmonies," says Erotion, "yet high thoughts and
ministrations bring no recompense of the world's
fame." He closes his speech with the prophecy
that Hesperia will live to triumph over all her
foes. When slavery fell the words of Erotion
seemed about to be realized, but when the en-
slavement of the laborers of all of the artisan
classes took place, when Mammon resumed the
throne of power, the day of Hesperia's full
triumph was postponed. When it shall come
none of us can tell, but some day, perhaps far
away in the future, Liberty shall reign supreme
over the entire earth.

The second part of this wonderful poem is entitled "Fraternia," and refers to the work accomplished in Philadelphia, the cradle of American
liberty. The invitation to Liberty and Love to
dwell with the American people and be their
rulers is given in the finest political language.
The Revolutionary fathers, with their serious,
care-worn faces, are sitting in solemn council,
trying to find some one capable of ruling their
land in a spirit of justice. They offer a crown

to one of their greatest leaders, and he refuses to accept it. They seek some one to lead them when Erotion and Astræa appear in their midst, weary and worn with their journeyings, pale and haggard from much suffering, yet true to their devotion to the principles of right. They are welcomed and are given a royal greeting. The patriots are eager to crown Astræa, or Love, as their Queen, and Erotion, or Liberty, as their king. This portion of the book, Fraternia, is dedicated to Lucretia Mott. It is impossible to fully describe the rare beauty of this section of the poem. It must be read to be appreciated. The fair city, Fraternia, as Philadelphia at first promised to be, gave refuge for a time to the spirit of Liberty and Love, but Hesperia lost her loved parents and imagined that they had gone back to their lonely mountain home, there to enjoy their freedom undisturbed by any tyrant or foe in the human form. They placed Hesperia in charge of a lady who was honored by all men, and who sympathized with Hesperia in her loneliness. This woman was Llamia, who sought to soothe her. The story of Fraternia is filled with many excellent thoughts, with one of which we close our review as follows:

> " It is easy to make rules
>   For others, set the golden word on high,
>   For all the world to follow save ourselves.
>   We claim exemption by especial plea
>   And hope to pettifog our way to heaven."

Lucretia Mott, acknowledges the dedication in the following letter:

"ROADSIDE (Near Philadelphia),
December 20, 1870.

"MY DEAR FRIEND:

"I have suffered thine of the 8th inst. to remain too long unacknowledged, hardly knowing what ought to be said. Long accustomed to have my name held up to reproach, I learned 'to endure hardness.' Now, that the tide is turned (save as to Woman's Rights), it is not so easy to receive adulation and complimentary notes, and make just the right returns. So if thy intended honor be not duly acknowledged, please make allowance for ignorance.

"Sincerely thine,
"LUCRETIA MOTT."

The story of Hesperia is continued in Part Third under the name of Llamia, dedicated to William Lloyd Garrison, and his noble coadjutors, the men and women of the Anti-Slavery Society. Llamia is the Serpent of Policy, who rules America, both North and South, by means of her siren-like power. In her home Hesperia is placed, as she leaves Fraternia. Here Llamia continues her direful machinations and attempts to wed Hesperia to her foul son, Slavery, but she is foiled, and Hesperia makes her escape, only to be recaptured and held in her power until the poet, Calios, Hesperia's soul counterpart, breaks the spell and sets Hesperia free. While under Llamia's power, Hesperia is nearly slain by the fearful intrigues and conspiracies that Llamia uses to maintain her sway over her victim's mind. This captivity only serves to make Hesperia and the friends of Liberty everywhere the more determined to destroy Llamia and her son when the final contest is waged.

Part Fourth of the story is called Crescentia, dedicated to Frederick Douglas, champion of freedom, and to the Southern Loyalists. The theme of this portion of the story of Hesperia deals with one of the Southern cities, probably New Orleans, and gives a brief pen picture of the conditions of the people, and their feelings during the few years prior to the war, under the influence of Llamia and her son, Slavery.

Part Fifth is entitled Athenia, and refers to Boston, and is dedicated to Wendell Phillips, the friend of humanity and the master of eloquence. Even Athenia is under the domination of Llamia and Slavery, for her citizens permitted the fugitive slaves to be taken back into bondage from their city, so great was their fear of the political power of the South. For this subservience and truckling to America's evil genius, the spirit of Freedom pronounces loud and deep curses upon Athenia, who is made to pay the penalty of wrongdoing in the long, bloody Civil War that came to destroy the power of Llamia and Slavery.

Mr. Phillips, in a friendly letter, acknowledges the dedication and the receipt of a copy of Hesperia in the following words:

"Why did you send me this superb copy of your fine poem? 'I never deserved it,' as Charles Lamb used to say, when his crony poet, Barton, sent him a fine haunch. 'I never would have given you as fine a thing.' Well, it is because you are the more generous; but I can tell a good thing when I see it almost as quick as you can, so have that right and title to the volume that Coleridge claimed when he borrowed a wise book and never returned it, viz.: that he 'valued it and knew its use better than the assumed owner.' I think, judged by that test—the pleasure it gives—I have a clear title to this flowing of soul into gorgeous touching lines. Let me congratulate you on having, as Byron sings: 'Wreaked your thoughts upon expression, and thrown soul, heart, mind, passions into words,' so successfully and sweetly.

"Faithfully yours,
"May 4, 1871."   "WENDELL PHILLIPS."

We take this opportunity to state that Mr. Garrison and Mr. Douglas were also both warm, personal friends of our subject, and expressed themselves as much pleased with the poem as a whole, and especially with the compliment paid to them in the dedication of certain portions of it to them.

Book Second, in Hesperia, deals with the history of the Indian tribes upon the American soil. The first, being a most charming poem couched in exquisite language, and abounding with splendid figures of speech and fine imagery of thought, is the sad, romantic story of Ouina and her parents. As we have already adverted to this, we need not dwell upon this beautiful poem any further than to call our readers' attention to its rare beauty, that they may read it for themselves.

Part Second of the sad story of the Indians is entitled Laus Natura, dedicated to Walt Whitman, the poet of Nature. It is a most pathetic song, and the refrain of the prelude in the words, "How they wave," referring to all of the vegetable and floral kingdoms, all the different manifestations that the Indians perceived in Nature, is most pathetic. The pleading of the Indian people through their different tribes for justice is most vividly portrayed. The story is told in exquisite language, and the pathos of its diction touches the heart of every reader. This poem should be in the hands of every lover of justice in America, and will cause the cheek of every thinking man and woman to tingle with shame as the wrongs of the helpless Indian people are brought to view. As we read, we can hear the eloquent tongues of Powhattan, pleading for justice, gentle Pocahontas pleading for the captives

and endeavoring to establish peace, the great
Massasoit, from the rocky shores of New England, sends up his pleading cry from the depths
of his mild spirit for justice and right, until at
last he was compelled to rise to defend his own;
stately King Phillip, with eloquent tongue and
sterling devotion to his country, the great patriot
of the Narragansetts; Canonicus, Miantonomo,
Canonchet, Garangula, Tecumseh, the mighty
chieftain of the War of 1812, the eloquent Logan,
the betrayed Osceola, the wronged Pontiac, and
the lordly Sagoyawatha, all, all are heard
from their tombs relating the sad story of their
wrongs; and crying out for redress.   No Spiritualist can read this wonderful poem without
being stirred to a sense of duty in regard to his
relations to the Indian.

Mr. Whitman acknowledges the receipt of a
copy of Hesperia in the following words:

"WASHINGTON, D. C., May 5, 1871.

"MY DEAR MADAM AND FRIEND:—I was ex-
pecting to visit New York early this month, and
intended to call and thank you for your beautiful and valued gift of Hesperia—but finding I
shall not go now for two or three weeks, I write
to acknowledge the receipt of the poem and to say
that when I come on, I shall personally call and
pay my respects.   WALT WHITMAN."

The closing portion of this beautiful story,
under the captions "Red, White and Blue," is

entitled "The Benediction," and refers to retribution, compensation and prophecy. It is dedicated to "Ulyses S. Grant, the earnest patriot, the faithful servant of the people, the true friend of the oppressed and long abused Indian, the citizen soldier who prefers to exchange the laurels of war for the olive branch of peace."

This poem shows that the law of retribution for the evils of slavery, and the injustice done to the Indian was most certainly felt. Also that the law of compensation meted out to the people who had suffered wrong, at last, their measure of justice, and made all the people of the earth to know that right had conquered wrong.

The prophecy indicated a brighter and better day for the Nation, the promise of the Spiritual millenium that shall bring in a universal reign of peace. President Grant sent an autograph letter in acknowledgment of the receipt of the copy of Hesperia. After suitable greeting, General Grant says:

"I have the honor to acknowledge the receipt of a copy of Hesperia which you were so kind as to send me. I beg that you will accept my thanks for your very kind expressions, and for the volume which I hope to read at my earliest leisure.   Very respectfully,

"U. S. GRANT.

"Executive Mansion, April 17, 1871."

In addition to Hesperia, and the several volumes of Discourses that we have referred to, besides many minor poems of great merit, she has published two other works, the one philosophical and scientific entitled "Psychopathy," and the other, "The Soul in Human Embodiments." Psychopathy is divided into eight chapters, all of which deal with the different types of life, foods, and their value, and various things pertaining to a thorough understanding of the human organism. The first chapter deals with the Physical and Spiritual Basis of Life. The second treats of the Influence of Spirit over the Organic Functions of the Body. The third, of the Influence of Food, raiment and surrounding conditions and atmospheres upon the Human Organism. Fourth, of Psychology, Mesmerism, Magnetism, and Electricity, as healing agencies. Fifth, of Social Life, including Marriage and Parentage. Sixth, of Actual Magnetic Poles and their corresponding nerve centres, their relation to Psychopathic treatment. Seventh, of volition. Eighth, a resume of the entire series.

Both "Psychopathy" and the "Soul" are filled with sublime thoughts, couched in the most scholarly language, scientifically applied, and philosophically considered. It would not be fair to the scholarly attainments of the authors of these works to epitomize their teachings in a brief review. It was said of Spinoza that his premises in philosophy being granted, his conclusions must inevitably be accepted by all of his students. The same statement is true of the teachings of the guides through Mrs. Richmond. The logic of Psychopathy and the Soul is most complete, and unanswerable from the standpoint of the majority of the readers of those works. If a man or woman desires to think, or wishes to be compelled to think, these works should be placed in their hands. They cannot fail to be benefited by the careful study that these books require. Therefore, we can say in passing that the literary standing of "Psychopathy" and the "Soul" is among the very first works on those subjects in English literature. The ideas are expressed in language that any thinking person cannot fail to comprehend. These books should be in the hands of every Spiritualist on the globe.

One of Ouina's serials is worthy of especial mention in this work. It is entitled "Zulieka," and was published in the columns of "The Progressive Thinker," in the Winter of 1892 and 1893. It is considered one of the finest works that has been given through her organism. It deals with romance, fact, fiction, politics, psychic experiences, and occult arts in a most intensely interesting and instructive manner. The story was planned and written by Ouina entirely without the knowledge of the medium, as she was in an unconscious trance state under Ouina's control at the time. It seems that Mr. J. R. Francis, the able and enterprising editor of "The Progressive Thinker," one day asked Ouina for a contribution to its columns. She promised him a story, and the result of her promise was the weirdly beautiful romance "Zulieka." Ouina has a sanctum all to herself in the medium's home, into which she would take Mrs. Richmond in the trance state, write chapter after chapter of the story in orderly form; then lock the manuscript in her desk until it was called for by Editor Francis. Mrs. Richmond never read one word of the story until after it had been published in "The Progressive Thinker."

In order to fully comprehend this marvellous story from the skies, our readers must study it for themselves. The occult realm is visited by the writer in a most realistic sense, and the facts underlying Occultism are clearly presented to our view. The reader is carried away by the beautiful pen pictures that reveal so much of the wondrous beauties of the two worlds which are made to appear as closely united in one. It makes one almost sigh for like experiences so vividly realistic do the scenes depicted by Ouina appear to all.

The story is full of useful lessons. A broadminded English nobleman weds the daughter of a Parsee mystic in India, and with his bride resides for a time in the beautiful island of Ceylon.

This marriage was a union of souls in the most complete sense. Three years later the child Zulieka was born. The young couple delighted to indulge in psychic experiments, and had two attendants in their household named Hiejoh and the young nobleman's private secretary, who bore the peculiar name of Spyx. Through these psychics, the earl obtained much useful information and instruction in occult phenomena. Through his long continued studies of occultism, the earl familiarized himself thoroughly with the esoteric and exoteric phenomena of the Orient, and through the mediumship of his two assistants the spirit-world was able to warn him of danger to himself and household, and rendered it possible for him to aid others. On a trip to Calcutta he met two wonderful mediums from America, who warned him of danger to his life, and gave him some useful information of a philosophical and scientific nature. These American mediums enter at intervals into the story, and always present some of the most instructive phenomenal manifestations and positive tests.

Summoned to England by the transition of his father, the young earl is saved from an assassin's hand by the occult forces around him, as he had been repeatedly saved from danger by the same power on other occasions Zulieka develops into a wonderful medium, and through the chance visit of the American mediums already named, she gives some startling phenomena at her father's castle. Even in childhood Zulieka was possessed of great wisdom, and did not require the school training usually forced upon children. So completely in touch, and so perfectly in sympathy with the spirit-world were her parents and herself, that her own intuitions familiarized her with every department of knowledge. On one occasion, she was appointed to bestow some prizes at a charitable school for boys. By her own clear reasoning, and leading questions, she taught the boys to see the evils of the giving of prizes, and led the teachers to abandon the pernicious practice forever. Assisted by her father, she accomplished the metamorphosis of the charitable institutions, patronized by the so-called nobility, and made them homes, in deed, as well as in name, for the inmates, who were not permitted to feel under the new regime, that they were dependents upon the bounties of strangers.

The questions of civil right for the English workingmen, the farmers, mechanics, and miners upon his estate, and elsewhere in the United Kingdom, were laid before the earl by the occult powers around him, who led him to see that suffrage was their inalienable right. Guided by his humane instincts, his wife's intuitions and Zulieka's revelations, the young earl metamorphosed his estate and tried to better the condition of his people. His guides in the other life soon

made him feel that his property was a burden,
and led him to see and feel that it was not his
by right, for he had never earned it himself, but
his people, who had developed the estates,
opened the mines and erected his villages, were
really the ones in whom the titles to his property
should be vested. Bereft of his faithful wife,
the earl returns to Ceylon with Zulieka, renounces
his title, and deeds all of his property to the men
and women upon his estates, who, through this
means, become English freemen, land owners,
vested with full political rights. This was a direct
blow at the English nobility, and caused even the
royal throne to tremble. Who of us can say
but that Ouina has probably shown the English
philanthropists a direct path by which they can
find a solution for their political difficulties and
the restoration to the people of their full legal
rights? Let one or two powerful noblemen be
made to see this, as did the hero of this story,
and who will be able to measure the result?

These practical ideas are so nicely woven into
the occult teachings of Ouina, as to make them
appear one to the reader, while references to the
applied sciences and the advanced thoughts of the
teachers in spirit life present a continued series
of new ideas to all. The story is full of oriental
expressions as well as occidental. It is simple,
direct and plain, yet has a perceptible vein of
mysticism running through it that makes it very

entrancing to the reader. It also awakens a
desire to investigate Spiritual phenomena, and
leads one to consider the spirit-world as real and
as tangible as the one in which we live. The
flowery language of the East, and the plain
modes of expression of the West, show the wonderful versatility of Ouina in weaving these two
forms of expression so nicely together. It also
shows with what ease Ouina's medium can be
made to respond to the inspirations that are
borne in upon her brain. It is a story of great
interest to all Spiritualists, and shows what can
be done through "a child of two worlds," as
Zulieka is called, to make the world better. If
the blending of thought and effort in mortal and
spirit life can make even one soul truly free, it is
proof enough that mortals, especially Spiritualists, should unite their thoughts and efforts here
to bring in that ideal state in which the principle
of co-operation shall govern, and make all men
truly free and equal. The story of Zulieka should
be read and re-read. Then the teachings therein
contained should be lived out practically, and
taught by the improved lives and nobler deeds of
all mankind.

The following from Mr. French in reference to
Zulieka is taken from the Progressive Thinker:

"A GIFTED ORATOR SPEAKS."

"To the Editor:—I am greatly pleased with
Mrs. Richmond's story. She is, indeed, one of

the few who seem at home in every field of intellectual labor. Nearly a quarter of a century
have I known her. Before assembled thousands
at our camps and conventions, and also in the
parlor with friends, she never fails to please and
instruct. Hers has been, and still is, a grand
work. She brings to every place a quiet dignity
worthy of her position, and scatters with graceful hand intellectual and Spiritual gems, which
glitter in the pure light of inspiration. Her
work will live after her and speak her praise
when critics have passed into silence.

"Clyde, Ohio. 'A. B. FRENCH.'"

"We are constantly receiving words of commendation of Mrs. Richmond. That her story
is the one great attraction at the present time
among Spiritualists, we know, and we are glad
to receive words of praise for her from one so
gifted as A. B. French."

If it has not already appeared on these pages
in a specific statement, the reader has certainly
been made aware of the fact that every discourse
given through the lips of our subject is impromptu
as far as she is concerned. That no course of
reading or study has ever been necessary, that
there is in fact no preparation on her part, except the willingness to be the instrument of her
spirit guides in these utterances.

Concerning the published discourses, particularly those printed in the Spiritualistic journals

regularly for years and those published in the secular press, it is true that she never saw them until they appeared in print from the short-hand reports of such eminent stenographers as Pitman, Yerrington, Clancy, Graham, Griffin and later, Wm. Richmond, no corrections in these utterances being necessary.

When a volume was to be compiled of discourses already published (as in London by J. Burns) or of those delivered before the Society in Chicago, if any supervision was necessary, any proof-reading required, Adin Augustus Ballou has been the ever willing spirit to perform that task, and taking control of the medium has with ease and facility employed printers' signs, (which the medium never learned), which he knew as a practical printer while here.

The guides revised and condensed the lessons on the Soul from Mr. Richmond's reports, and Benjamin Rush controlled the medium to revise the manuscript and make the original drawings from which the plates in Psychopathy were made, using hand and brain with equal facility.

Ouina has a literature of her own. Through her medium, Watèr Lily, (as she calls Mrs. Richmond), she for some time edited the childrens', department of the R. P. Journal under the pretty and suggestive vignette of a basket filled with flowers—called *Ouina's Basket.* Afterward she had charge of a similar department of the

Spiritual Offering (then published by D. M. and N. P. Fox), from which was compiled a few stories and poems as a Christmas offering. Her brief and more lengthy stories, fairy tales and poems for children, small and large, would make a valuable acquisition to our literature, now devoid, almost, of anything especially adapted to young folks. In all this wonderful work our subject can more truly say than an eminent lady novelist was reputed to have said: "I did not do it, it was done *through* me."

In all this we are strongly reminded as we write, that while our subject ever modestly disclaims any credit to herself for the merits (literary or otherwise) of her work, still there must be an instrument; *apropos* to this it was related to us by a friend in Washington that on one occasion a lady, supposed to be rather brilliant in intellectual ways, insisted upon accompanying her friends to one of those evening *conversazionnes* given in the Capital City, referred to by Mr. Bacon. On her way there and in the course of the evening she ridiculed the idea of "spirits" and "spirit control," but the ready answers of the guides and the improvised poems challenged her attention. When questions were permitted she asked: "Why cannot I be controlled to make poems as well as this lady?" (referring to the medium). The reply came very quickly and distinctly, "We do not create brains, madam we only use them." We were informed that the lady never ridiculed Spiritualism again; but became interested from that hour.

Before concluding this portion of the consideration of our subject's literary labors, we must mention her little book, "Ouina's Canoe." It contains a series of instructive lessons for children in the form of stories. From letters to Mrs. Richmond from England we learn that the children of our English brethren were delighted with this book, such stories as "Joe, the Hunchback," and "Rosy Toes" being very popular there. These stories led the children to take a deep interest in Spiritual seances, and made them long to know Ouina personally, as well as the other spirit guides. Such a work as this is greatly needed in Spiritualism, and Ouina's Canoe, full of stories, just fills the niche. It should be introduced into the Sunday Schools of the land, so that the children everywhere can be led to see the beauties of Spiritualism.

From the foregoing brief reviews of her literary labors, our readers will see that her pen has been kept at work in many fields, with great profit to those who shall follow her as gleaners. We have not considered the multitudes of letters, personal and otherwise, that she has penned, nor the poems given by Ouina, and afterwards written out, all of which constitute parts of her literary labors. We present some of her poems in this and the following chapter, as well as other parts of this volume, specimens of her average verse. Under the inspiration of the spirit world we can see that a versatility of gifts may be bestowed upon one individual, when that individual is ready and willing to give credit to whom credit is due, and to permit those gifts to become blessings to the world, as our subject has sought to do with those that heaven has so generously bestowed upon her.

In the next chapter we will present a few poems and discourses out of the thousands that invite us, for our readers to enjoy.

CHAPTER XV.

LITERARY WORK—CONTINUED.

IT would be unfair to our subject to turn from the consideration of her literary labors without presenting to our readers specimens of her published work as a lecturer and writer at different periods of her life.

We here present some of the thoughts that were given through her lips in childhood, which were written out by her father, edited and published by him long years ago. We feel that our readers will take a deep interest in these few excerpts from Mr. Scott's diary, as it would be impossible for a child of twelve years, in her normal state, to give utterance to any such ideas as are contained herein. Our readers will notice the beautiful language and the dignified expressions of thought advanced, indicative of a mind well trained in the schools of logic, capable of thinking for itself, and advancing its ideas in logical order. The first is an article entitled ''Sunset in Autumn,'' written in September, 1852, under inspiration. Our subject was then twelve years of age:

"The last rays of the setting sun linger lovingly among the trees, and gild the domes of the distant mountains; then swiftly change, leaving the western sky aglow with a flame of splendor.

"The birds warble their vesper songs, then quickly seek their nests.

The breezes sigh for a moment under the leaves and grasses, then die away, murmuring faintly, 'Rest, rest.'

"The lake, in whose placid bosom is mirrored each tint of the sky, slumbers quietly in its bed of forest trees, whose gorgeous foliage sweeps gracefully along the shore like the folds of a crimson curtain. All Nature seems hushed to sweet repose, save when the whip-poor-will breaks the calm stillness with his melodious complainings.

"Man alone pauses not; filled with unrest and mad pursuits of ambition, he struggles on. Yet, in such an hour as this, how is the mind invited to regions of higher thought! The earth and heaven seem blent together, and on the wings of the twilight fair forms appear, soft voices seem to whisper of peace. We seem to be near the abodes of the angels, and to blend our hearts with theirs in solemn songs of praise.

"The earth and lake and sky, the birds and fields and forests, the stars and voiceless depths of space, seem pervaded by a solemn presence encompassing and o'erruling all."

We next introduce a communication from Spirit Ballou, given February 15, 1853, less than one year after his entrance into spirit life. Our readers can readily see that it would be absolutely impossible for a child in her thirteenth year to give such thoughts as these without assistance from some power outside of herself. The subject of this address is "The Spheres."

"Thinking that this assemblage is fully satisfied of the *existence* of spirits, I shall now endeavor to explain to you in what manner they exist after they leave the earth. I know of three *spheres* in the spirit land, one terrestrial, one *super*terrestrial, another celestial. Each sphere has *seven circles*, and these in turn are divided into *seven societies*. Each of these spheres, circles and societies represents a degree of development, those in the *terrestrial* corresponding to the development of the earth's inhabitants. For instance, any person on earth, whose development would correspond to or fit him for the *first circle*, of the terrestial sphere, would enter that circle on leaving the earthly form. But a person on earth can only ascend to the sixth circle, because, should that person attain the development of the *seventh*, he or she could not remain upon the earth nor in the terrestrial sphere, that circle representing the transition from the first to the second sphere; and the spirit then throws off its lower body and takes on a more celestial form, no pain or sickness accompanying such a change in our world. You perceive by these remarks that progression is the law governing all spirits, whether *embodied* or *disembodied*. There is no *retrogression*.

"The spheres or circles referred to are *states* or *conditions of mind*. The darkness which now pervades earthly minds concerning life in the Spiritual world will soon be swept away by this open communion. Instead of fear in your worship of God, you will know only love, for *love* and *truth* arc the attributes of God."

Eight days later, on the 23d of February, 1853, in the presence of three hundred people the following address was given:

"We rejoice to welcome so many here assembled for the purpose of hearing from the spirit land. We doubt not you have come with a sincere desire for instruction.

"This is a glorious age in which you live; an age long sought by minds of earth—long foretold by seer and age. Greatest—because between your world and the spirit land a means of communication has been revealed. A most glorious thought! One which makes sad hearts throb with joy. We come to tell you of the happiness that this communion gives your departed friends.

"We come to tell you that your bodies shall go back to the dust, whence they came, but the spirits shall ascend to the 'mansions not made with hands.' There is happiness for all. Not *perfect*, nor immediate, but each one, according to his deeds and conditions, shall be happy. Everyone shall have such happiness as he is fitted to enjoy and comprehend.

"We come to tell you that *love* shall conquer *hatred*, and that these communings shall never cease. You are requested calmly and candidly to consider the subject. It has proofs for every sincere mind. Ignorance alone enslaves the world, and bars the door of truth. But there is promised to all this blessed boon, 'The light that lighteth every man that cometh into the world.'

"The first step being taken (in Spiritualism), *i. e.*, to open communication with the inhab· itants of earth; the next will be to tell of the condition of spirit existence. *Love*, *truth* and *purity* are engraven on the arches of the soul's temple."

We now present an extract from an address on the subject, "Evidences of Immortality" given through our subject's mediumship, when she was fifteen years of age. We consider it of great value and feel certain that our readers will enjoy the brief extracts we have made:

"Before the planet Neptune was discovered, the astronomers in the Old World were saying: 'To make this plan complete, this geometric ratio certain, there must be another star yonder, beyond the reach of our telescopic range of vision.'

"The eye of mathematical faith had seen it there—the student had beheld it glimmering through the midnight lamp, when he drew the circles of the solar system, and measured their geometrical ratios. Sure enough, when, within the last century, the most powerful telescope was brought to bear on that portion of the heavens, there was the remote star glimmering away as though it had been discovered countless ages ago, as it undoubtedly was created. So with the eye of faith, the eye of Spiritual science, the eye of absolute certainty, minds of the past have said:

" 'Somewhere in all this range of Spiritual truth, there must be a means of communion between the two worlds. The gateway of death must be unbarred, and there will be discovered a mental telescope, whereby we can see the fixed star of immortality gleaming and know that it is there.'

"The telescope of modern science, whose premonitory symbols were mesmerism and psychology, has at last been pointed in the right direction. It has swept around and around the circle of cause and effect—around and around the circle of religion and science, until at last it has pointed its lens directly in range of the star that reveals with certainty the future circumstances of the human soul. It gives three-fold evidence—physical proof, mental proof, Spiritual proof. The last is greatest, since the spirit alone can judge of Spiritual things, and thus opens the wide vista of knowledge so positively, so undeniably, that those who have traversed it can tell of its truthfulness. But of this proof we can only say, pursue it even as the astronomer pursues his science, the chemist his, the geologist his. In one night, in a single hour, you cannot be made familiar with all the evidences. We can only say, study your souls as you do your bodies, pursue the science as you do any other. Make the lamp of the human spirit the subject of your inquiries and investigations, and, like the happy astronomer who triumphed in the exercise of mathematical faith, you too shall triumph in the certainty of Spiritual knowledge.

"Greatest and best of all, the divinest evidence is that which comes to the human spirit in its hours of exaltation, in its moments of intuition and inspiration, when it is brought vividly in contact with the upper world. There is no questioning, no setting aside, no pushing away. The senses may cry deception, the intellect may say it is false, but the spirit, calm in the majesty of its own intuition and certainty, rests upon the mountain top of truth and says: 'We know whereof we testify. It is not blind faith; it is not fictitious logic. It is the certainty of absolute knowledge that causes every human spirit to shrink away from error, darkness, oppression, and bigotry.'"

We have alluded to the wonderful lecture on the "Gyroscope," given in 1857 in the city of New York. This lecture is so valuable that we produce it in full. We ask our readers to compare it with a lecture given in 1887 on the subject of "The Shadow of a Great Rock in a Weary Land." These two lectures, given exactly thirty years apart, will prove the claim we have made throughout our work, that her guides have endeavored to lead the thoughts of the people onward and upward in their search for truth. They also show that there has been no standing still on the part of those guides, but that they have ever been ready to present new themes for the consideration of all thinking men and women, whenever they deemed that the human mind was sufficiently unfolded to receive those new teachings.

The reader will bear in mind that the discourses here presented have been taken (not *selected*) from volumes containing many, any of which might be selected, and perhaps there are others that might be considered finer,—but these were the first that the eye rested upon, and perhaps serve to illustrate the versatile powers of the controls of the medium as well as any. The lecture on the Gyroscope is as follows:

The Gyroscope.

PRAYER.

"Our Father! on all occasions we offer the spontaneous outpouring of worship which ever wells up from the depths of thought and feeling within our souls, as natural and as pure as does the fountain of water burst from its deep-bedded rock, seeking to aspire toward the sunlight, catching with its spray-diamonds bright gleams and flashes as they are given off from the great center of the solar system. So our thoughts and feelings, having their origin, their source, and their life in Thee, are seeking forever to gush forth, expanding in Thee, seeking forever to reach the sunshine of Thy love, that Thou mayst crown them with the perpetual rainbow-tints of everlasting beauty.

"On this occasion we would approach Thee with thankfulness and love. As the external earth is free from the icy chains of a long, protracted Winter; as Thy children have again and again breathed forth their hymns of thankfulness to Thee that the dreary Winter is past; that the poor and lowly and desolate shall no more cry for bread in vain; but that the earth, responding to Thy voice, is again yielding the rich germs and shoots which, in the Autumn time, shall bring forth the harvests for those who labor; so, Father, perhaps we may feel that the Winter of a long state of materialism may pass away, and the spring-time of love and hope may call forth the shoots and blossoms of thought and feeling, until, in the Autumn of Thy unending eternity, there may be gathered into the granaries of eternal thought and feeling, into the store-houses of that 'mansion not made with hands,' the fruits and the grains of our souls.

"Oh, may we feel that Thou art sowing seeds in our hearts; that though many fall on stony places or among thorns and briers, ours is the duty to tear the thorns away, and cherish the germs; to remove the rocks, that the shoots may not be dwarfed, or that the unfoldment may not be imperfect; and that for ever are the capacities of the soul expanding, giving to us the germs of knowledge and truth, which we may cultivate and unfold, believing that in the end they will yield the harvest in tenfold proportion O Father! we bless Thee for this thought, and for every blessing; we praise Thee for every capacity of life; that even as Thou lovest Thy creation, we would acknowledge that love by loving Thee in return.

"May we breathe words of truth—truth that never grows dim, but constantly brightens as it unfolds in the minds of Thy children, and which, like the diamond, grows bright and more bright as the rays of Thy love are thrown upon it, as they reflect the beauty of Thy divine life. O Father! we bless Thee for ever and for ever.

DISCOURSE.

(Subject selected by a committee from the audience.)

."The name, Gyroscope, is a scientific one, and there are perhaps few in the audience who understand what the thing referred to signifies. When we consider it strictly with reference to the name, it simply signifies *a view of motion*, consequently, whatever is in motion may be called a gyroscope; if that motion is presented to you in an harmonious manner, or in a circular direction. But it is particularly applied to a certain philosophical instrument which, by men of science, is considered a toy, a plaything, but which had its origin in the mind of a man who penetrated into the mysteries of Nature's laws; and in considering the laws of motion, this problem was, in his brain, resolved into a demonstration, and the result is this instrument known as the *Gyroscope*.

"We think the question was in this form: '*What are the Laws or Principles Controlling the Movement of the Gyroscope?*' All bodies, all substance, all atoms of matter possess, intrinsically, a life and a motion. Rest is said to be a capacity or a quality of matter. Rest is directly opposed to motion. It is said that rest is as constant as motion. We do not think that rest is a state of matter, but that it has only an existence *relatively*. Trace the geological upheavings of granite life in the formation of planets and worlds; trace the principles of life as they outwork themselves in every form of existence, and it will become apparent to you that, although compared with the earth the particles of matter composing it may be said to be at rest, yet with themselves compared, they are in motion, eternally breathing, aspiring, giving forth, inhaling, and exhaling, whereby the forms of life are outwrought and perfected. This is mechanical motion.

"Another motion is the upheaving of the earth by earthquakes, which is geological motion. The motion of gravity is inherent as well in small particles of matter, in mechanical action as in planets, systems, suns, or stars; for if the principle be perceived in larger bodies, then it must be perceived with regard to the movement of every atom of matter that exists, however imperceptible that atom may be to the external senses.

"Consequently gravity, strictly and intrinsically defined, is the tendency of all substances toward a center, and of the same substances in kind to a common center. This has been defined as attraction.

"The attraction of gravitation is that which draws things toward a center, as we have explained. The attraction of cohesion is that which draws substances having like or opposing qualities and density. The attraction of repulsion, so termed by men of science, is simply a name, possibly a principle; is the law of all formations of

matter, of planets, and of worlds. Attraction
signifies a coming together, a blending, with regard to circumference, intensity, momentum and
force. Repulsion signifies a separation with regard to some or all of these laws; consequently
the attraction of repulsion in the formation of
planets and worlds, of suns and particles of matter, is that which prevents worlds and suns from
coalescing or commingling to a central point.

"If the attraction of gravitation, in contradis-
tinction to the attraction of repulsion, were always
to have the sway, then worlds would never be
defined, or rendered distinct; each particle of
matter would be assimilated with its neighboring
particle, and the sun would be still as small as
the minutest particle in creation. But this attraction of repulsion may also be defined, not simply
as attraction, but as a *principle*, because really,
positively, and technically, two things never come
in contact by a law of gravitation, because this
law of repulsion is always active. Two things
may approach so closely that the eye can detect
no intervening space, but there is never an actual
contact of any two particles. And this *'film of
resistance,'* so termed by one of your scientific
men, is none other than the attraction of repulsion, or that which prevents all bodies or distinct
particles which compose bodies, from blending
or coalescing, by the laws of gravitation and from
the force of revolution, beyond a certain point.

" The Gyroscope is intended to illustrate this principle that *motion is as constant as rest*, and that momentum, as distinct and positive in its nature from absolute force, exerts more influence upon the revolution of bodies than all the attraction or repulsion that the scientific world has discovered.   What is momentum ?   It is the power of motion, or in other words it is a constant motion, multiplied by the force or weight of the object; and although the object may be but one-tenth of a thousand the momentum may raise its force to one hundred or one thousand times its weight. Apply this to the Gyroscope.   It is set in motion, and one end of the framework surrounding the ring being placed upon a pivot, the ring and frame in which it is placed will revolve around a common center, and the other end will not fall. Why ?   Simply from the reason that the momentum given to the wheel or globe more than equals the weight of the instrument, or the attraction of gravitation; or in other words, because, although the weight of the wheel may be but one-tenth, the momentum compared to the force applied is one thousand.   The natural law of gravitation is for the time suspended, and where there is no atmospherical resistance or friction from its own axis, and this motion was inherent, instead of being externally applied, it would revolve for ever.

"Now apply this proposition to the formation

of planets, not as the law of attraction nor the law of repulsion, but as the law of momentum, which is the result and life-principle of motion. This is the constant outworking principle which pervades all bodies. Momentum is the real law of all spherical, all solar, and all systematic formations in the vast universe of Deity. No man of science has clearly defined why this wheel, or this globe, refuses to acknowledge the general laws of gravitation; but it is because this instrument has within itself a center, which, for the time being, is superior to the attraction of the earth; and this is obtained simply by the laws of momentum. Continued force would not do it.

"A continued force is defined in this manner: A ball of ten thousand times larger dimensions than this simple wheel of the gyroscope, if placed at a certain elevation from the earth, would fall, though its attraction might be half equal to that of the earth. But this law of momentum is a *positive motion*, and produces in each atom a self-existent principle, which must outwork itself in some form or other; and when that form is no longer required in the center of the solar system, it must seek its center elsewhere.

"It is not by centrifugal or centripetal force that planets are kept in their orbits, but by the law of central life, simply because they are outworking the life-principle within them, and that life-principle is motion. They can no longer remain upon the sun, or upon the center of the universe, and fulfill the laws of their motion, because they are at rest in reference to the great body, in reference to the sun. For instance: the atom which assists to form the flower, seemingly to us, is at rest. Why? Simply because the larger body, the earth, has a motion which is more rapid than you can perceive.

"The slower motion of the planet is not perceived, but yet it is outworking its destiny within the arteries and veins of its constitution, by vibratory motion is outworking a little system of its own. So stars are but the blossoms of the suns, which bud and bloom because they cannot rest. They find their birth within their central motions; they seek to bloom where thoughts and feelings can best prove their intelligence and power—the power of our Father.

"The only difference between the gyroscope and the solar system is, that the gyroscope, relatively speaking, possesses no inherent power of motion distinct from the earth; the motion is an outside or an external one, which is simply given to illustrate a principle in the planetary world.

"In the revolution of the moon around your earth, the motion is inherent, and it is outworking itself by establishing that motion. When the gyroscope is put in motion, it overcomes the resistance of the brief space of atmosphere in which it moves, and while the momentum lasts, it becomes a satellite around the center of its motion or the pivot.

"This resolves the science of astronomy into a simple problem by a positive rule, and the veriest child, or the man who has never read a book, and does not know how to read or spell, can trace in the skies, in the earth, in every existing body, the principles of astronomy. For the sun and its system are but a type of that which is moving around you daily. A consideration of the motions of the vegetable and animal kingdoms, an analysis of the chemical properties of the mineral kingdom, will present to you a force, a life, as self-existent and positive as that which controls suns, stars and universes, in their revolutions around their centers. We would like that we had this instrument, the gyroscope, by which to illustrate, but those who have never seen one will feel interested to examine for themselves. The principles, we have said, which control the gyroscope in its revolutions are simple, and being simple are natural, and being natural, they represent the true type of Nature as manifested in all of her revolutions.

"How does the gyroscope apply to the mind? We will make the mind a thing, a force, governed by principles and laws analogous to external astronomy, and we will prove to you that the mind, in its revolutions, is acting more or less within the semblance of the solar system, that there is a sun around which thoughts, like planets and satellites, revolve—that sun being the life-giving principle which God has given to the human soul. Ultimately, astronomy, geology, mineralogy, all the various sciences which seek to penetrate into external nature, must combine; they must be resolved into a single principle, a universal science, a knowledge of which can be obtained by the most unscientific person, else they will not serve the purpose of true science.

"Astronomers, taking upon them the dignity which they ever attach to that single investigation, have produced books which have no particular bearing upon the subject, and which can not be comprehended by men without much research. The first principles of the science must be reached before the facts can be understood; the first laws of their being, the great and distinct elements of life must be brought to the mind of the pupil, else it cannot understand why a planet moves, what is the use of one, or whether it moves at all. Thus, the science of astronomy has been too visionary, although conceived to be so perfect mathematically. It may be perfect mathematically, but not demonstrably or illustratively; for no child, although he may measure the distances of the planets and suns, knows what gives planets and suns their origin. What is it? 'We do not know,' say the men of astron-

omy. If you do not know, then you do not
know what you are investigating, and your mathematical investigations are comparatively useless,
and your pupil will look upon the stars as simple
multiplications of the bodies in nature, not serving any particular object in creation, except to
demonstrate to how great an extent Deity might
tax the mathematical powers of humanity.

" The geologist claims to penetrate into the
origin of the earth, to ascertain the laws by which
earths are outwrought and perfected, and they
must have originated from something, but what
that something is, like the astronomer, he is in
doubt. Consequently, children are led back
thousands of years, where stratifications of soils
are heaped upon each other, where waters are
gathered together in the depths of the ocean;
and the conclusion is arrived at, according to the
laws of geology, that once this earth was a mass
of burning fluid, impalpable, self-existent. But
'what caused it to be so?' asked the child. The
geologist must answer, 'We do not know.'

"Again, the chemist—in ages gone by called
alchemist—is endeavoring to analyze the properties of things, or the principles which enter into
their more immediate assimilation. Consequently,
the chemist becomes the most scientific man of
the whole. The astronomer has only the form
of the universe, not the spirit. But the chemist
confines himself too much, like the others, to

formulas and theories and speculations, which have not their bases upon principles. Interrogate the chemist, and he will tell you that certain combinations will produce certain results. Why? Because they are alike in their properties.

" But what is that chemical attraction, what is that law, which causes certain particles imperceptibly to blend and form a newer and more powerful combination? What causes the simple elements composing water to be different in combination with other elements than when in their original state? Because they have produced a new capacity—because they give forth a more perfect formation; and the oxygen and hydrogen, resolved into their primaries, enter into new forms, and water becomes an element of life and beauty, as traced through the animal and vegetable creations. Well, then, we have the real laws and principles which illustrate perfectly and emphatically the forces of Nature, which govern as well the chemical, geological, and astronomical world, as they govern mind and spirit.

(At this point a gentleman came forward to the platform and produced a Gyroscope, which was set in motion.)

"We were applying the laws of the Gyroscope to the mind; but it seems that some kind friend has brought one, which we will use—not technically, perhaps, but we will present to you, and afterward you can examine one for yourselves.

"Our audience will remember, when examining this instrument, this one mathematical proposition which we have stated—that the momentum of a body in its revolutions, or in its motions, is equal to the weight multiplied by the force of its revolution. You all perceive that the revolution and momentum gradually lessen as the motion diminishes. Were that motion inherent, self-existent, that wheel would continue to revolve, as now, for ever. The pivot upon which it revolves may be the axis of a planet, the motion may be the momentum, the inherent life principle within it; and this motion, multiplied by the weight of the instrument, you will perceive is sufficient to keep it revolving. You would naturally suppose that when one end is placed upon this stand, the other would fall. Why does it not? Simply because the motion given in that direction, and in that particular orbit, more than equals the weight of the instrument or the law of gravitation, which would draw it toward the earth. But as that motion ceases, the attraction of the earth or the weight of the instrument produces a different result. The effect for the time being is to disperse the atmosphere, and overcome the laws of gravitation, and thus revolve in an orbit of its own. Now, if that motion was inherent, it could not be drawn to any planet, but would fly off into space. Attach a single thread to this center, and it may be suspended in the air, and by this means you see that it would turn in a certain direction as now, and would have a particular center around which it would revolve; and this attraction being more than its motion could overcome, it could not fly off into the room, to become a satellite around this center. Why? Simply because the attraction to this point is greater than the momentum, or its inherent life principle. But while the motion is kept up, it can not fall, it can not rise, because the motion is in itself. So the moon revolves around your earth, and the earth around the sun; and the atmospheric influences which these may represent are not in motion except as regards the sun. The earth revolving in its orbit produces its own atmosphere; and the atmosphere is at rest with regard to the earth, but it is in motion when viewed from the sun.

"*Motion is as constant as rest.* The stars which are known as fixed stars in the heavens are so called simply because their distance and magnitude are so great that their motion can not be perceived; they are at rest with regard to this earth, but with regard to the laws of their own revolution their motion is as constant as their seeming rest. Your sun is at rest to you because it is larger—because in its magnitude it presents so great an area of attraction, that you perceive no other motion than your own around it. But could you be placed at a distance from the sun,

so that the attraction of another sun could be
perceived, you might see the revolution of that
ball around the other, its natural center, which
would be equal to the revolution of this wheel
around this pivot.

"We have simply endeavored to give the principles, not the technicalities, as applied to the
Gyroscope, or the principle of motion as applied
to this instrument. It has a concentrated, spherical form. Suppose, now, that this wheel was a
combined mass of fluid, having no particular
form except in essence, and the atomic particles
by some strange law of attraction—not chemical,
not cohesive, but of life and motion—were drawn
together to produce this wheel, and gradually
their motion becoming greater and greater, and
more powerful, and the momentum was equal in
itself to the attraction of the sun; then they
must, from the necessity of their own self-existent life, become a planet—not by any law of
centrifugal force or power of repulsion, which
drove it from the sun, but from the necessity of
its inherent life-principle; it must become a
planet, and it must revolve in a spherical form,
because it is a sphere itself; and as it revolves,
that sphere, corresponding to the sphere of some
other planet, must outwork itself in that form,
as this must revolve around that.

"We hope that astronomy will be resolved into
a practical science; that men, and women, and

children, may gaze into the sky and see not only
stars, like bright and beauteous points, begem-
ming the night, but like beacons set to light them
in their eternal journey, and as living, breathing
things, freighted with divine beauty, inhabited
with divine beings, until, by a chain of light, not
electricity, a telegraph may be extended around
the universe, and a girdle be placed thereon, that
men through the eye of science may see the
worlds, and know that this is astronomy, the
science of the heavens. And thus must be the
principle upon which men of science shall base
all their investigations, else astronomy will be as
now, a mathematical science—never resolved into
a practical one.

"But, as we said before, chemistry, geology and
astronomy, must be united; for, unless you understand what causes the particles of this metal to
adhere to each other, you can not understand the
laws which cause them to move harmoniously.
Then motion is as constant as rest. The crystals,
the iron and the steel, all things ponderable or
in imperceptible gases, or becoming solid as the
diamond, when analyzed by chemistry, must
have undergone a revolution, a change—not only
chemical, but perhaps, geological and astronomical.

"We have endeavored to give our ideas as
clearly as possible. If we have failed to make
the subject plain, we hope you will attribute it

to the fatigue of the brain of the medium, owing to her labors during the week. Hoping that the gyroscope of your minds will lead you to an investigation of the laws which control the elements of the soul, of thought, as well as the external world; hoping you will commence your investigations with the great center and work outward, as do stars, suns, systems, planets, vegetables, minerals, animals, men, until at last you have found, by knowledge of principles, as well as facts the great laws that control in their beauty the universe of matter, we leave you to your meditations."

We now present the lecture on the subject, "The Shadow of a Great Rock in a Weary Land." [This discourse, with invocation and poem is published in pamphlet form.—ED.] The depth of thought herein expressed, the beautiful language with which that thought is clothed, and the simplicity of its expression, make it a most remarkable production, even from so gifted an instrument as we consider our subject to be. Thirty vanished years lie between the time of the production of the lecture on the "Gyroscope" and the one we are now considering. The mutations that time has wrought in material things are also perceptible in the Spiritual growth of the people of this nation, as will be seen from the difference in expression of the thought in these two discourses. We consider the lecture on the "Gyroscope" one of the most remarkable philosophical theses that the nineteenth century has produced; and this lecture, on an entirely different subject, enters largely into the field of religious thought, consequently must be measured from a different standpoint; but both of them only go to show that every philosophical subject can be treated from the standpoint of religion, and every religious subject from the standpoint of philosophy, so that the interblending of the two will produce a higher order of thought and give a broader view of all questions that are treated in this comprehensive manner. We commend these two lectures to the careful consideration of all our readers:

"THE SHADOW OF A GREAT ROCK IN A WEARY LAND."

(Delivered at Boston, Sunday, March 13, 1887.)

"Thou art, O God, as the shadow of a rock in a weary land."

"Whoever has journeyed across a great desert, whether of Arabia or the desert of your own Western plains, well understands this Oriental expression unto God.

"You think, who dwell amid the mists, and the clouds, and the rain, and the shadows of your climate, or those who dwell in the ever mist-laden climate of England think, that the sunshine is the greatest blessing that can come. In its

light the spring-time flowers are quickened into
birth, in the summer time your harvests are
ripening, and the great flow of life responds to
this quickening power. But out upon the plains
the merciless sun beats down upon the weary
traveler, there is no shelter from morning unto
eventide, he must go on and on. The great red
sun rises unpityingly in the morning; it ascends
unto the zenith; still he must plod on his weary
way; over the sands that burn his feet and reflect the glare of the midday sun; until eventide
comes there is no respite. Along the borders
of the desert in Arabia, where the ancient no-
madic tribes were wont to assemble, were great
rocks thrown up in some of the wonderful con-
vulsions of nature; and if, perchance, the wanderers could reach the shelter of one of these
rocks and rest at midday, it was the greatest
boon to the travelers, the glare of the sun nearly
blinding them in the great waste; so to find shelter
beneath one of these rocks was the only boon to
the pilgrim or traveler journeying in the desert
when they were approaching Jerusalem, the gate
toward the desert being the smallest gate in that
wonderful city, the travelers hurried that they
might find the protecting shelter of the wall,
even though they could not enter the gateway
after nightfall. Thus it is that the human heart
prays for the shadow. It is often considered
when people are in sorrow, when they are in the

midst of doubt, in the shadow of gloom, that
darkness or shadow is the great curse of the
world; but it is beneath the shelter of the Alpine
rock, underneath the drifted snows, that the
small flower finds its germination. Far upon
the heights of the Rocky Mountains, where the
tempests have full sway, you will look in the
crevices of the rocks and find the blushing mountain pink, and the beautiful petals of the mountain lily, growing securely beneath the folded
palms of the giant rocks, you are filled with joy
to find the blossoms there.

"In the shadows of material life you cry out
for greater prosperity. Was it not in the arid
wastes of prosperity, the great wide desert of
human success, that Egypt was sunk? Was it
not the burning, scorching sand of material
power that quenched the light of the primal
nations of the earth? Is not the earth itself
typical of what befalls nations in the glamour
and glare of material prosperity alone? Look
to ancient Egypt, the Empress of all the Eastern world, unto her came the riches of every
land, and into her treasuries poured offerings
of gold, silver, and precious stones; her cities
and temples were builded to the sun, yet the
sun of material power quenched her life and
she might have well prayed, 'Oh, for the shadow
of a great rock in this weary land!' Weary with
success; weary with the routine of prosperity;

weary with kings who governed the power and
wealth of the world; weary with all the pride and
glamour of material pride and conquest! There
is no desert greater than that of unlimited success. You might ask for some rain-drops to
descend, for some dews to fall, that, like tears,
should give you shelter. On the way to that
material power, that thriving only on prosperity,
forgets the weariness and desolation of those who
toil, forgets the shadow that broods above those
who mourn, there is no respite. You may take
the lesson of ancient Rome, the empress at one
time of all the civilized world, after Egypt; you
will find into the sunshine of her prosperity there
came the desert sands of human desolation, vanquishing the Orient and the Occident, her son of
splendor had arisen to the zenith, then the greatest of all her prophets might have cried for the
'shadow of a rock in that weary land.' Modern
Europe is crying out today from the desert wastes
of the worship of Mammon, from the desolation,
travail and pain of the monarchies of the world
the cry goes forth for this shelter, this one Rock
of Truth that shall bring them strength.

"The symbol of the ancient prophets is in the
world today. Every human life covets prosperity, every human heart rebels against adversity;
the individual sorrows that beset you form especial griefs; each individual life complains of its
own bitterness; there are no trials you think so

hard as those that you each, individually, have to bear; every mother whose darling is laid away to sleep in the grave, feels that there never was grief like hers: every child left to mourn her on earth, feels that no one ever mourned so much for a dearly loved parent; when wealth and prosperity seems to take wings and fly away you feel, each of you, that the hand of fate is laid more heavily upon you than upon any other; but look, if you can, with unbiased eyes at those who have prosperity, unqualified prosperity; would you change places with a king or worldly magnate? Do you think you would change the shadow of your rock, the shadow with the brightness of its refreshing tears, the adversity that brings with it patience and growth, for the unalloyed splendor that satiates and wearies? If you ask for the crown of kings it brings you bitterness, trials, doubts, suspicion and fear of death. If you ask for the prosperity of riches, it brings you what? All worldly praise, all empire over human things, but over the heart no power. Seared by the sunshine of continued prosperity, those who revel in what the world offers of material life and power, often cry out in the satiety of wealth and luxury for the shadow of the rock.

"What will you have; continued sunshine? Then the flowers that spring up in lowly places will not grow in your hearts; you cannot find violets on the desert; the lilies of the valley do not blossom in the garish light of the sun, even roses in tropical climates bloom and fade away before the summer has fully come; so do they hasten on to their bloom and their decay. What will you have; unqualified earthly prosperity, that you may sear your conscience over with gold, and obscured in the light of its material splendor forget the refreshing tears that bring forth the flowers of patience and fortitude? We tell you that the shadow of the rock is the safety of the world, that the great sorrows that sweep over human lives are the refuge and strength that God gives to man. We tell you that the grief you feel for those who have passed beyond the shadow of death, is the shadow that leads to immortal life. We tell you that when the wings of adversity brood over you it is the shadow of God's rock of safety.

"One who spoke in your midst more than a quarter of a century ago, said to his congregation of several hundred people: 'I never had a sorrow that I could spare.' He felt the need of the shadow, he felt that in the walks of silent grief and discipline, the great truths of the world are nourished into being; and as the wind blows the seed into the crevice of the rock and it germinates there, or the winged bird may bear it to the mountain height in his beak, so the seeds of truth, and love, and hope, and fortitude, are planted in human hearts; but woe unto those who have only the sunshine of material prosperity! Their lives are short in happiness, they blossom as poppies for an hour; they are like roses in the tropics, that early spring to bloom and are early to depart; or flowers that yield no splendid fruition. So lives that have not grown up through the shadow into the glory of perfect truth, they do not know of God's presence in their midst.

"The side of heaven that is turned toward man is the shadowy side; it is needed; with your eyes of earth you cannot see the perfect light of truth, it would blind your vision; you would be dazzled by its perfect power. So the great rock broods between you and the perfect light that in its reflected rays you may grow toward immortality. You cannot bear the great heat-light of prosperity; when the world has conquered selfishness then all material treasures will flow toward mankind; but never believe until then, that human hands will receive without labor, or that labor will cease to be in some instances oppressive. It is needful that men shall toil, it is needful that they shall have for their bodies the sustenance that they win, it is needful in spirit that they climb up to the jagged height to win the glory that is to be seen beyond.

"If one should pray for the shadow the whole world would cry out in alarm. But what is the meaning of the shadow? When the sun has gone and the golden pinions of the sunset are

folded away in the softest silence, and the gray
night dawn has not yet come, the very voices of
the stars are heard in the skies, and man
exchanges the glamour of one sun for the splendor of a system of constellations, the whole
heaven is full of suns; the glory of the starry
firmament would never have been revealed to
the vision of man but for the 'shadow of the
rock' in the nature that brings the repose of
night. Still you complain when the day is gone,
of the allotment of the hours of rest that takes
you away from Mammon. Even thus it is, if
the shadow of refuge be not in the weary land
of earth you become satiated with material
things, bloated with the pleasures of the senses;
the prosperity that is coveted is despised as
soon as it is won; the ambition that men seek
to have crowned with laurel and bay, they find
is but a fading garland after all. The glory
of spiritual truth is nourished in the shadow;
the wisest provision of nature is that germination never takes place in the light. Study
nature as you will her seeds are sheltered beneath the sod, her generation is hidden in its
primal sources, and silently and beneath the
shadows, every form of life has its birth.

"Under the shadow of what is the light of
truth beyond, man's spiritual being has growth
and unfoldment ; here beneath the shadow of
the rock of material things he finds shelter

until the spiritual germs begin to grow, then he may throw off the shadow, it has partially tempered the light to his understanding, has fed from the fountain source and he can bear the light; but even then the great wings of God's Love overshadow him according to his state, he only has the truth that he can bear; let no one make the mistake and believe that if the truth was present in its entirety he could understand it today; let no one believe that if God's love were shown to him in the especial way that he desires that he would be satisfied; let no one make the mistake because the materialist or atheist or blind worshipper of the senses has said, 'But if I were God I would have no sin, no sickness, no suffering in the world.' No, not if you were the God of the senses; but if you *were* God, and had charge of immortal souls, you would make the shadow of the rock manifest to them in order that they might behold the light, and prove that the great background of material things, which constitutes the shadow, is that upon which the glory of the Angel is painted. The materialist, as a God, would have a world that would be a desert, for the sun would shine all the time, and the shadow of the rock would never be found.

"Behind this wonderful shelter in the midst of the arid wastes and wildernesses of life, under this protecting shadow of grief, all souls are nurtured.

"Speak of blessedness! It is when the shadow falls above the tomb, and the tears are shed there for your loved ones, that the shadow of a great rock is felt, and you wonder that God's hand is not stretched out to remove the gloom; soon from between the crevices of the rock, from the great splendor that is above, in your grief there comes the strength, and the trickling waters of spiritual life flow down into your hearts, your pain is assuaged. The joy that comes of resignation is much greater than the joy which preceded it, as is the height of one who climbs from the valley greater than that of the one who remains in the shadow; then out of this resignation comes the knowledge of the great light that is beyond. How could you, immured in time and sense, know of immortality had it not been for that 'shadow' in the weary land of earth?

"Watch those who follow in the treadmill of fashion, butterflies who hover around the lamps that destroy them, votaries of pleasure whose whole seekings are to satisfy the appetites and tastes until they are turned away human wrecks; watch those who follow any physical appetite or passion; you will see them as weary travelers on the desert of human life, parched and thirsting; and then if only they can reach the shadow of this great rock, that would give them brief oblivion; then watch how, beneath this sheltering shade, when their sins are repented of, when

their weakness is forgotten, when their spiritual
strength rises within them to overcome, when
they are ministered to by angels in the shadows,
watch the dawn of the higher life; see how the
wrecks revive; see how chastened and subdued
from material conquest and material discord,
they rise to a knowledge of the spirit; then question if you can the wisdom of this surpassing
shelter. That which is typified most fully in
this wonderfully poetic explanation is: the rock
was the symbol of God's unchangeableness, was
that within it were held all germs of life, all
known forms of being that have been enfolded
and laid away in the crevices of the rock and, by
the trituration, and trickling of waters, gradually
that which rests in the shelter of the rock suddenly upsprings as flowers; there also are, oftentimes, cooling drops that quench the thirst of
the traveler.   In the great alchemy of nature all
things revealed are illustrations of truth to those
who perceive nature aright; and so that which is
in and around you by which life is overshadowed,
would seem useless when you interpret it in the
light and glamour of the material senses.

  "Let no human heart make the mistake of supposing that the great, white light of spiritual
truth can be turned loose upon the world and
man survive it. Even as those who ascended
with Christ to the Mount of Transfiguration fell
down before the burning light of the angels and

spirits whom they saw; Moses, Elias, and Christ
transfigured before them, so if, instead of in the
shadow, you were upon the white side of the
rock of spiritual truth, you could neither bear
the transfigured Christ of truth, nor could you
even bear the resurrection in the form of the
angels of those whom you love.   Spirits have to
descend to mortal states; those who pass the
shadow of death come back and gently knock at
the outer door of your dwelling; they must appeal to the shadowed light in your senses or you
do not understand them.   What would you do
with the rare gleam of immortal life thrown suddenly in your mind, if you had never thought of
it before?   You would feel that your mind was
exposed to the sun pitilessly; you would have
some shade fall between you and this light.
Have you never known that a stupendous truth
constantly forcing itself upon the outward human
consciousness has made men mad?   The whole
world would go mad in the unqualified sunshine
of spiritual truth until they grow to understand
it.   Teach a child geometry and the child will
be an idiot; teach it the small numerals and the
child will grow to geometry in due course of unfoldment.   You must place the shadow perhaps
of ignorance, between perfect knowledge and the
state that cannot bear perfect knowledge.   Men
have blamed priests and initiates in the ancient
temples for veiling the truth from mankind; they

were but instruments in the hands of a higher
power and veiled that which could not be understood, until the world grew to the stature of spiritual comprehension. You may understand the
meaning of a triangle today, and the mystic
meaning of the sphere, and the circle; but in the
days when these were symbols of divine truths the
masses could not understand them, they must be
veiled until the people grew to the knowledge of
their meaning. The whole world is a school for
adepts today, but in ancient times the divine
geometry of the skies was veiled in symbols that
mankind could not understand, because of their
ignorance, and only doled out to them in piece-
meal, until at last the world should grow to the
stature of those who had first received these
primal truths.

"You may stand in the temple of nature today
and unqualifiedly receive some of the divine
propositions of the universe; but there are others
that are hidden, they are wisely hidden for you
would not perceive them even if they were revealed; if an angel, speaking the language and
thought of the absolute truth of the celestial
heavens, were in your midst today you would not
understand that which was taught. Many people
say, 'I know I have grown to an appreciation
and understanding of what I once rejected.'
Compare what you receive today with what you
received a quarter of a century ago; compare the

average thought in the world today with that of
fifty years ago, you will find that that which
could not then be spoken, which people did not
understand, which they have grown to realize,
has now become the common phraseology of
mankind. A half of a century, or quarter of a
century, has sufficed to create a new language;
new forms of thought; new orders of ideas; and
has introduced into existence a whole superstrata
of a new mentality pertaining to man's spiritual
being. This has been variously introduced: in
the form of psychological words and phrases; in
the form of man's perceptions and gifts; but the
whole have revolved around the one center of
spiritual truth that is in the world today; and
the shadow under which you have rested will still
support you until you grow to the knowledge of
that which is more and more divine.

"If we were to form a prayer best adapted to
human need we should say continue the shadow
of the rock, O God, as long as human spirits are
veiled in human life, as long as human existence
is limited by human sensations; for so needful is
the shadow when one would have rest and
growth.

"Many people suppose that fruition can come
without germination and growth, that they can
attain the result without the needed steps; this
comes of the mistake of supposing that the kingdom of heaven could be attained without individ-

ual merit, it is the fictitious glamour and glare of
a salvation that is offered without each one walking in the shadow that has made theology a bare
and barren desert; but the Christ who walked in
the shadow of the Cross, who suffered pain; or
the Buddha who received the light beneath the
shadow of the wonderful Tree that gave unto
Asia her mystic, yet wonderful religion; all
prophets, teachers, and Messiahs, who have sym-
bolized the light of truth; have done so through
the shadow, by walking in the valley of self-for-
getfulness by turning man's thoughts to Spiritual
things, and to the knowledge that every material
pain is because of the material shadow.

"The great Christ-truth of the world has never
been won at a single bound, and no nation or individual leaps up to meet it without growing in
the shadow and being nurtured in the darkness.
We know what individuals will say: 'Still I think
I have had my share of the shadows,' but do you
know what it means to have your share of the
shadows? If you have noticed the light when
the sun is veiled by the mists the shadows are
not usually so marked, and that in exact proportion to the depth of the shadow so is the brightness of the light. The electric light, which
flashes in upon the darkness of your crowded
cities, makes the distinct outlines of every leaf and
twig, almost the silken hair of a lady's tresses
is reflected in shadows at your feet; what does

this mean? In exact proportion as the light is white toward which you are tending, so will the shadows be deep. Those who live in the twilight state that is neither light nor shadow, have less knowledge of that toward which they are tending. Never covet the veil of thin mist that divides you from the shadow, for it divides you from the light also; by the sign of the shadow you know what light is yours.

"God means that every soul shall be tested by the hand of the shadow that is his; even in the outlines you despise; and if as did Richard III., you make faces at your own shadow, and call the life accursed that is reflected there, then remember that the shadow which you persist in seeing is only there because you are there, and if you could turn courageously toward the light you would behold no ungainly shadow at all; we mean that human selfishness, human pride, human ambition and passion constitute half the shadows that are seen, and that needed shelter within the shadow of the rock is all that God implies by any sorrow or suffering that comes to man. Whoever heard of an *absolutely unselfish* life that felt suffering? Never doubt for a moment that most of the pain that each life bears is not for another but for wounded self. If you really have compassion for another, the effort to remove their grief, the sympathy for their sorrow, will make their sorrow greatest not yours. No nurse entering a hospital sits down and wails over the suffering that is there; no one sees the miseries of the world who deplores them without an effort to alleviate them; the cheerful physician relieves pain and becomes valuable, and both nurse and physician are content to alleviate the suffering.

"The great wisdom of God is manifest, that just as soon as you turn away from the contemplation of self, you turn more and more toward the light, and that which was the shadow becomes the light.

"In the great glory and wonder of Spiritual existence earthly brightness would fade away, and in the midst of celestial splendor no glamour of gold, no consciousness of the splendor of earth and its sun can ever come; you turn as gladly to walk the pathway of pain as of pleasure, knowing that all ways lead unto truth. The carefully attuned and adjusted life does not cry out for Truth and Love and Wisdom, which are as much greater than happiness as is the light of heaven greater than the light of earth. So you may perceive that even now rising beneath the shadow of God's love, beneath that great rock of strength and safety, beneath all that seems discordant and terrible in human life, the white lily of immortality is blooming within your souls and the germ, expectant, but waits for your state to come forth and adorn and beautify the outer world. Now that the great desert of Mammon has been

encompassed, you are approaching that wonderful Shadow of the Rock of Eternal Truth,
wherein all germs are nurtured and all divine
possibilities are hidden; and at last the giant
power of God's love shall reveal unto each the
wonderful ministry of the shadow, and you shall
behold how fair and perfect is that wisdom that
leads you to rest beneath the Shadow of this Rock
in the weary desert of your earthly pilgrimage."

We find it opportune to insert here a most
beautiful poem entitled *A Tribute to Alice Cary*,
copied from the files of the Banner of Light,
May 13, 1871. The circumstances of its production were as follows:

Soon after the founding of Sorosis, really by
Alice Cary, the people of America who loved the
"twin birds of song," Alice and Phoebe Cary,
were called upon to part with both of these sweet
singers, as far as mortal presence was concerned.

Alice Cary had passed on since the meeting of
Sorosis preceding the one to which we now refer,
and this was made the occasion of a memorial to
the arisen poetess by the literary ladies who
belonged to the club.

Mrs. Charlotte Bebee Wilbur, an early speaker
on the Spiritualistic platform, one of the most
pleasing and scholarly lecturers of that memorable "first decade," was the honored president
of Sorosis. After other exercises, the president
called upon our subject, much to the latter's

surprise, and without a moment's hesitation the following improvisation was rendered.

TRIBUTE TO ALICE CARY.

Because the broken lyre-string hath no sound,
The faded rose distills no dewy gem;
Because in stranded shells no pearls are found,
The shattered casket holds no diadem,
  We will not weep!
   But the lily-bell,
   In the dewy dell,
   Chimes a mournful knell.

Because the Autumn leaf grows brown and sere,
And Summer splendors crimson to dull gray,
Because the Spring returns but once a year,
And purple fruitage crowns the bloom of May,
  We will not weep!
   But the violet,
   With blue eyes still wet,
   Must thy loss regret.

Because the lowly creeping worm can die,
And be forgotten in the mould and rust,
While, Iris-winged, up springs the butterfly,
To feed on honey-dew instead of dust,
  We will not weep!
   But the buds of Spring,
   Must their flowers bring,
   On thy bed to fling.

Because the shattered shell prisons no bird,
We look in vain for last year's dear delight;
Above our heads the rustling wings are heard—
The skylark singeth sweetest out of sight—
  We will not weep!
   When the night is still,
   Sings the whip-poor-will,
   With mournfulest trill.

Happy were they who dwelt anear thy heart,
Baptized and blest by friendship pure as thine;
Who drank thy love's clear waters whence they start,
From fountains that flow near the spirits' shrine.
        We will not weep!
            In the willow vale,
            The lone nightingale,
            Will thy flight bewail.

Thy songs fly after thee like white-winged doves,
Cleaving the higher air where thou dost roam;
Then, slow returning, like thine early loves,
Within the hearts that bless thee find a home.
        We will not weep!
            But in love's pure urn
            The heart-fires will burn
            For thy sweet return.

Now is thy harp attuned to sweeter lays
Than ever thou couldst chant in human speech;
To symphonies of rapture, sounds of praise,
We strive in vain with earthly sense to reach.
        We will not weep!
            For a lily white,
            Swings downward to-night,
            To chime thy delight.

Thy kindred poets greet thee with a song
Olympus and Parnassas never won.
Drink, drink the glad nepenthe, and grow strong!
We follow thee when earth's dark night is done—
        We will not weep!
            For an asphodel
            Floateth earthward to tel!
            "It is well—'tis well!"

We cannot refrain from introducing here one
of our subject's most charming poems delivered
in Washington, D. C., in 1870, the subject of

which was suggested by a professor from the
Smithsonian Institute:

THE BEAUTIFUL LAND.

There's a beautiful country, not far away,
  With its shores of emerald green;
Where rise the beautiful hills of day,
  From meadows of amber-hued sheen;
There beautiful flowers forever blow,
With beautiful names that ye do not know.

There are beautiful walks, star-paven and bright,
  That lead up to beautiful homes;
And beautiful temples, all carved in white,
  Crowned with golden and sapphire domes;
And beautiful gates that swing so slow
To beautiful symbols ye do not know.

There are beautiful valleys and mountains high,
  With rivers and forests and hills;
And beautiful fountains leap up to the sky,
  Then descend in murmuring rills.
There beautiful life-trees forever grow,
With beautiful names that ye do not know.

There is beautiful music borne on the air
  From rare birds with flashing wings;
And beautiful odors float everywhere,
  Which an unseen censer flings:
And a beautiful stream near that land doth flow,
With a beautiful name that ye do not know.

Across this beautiful, mystical stream
  Flash rare scintillations bright;
And many a witching, mysterious dream
  Is borne on the pinions of night;
And the stream is spanned by a beautiful bow,
With a beautiful name that ye do not know.

And beautiful gondolas, formed of pearl,
  Come laden with wonderful stores;
While beautiful banners their folds unfurl
  To the dipping of musical oars;
And beautiful beings cross to and fro,
With beautiful names ye do not know.

Would ye know the name of that beautiful land
  Where the emerald waters roll
In gentle waves on a beautiful strand?
  It is called the Land of the Soul;
And the beautiful flowers that ever blow
Are the beautiful thoughts ye have below.

And the beautiful pathways are your life deeds,
  Which fashion your future homes,
And the temples grand are the world's great needs,
  While your saviors have reared the domes;
And the beautiful gates that swing so slow
Are the beautiful truths ye have learn'd below.

The beautiful valleys are formed of thought,
  Of all that world has been,
And the beautiful mountains are tears outwrought
  Through immortal sunlight seen;
And the beautiful life-trees that ever grow
Are the beautiful hopes ye have cherished below.

All the beautiful melody is prayer,
  That is echoed in music's powers;
And the beautiful perfumes floating there
  Are the spirits of all earth's flowers;
And the beautiful stream that divides you so
Is the beautiful river named Death below.

The beautiful flashes across the stream
  Are your inspirations grand,
While the beautiful meaning of every dream
  Is real in this fair land;
And the beautiful million-colored bow
Is formed of your tears for each other's woe.

The beautiful barges are all the years
　　That bear you away from pain,
And the beautiful banners transformed from fears,
　　Are returning to bless you again;
And the beautiful forms crossing to and fro
Are the beautiful ones ye have loved below.

Who has done more to soften—nay, to illumine—the thoughts of death than the loving, gentle Ouina?　Three years after the above beautiful picture of the future home was given to the world, she painted another upon the minds of a London audience, and so well do the two harmonize in spirit—the former a resplendent word-picture, the latter the very essence of soul perception—that we hang them side by side, feeling that the one will but add to the beauty of the other:

DEATH.

O beautiful, white mother, Death!
　　Thou unseen and shadowy soul—
　　Thou mystical, magical soul—
How soothing and cooling thy breath!

Ere the morning stars sang in their spheres,
　　Thou didst dwell in the spirit of things,
　　Brooding there with thy wonderful wings,
Incubating the germs of the years.

Coeval with Time and with Space,
　　Thy sisters are Silence and Sleep—
　　Three sisters, Death, Silence and Sleep;
How strange and how still is thy face!

In the marriage of Matter and Soul,
　　Thou wert wedded to young, fiery Time—
　　The now hoary and snowy-haired Time—
And with him hast shared Earth's control.

O beautiful Spirit of Death!
   Thy brothers are Winter and Night—
   Stern Winter and shadowy Night—
They bear thy still likeness and breath.

Summer buds fall asleep to thy arms,
   'Neath the fleecy and soft-footed snow—
   The silent, pure, beautiful snow—
And the earth their new life-being warms.

All the world is endowed with thy breath,
   Summer splendors and purple of vine,
   Flow out of this magic of thine,
O beautiful Angel of Death.

What wonders in Silence we see!
   The lily grows pale in thy sight;
   The rose, through the long summer night,
Sighs its life out in fragrance to thee.

O beautiful Angel of Death!
   The beloved are thine—all thine!
   They have drunk the nepenthe divine,
They have felt the full flow of thy breath.

Out into thy realm they are gone,
   Like the incense that greeteth the morn;
   On the wings of thy might they're upborne,
As bright birds to thy paradise flown.

They are folded and safe in thy sight;
   Through thy portals they've passed from earth's prison;
   From the cold clod of clay they have risen,
To dwell in thy temple of light.

O beautiful Angel of Life!
   Germs feel thee and burst into bloom;
   Souls see thee and rise from the tomb;
With rapture and loveliness rife.
   On earth thou art named cold Death,
   Dim, dark, dismal, dire, dreadful Death,
But in heaven thou art Angel of Life!

We are one with thy spirit, O Death!
We spring to thine arms unafraid;
One with thee are our glad spirits made.
We are born when we breathe thy full breath,
O mother of Life, lovely Death!

In wandering among these blossoms of poetry from Ouina's affluent hand we are tempted to keep on calling as fancy dictates until our volume would overflow—and even then we might go "on and on forever," never wearying. We have come upon the following dainty bit of love, beauty and delicate satire—and cannot resist inserting it here; then we must pause and hope for the time when these jewels shall find a fitting setting in a volume of their own.

The editor of the Medium and Daybreak thus publishes:

"A very busy individual reproached a friend of less industrious tendencies for his usefulness. Our subject hearing of the circumstances, was controlled by her spirit-guide ' Ouina,' to write the following poem. The Tarantula is a species of spider plentifully endowed with the utilitarian instincts of that *genus* of insects; the Humming Bird is exclusively a 'thing of beauty.'

A SONG OF USE AND BEAUTY.

Could I Sing, this Would be My Song

Of Tarantula,
Weaving web of silken woof;
House complete from floor to roof;
Perfect, safe, and plunder proof;
Good Tarantula.

Toiling, toiling ceaselessly;
What a home ! How skilfully
All is wrought, and thriftily !
      Wise Tarantula.

      Ah ! Tarantula,
Soft thy silken tapestry,—
Fold on fold of drapery;—
Deftly done, and daintily;
      Say; Tarantula,
When thy wise work was begun,
Didst thou say, "when all is done,
And the goal is truly won,"—
      Brave Tarantula—

Life will then be all complete;
All its fortune at my feet ;
I shall have rewards most sweet ?"
      And, Tarantula,
Were thy dreams visions of rest,
Of a home by kindness blest,
Of a life in graces drest ?
      Tell, Tarantula.

          ————

      Of a Humming Bird,—
Dainty, dazzling, starry thing;
Woven rainbows on each wing !—
Fluttering and fluttering
      Till the air is stirred
With the wondrous winnowing
Of the restless, tireless wing;
Nothing doth it sing or bring;
      Witching Humming Bird.

      In and out my Bower ;
Dip thy beak—thou knowest well
Where the nectar fountains swell—
In the honeysuckle cell ;
      Dewdrops for thy dower;

Flitting in and out again ;
Sipping sweets without refrain ;
Nothing can thy flight restrain—
          Pleasure, beauty, power.

          Idle Humming Bird ;
Wantoning the hours away,
In thy ceaseless aimless play;
Caring only for today.
          Who hath ever heard
Of a playful pretty thing,
Living always on the wing,
No home, and no song to sing ?
          Naughty Humming Bird !

          Of a friend, who came
One day to my Summer bower,—
For a walk and for a flower—
Spending there a charmed hour;
          Naming the sweet name
Of one loved whom we had known;
A sweet spirit, who had flown
From this world, and whiter grown
          Up in Heaven's flame.

          Then we talking trode
Through the garden, at the gate
Lingering, in the sunset late;
Then we spied, in all its state,
          Tarantula's abode.
Laughingly I named the skill,
And the stern, untiring will
Which had wrought that house so still,
          Nearer then she glode.

          "But Tarantula
Hath a horrid house," said she,
" Look, he kills a honey bee !
Skill indeed for misery—
          Sly Tarantula !"

Sudden paleness, as of pain,
Touched her face; no word again
She spoke.   Thy shaft was not in vain,
    O, Tarantula !

———

    Of a forest glade,
Where the mottled mosses creep,
And the pied wind-flowers peep
From the shadows dark and deep.
    In the deepest shade
Is a thicket, overgrown
With the wild clematis blown;
And the tendrils it hath thrown
    Have a bower made.

    Softly, not a word;
Gem of beauty never prest
Brow of maiden, nor her breast,
Lovely as this dainty nest;
    And one tiny bird,
Waiting, waiting patiently
For the life that soon will be
Which she feels, but cannot see—
    Patient little bird.

    Now the air is stirred.
Witching wings are hurrying;
Hastening, and hurrying;
All the leaflets flurrying;
    And they bring this word.
"Far away from glade and glen,
Over field and over fen,
Near the haunted homes of men,
    I have buzzed and whirred;
All the drops of honey dew
I have gathered sweet, for you—
Mate of mine, so fond, so true."
    Darling Humming Bird !

Mr. A. M. Griffin, in his review of Mrs. Richmond's work in Chicago, called especial attention to a lecture by her before the Philosophical Society in that city. As that lecture was listened to by some of the ablest thinkers in the city of Chicago, it has been deemed advisable to reproduce another in this work, given three years later before the same Society, for the benefit of our readers; hence we subjoin it without comment, together with the discussion that followed its delivery, on the part of the members of the Society. Having read the lecture with a great deal of care ourselves, we feel that it is wholly in keeping with the spirit of this work that its thought should find place upon these pages, in order that others may enjoy the same privilege that has been ours. We consider it one of her best efforts.

"THE HUMAN MIND."

Impromptu discourse by the guides of Mrs. Cora L. V. Richmond, before the Philosophical Society of Chicago, March 6, 1886.

Introductory remarks by the Chairman, Sidney Thomas, Esq.:

"I have been called upon at this time, before introducing the lecturer of the evening to announce the subject. I am certain I have not communicated this subject to any one else. First if I have settled upon a subject it certainly has been since I came in the hall this evening. This Society has discussed during the recent course

various subjects and now that we are about to
be addressed by an alleged spirit from another
world, it occurred to me that it would be a wise
thing for the Philosophical Society, to try the
distinguished speaker for some information concerning matters that are not within the reach of
mortals, yet in selecting this question I saw at
once that it would be very easy to secure a subject that would allow the spirit on pinions to soar
before us in a forty-five minutes' talk concerning things about which we know nothing, and
with reference to which we could hardly give
time for discussion.   The problem to me was to
select a question that should be so far within the
province and practices of this Society as to
enable us, in some manner, to pass judgment
upon what we hear, and on the other hand to
select a subject so substantial and practical that
what should be said might be of some use to us,
that even might advance us somewhat upon this
subject.   Now the subject which I am about to
announce, I do not announce it in one or two
words because I desire to confine this visitant to
a specific line of thought, consequently I had
thought it necessary to have a long subject that
will not only indicate the subject generally, but
open out a line of thought.

"Now we have discussed many subjects this
Winter.   Among the subjects which have been
before the Society and with which it is somewhat

familiar is the subject of the mind or spirit. The opening lecture was upon the 'Thinking Faculties.'

"You will remember sometime afterward the lecture of Judge Russell upon 'Individuality,' and lastly you all have recollections of the lecture by Mr. Lancaster, supposed by many of this Society to be as complete a statement of the materalistic hypothesis as could be made. Now having discussed that subject under these heads and incidentally in connection with other lectures, I thought I would ask that the subject to be discussed to-night should be upon the Mind, Soul or Spirit. Assuming, perhaps, that it will be considered that man is not a unit but a duality, that he is not a mere material being but has a material entity and a Spiritual entity, whatever that may be.

"I have written out the question, 'The Human Mind, its Origin, Nature and Destiny.'

"I want to say one more word. In the discussion of this matter we have attempted on several occasions to discuss the material basis of thought; we have endeavored to obtain some information in the line of biology, and see whether the mind originated in the germ of life, whether it originated at birth, or whether it has been afterward developed by experience.

"'The Human Mind, its Origin, Nature and Destiny. At what period did it begin in time?

What room does it occupy in space? Is it a substance or force? Is it a cause or an effect? What specifically is its shape, size and substance? Upon what principles or by what properties can it resist destruction?"

"If this subject is satisfactory it will be given for the lecture. The lecture shall be limited to forty-five minutes.

"Now this whole matter is entirely new to me. I don't know whether spirits are limited to time and space or not, but the members of the Philosophical Society are.

"The lecture should not occupy more than forty-five minutes, so that there will be time for discussion and the lecturer will have an opportunity to rely to the critics afterwards."

Mrs. Richmond arose and, speaking under control of her spirit guides, said:

"Mr. Chairman, it is our usual custom to open every address with an invocation. And if it is not in violation of the rules of this Society, we would like to do so on this occasion. All who feel moved are invited to join in the invocation.

INVOCATION.

"Infinite God, Thou source of all life, all intelligence; Thou guide and ruler of every living thing; Thou who movest the visible world by law, and who governest the invisible world by the law of perfect knowledge and love, unto

Thee we turn with thanksgiving, and praises for every blessing; for those blessings, which unto Thy children on earth are revealed in answer to their human needs, for those blessings of the mind that are given for their mental needs, for those deeper and diviner aspirations emanating from within, yet palpable and ever living, which come in answer to their spiritual needs. We praise Thee, for the abundance of every blessing, for that life and light that in the human form enfolded, still is made manifest in the aspirations that are one with Thy life forevermore. By whatever name, man may address Thee, in whatever form the worship of the spirit may be made known, still would the aspiring hearts of Thy children go outward, upward and inward, unto Thee, forever praising Thee, for all life and light. Unto Thee who art the guide of angels, ministering spirits, and men, and Who hast given in every age the evidence of that power to mortals we would render homage and praises now, and evermore. Amen.

"Mr. Chairman will you kindly announce the subject for the evening discourse?"

The chairman announced :

"The human mind, its origin, nature and destiny; at what period did it begin in time; what room does it occupy in space; is it a force; is it a cause or an effect; what specifically is its shape,

size, and substance; upon what principle, or by
what properties can it resist destruction?"

Mrs. Richmond then delivered the following
address:

"Mr. Chairman and Members of the Philosophical Society:—The subject announced by
your chairman is of such vast scope, so wide and
far reaching in its nature and would require not
only perfect knowledge of the principles governing the subject to be treated, but also sufficient
time to express that knowledge, that we will
answer simply that should the time allotted fail
to be sufficient to express our views upon the
theme announced, you will please to consider the
nature of the subject and that it has occupied the
attention of the most profound minds of earth in
all ages, and even if we should be able to give
perfect answer to the question or series of questions which your chairman has suggested, we
are by no means certain that the members of the
Philosophical Society would be able to understand it, yet as brief as possible, under the circumstances, will be our answer. We know that
as perfect attention as it is possible you will give
to that reply. What is meant by the word mind
is qualified in the remarks of your chairman by
including also spirit or soul; the word mind is
supposed to be human intelligence and to cover
the entire ground supposed to be occupied by
the words spirit and soul also. In our definition

we shall make the three words fill the answer
to these questions embodied in the theme. We
shall divide the subject to be treated of into
mind, spirit and soul, and shall treat these as
constituting the entirety of human intelligence;
by doing this we shall be better able to express
what we mean, and we have no doubt perhaps
satisfy you as fully.

"The terms 'mental philosophy,' 'mental
science,' and other kindred terms expressing the
knowledge humanity has concerning the mind,
nevertheless, must be very inadequate to express
what we mean by the added words spirit and
soul.

"We consider the soul, from the spiritual
standpoint, to be the innermost essence, the absolute entity, which we assume has an existence
and which we have just as good a right to assume
has an existence as the materialist has to assume
the atom; we assume this soul to be the complete entity of all mind, and that primarily it is
non-created and immaterial, has no existence in
time and space, is not connected in any manner,
except by acting upon matter, with the laws that
govern material things. We assume the soul,
the entity, the intelligence, eternal in its nature
and therefore indestructible.

"Spirit, as the word implies, we assume to be
the breathing of the soul into matter, the inbreathing of this immortal entity into the life of

earth, and the spirit may be said to be the theme, or intention of the life of the soul in its expression through material forms. The spirit of man is limited, therefore, as to its expression; the soul is not limited by that expression in time and space. The spirit of man is expressed in the intention and fulfillment of the complete cycle of earthly existence. The soul is not expressed wholly in that cycle but only in eternity. The mind is the active intelligence, expressed through the brain and form of man, of the spirit animating the individual form, depending upon organic laws for its expression. The mind is more limited than the spirit, as the spirit is more limited than the soul. The mind is governed in its expression by the limitation of time and space, the material organism, and whatever else pertains to the human structure. Nevertheless the existence of the mind, its contact with matter, and all that it reflects through sensation, cannot sufficiently be explained by what we term the purely material process. The *a priori* knowledge to which Kant refers, the power embodied in the mind of knowing something that has not been experienced or taught, that the senses cannot discover, that the material processes of life cannot adequately explain or unfold, all prove that the mind is the result of the two-fold action of spirit and matter, that while the mind may change from day to day in its

knowledge and expression, the quality that
causes it to be mind, or the consciousness, the
power that imparts the reason, the aspiration,
the power that imparts the understanding, as
Kant would express it, is that which is beyond
the senses and in the realm of soul. In the whole
realm of German metaphysics, we have Kant,
Hiegel, Klopstoch, Wiedel and perhaps a score
of others who attribute qualities to the mind
which we think belong exclusively to the spirit,
the mind being rather a mirror in which both
material and spiritual powers are reflected. On
the one side the mind reflects what the senses
convey, but if there were not something imparted
from within to the mind, capable of receiving
that reflection, there could be no impression
made beyond that of the mere physical life of
man. The very existence of that something is
proof, in our opinion, that the source of the mind
is beyond the senses and above matter, and
whatever may be the process by which we arrive at this conclusion, the whole world of philosophy gives evidence that the material functions
of life cannot possibly generate anything beyond
their source, that nature never upbuilds, in all
her realm, powers that are wasted, that she does
not in augmenting her resources destroy them in
the augmentation. Therefore, if it be true that
the mind is the result of matter, and has no *a
priori* sources of existence, yet that the mind can

conceive of an *a priori* source of existence, if it be true that spirit is matter, that all human conception of spiritual existence has its foundation in matter, then it is evident that in this one instance nature does not conserve her resources, that she builds a structure for which there is no foundation, gives man capacity for something for which she has no answer.

"We will not dwell upon this hypothesis, but state our views, after which, of course, you are at liberty to exercise the same kind of reason and judgment upon them that you do concerning other topics; bearing in mind, however, that if there is a realm of spirit as we assume, if there is beyond spirit a realm of soul, as we assume also, that realm must require from you the exercise of the faculties that belong to it for expression, and as it requires a musician to understand music, a poet to understand poetry, so that which relates to the realm of the spirit cannot be measured by the narrow limitation of the kind of thought that you employ for the realm of matter.

"You investigate astronomy with the material faculties of observation and mathematics; you investigate chemistry by such process as your experience reveals, but prophecy, inspiration, the realm of the spirit, that which belongs to the soul you do not claim to investigate with your spiritual faculties, but attempt at the same time that you are endeavoring to analyze them by material processes, to disprove their existence merely because they are not amenable to the usual material laws.

"The mind is the most external expression of the life of the soul (which is an eternal entity), begins with the physical organism, expresses itself just so soon as there is a vital germ that constitutes physical life, is the first impression made by the spirit upon matter, beyond organic sensations, and is, as said before, from the spirit, which is before mind, as spirit is the inbreathing of the life of the eternal soul. The mind begins as soon as the experience of the spirit begins its action upon the material life, and expresses both the impressions of matter and of the spirit, as said before, being registered upon the brain which is the mechanical apparatus for expressing the mental power. Yet every nerve, every center of ganglia, every globule in every vein, every fibre of the material body, every vibration of that subtle organism which is not known and defined in science, and all that which is known as the mechanism of the human body, contains expression of the spirit. The mind, however, is regulated in its expression by whatever shall chance to be either the organic tendencies, or the spiritual processes that lie beyond them. These two, the spirit and the organic tendencies, commingling in the human organism, constitute the basis of what may be called the mind.

" Just so soon, as said before, as sensation begins, the mind begins, as the intention of the spirit begins to express itself so the mind animating the visible human being is expressed in the smallest infant. The greater attributes, the tenacity of the will, reason and continuity of purpose, begin just as soon as there is conscious life, and gradually unfolds itself to expression as that life increases in physical power.

" This mental process, which you denominate reason, is not the only mental process. Whatever consciousness there is in the human organism that recognizes its own existence, whatever power there is that is capable of comprising, judging, aspiring or in any way expressing itself, that is mind. And when the mind has sufficiently established itself in the human organism by the maturer years of that organism, then whatever spiritual power constitutes the primal, *a priori* impetus of that life begins to be expressed, and · the whole range of the individual mind, limited as said before by organic processes, by what you term accident of birth, by the limitations of the senses, by certain hereditary tendencies, still must express the intention of the spirit, but if it does not so express the intention, if it fails in some degree, there is still the *a priori* consciousness, which is aware of much that has not been expressed. There is no human being, perhaps, possibly none before the speaker this night, that is not aware of certain powers, certain latent possibilities, certain aspirations that are not expressed because of the limitations of the human organism, but if it were the human organism itself that gave rise to these aspirations, were in fact the source of aspiration then, as said before, it would simply prove that matter is capable in her final efforts, the acme of creation, of not conserving all her powers, leaving this vast realm to which man aspires, and which in the mind is reflected, without fruition and purpose.

" The powers that relate to the individual mind may be classified thus: The mind that is aware of sensation, the material mind; the mind that is aware of the mental process independent of the sensation, the reasoning mind; and the mind that is aware of aspirations and powers beyond the possible realm of sensation and reason, while still confined and limited to the realm of sensation, the intuitive mind. In its expression the mind is capable, as instanced in the power of mathematics, of conceiving of that which it is not possible to demonstrate to the senses. It is impossible for you to count in time and space the number of miles or of the vibrations of light, or any other gigantic mathematical statement connected with your earth and the remotest planets of your solar system. Who ever counted a billion, or even a million, actually ? And yet by the principles of mathematics, by processes

purely mental, you realize these vast numbers,
state them, and understand fully their meaning.
The same is true of abstract principles in philosophy.

"There is no empirical knowledge that can
give man any idea of the statements known to be
true in the realm of moral philosophy.   There is
no absolute experimental test that can be brought
to bear upon the existence of the mind itself;
and however subtle the anatomical, or chemical
analysis of the human body one instant after the
decease of that body, no traces can be found of
this subtle, this absolute power, which constitutes
all that there was of the individual; yet chemic-
ally there is apparently no change, and no law of
anatomy or physiology can in the least explain
the difference between the form of man a moment
previous and a moment after the decease of the
body.   In one instant there is mentality, there
is a spirit acting upon the vital forces, the next
instant there is what is called death; but chemic-
ally in the one instant there is no change.   Yet
that force which makes all there is of intelligence,
that power which expressed itself in the mind of
man is thus forcibly removed; yet this very process is not capable of being discovered, because
in a realm into which science has not physically
penetrated.

"The origin of this life, the foundation, the
basis of all human existence, which is beyond

the mere generic existence, is therefore in that
realm which, as said before, we denominate the
realm of the soul, which is allied to the Infinite
consciousness or what one of the most eminent
German philosophers has declared Infinite substance. We do not accept the word substance,
because that relates to something inferior, we
prefer the word consciousness, or *essence*, because that relates to primal being, whatever that
may be, whether that primal being be all spirit,
as Berkeley and those of his school declare, or
whether you choose to prefer that it shall be
called matter, the expression of life indicates
that in connection with the human mind and
spirit, that which we call the power, the vitality
of the mind, and which constitutes the essential
life of man is volition, and this volition is the
measure of human perfection. Whatever is in-
voluntary in the human organism is not therefore
mental (*i. e.* spiritual), volition or will of man is
purely a mental (*i. e.* spiritual) quality; is the
action of the spirit upon the vital functions of
the body, producing such energy and power
through the mind. Each attribute is there in its
turn expressed, what the spirit wishes to portray.

"All men are not equal in their earthly expressions; some are born geniuses, some have
powers of mental philosophy and others of physical science, some have adaptation to one form of
thought, and some to another, minds seem to

be unequal. We claim that the souls of all men are equal, that in the original essence, or '*esse*,' the life of every individual is equally perfect; we claim that the spirit expresses in the individual organism the limitations that time and space contain, but that the mind is still more governed by these limitations, that all the inequalities in human life are not the result of inequalities in the primary '*esse*,' but inequalities in the human environments; we claim that mind has its duration only by the sufferance of the spirit, not in the least by the existence of the body. We claim that the mind has its duration from the soul and that, therefore, the source of mind is indestructible, not because it may express itself forever through the sense, but because the source of it is in the only real, indestructible existence.

"Mind does not occupy space or time, it exists only in connection with time and space as the expression of the spirit; its source of existence is immaterial. The soul is the immaterial entity, and therefore not limited to time, nor space nor any conditions of matter. If limited to time and condition of matter then the soul and its spirit and expression of mind, would be but refined matter, but as soul has existence of itself, and as its existence is within the Infinite, so that which relates to time and space can only affect the mind in that expression of man's mental being which is the register for material things, but whatever the mental being registers or requires spiritually, cannot be governed by time and space. The affections, aspirations and thoughts of morality, everything that relates to abstract principles, every idea that is not fraught with reference to your physical organism cannot therefore be governed by time and space. When your minds are dealing with time and space, with things instead of subjects, with the material organism instead of themes, then you adapt your mental methods to time and space. It is a law of the spirit that it adapts itself to the conditions in which it seeks expression. As the musician, in his knowledge of music, is not limited by the imperfection of the instrument upon which he plays, but in the sound that he expresses he is very much limited by accuracy or imperfection of the instrument; if the instrument be out of tune he still will not make harmony though he be a master musician, and if the instrument is in tune he still will not express all the harmony that is within his mind, so the spirit, in expressing itself through the human organism, may be limited to the limitations of that organism as far as time and space are concerned, in the province that the mind cognates time and space; but in the province that it is not governed by time and space the mind is unlimited by them.

"The powers of the body are limited, the powers of the spirit however relate to another and vaster realm where there is no time and no space and no limitations of a material kind, and where whatever limitations there may be, they are limitations of the expression of the Spiritual nature and not of the material nature.

"The world of human sensation is acted upon by mind; registers whatever the mind perceives, but you must be aware that the same sensations record themselves differently to different human minds and that no two of you listen alike, or see alike, or perceive alike, and that this cannot be owing so much to differences in your physical senses as in your mental perceptions, and that your mental perceptions are governed by the activity of spirit that is there, its alertness, its power over the brain, its ability to register carefully that which is perceived. The artist whose sensations are quickened by his fine perception of coloring, in no wise sees the landscape as does the material man of toil who only measures the soil in feet, rods and roods for its cultivation.

"He who listens to music, if his ear is not attuned by his mental perception, and his mental perception by his spirit, to harmony, in nowise perceives the music as does the one whose faculties are so awakened, and the power that enables you to perceive. This may not be registered in any particular physical locality, as the phrenologists assert, but may be the attuning of the entire fabric of the human body by the spirit which merely placed the register in the brain to record the harmonies of sound. Every object, therefore, which the eyes see (or that produces an impression by the vibration of light upon the retina of the eye) you do not all perceive, you may be gazing at something and not see it all. If the mind is alert at every avenue of sensation you perceive many things. The mind must be quickened still more, the perceptions must be more and more enlarged before you are able to see all the things that are about you in material life and yet are within range of your senses.

"The vibrations of light are limited by you to your vision, the vibrations of sound are limited by you to your perception of them, in the vast realm of light, in the vast realm of sound are millions of vibrations that you do not perceive with the senses that the mind is capable of recording, and beyond even spectroscopic analysis of light you can readily realize that there are thousands and thousands of vibrations which no human skill has yet been able to imprison. Such is the nature of mind that, under the inspiration of that knowledge that comes from within it makes the whole visible world luminous; such is the nature of mind that, if not endowed by that knowledge that comes from within the whole visible universe is opaque; such is the nature of mind that unillumined, uninspired by this *a priori* knowledge, which some call aspiration and others term inspiration, there would be no consciousness whatever of the various processes or laws of life going on about you; such is the nature of mind that under the inspiration of that very power which is the least palpable to your senses, which has no visible centers of registration, which cannot be traced to nerve centers or ganglia, which cannot by any process be traced to any physical location, you still have the highest knowledge, the loftiest perception of truth, of all that governs the world in a moral sense and all that gives hope to humanity in the sense of progress and aspiration.

"We will say that the body is a carefully constructed mechanical instrument, through which the spirit of man, by divine intent, expresses in the mind such portions of this divine existence as the human organism renders possible; we will say that the soul of man is that ultimate immortal essence, uncreated, without beginning or ending; having therefore in itself the source of knowledge, from which all intelligence *a priori* must come, and to which all experience must at last render tribute. We will say that the human mind, governed merely by physical conceptions, is limited to the limitations of the body, but the human mind under the luminous power of this Spiritual life which cannot be measured, which cannot be limited, which cannot be stated in time and space and other material limitations, must at last cope with all the problems of material existence, revealing the very nature of the mental process by which these questions are possible, and illuminating all that realm which now lies obscured to human perception, merely because man insists upon studying the Spiritual realm with the microscope of materialism instead of the telescope of Spiritual perception and inspiration. Whoever turns his lens toward the dust will find the dust reflected there, but whoever turns his lens toward the sky will find the stars reflected, and whoever would study the laws of mind in the mere material formation, will never get beyond those material formations, but whoever studies the laws of the mind in the realm to which they belong will find an answer to every question, fulfillment to every hope, analysis to every problem, and inspiration for every need of the mind that so aspires.

"Mr. Chairman, if we have not fulfilled our allotted time we still feel that we have made our statement of general principles as perfect as would be possible unless we had time to devote to several discourses, taking up the different branches of the theme, and if we have neglected any one especial branch which the question involves we shall be very happy if you will remind us."

The Chairman then spoke as follows:

"I must say to the Society that I am surprised

In fact the word is not adequate to express my feelings at this time. I forgot in introducing the speaker to you to say that authenticated by un-questionable evidences, she in Wisconsin when a girl at the age of eleven years was taken from the district school, and developed into a trance speaker, and has not acquired any knowledge from the schools since, has had no opportunity of doing so, but has acquired an international reputation as a trance speaker; now knowing this I did not select the subject because it was a dif-ficult one, I had no desire to puzzle the speaker, I was asking for information, although I congrat-ulate myself upon the subject as being one of the most difficult questions that the human mind ever attempted to investigate. You are witness to the logical and consecutive manner in which the subject was opened, defined, and carried through. Now the subject is open for discussion, and I hope the interest of this meeting is now to begin. We are largely represented by material-ists who have made this subject a study, and I hope no one will be at all backward; do not let one single moment go to waste, the lecturer will then reply. If you cannot make a speech you can ask questions."

Judge Booth: "I am not quite sure that I grasp the statement of the speaker, but if I un-derstood the statement it is that man is threefold; first, the immaterial soul that is self-existent and indestructible, and that all souls are equal. Next the spirit which is encased in every soul breathing upon and through matter, and that the expression of this spirit through material substances and material organisms constitutes the mind, that without this as a matter of course there is no mentality, that the spirit operating in and through matter constructs its own instrument, its own organism by which all that is mental in the human being is its characteristics and its powers. The question arises right here if this be the case, then where there is a separation of the immaterial part, when the soul and spirit withdraws from the body, does the mind cease to exist? And what is death, what is it that dies; is it the mind only that dies? Because if it depends for its expression upon human organism, if it is the result of this affluence of the soul which we call spirit operating in and through matter, is it not death which must be the result? And if such is the result, after death all entities are reduced again to a condition of equality; that at the starting-point of the soul the original entity that which is indestructible, all souls are equal, then when the mind ceases to exist are not souls again equal? If such is the case does it matter very much consequently what the expression of the soul, through this affluence that we call spirit, is here in the mortal state? I would like to ask some questions. I have no doubt that the answers would be a great deal more interesting than anything I can say by way of criticism, by way of following out the line of thought which has been suggested to your mind. One question which I should like to ask, and for which I should be much pleased to receive an answer, particularly, what is death? How does the spirit, the disembodied spirit regard this great event, to which we are accustomed to look forward with dread and perhaps with terror; how does it appear to the disembodied spirit in retrospect. Has the spirit consciousness immediately after coldness wraps the suffering form, or does the consciousness awaken slowly like that of the infant? Is there a gradual process of awakening which the spirit has after passing through this change, or is there in death any change whatever in the spirit of that affluence from this entity which we call soul? And again is the human being alone endowed with a soul, or have what are sometimes called the lower animals also souls? That they have minds there can be no doubt on the part of any one who has made their acquaintance, and if they have minds, are not those minds produced in the same way as any other physical organism through which the different phases of mind has its expression; is not that builded up in the same way by this affluence from the original, uncreated, self-existent, indestructible, immaterial entity, which the lecturer speaks of as soul?

Mrs. Cora L. V. Richmond: "Mr. Chairman, it is our usual custom to employ the fewest words possible in expressing our ideas, as those will bear witness to who are accustomed to hear us. The questioner evidently has great confidence that the spirit addressing you has a mind, or he would not expect us to bear in mind the succession of questions which he has asked culminating in one. In the first instance we must correct his statement. We did not say that the spirit fashions the body in which the mental expression is to be made, we said the spirit expresses itself through the body, but if governed by such limitation as the laws of material organization enforce, then the mental expression through that body is limited to those laws. We believe you will bear witness that we said this. So the spirit not creating the body in all of its conditions, cannot therefore govern fully its expression, whether it shall be perfect or otherwise. Then the gentleman wished to know, or said, that if all souls are alike that after the dissolution called death, between the spirit and the body, is there therefore no mind? We answer, your minds die daily, at least we hope they do. You change your minds continually, that as the thoughts you had ten or twenty years ago, you by no means entertain today. The Philosophical Society, though not intent upon destroying the mind, is nevertheless intent upon changing the mind continually; very

likely many of you have not the same mind
to-day that you had when you first became members of this body.

"Paul said, 'he died daily,' this of course was
not his body merely but his mind and spirit, the
condition of overcoming the errors of the past.
Now when the dissolution called death takes place
the spirit preserves all that is essentially of the
spirit in its mental process; but you no more require the mind to express your Spiritual life, as
we have defined the mind, than you require a
musical instrument to write a musical composition. Of course if you are playing to people who
cannot read the composition you must interpret
it for them. Your minds are the interpreters
between your spirits while you occupy material
forms, when you cease to be material and live in
the spirit you become more than a mental being,
you are then a spirit; it is face to face instead of
through the dark and varying glass of man's mentality.

"The culminating question was, what is death,
what is this dissolution separating the spirit from
the body, and in the dissolution are all souls
again equal, and what view do disembodied
spirits take of death in looking back upon it?
We will answer that death is the withdrawal of
the spirit from the body either voluntary or in-
voluntary. When you ask if voluntary, we point
you to the suicide, or we point to some instances

of sudden death where the physicians are not able to give an adequate account of any diseases affecting the organism, where in perfect health seemingly the spirit departs and does not return. The questioner has forgotten that the realm of spirit was not included in what we were to define, that is beyond death, but he is at perfect liberty to ask the question if he is permitted. We will answer then that when there is dissolution between the spirit and the body, the spirit is not destroyed; that is, the theme of each individual life which makes up what we call the spirit of that life, like the theme of a sonata or the theme of a discourse, is carried forward to the flowering, the blossoming or the fruition in the spirit state, so that you are not then at once in the realm of the soul, but you are in the realm of the spirit, which is the state of those who have departed from the earth, and that Spiritual state is composed of all that constitutes your individual or personal expression here. However long or short the duration of that Spiritual state may be, the soul alone is immortal. But the greater always includes the less, and the soul includes this Spiritual state after death in its possessions, so that the disembodied spirit is the augmentation of the life experienced here, or expressed; meaning that whatever is valuable in your earthly existence or expression, the spirit retains that value in what is termed the Spiritual realm. The

spirit that is expressed by your human life looking from that state, the disembodied human
spirit, views death, when death has been attained,
(here you must of course take the personal testimony of the one addressing you, since you
have no means of proving it until you die), as a
man looks upon his release from prison.   The
process of death is fearful only on the mortal
side, on the Spiritual side it is awakening.   All
do not pass through the change called death in
the same manner, simply because all approach it
differently; one is prepared, another is unprepared, one is fearful, another has faith and hope;
one is wicked, another is full of goodness; every
one approaches death in the light of his or her
own conscience.   When the change comes every
one looks upon death in the light of his or her
spiritual possessions.   If those possessions, which
are the qualities of goodness and truth and
knowledge, are limited, the spirit looks upon
death as making him a pauper.   If the Spiritual
possessions are great, as in the light of wisdom
and love, and truth and good deeds, Spiritual
possessions must be measured, the spirit looks
upon death as the one hand that releases him
from prison.   Both of these statements may be
considered.   But all human beings have some
portion of each experience in passing from earthly
life; all are limited in some degree on awakening to Spiritual consciousness, that is the con-

sciousness that there is a Spiritual life beyond death, which measures his or her condition by this inward monitor. We do not say that one loses consciousness even during the process of death, but one is not conscious of what process is going on, even though one is conscious. For instance, one may be undergoing the change called death and not know it, the mind may be illumined and all the faculties still be in active existence, but so much more quickened that one will think 'this cannot be death.' Death is the awakener instead of that which puts one asleep. The mortal body, it is true, not only slumbers but decays, but the very process of mortal decomposition during the change called death, is the process of awakening in spirit life. You are asleep, you are comparatively dead while limited to the physical body. Spirits only are alive.

Judge Russell, one of the regularly appointed critics, spoke as follows:

"Mr. President, Ladies and Gentlemen: I confess I have never been put in any position where I feel so embarrassed as I do at the present time. I am troubled with a conflict of emotion. You have all, as I have, enjoyed the remarks of the lecturer to-night. Reverie to me has always been pleasant and also pleasant dreams. I will lie awake of a morning saddened by them because they were pleasant, but we have something else to do than to indulge in our propensity to dream; we need to consult not alone what is pleasant, and what is agreeable, but what is real, whether that be pleasant or whether it be unpleasant. In fact, mankind through experience during his whole existence upon this earth, has settled down to the opinion that the very things which they are interested in, above all other things, that subject which above all others they need to make no mistake about is what things are real. Now I read at the time of its publication, Mrs. Elizabeth Stewart Phelps' book entitled 'Beyond the Gates,' I perused it with intensest interest, as a work of fiction it is a most magnificent success. So I say with respect to this lecture on the Human Mind, as a fiction it is a grand success. But I have in my capacity as one of the critics to call your minds back at last to the plain straightforward everyday question, is it real? Now mankind have to-day only a few things, a few tests by which they may determine the difference between dreams and realities, and the first great and only principle is this, proceed from the known toward the unknown. What is meant when we say, 'explain a thing, explain to make more plain,' we mean simply this, that that which we do not so well understand shall be expressed in the terms of those things which we understand better; the unfamiliar should be expressed in terms familiar; the complex expressed in the terms of those things which are simply elementary. Now if I understood what an essence was, if I had ever felt an essence, if I had ever felt anything or seen anything or in any way experienced any symbol which by any means of application could be explained to me in its motive and application to mental science, then I would have some leverage whereby I might understand and explain that which has been vouchsafed here. But of what avail is it to me, to tell me that the soul is an essence? They might just as securely and as well put some other word in its place, they might just as well have used some Latin or unusual Greek word, as the word essence conveys no sort of conception to my mind, of the human mind, that I understand any better than I do essence. Now it may be, of course it is my inability. Those who take plain home terms have led the way to learning things, and that I believe to be the right way of proceeding. We want propositions to be susceptible to analysis, we want figures to represent things which are susceptible to analysis, and we usually analyse those propositions, those things down to their ultimates, so far as we can go, so that we may know they are real and elementary. If a thing is expressed like a steam engine; what is a steam engine? A steam engine is a thing composed of iron, we know what iron is, and has wheels about it, we know what wheels are, and is put

together in shape like a picture which you can
see, then we get some idea of it, then we can do
something with it, then we can put these wheels
and iron together in shape when we have comprehended why an engine is put together, then
we can conceive of things from words made visible every time. But to my mind the subject
which has been treated on to-night is wholly beyond the power of anybody to realize in any
wise."

Mr. Orchardson: "I was going to make a few
statements in the light of inquiry as to whether
it would be desirable to have our identity forever. Take the first hundred people you meet
and they are all imperfect, none of them physically or mentally are perfect, and to stamp these
imperfections on them forever, in my judgment,
would be a great calamity. I saw a man punch
his ticket at a restaurant the other day, a com-
mutation ticket, and he inquired if they did not
always give cigars with meals, a soul like that is
certainly hardly worth perpetuating. I think it
would be a terrible calamity to take the human
race in its present undeveloped condition and
make their identity forever, because it is through
their mental and physical peculiarities that their
identity is discovered and I would prefer finding
myself according to the law of evolution, or
finding mortals with far better mental and physical capabilities than I possess. I would rather

lose my individuality than have no greater capabilities for recognizing and understanding my relations to my surroundings. The best way we can judge of anything as to whether it is a true discovery, is whether there is anything to illustrate it. For instance, if a drop of water that has arisen in evaporation fall again to the face of the earth, it loses its identity by reason of evaporation, but it is just as valuable a drop because it contains just as many particles as it did before evaporation, but when it rises in evaporation each drop becomes a part of myriad other drops. If the drop of water loses its identity, why does this law not hold good in relation to human beings?"

Mr. Lancaster: "A human being is a very singular animal, I found that out long ago. While he has a body which is only capable of being in one place at a time, he is still inhabiting two worlds; one world exists independent of his thought, or his feelings, or his imaginations, or his hopes, or his fears; the other world is the world of his imagination, and his hopes, and his fears, and there is not one human being in ten who can distinguish these two worlds from one another. Now when a barbarian puts a few sticks and stones in the form of idols and kneels before them imploring a power that he thinks resides therein to ward off the destructive forces of the universe which everywhere impinge upon him, he is doing precisely what we expect him to do, giving intelligence to forms as he presumes it would be, as he sees and thinks it is, it is just exactly what the barbarian would do. Why, long ago on the plains of China these human beings got together, supposing the earth to be flat, to build a great big tower to get from this flat place up into the heaven where God was supposed to be Yet if you had approached those people who were building that temple and represented to them that it was all a piece of nonsense, they would not have believed it; but if by any manner of means they could have conceived of this universe as a great many of us conceive of it, they would not have needed any argument, they never would have tried to build that tower of Babel. So it goes on through all the past history of mankind, through all the angelic hierarchy, through all the forms of Christianity up to the very highest belief of Matthew Arnold, the same thing runs through the whole history, and men, judging the universe and the things in it, from the standpoint of their imagination, their hopes, and their fears, and their emotions here, is one thing; judging from the standpoint of scientific and verifyable evidence, as things really exist independent of man here, it is very different. Now I would not do this lecturer the indignity, neither will I do this audience the indignity, for a moment to infer that this question has

been looked at from any other standpoint, or
that the method of dealing with this question
here to-night can possibly be from any other
standpoint than the standpoint of the imagination, the hopes, and the fears, and the emotions.
As a man's idea is about a thing, it don't make
a particle of difference whether it is so, it is
provided he thinks it is. For as a human being thinks, he makes precisely the same course
of talk as if it was absolutely so. Hence a great
many things in this world are as one thinks they
are. And there are men in the world, rather
there are such men as James Watt, George
Stevens, Huxley and Tyndall, and a great many
minds of that kind that deal with things in a
very different manner. But what we have
heard to-night exists in an entirely different
realm, from any where the method or manner
in which questions of this kind are discussed can
be applied. I must say from this standpoint,
the standpoint of the imagination, that this is a
very good lecture. I heard Andrew Jackson
Davis, about thirty years ago, and I must say
that this lecture is an advance on that. I think
it all belongs to that realm of thought that was
exploded thirty years ago. I have not the least
objection to it. I have no doubt the world is
full of this kind of thought, that it always has
been and always will be, consequently from that
standpoint I must commend the lecture."

Mr. Zimmerman: "The idea which the speaker has given us, is one which is dominant in the minds of every one. He has not revealed any new things but has limited himself to the old statements reiterated over and over again, in harmony with the wishes of mankind, not with truth or with science. It is catering to our desires and not to the cause of philosophy. The statement of what the question involves, that was put by the president, is so erroneous, I feel in duty bound to give the truth upon the subject and criticise it with some severity, and that is that in all statements that have been made they are not in harmony with science or the knowledge of the present day, they are in harmony with such knowledge as men had thirty, fifty or a hundred years ago. The theories which we are called on to prove or disprove have their origin in sentiment and not in philosophy. For instance the statement begins first with the body, second to that there is the mind, and from the mind springs the spirit, and from the spirit springs the soul, from the material body comes the immaterial mind, which is indestructible, the body alone is destructible. How can two things that cannot go together one produce the other? How can a material body produce an immaterial thing? The idea itself is erroneous, just as the theory of the immateriality or materiality of water and heat. A few years ago heat was considered material as it came from a material substance, and the explanation of it was perfectly philosophical, and perfectly stated until a few scientific men got together and finally overthrew that theory altogether.

"So the mind is said to survive, while the body does not. Now the way in which the mind survives is simply this; a person has an idea which he communicates to another through the body by writing or speaking, it makes its impression upon another mind, one material sets another material in motion until this impression is made, that is all there can be to this theory. How can an immaterial substance spring from a material thing? It is an assumption which never has been proved, and I hold never can be."

Judge Waterman: "I shall not speak this evening but there are a great many strangers present and I fear they might go away thinking the critics less intelligent than I know them to be. Judge Russell said he did not understand the word essence, and yet I heard the Judge in an address which he was making to the courts say the essence of things was so and so; then in a very learned manner he spoke about the spirit of the laws, saying that the gist of the question is this, now I would like to have Mr. Russell explain the meaning of the word gist. We are in the habit constantly of employing words which if you call upon us to give their definition it is utterly impossible to do so, and yet we all understand very well what we mean by these things.

"Now it may be that man is a unit, and it may be perhaps that his mind is merely something which rebounds from an impression made upon it. It might be well to compare it to a drum, you pound upon a drum, and it gives back a sound in accord with the stroke, and it is insisted substantially by certain materialists that all there is of the human mind is simply an organism, that there is a brain and that certain sensations or certain impressions made upon it, cause it to rebound, and that that is all there is of consciousness. Well, if it be so, we are reduced to this position, we absolutely know nothing, have no knowledge upon anything. Either there must be a mind or consciousness that sits in judgment upon the sensation which comes to it, and determines what is true in relation to things, or else we have no knowledge. If our minds are merely like a drum which responds to the stroke that is made upon it, then we have no judgment at all, we do not know whether we are two or four legged creatures, because our judgment is simply the result of an impression which is made by the stroke which is given upon this instrument, which for the sake of speech, is located in the brain. Now every man recognizes that through his life time from the cradle to the grave, that he has a consciousness which is able to sit in judgment upon the facts that come to him and other things. Is it not so when two opposite possibilities are presented to him to determine which he will follow?

"However much a man may be carried away by this subtle material philosophy, they know at heart it is not true. It is a little singular that the materialists of today, the materialists who occupy the ultra position upon the question, are right straight where the Calvinists who occupy the ultra position of faith are. The Calvinist is all faith; his whole faith is based upon the word of God, and the declaration made there, that in the beginning God fore-ordained everything, consequently He must have fore-ordained happiness or misery, must have fore-ordained one to believe in Calvinism as well as in anything else, and must also have fore-ordained him to judge whether Calvinism was the true theology. Materialists walk right straight up the same position and say the mind is a drum or bell, that some bells are made different from others, of different metals, but after all is a bell, a bell giving forth sound, a note low, high, harsh or soft in accordance with the stroke that is made upon it. But there is really no judgment to determine what sort of a sound it shall be, or what sort of a stroke it shall be. Now if their theories are true, let us end the Philosophical Society forever, and not attempt to sit in judgment, and in conclusion

upon anything when our conclusions are determined by appliances made according to materialism, or by some organic construction of our brain,
and the waves that happen to play upon it."

Mr. Rawson: "May I ask the name of the
spirit who addressed us?"

Mrs. C. L. V. Richmond: "Mr. Chairman, it
was suggested I believe in the business portion of
this meeting that you change the constitution of
this Society, we might, if we were members,
suggest that you change its name also. We responded to the regular critic the first one appointed, in answer to his questions; the second
critic we sympathize with, he was very diffident.
he was suffering from embarrassment, and we
trust that will explain what he said, as in philosophy there is no excuse for it. You summon
Hercules and you ask him to build block houses
for you; you ask for Apollo and wish him to play
Yankee Doodle, and if he does not do this you
cannot understand him, then why invoke him?
If the subject is beyond the realm and comprehension of the Philosophical Society, why was
the subject proposed? We did not select it, we
did not fashion the words of the theme which
was suggested, we presumed that the chairman
of the meeting was sufficiently acquainted with
the infantile nature of the requirements of the
Society to choose a subject in keeping with their
understanding. If the gentleman wants some-

thing more tangible than the word 'esse,' described as essence, will he please answer if he has ever felt an atom, if he has seen an atom, or held it in his hand, or analyzed it, or knows what it is? and if he has not, then when the materialist tells him that everything in the universe is the result of the ultimate atom, or the aggregation of atoms, why does he not say, I do not understand you? These are foolish words. A subject that has occupied the attention of all minds of all ages, is certainly not beneath you, and it may be above you, if it is, then your Society should strive to attain to its altitude. If the manner of treating the subject was beyond your grasp, we beg your pardon. We thought we were using plain words, our language was such as, one gentleman said, was exploded thirty years ago, therefore being within your infantile recollection at least. We used words to express the definitions that we were asked to make, if we did not make that to your comprehension we are sorry. If the fault is in our language you have a right to criticize it. But the subject certainly is one that has not only been treated by the materialist but by such philosophers as Kant and Hiegel, by such men combining poetry and philosophy as Klopstock, Wiedel, Jacobi, and by those minds that you are accustomed to consider authority upon the mind.

"We believe none of the gentlemen referred

to by one of the critics have ever treated of
mental science, any subjects that aim at knowledge, in that direction they have relegated to
that realm that is called the 'unknowable.' Perhaps that realm may not be unknowable to all.
One of the critics must have been listening while
standing on his head because he exactly reversed
what we said.   He stated that we said the body
is first, and from this the mind is evolved, from
the mind the spirit, and from the spirit the soul,
we said nothing of the kind, we said that the
soul is the primal 'esse' or entity, that from the
soul the spirit emanates, creating in its contact
with the material body that which is called the
mind, so that the gentleman made a man of
straw, and then proceeded to knock him down.
Concerning the statement of another that the
views entertained were in harmony with something he heard thirty years ago; we know that
this is a very enlightened age; we know you have
made great progress in thirty years, but we have
yet to learn that any Philosophical Society claims
to have transcended Plato, or, that others, in
the realm of philosophy, in treating subjects
that pertain to man's spirit or immortal nature,
can transcend the teachings of Socrates.   You
may consign these philosophers to the dark ages,
in this age of steam, electricity and other mechanical contrivances, but if you do you will lose
all that is really valuable in human life.   One

critic says he could understand the statement of a steam engine, we doubt it; unless he could build a steam engine, and know the relation of all its parts he could not understand it. The first steam engine that was ever run was examined by gentlemen, considering themselves just as wise as the members of the Philosophical Society, who declared that it could not move; yet it did. If we mistake not all discoveries have been relegated to that realm to which our discourse has been consigned by the critics, the realm of the imagination. All hail to the realm of the imagination! Galileo, Herschel, Watt, were 'dreamers' until they built the illustration of their dreams (block houses that brought them down to the comprehension of the people). Spiritual truth has been in the world during the infancy of the race, and has been recognized only by geniuses, prophets and seers, if you represent the manhood of the race meet it on that level.

"One gentleman said that this is beautiful, because it is in the realm of fiction, and, therefore, as a dream he had no fault to find with it. Then does he say that all who attest in the present day to have witnessed and received intelligent communications from the spirit world are living in the imagination, in the realm of fiction? Does he say that Prof. Wallace, one of the best naturalists in England, and Prof. Crookes who gave three years of time to the investigation of psychical phenomena, the late Mr. Varley and Prof. Zollner, and a score of living scientific men are living in the imagination ? Does he say he has taken no notice of the evidence that is in the world and has been for thirty years ? but has been content merely to listen to a few discourses ? If he has only listened to theories he might call them imagination, but the evidence is here. There are millions of people in the world who know of Spiritual manifestations, and thousands who know of that realm that has been treated of to-night. If he is so unfortunate as not to know of it, then he should correct his ignorance at once, study the subject that other people have studied, devoting not a single moment to intellectual theory or the 'imagination' which he has attempted to state, but years, a lifetime to the truth. We thank the last speaker for his remarks, but we are sorry that he tried to help us, because while it is true that he ought to say something to place the Philosophical Society on a higher footing, intellectually, before the visitors who are here, it might seem that he was endeavoring to assist the speaker."

The Chairman: "A member of the Society wished to know if the spirit addressing us, would state his name? I would also ask if spirits have any means of ascertaining the advance thoughts of the day?"

Mrs. Cora L. V. Richmond: "Mr. Chairman,

the answers to similar inquiries have been so er-
roneously received that the spirit has great hesitation in answering. In the first place he had
no personal acquaintance with the Philosophical
Society, nor any of its members, therefore you
will have no means of knowing the truth except
the authority of the speaker. The name as given
in a recent address was Adin Augustus Ballou,
son of the Rev. Adin Ballou of Hopedale, Milford, Mass., having been in spirit life about
thirty-five years, and has such experience as
his individual intelligence has enabled him to
gain.

"The spirit during that time has become acquainted with the thoughts of the present time.
Since, while mortals are very ignorant, as a rule,
of what the spirits are doing, that ignorance is
not reciprocated by them. The spirit world is
familiar with the current thoughts of men, because where they are valuable many of them may
come from the spirit world, where they are not
valuable the blemishes are easily detected, because like a blot upon the sun, they make themselves manifest in the shadows of your daily
lives."

[This address and attendant discussion is also
published in pamphlet form.—ED.]

The following has been much admired, and
was first given in England, 1874:

FROM SUNSET TO DAWN.

I stood on the brow of the hill; to the West
The sunset glories were tenderly prest,
　And out of the silence of evening's breast
　Flushed wave upon wave of amethyst,
Mingled with golden and crimson flame,
Whence sudden pulses of glory came;—
　　　Chime on heather bells.

Each pulse was a petal of rare delight
That unfolded and fashioned itself to my sight;
　Then a viewless face, an impalpable form,
　Yet a presence distinct 'mid the coloring warm
Came out of the splendor of sapphire and gold,
Enfolding, pervading, with portent untold;—
　　　Chime on heather bells.

Then I sang; and my singing seemed sacred and tender,
Full of fervor and fire and a musical splendor,
　Until all of the raptnre flew out of my soul
　Far, far on the song-wings to some distant goal,
Leaving silver-gray silence, a spell without name,
'Mid the ashes of song and the sunset's dead flame;-
　　　Chime on heather bells.

There the cold, silver-gray of the twilight enwound
In a shivering mantle the still earth around,
　And the waves of the sea broke in sobs at my feet
　With a sighing and longing of pain, bittter-sweet;
The pitiful tale of a strange, deep despair
Swept over and through me, enchaining me there;—
　　　Are ye there, heather bells?

Like the sound of the winds in their sobbing and cryings,
Restless waves of the deep with their moanings and sighings,
　Like the far-stifled roar of the populous city,
　Of those seeking vainly for pleasure or pity;
Deep and deeper, like tremblings of far-away thunder,
Or terror of earth when the earthquake strides under;—
　　　Ah! ye weep, heather bells.

Like lost souls engulphed in shame for sinning,
Without hope of pardon, no respite e'er winning,
  The sound of great wrongs heretofore unrequited,
  Ages of Hope-buds, and Love's promise blighted,
Bitter, dead sea-fruits, dashed on the bleak shore
'Mid tempest and lightning and winds wrathful roar;—
    Are ye dead, heather bells?

Meanwhile all the stars had bloomed in their places,
The clear, sapphire dome was resplendent with faces,
  Still and white the Madonna of night whispered low
  To her mystical daughters who passed to and fro,
And they silently passed on their wonderful way,
Making *real* the visions called *dreams* in earth's day;—
    Sleep now, heather bells.

Yet still amid all was the sound of deep sorrow,
That 'mid all the splendor no surcease could borrow,
No respite to-day and no hope for the morrow.
Never more will the waves of woe be receding,
O God! will it cease not this moaning and pleading?
The sound that I hear is the Earth's heart a-bleeding;—
    Not now, heather bells.

O Angel of Earth! O thou ancient, blest Mother,
Thy children are thine; they will have thee, none other;
  They will love thee and bless thee, Earth Mother so olden
  Thy spring shall return, thy gray hair be golden;
The wars that have rent thee shall blossom to peace,
The wrongs that oppress thee shall ever more cease;—
    Chime now, heather bells.

Meanwhile all the amethyst silver-gray sheen
Of heather and sky were merging in space,
  The line of the distance that slumbered between
  Was lighted and thrilled by a wonderful face—
The face of the NEW DAWN pressed o'er the dark moor,
Parting the clouds by the morn's purple door;—
    Chime out, heather bells!

At the Chicago National Convention in 1893, Mrs. Richmond was made chairman of a committee of nine to prepare a paper on Spiritualism for the World's Parliament of Religions then in session. As the delegates to that convention had so much to perform, the committee was unable to get together for the consideration of the points to be presented in the paper at the Parliament. An informal discussion, however, took place among the nine members, and, by the unanimous wish of the majority of them, Mrs. Richmond was delegated to prepare that paper. This she did under the direction of her guides in a masterly manner, which paper was duly presented to President Bonney, received by him, and incorporated as a part of the proceedings of that great Parliament. We have received letters from all sections of the United States commenting favorably upon this splendid paper, and have deemed it wise, after consulting with the guides, especially with Spirit Ballou, in regard to the matter, to introduce it as a specimen of her literary work. It will stand the test of time, and many decades hence, will be read with interest by all classes of thinkers as one of the clearest, ablest, and, at the same time, most concise statements of what Spiritualism is to the world that has ever been given by or through anyone. We feel that our readers will find much food for thought in this essay.

PRESENTATION OF SPIRITUALISM.

To the World's Parliament of Religions, Chicago, October, 1893, by the guides of Mrs. Cora L. V. Richmond.

" 'God is spirit, and they who worship Him must worship in spirit and in truth.'—Jesus.

" 'Now, brethren, concerning Spiritual gifts, I would not have you ignorant.'—St. Paul.

" 'Millions of Spiritual beings walk the earth both when we wake and when we sleep.'—Milton, Hesiod.

" 'A little cloud is rising in the west not larger than a man's hand, which will one day overspread the earth; that cloud is Spiritualism.'— Lord Brougham.'

" 'I have not had time in the midst of a busy life, while solving the problem of human freedom, to investigate the phenomena of Spiritualism, nevertheless, I believe its philosophy and phenomena are true, and that Spiritualism will be the religion of the future.'—Theodore Parker.

" 'Sooner than we imagine the day will dawn when a godless science will be an unscientific absurdity.'—Giles B. Stebbins.

GENERAL STATEMENTS.

"Spiritualism, as a name, is synonymous with all that relates to the spirit:

"1. The universal spirit pervading and governing the universe as Universal Intelligence;

"2. The individual spirit whether expressed

in the earthly environment or in the larger freedom of the higher realm.

"Specifically, the name applies to the religious, philosophical and phenomenal aspects of a movement that had its modern beginnings in a series of manifestations Spiritual, mental and physical, forty-five years ago.

"This movement and these manifestations came unsought by those in mortal life; they appeared almost simultaneously in the different portions of this country, and very soon after in different parts of the world.

"The manifestations and the name Spiritualism, in fact, the movement as a whole and in its several parts, were the result of impelling intelligences outside of and manifestly beyond human beings in the earthly state.

"For convenience only, and without any intention of dividing any portion of the subject from the whole, and without forgetting that the name in its entirety signifies all that has ever been expressed from the realm of spirits to those in mortal life, and all that has been unfolded by aspiration and inspiration from within the human spirit, the writer will divide the subject into three general headings, viz.:

"1. The Phenomenal Aspect.

"2. The Philosophical Aspect.

"3. The Religious Aspect.

"The writer is convinced that this method of

presentation will better represent all classes of minds who are interested in this stupendous movement either as a whole or through any one of these especial departments.

PART I.

"In the presentation the writer will reverse the order by considering first

THE RELIGIOUS ASPECT.

"If, as St. Paul declares, 'faith is the substance of things hoped for, the evidence of things not seen,' the most exalted faith must be synonymous with the most positive knowledge, and the word 'faith' must have been misinterpreted in its essential meaning by most denominational religionists.

"Those who accept Spiritualism as a new manifestation of, or a new religion (always using the word 'religion' in the largest interpretation) do so upon the following basis:

"1. The Supreme Intelligence; the Mother-Father, God; the Over-Soul; the Divine Parent, or any other name or term that the individual may choose as synonymous with Infinite Good, the Love, and Wisdom.

"2. The soul (or spirit) as an immortal entity, forever *en rapport* with the Eternal, Infinite Good, continuously seeking and receiving evidences of the loving All-Presence; as the sun is the light of the visible universe, so this Infinite Love and Wisdom is the light of all souls.

"3. The recognition of the divine message from God to Man, either by direct perception awakened in Man or by inspiration from higher realms of spirits and angelic beings.

"4. The recognition of the *Great Messianic Teacher* or *Teachers* as the voice of truth to the world.

"Those who receive Spiritualism in its religious aspects are :

"1. Christian Spiritualists, who accept the Christ life as impersonated in Jesus of Nazareth as the highest expression of religious revelation of truth, and who consider that, without denominational or sectarian definitions, the life and works of Jesus are the highest guidance, but who also recognize that every age has been blessed with Spiritual teachers chosen to bear to earth the message of immortality and the love of God to man.

"Most of these Christian Spiritualists are members of different Christian churches. There are to be found in every denominational church in Christendom those who accept spirit communion as taught by Spiritualists as a part of their religion.

"2. Spiritualists who accept the word 'religion' in the broadest possible interpretation of its meaning; who recognize the religions of every age as having their primal basis in inspiration, and who are willing and ready to accept the *truths* received in any and every form of faith; who consider that Zoroaster or Zardhust, Moses, Buddha, and Jesus were the interpreters of truth to the age in which they lived; that the prophets, seers, and others endowed with Spiritual gifts in every age have been the means of presenting Spiritual truths to man; that Spiritual gifts as witnessed today among the media for Spiritual manifestations are similar (making due allowance for the difference in the general state of humanity) to those that have occurred in past times, especially those accompanying every new dispensation or manifestation of religious truth, and are particularly similar to those mentioned in Paul's epistle on Spiritual gifts.

"3. There are still others who believe Spiritualism to be a new dispensation of religion; not only as a new statement of old revealments, perpetuating the good in all past religions, but a new and living inspiration from the Infinite as the light of this day, and they believe that Spiritualism, in its entirety of phenomena, philosophy, and revelation, forms the basis of the new religion.

"Spiritualists have no sectarian creed, articles of faith, or statement of belief excepting the truth as perceived by the individual, each according to others the privilege of worshiping God according to the dictates of conscience.

"There is a feeling of fellowship with all, and they meet on the common ground of universal Spiritual truth.

"God is manifest in Infinite Love.   Universal Fraternity of Souls.

PART II—THE PHILOSOPHICAL ASPECT.

" 'There are more things in heaven and earth, Horatio, than are dreamt of in *your* philosophy.' —Shakespeare in Hamlet.

> " We all are parts of one stupendous whole,
> Whose body Nature is and God the Soul."—Pope.

" As religion is love (love to God, human brotherhood).

" As science is demonstrated *truth* or knowledge, so philosophy is *wisdom*.

" The *philosophy of Spiritualism* is the inblending into the one perfect whole of all its parts; the union of its phenomena, and spirit, the meeting and merging of its body and soul.

" To many, perhaps a greater number of thoughtful minds than most people are aware, the philosophical aspect of Spiritualism is its most enchanting, and, as it seems to them, its most comprehensive side.   To the writer it is one side of the equilateral triangle of which the phenomenal portion is the base and religion the other side, which triangle solves the circle of immortality.

" The logical perfection of the philosophy of Spiritualism is the primal statement.

"Its harmony with the highest ethics in the undoubted elevation of purpose of the individual, and the whole human race by the substitution of individual growth and unfoldment into spiritual *perfectness* for any other method of attaining the highest good here and hereafter. Its propositions are:

"1. That the present and continued existence of the conscious spirit, the *ego*, inheres in the soul, and is not an especial bestowment of the Infinite or the result of contact with the human organism.

"2. That whatever may be the ideas of individuals or classes concerning a conscious, *a priori* existence, or previous state of individual intelligence embodied in each human life, there is but one philosophical conclusion, based on the phenomenal and intuitional evidence of Spiritualism, *i. e.*, that the change called death (or separation from the body) is not only a natural change (inherent in all organisms), but that it is the next step in the existence of the spirit, releasing or setting free its activities in the next state or realm, and as perfectly in accordance with the Divine plan as is the birth into the human form.

"In fact that the next step or state is the legitimate sequence of existence here, and that each human spirit takes up its line of active individual life in spirit existence, just where, as an individual spirit, the thread seems broken or disturbed at death.

" 3. That the spirit realm includes whatever spirits are, or need, in that state of existence, as the earth state includes whatever is needed for earthly expression.

"4. That the fixed states of happiness or misery are not possible in any state of the spirit expression, but that each spirit, according to growth, continues the individual activities and unfoldments, and all advance from lower to higher conditions by gradual states of progression through unending cycles.

" 5. That no spirit or angel is too exalted or holy to reach and assist those who are beneath, and none too low to be aided by those above.

> Cycle on cycle must the ages move,
>   Onward and upward must all spirits tend,
> Seen in the perfect light of perfect love,
>   All in one supreme purpose ever blend.

"6. That the various states in which spirits find themselves after their release from the environment of the sensuous organism, the relative and absolute principles governing those states, the interblending of spirits in more perfect, with those in less perfect conditions of unfoldment; the communion with and ministration to those in earthly existence; in fact, that the principles governing the spiritual realm and the wisdom by which that realm pervades, encircles and governs the whole of life are made known.

"The *Philosophy of Spiritualism* is the *Philosophy of Life*.

"Material science has claimed to prove the indestructibility of the primal atom, or whatever is the ultimate term for matter.

"Spiritualism does prove the immortality of individual soul by bases, deductions and proofs as undeniable as the principles of mathematics.

"In its final definition, it is the philosophy of philosophies, as it is the religion of religions, and (if need be) the science of sciences.

"It includes the primal and final statements of matter, the primal and final terms for mind, the primal and final principles of spirit in the eternal entity, the soul and all that relates to state and conditions, degrees and stages of expression, all that relates to being, and includes every portion and factor in its statement of the whole.

PART III.—THE PHENOMENAL ASPECT.

"This phase of the subject is sometimes designated scientific, although the writer does not think, individually, that the words *science* and *scientific*, as usually understood, can be applied to the investigation of even the phenomenal phases of Spiritualism.

"Forty-five years ago, scientific men like Professor Robert Hare, of Philadelphia; James J. Mapes, of New York; and, later, Alfred R. Wallace, Professor Crooks and Mr. Varley, of Eng-

land; Camile Flammarion, of France; Professor
Zollner, of Germany, and scores of other scientists of note, investigated the physical phenomena
of Spiritualism and have uniformly declared that
there is no law of material science with which
they are familiar that can explain these phenomena; and that they have recourse only to the
solution always claimed by the manifesting intelligence, viz.: that the source of the phenomena
is disembodied spirits working through means
and methods entirely unknown in any human
science.

"As the result of the experiments in investigating the phenomena of Spiritualism, made by so
many eminent, scientific men in all parts of the
world, extending over the entire period of forty-
five years in which Spiritualism as a name and
manifestation has been in the world—from the
small rappings, near Rochester, N. Y., to the
various and multitudinous phenomena of today—
there has been but one conclusion among scientific men, viz.: that the cause of the phenomena
is immanent in the phenomena, that both are
demonstrated beyond the possibility of a cavil
or a doubt; and that to investigate the physical,
mental or intuitional phenomena of Spiritualism
separately from the whole subject with a view of
ascertaining another cause than that of the action
of spirits, is as much a work of supererogation
as to investigate the phenomena of the light of

day with a view to finding another source of light than the sun.

"The phenomena, philosophy and inspiration focalize around persons who are called 'mediums,' that being the name bestowed upon them by the manifesting intelligences, the spirits who act upon and through them. At the present writing there is no knowledge among Spiritualists as a body, or investigators within or outside of the ranks of Spiritualism as to what constitutes mediumship.

" Mediums are chosen by the spirit intelligences desiring to manifest, from among all nationalities, races, classes and conditions of people. Although the particular gift or phase of mediumship may seem to depend upon, or be modified by the mental and physical or other states of the individual, the mediumship *per se* seems to be determined by the choice or action of the spirit intelligences governing the manifestations.

"The difficulties to be met in approaching this investigation from a purely scientific standpoint are very clear, even if the word 'scientific' shall be made to mean every kind of investigation.

" These difficulties we briefly state. Physical phenomena are usually the basis of scientific investigation, and, naturally, along that line the investigation must be from effect to cause;

therefore from the first the investigation must be confined to results merely. Sometimes science arrives at a perfect knowledge of results, usually only approximately at causes. With the phenomal as well as all other phases of Spiritualism the cause is immanent from the first, and science has nothing to do but to make a statement.

"This may be illustrated thus: if one hears a rap at the door of his room or dwelling, and on opening the door he finds a friend, or any person or thing whatsoever, as the cause of the sounds, he at once loses interest in the phenomena of the sounds, and is occupied by the larger interest of receiving his friend. There is nothing to be solved. If, however, he repeatedly hears the sounds, and on going to the door discovers no person or thing that could have produced them, he commences his investigation to discover the cause.

"From the very first manifestation of the phenomena of Spiritualism to the last, the cause or source of the phenomena has been as manifest as the phenomena.

"By as intelligent methods as language, signals, or any established system of communication between mind and mind in human states, these Spiritual intelligences have been recognized. Invariably they have declared themselves to be individual spirits who once lived in earth forms, accompanying the declaration by evidences of personal identity entirely separated from and independent of any individual in the earth form at the time of the manifestation.

"The cause of the phenomena is, therefore, so clearly identical with the results as to make a scientific investigation, on the basis of discovering a new cause, entirely impertinent. To ignore the knowledge already gained is totally unscientific as well as illogical. Therefore, all investigations of Spiritualism *de novo* claiming, *a priori*, that the source of the manifestation is still unknown, is equivalent to ignoring the whole subject.

"Doubtless the methods of communion between the two states of conscious existence, the one preceding and the other following the change called death, will be formed into an interesting branch in the future study of Spiritualism, or will be revealed from the same realm by the same intelligences from whence the movement as a whole has been impelled into mortal life. Possibly that study may lead to scientific data upon which to predicate knowledge of the methods by which disembodied spirits communicate with those in the human environment.

"Thus far there has been no formulation of facts, because none was needed, each particular manifestation being given for the specific purpose of conveying the intelligence desired from disembodied spirits to those in human life; and since

the philosophy, or *rationale*, of the whole subject includes both cause and result, and since
these resolve themselves into the one word Spiritualism, the subject in its entirety is before the
world, and the subdivisions may be open to
study.

"The conclusions are invariably the same,
whether arrived at from the supposed scientific
method or the result of philosophical deductions,
or revealed by distinct inspiration, viz.: individual human intelligences existing beyond human
states, (and presumably immortal) do manifest
under conditions not known by those existing in
human life. The demonstration of this and what
it naturally leads to in all that pertains to the
relation of spirits, embodied and disembodied, to
each other and to the whole universe, constitutes
the realm of Spiritualism.

"That there is no solution for the phenomena,
physical, mental, or spiritual, in the known
realm of science; and that, while the methods of
communion between the two states are still unknown, the evidence of the existence of disembodied spirits, and of their communion with this
world is demonstrated.

"Spiritualists are by no means tenacious as to
terms, and the writer is perfectly willing to state
that, to those who pursue the investigation along
the lines of exact science, there is the fullest
appreciation of their work; but the majority of

Spiritualists, in viewing the whole subject, consider that the whole subject is beyond the realm of exact science and within the realm of revealed or intuitional knowledge.

"Whatever view may be taken of the scientific investigation of the whole subject, or of its physical phenomena only, it is the proper place here to state that all scientific minds who have investigated the phenomenal phases of this movement readily admit, and many of them openly declare, that Spiritualism will compel a restatement of science, either by the readjustment or the re-creation of scientific bases and terms; in the recognition of a vast unexplored realm between the kingdom of spirit and the heretofore recognized domain of science, whether that realm shall include a 'fourth dimension of space,' as suggested by Professor Zollner, or whether it will be found to be a realm of occult forces impinging on the material and spiritual states, and interblending with each, or whether the results will prove the methods of communion to be simply the setting free of individual volition. The final adoption of either of these methods, or of any other not named, must be determined by future revealments, and in any case the new statement will be incorporated into Spiritualism as a portion of its entire statement.

"Scientific minds in Spiritualism epitomize the whole subject as follows: 1st, the existence

of the individual human spirit; the continued
conscious existence of the individual spirit after
the change called death; the intercommunion of
the two states by the voluntary action of individual disembodied spirits to and through those
existing in human form; by automatic action
upon the brain or any part of the human organism without the conscious concurrence of the
individual acted upon; 2d, by action upon sen-
tient or non-sentient objects without the intervention of any human being, excepting that these
manifestations usually occur in the presence of a
medium who does not voluntarily aid in their
production; 3d, by action upon all bodies and
substances upon the earth or in its atmosphere,
without the intervention of any human agency,
and by methods not known in any existing
science.

"The scientific statement is: *knowledge* of a
future life, *demonstrated* truth of immortality.

PART IV.—A RESUME OF ITS WORK AND INFLUENCE.

"In a movement wholly impelled from the
realm of spirit and borne forward on the wave of
inspiration, although intelligently met and aided
from the first by many among the ablest minds
of the earth, it is utterly impossible to name or
number all those whom it has reached.

"Societies have been organized in every State
in the Union, and in all parts of the world as

centers for those who have had individual experiences, and to receive the manifestations and ministrations from the spirit world; but Spiritualism has spread rather by individual experiences than by organized efforts.

" As early as 1860, the late Archbishop Hughes, of New York, estimated that there were ten millions of Spiritualists in the United States alone, *pro rata* there should now be thirty millions. Spiritualists claim no definite number, and numbers are unimportant in a statement of truth. If its principles and its manifestations be perceived by but one, all the world must follow.

"The organization of Spiritualists into local Societies and now into a National Association is rather for the purpose of fellowship and mutual protection than for any sectarian purpose, and also for the purpose of making available the manifestations and ministrations, as well as the spiritual teachings given through the media.

"As a whole movement, the scope of its influence is measureless. Its manifestations extend into every department of human thought; its presence in the world has changed the entire attitude of thoughtful minds concerning the problems of death and the after life, and their relation to human states, at the same time opening up for investigation a vast inter-realm, including the latent possibilities of the human spirit while in the earthly environment.

"It has reached the man of science in his laboratory, or study, and within its rare alembic, has rewrought the demonstration of immortality

"It has walked into the churches of all denominations, religions and tongues; has stood beside the clergyman or priest or ministrant, and has whispered the message of immortal life, saying: 'Are they not all ministering spirits?'

"It has proved itself a solvent of all religions and philosophies by correcting erroneous ideas born of imperfect human interpretations concerning a future life, and substituting knowledge.

"It has restored Spiritual gifts and made them a portion of the recognized opinions of the human race.

"It has made thousands and hundreds of thousands to acknowledge it by name within and without the churches, within and without established schools of philosophy, within and without the walks of science, by knowledge alone; and thousands of others to accept its evidence in the form of belief based upon testimony of others.

"Its sources of inspiration are the invisible hosts.

"Its teachers and messengers are the great, the wise, and the loved ones who have passed on.

"It has opened a royal or inner way to knowledge for many who are its chosen instruments, by touching child minds with facts and data, with scientific and philosophical knowledge, with wisdom far beyond their years, and with eloquence unknown to mortal art.

"It not only has created a literature of its own, in hundreds of volumes of experience and philosophy, and scores of periodicals publishing its demonstrations and advocating its propositions, but it has pervaded the best literature of the age, touching and illumining the minds of such writers as Dickens, Thackeray, Longfellow, Phelps and scores of others with its living presence.

"Its uplifting influence is felt in every life that accepts its truths, and in the whole world by making the aims of life here consistent with a continued existence, primary steps in the external pathway, and by making the basis of life *spiritual*, not material.

"To a materialistic and unbelieving age, it has demonstrated the existence of the human spirit beyond the change called death.

"To those who had 'hope' and 'faith' through any form of religious belief in a future life, it has added knowledge, and to both has opened the gateways that had not even been left 'ajar' between the spiritual and material realms.

"It has removed the fear of death, and of what might come to the spirit after dissolution of the body, by a knowledge of the states and conditions of those who have passed beyond that change as declared by the testimony of disembodied spirits, who must be in the very nature of the case the

only authentic source of information upon subjects pertaining to that future existence.

"It has bridged the chasm, spanned the gulf
between the two states of existence by the iris
archway of love.

"Immortal messengers have brought the knowi-
edge of their state of existence and have announced in unmistakable ways the nearness of
that so-called ' undiscovered country.'

" Invisible hands have re-kindled the fires upon
the altars of inspiration that had long been desolate.

" Angels and ministering spirits have anew attuned the voices of mortal to immortal songs.

" And they have ' rolled away the stone from
the door of the sepulcher' of thousands of human
hearts who thought their dead lived not.

"Its authority is truth wherever found;

"Its sacred books the inspirations of every
age;

" Its oracles and priests, those whom truth
annoints and inspiration calls; its creed the un-
written law of knowledge, wisdom, truth and
love;

"Its ceremonials the service of a noble life;

"Its communion is with kindred spirits and its
fellowship with all.

"Its altars the human spirit; its temples living
souls.

"It is the open door, the present light, the

demonstration, philosophy and religion of the immortal soul.

"Calm-browed and unafraid this mild-eyed, open-visioned Presence views the heretofore and the hereafter, the present and the future, with equal interest and courage born of perfect truth.

"The 'well-springs of eternal life' are hers, and she bids mortals drink fearlessly at their living fountains.

"The ' bread of life ' is hers, and she bids all spirits partake freely from the all-bounteous store.

"From the vintage of the spirit the wine of her everlasting kingdom is distilled in streams of living inspiration.

"Poets quaff as this golden goblet is pressed to their lips and sing the songs of the spheres.

"Sages gather from its open treasure-house the wisdom of the skies.

"Seers and prophets, inspired anew, reveal again the forever old, forever new, immortal theme.

"The mourner forgets her grief and dries her eyes while listening to the messages of love.

"The weary find rest in its all-reposeful and eternal ways.

"The weak find strength in its unhindered helpfulness.

"Crime, sin, and all human imperfections and shadows fade gradually yet surely before its all potent light.

"The whole world touched, awakened, thrilled, aroused from the lethargy of material propositions and dogmatic assertions, from charnel houses of the senses, the tombs of death and despair, from sepulchers wherein their hope and faith and highest love were well-nigh buried, turns toward this new day-dawn saying, 'Is not this the light that lighteth every man that cometh into the world?'"

We deem this an opportune time to call our readers' attention to the wonderful poem, "Heaven's Greeting to Columbia," that was given through the mediumship of Mrs. Richmond in the Columbian year, 1892. This poem is replete with instructive ideas, historical data, and idealistic prophecies of that which is in store for our beloved America. This poem received many favorable notices from the press of the country, and had an extensive sale at the various Spiritualistic camps during the seasons of 1892 and 1893. It made a beautiful souvenir of the World's Fair. The beauty of its thought and perfect rhythm constitute it one of the most remarkable productions that our subject has ever given in the line of poesy. Its value is, as an entirety, too great to admit of a partial review, and we have not space to give it in full for the delectation of our readers, but it can easily be obtained and would amply repay perusal. If heaven, through the ministering angels, can be made to bless Columbia with freedom of thought in social, political and religious matters, then shall our people be free indeed. This is the aim of the emancipated hosts of heaven, the leaders of thought in both worlds, who are endeavoring to usher in a brighter light for the guidance of all men, by removing slavery of caste, of dogmatic theology, bigotry, and superstition from every department of life. We commend this poem to our readers for we feel that a practical application of the sublime thoughts it contains will make all men better, through being permitted to read the inspired words contained therein.

In connection with our subject's literary labors, we with pleasure record that much of the success with which these works have met, is due to the unswerving fidelity and conscientious devotion of William Richmond. During the past twenty years he has been constantly by our subject's side, endeavoring with his kindly words of sympathy and affection to sustain her in her public labors, and to aid in preserving the inspired thoughts that have fallen from her lips. He felt that these discourses and teachings, and the poetic pearls that fell from her lips should be preserved for the benefit of the world at large. He devoted himself to the study of stenography in order that his might be the hand to transcribe these words, and to give them to the world.   In a short time he had acquired a complete knowledge of this magic art, and since that time has taken several thousand of the name poems for the benefit of the friends receiving them, has reported the class lessons (see Soul Teachings and Psychopathy), he has also transcribed all of her Sunday lectures and the poems given by Ouina at the close of her discourses.

He then felt the necessity of presenting these thoughts to the world in the form of books and periodicals. He set himself to learn the printer's trade, and soon became an expert compositor. Then he was master of the situation. He would take the lectures, lessons and poems in shorthand, write them out for the press, and with his own hands, would set the type, sometimes, indeed, doing compositorial work from the shorthand notes, correct the proof, fold and mail the discourses to all parts of the world. This office has been no sinecure. He has faithfully discharged his duties, absolutely without other reward than the love of the cause.

His confidence and perfect trust in the guides must not pass unnoticed. He has endeavored to be their true recorder to the world, after their instrument has given him the thought; and most faithfully has he discharged this duty. Month after month, year after year, with complete self-abnegation, has he devoted himself to this work. In his soul he has felt the value of these teach-

ings, and in the compilation of the lessons upon
the subjects of Psychopathy and the Soul in
Human Embodiments, he has proved how boundless was the value of his services to our subject
and to the world. In fact, the work of the two
is so interblended that it is hard to disassociate
one from the other. No more unselfish worker
in our ranks can be found than William Richmond. He has more than ten thousand name
poems in shorthand notes ready for use when
the occasion for their production shall come.

For many years he has reported for the Spiritualistic press the discourses given by the guides.
He reported and published the ''Weekly Discourse'' for several years. When the financial
stringency became too great, the publication of
these discourses was discontinued; but he, real-
izing the importance of these lectures, kept his
stenographic notes of every one of them, and has
them now in his possession for future use. He
feels, as do all of our subject's most intimate
friends, as well as most minds conversant with
these themes, that the time will come when these
discourses will be transcribed for the benefit of
the world and placed in an enduring form before
the reading public. Pecuniary reward for those
arduous labors has never entered into his thought,
nor has he murmured under the burden that has
been laid upon him, for he has felt that the reward of the spirit would more than compensate

him for his years of toil in the service of the
spirit world while here on earth. Spiritualism,
as manifested in the teachings of the guides, has
always been his first consideration outside of the
care that he felt was due his beloved wife, and
faithfully has this pair obeyed the injunctions
laid upon them by their guides.

· Mr. Richmond felt that the life work of our
subject was of such paramount importance to the
history of Spiritualism that he undertook, several
years ago, to compile the same from such data
as he could obtain from her friends. Finding
this task too great to be carried on in connection
with his other multitudinous duties he put the
thought one side for a time and finally committed
the work to our hands to be carried on to its
completion. Whatever material he had in hand
he generously turned over for our use, and has
aided in every possible way the preparation of
this life work; reserving the more sacred collection for the more sacred work that only the most
loving hand can be intrusted with, and that he
alone of all the world must be the one to prepare, viz.: a full account of the higher, inner
teachings, given by the guides of our subject, and
her biography. His is a genial, kindly nature,
and wherever he goes he makes friends and keeps
them. In many of the letters that we have examined, high testimonials of the personal regard
of the writers for Mr. Richmond have been given.

His sincerity, devotion to principle, love for the cause, and desire for its advancement, are well known to all his friends. He is an earnest worker and a true Spiritualist, and we feel that we speak for all of our readers in uttering this thought that he, and his Spiritually endowed wife may long be spared to minister to the Spiritual and intellectual needs of the people of earth.

CHAPTER XVI.

LETTERS FROM PERSONAL FRIENDS AND OTHERS IN APPRECIATION OF THE WORK.

IN the account of anyone's life or work, to omit the opinions of personal friends, who know the subject best, hence love her most, would leave the work sadly incomplete. From all quarters of the world have come in tributes of praise to our gifted subject, breathing forth a spirit of love, which, if extended to all of the human family, would make the world a brighter and happier place for all the children of men. It is the appreciation of the *real soul worth* of the individual that makes one able to reach understandingly that friend's real self. These friends of our subject, who have thus written, have entered deeply into her soul life, and have expressed what *they* feel, concerning the truth that comes forth from the sanctuary of her inner being to the outward world, in these tributes of affection that they lay upon the shrine of her life. Friendship has been too often confounded with acquaintance; therefore, the seeming falling away of friends from one's life has brought in a great deal of bitterness to the

individual. No real friendship, however, can
ever be thus broken; because, if there be a relationship formed between individuals based upon
other than that of the soul, there will be in
time a falling away or breaking up of the ties
that bind them together. If, however, these ties
are formed from the soul-side of life, like the
flowers that bloom in the world supernal, the
flower of Friendship will forever bloom as bright,
and shed its fragrance over the lives of men with
undiminished splendor and sweetness throughout all eternity. To have a friend, is to have a
treasure that is everlasting. To have an acquaintance, is like an ephemeris, which, with the
change of the winds or the departure of the
spring or summer months, leaves us as if it had
not been.

Hence, these friends of our subject, not acquaintances, through long association and appreciation of the real soul worth, through the laws
governing soul life, have entered into her life,
and she into theirs, in the way that has formed
a complete Harmonia in this expression of the
lives of the individuals. We append these letters, perhaps not consecutively, but as they have
been received, in order that our readers may
come to an understanding of what lies back of
the expressed personality of Mrs. Cora L. V.
Richmond. We cannot reproduce all that we
have received. We can only give a few from

those who have known her longest, loved her
most, and appreciated the great work that she
has done and is still doing for suffering humanity.

We had prepared a review of the Soul Teachings to be printed as a separate chapter in this
book, on reflection we have decided that it is
not necessary or best to publish it.

First; because the entire ground of the spirit
and effect of those teachings has been so ably
and completely traced in the letters of personal
friends of our subject, pupils of the teachings,
published in this and other chapters of this
book.

Second; because the space so filled would have
crowded out other matter that cannot be easily
obtained by the usual reader and cannot well be
omitted from this work.

Third; and most important, because the teachings are accessible to the reader in the volume,
The Soul in Human Embodiments, and no review or synopsis can possibly convey an adequate
idea of the scope and masterful completeness of
those teachings.

We, therefore, begin this chapter of letters with
one from the pen of Col. H. J. Horn; this letter,
perhaps, would properly have come under the
head of our subject's work in New York city,
but it is equally pertinent to the present chapter,
therefore we publish it here in full:

"27 Park Place,
"SARATOGA SPRINGS, June 15, 1894.
"MR. H. D. BARRETT:

"DEAR SIR:—Your favor of April 6th, asking replies to certain questions concerning Mrs. Richmond, and reminiscences of her early work in New York city, came duly to hand, but at a time when I was quite ill and unable to furnish a prompt reply.

"Previous to her advent as a public lecturer, there gathered in New York a band of noble men and women, sacrificing their livelihoods to their convictions, who avowed their faith in a new dispensation that was then dawning upon the world. These early apostles of liberal thought opened the way and prepared the public for the soul stirring lectures of Mrs. Richmond that followed.

"It is well, at this day, for Spiritualists to be informed concerning these pioneers, who renounced every temporary consideration for the promulgation of a cause that has since illuminated the world. Conspicuous among them were A. J. Davis, S. B. Brittan, William Fishbough, with Fernald, Baker, Harris, Ingall, Johnson, and Mrs. Fanny Green, and the indomitable Mrs. Katherine Dodge. She it was who, with material means, caused the 'Divine Revelation' and the 'Univercœlum' to be embodied in tangible form, and spread broadcast before the public.

"Then appeared Mrs. Richmond upon the horizon of awakened thought. She was at once popular and drew crowds of anxious inquirers whenever she discoursed, by her winning and persuasive eloquence. Her very presence seemed to give out a harmonious influence, which permeated her audiences, and as tidings of an inner life fell from her lips, they became, as it were, spell-bound in deepest interest. Again, all who listened were united to her in personal affection and regard. A sincerity and pathos marked every utterance, and her influence upon the progressive thought of the age cannot be estimated.

"Very truly and sincerely,

"H. J. HORN."

We cannot refrain from introducing at this point a letter from one of the gifted writers on the subject of Spiritualism and occult phenomena in foreign lands. While this letter was personal to Mrs. Richmond, it is so expressive of the high regard of the writer, Countess of Caithness, Duchesse de Pomar, that we take the liberty of reproducing it in full:

"PARIS, June 15, 1885.

"DEAR MRS. RICHMOND:—You will wonder who is your correspondent, as I have never had the pleasure of addressing you before, but when you turn the pages and see my name, I believe it will not be unknown to you, as that of a true, firm and devoted Spiritualist of many years standing, but one, alas, who is wholly debarred from enjoying your grand and eloquent discourses, from her residence abroad. Only two or three times many years ago was I able to profit by them through meetings at the Cavendish rooms; I cannot remember the date, but it must have been at least ten years ago. Since then I have eagerly sought to read your lectures in the 'Medium' and in the 'Banner,' but of course it is not quite the same thing as to listen to them, and imbibe at the same time, the powerful magnetic influence of the inspired medium. I think I have never regretted so much not being in London as I do at present; for I see from the papers that your two last lectures would have been most congenial to me, that of Sunday, the 7th, when you spoke of the important new epoch, which had dawned upon the world's history, the old dispensation having closed in the year 1881 (this being entirely my own conviction also), and that of yesterday, the 14th, when I see you were to discourse on Christianity, Buddhism and Orientalism, and their relations to the new religion; this also is a theme that most particularly interests me, for I am deeply engaged at present in writing a book entitled: 'Universal Theosophy.' You will therefore understand how earnestly all my thoughts are in the subject of your lectures, and how much I feel I might have gained from the teachings of your spirit guides, who no doubt know me, and know my thoughts, and are able to follow the progress of my work, and I trust take an interest in its success as a book, that may lead some who are still on the outside to enter in, and enjoy the rich feast of good things now spread on the great Father's table, for those who love and seek Him, and Her, the everlasting Mother, the Divine Wisdom, ' *Theosophia* '; and it is in this hope, I venture to write you as a sister Spiritualist and dear friend of many years, (although as yet the friendship has been all on my side), in the hope that through you, your guides might be willing to give me some bright ideas, some crumbs from the two loaves that were divided amongst the multitudes assembled around you on the two last Sundays.

"Dear Mrs. Richmond, pray tell me whether any shorthand notes were taken of the two discourses, and whether it might be in my power to obtain a copy or copies from the happy scribe by purchase.

"And now it only remains for me to assure you that you have in me a true friend, an old and ardent admirer, and to say that should you ever be induced to pay a pleasure and relaxation visit to Paris, I would do all I could to make you enjoy your visit, and prove to you how truly I admire and appreciate you. In the meantime, let me beg of you to excuse my want of ceremony in addressing you direct, without any introduction, feeling sure that my own fraternal sympathy would be met by yours in the same spirit, and that, though you may not feel drawn to me in friendship, yet your spirit guides will assure you that I am no stranger to them, for they have often witnessed my happiness and enthusiasm when reading your written lectures. Pray believe me then,

"Most sincerely and fraternally yours,

"MARIE CAITHNESS, Duchesse de Pomar."

Mrs. Lizzie Howard, from Clapham, England, in 1886, writes a most appreciative letter, saying among other good things: "May your life be full of peace and happiness, and may constant aspirations of love and sympathy help and cheer you in your ministrations." Her husband, Ben Howard, a gifted inventor, student, and *litterateur*, writes in the same spirit of appreciation and consideration, in the following words: "May you be spared on this planet for many years to come. Your life has indeed been a most useful one. I can truly say the first occasion on which I heard you speak marked an era in my life, and on each successive occasion when, after a lapse of time, I have heard you again, I have felt my better nature stirred and my lower recede. May every blessing be showered upon you and upon Mr. Richmond, whose kindly nature wins him friends everywhere."

If we had space we would gladly give our

readers the benefit of many personal letters from
friends in foreign lands, all of whom have written
in a spirit of loving appreciation of our subject
and her work.   If the good wishes these letters
contain could find fruition in her life, no shadow
of sorrow, no touch of pain, no clouds of darkness would be her portion during the remainder
of her life, but the eternal sunshine of joy, made
possible through the practical application of
human sympathy and love would be hers forever
more.

We cannot fail to appreciate the fact that those
who knew us in our childhood become better
acquainted with our real selves than as if they
had met us in later periods in life.   Hence it will
be of interest here to introduce a letter from a
gifted writer in the Spiritualist ranks, Mrs. Orpha
E. Tousey, from whom we have already quoted
concerning her Buffalo and Dunkirk labors. This
letter enters into the spirit of Mrs. Richmond's
work, and will be of great value to our readers
as well as instructive to the general public in relation to the subject whose life we are endeavoring to portray:

"MR. H. D. BARRETT.

"DEAR FRIEND AND BROTHER:—It has been
said that genius has no pedigree, no parents, no
children, that its possessor cannot tell how he
came by it, and cannot transmit it to others.
But we believe it not.   Genius, which is only

another name for mediumship, is as much the product of natural causes as is any formation in the realm material, and when the world is educated to an understanding of the laws governing these things, the two worlds now designated as material and Spiritual will be so interblended that the word medium will become obsolete, for all will be mediums and walk hand in hand with the angels.

"Mrs. Cora L. V. Richmond was and is the child of Nature, childlike in her exuberance, her teachableness and impressibility, full of kindness and affection, her spirit vibrating as readily to the touch of sorrow as of joy, and as susceptible to the guidance of the angels as is the Æolian harp to the breath of the wind. Her mother before her was rarely gifted with mediumistic powers, and not only transmitted this quality to her child, but gave her up unrestrainedly to the guidance and keeping of the angels. More than once during her childhood, and later career as a medium, has she been rescued by her invisible guides from imminent danger. They have proved times without number that they are fully equal to the task of protecting her under all circumstances. In the fact of her perfect and unqualified surrender to angel guidance, lies the secret of her wonderful susceptibility and the development of those traits of character so lovable and so peculiar to herself, and has placed her pre-

eminent in a sphere of usefulness as a teacher
and lecturer. Her career goes to prove that book
education is not after all the great source from
which has sprung our greatest men and women.
Colleges and schools can only be secondary.
There is a power behind them that projects the
higher and more potent qualities of the man
or woman, and the great, active, utilitarian world
accords to men and women their rightful place,
after all, if they be but true to the inner self and,
with dignified and unfaltering steps, press forward in the work to which they are called by
their fitness thereunto.

"Mrs. Richmond from her earliest childhood
has, almost unconsciously to herself, been constantly moved onward and outward, going deeper
and deeper into the all encompassing realm of
truth; as a stream springing from the woodland
mountain, gracefully winding through flower-
gemmed valleys, around trees and about bould-
ers, hindered sometimes by rubbish and drift-
wood, or perchance struggling up some unusual
eminence, yet rolling onward into the wide plains,
an irresistible river, deep, sparkling, clear, mysterious and sublime, reaching at last the all em-
bracing ocean. All this shows the masterful power
of spirit, and the possibility of individual victory
in the midst of human environments. As we
behold her to-day, standing among earth's spiritually crowned and glorified teachers, in the zenith

of perfected womanhood, contributing so gracefully, and with so little friction and bluster, to the needs of human hearts, giving hope to the despondent, courage to the weak, and words of wisdom to the seeker after truth, we cannot forbear comparing her, as well as others of her contemporaries in mediumship, to the medium of Nazareth, whose personality we reverence; and we trust our comparison will not seem sacrilegious to any who are acquainted with the course of mediumship—what it has accomplished towards liberating, equalizing and enlightening the world, and what it has had to endure in the way of self-sacrifice. This so-called Christian Nation rests upon the teachings of the babe of Nazareth as the foundation principle of civilization. The Christian reads with throbbing heart and moistened eyes of the 'immaculate' (?) mother watching over her babe as the stars shone in upon his bed in the manger, of that child at the age of twelve, confounding those men, wise in the logic of the world, by the simple words given by the inspiration of a spirit at one with the All-Father, how, after a day's journey, he stopped at the tent of Martha and Mary, and taking up the little children blessed them, saying: 'Of such is the kingdom of heaven,' how he befriended the woman Magdalene, and the poor, needy and afflicted everywhere, causing the blind to see, the deaf to hear, the dead to arise by the magic touch of his hand; how he died upon the cross, how Martha and Mary followed him to the tomb, and rolling away the stone found that he had arisen; how in the calm of evening he appeared unto the eleven as they sat at meat, and upbraided them with their unbelief and hardness of heart, because they believed not them that had seen him after he had arisen.

" When we take a retrospective glance at the last forty-six years and realize what mediumship has done in this age of materialism and blind beliefs, this age of out-reaching investigation and ' bold experiments,' we can but feel that the mission of Christ is being renewed and multiplied.

"That Mrs. Richmond possesses those soul illuminating and helpful qualities in an unusual degree must be admitted by all who have known her. It is not for us to trace and present her life lines except to a limited extent. To her biographer and ever faithful and wise guides is given the pleasant task of giving to the world the more extended account, though we feel that no one will be able to fully compass her life work.

" Sincerely your friend,

"ORPHA E. TOUSEY."

We next invite our readers' attention to a letter from the pen of the Honorable Wendell C. Warner, United States Consul at Burslem, England. Mr. Warner for some years has been an able and is, at his best, one of the most eloquent speakers upon the Spiritualistic platform as well as deeply interested in the political affairs of this nation. At the opening of Mr. Cleveland's second term, Mr. Warner received a well merited appointment from his hands as Consul to Burslem, England. Brother Warner's long acquaintance with our subject and her work, entitles him to a prominent place in this history, for he can speak from the standpoint of appreciative knowledge. His letter is a mine of information for all those who care to enter into the spirit of the philosophy and religion of Spiritualism, as well as to comprehend the real meaning of the soul teachings of the guides of our subject. We append his letter in full:

"CONSULATE OF THE U. S.,
"DISTRICT OF TUNSTALL,
"MOORLAND ROAD, BURSLEM, Sept. 16, 1894.
"PROF. H. D. BARRETT,

"MY DEAR BROTHER:—At your request and that of Mrs. Richmond, I send you enclosed letter for your book of her life work. If the style of your work will admit it, please publish as written.

"I often think of you in connection with dear old Cassadaga, and long for the time when I can again be identified with its work. With deep sympathy for all your undertakings, I am, dear brother, Your obedient servant,

"WENDELL C. WARNER."

"I am asked to write what the work of Mrs. Cora L. V. Richmond and her guides has been to me. As well might I try to give a record of all heart-throbs, all impulses for good, all aspirations, for so closely have her work and influence been woven with the warp and woof of my life, that I can separate nothing of value that I spiritually possess from their divine ministrations. What Christ is to the Christian, what Mahommet is to the followers of Islam, what Buddha is to the dwellers in the Orient, what Luther was to the reformation, was Mrs. Richmond, Ouina and the guides to me. I cannot separate the three forces. They stand to me as the Trinity. Not afar off, not mere symbols of a bygone age, but living, speaking realities of today.

"When a boy climbing the hills of my Wyoming county home, knowing naught of Spiritualism by name, there fell in my way a book of lectures given by Mrs. Richmond when but a little girl. To me that volume was the first revelation of the higher life, the first key to unlock the mighty mysteries that brooded over me, and I clasped the treasure to my heart, wept over its inspired pages, and bowed before that altar whereon they have set the lights of God's last revelation to man. Their sacred words, breathed at many places during the years that followed were the inspiration of my life; but not until I had grown to manhood did I personally meet Mrs. Rich-

mond. Now nearly two decades have passed
since I first saw her standing under the maple
near her childhood's home, breaking the bread
of life to those gathered around her. Time can
never efface the picture. It stands wreathed with
its blush of Autumn leaves, the shimmer of
golden sunshine, and stamped with all the rich
poetry of smiling skies.

"What this Trinity has been to me and mine
during these two decades language cannot tell.
When every light had gone out, when the heavens
were black with despair, when we cowered under
the chastening rod, suffering as only parents'
hearts can suffer, it was Ouina's hand that led us
forth, it was Ouina's voice that bade us arise and
turn our eyes toward the light of the new morning. Ouina has always been my mother con-
fessor. To her I have gone yearly, laid bare
every secret of my heart, confessed every short-
coming, and received such strength and Spiritual
admonition as has better fitted me for the work
to come. From the guides I have learned that
all reforms must commence with the individual,
that Spiritual growth is a series of conquests,
that man cannot escape the overcoming of self
by fleeing from temptation, but that: 'He that
overcometh, shall all things inherit.'

"In Water Lily, my beloved sister, I have
found that blending of the human and divine,
that sweeetness born of two realms, that grace

that gives God's noblest crown to womanhood.
Strong in her personality, strong in her peerless
inspiration, possessing a fidelity to her guides,
and a confidence in their all-wise leading, such
as the world has never before witnessed, what
wonder that the words she utters fall like the
dews of heaven upon thirsting souls. But the
'groups of souls' to which they stand in the
same relation as to me and mine are scattered
throughout the world.   They dwell in the valleys and upon the hillsides of our own land.
They are found midst the hedgerows of England, the vineyards of France, and along the
classic Rhine.   In short, wherever the divine
truth of this new revelation has penetrated,
there are their worshipers, there dwell the soul's
kindred.

"That work which is carried on silently in the
hearts and lives of men cannot be measured by
any human standard.   But could we gather all
secret prayers that have arisen to bless Water
Lily, Ouina and the guides, could we gather the
rivulets of love that flow toward them in every
walk in life, could the hearts that they have comforted, the souls that they have blessed, and all
these tributes be united in one grand anthem,
earth had not heard such a Te Deum since the
angels sang o'er the cradle of Bethlehem.

"Words cannot express my love. I bow my
head and let the mighty waves sweep o'er me.

They surge and break in a language not known
to earth. But with every throb there arises a
prayer of thankfulness that this light was given
me, that my eyes were opened to behold the
glory of the New Dawn that they have heralded,
a dawn waving with gold and crimson banners,
ready to enfold all who shall perceive the light
of the morning. With tears flowing fast as April
rain, I pray, 'God bless Water Lily, Ouina and
the guides.'

"WENDELL C. WARNER."

We now introduce a letter from one of the
most philosophical minds and scholarly writers
connected with this New Dispensation, Mr.
Frederick F. Cook, who has long been a friend
of our subject. He is thoroughly conversant with
her work almost since her advent upon the public
platform, and is able to give a clearer view of the
value of her teachings to the world than perhaps
any other writer now before the public. We
reproduce his letter in full, together with a communication from him to the "Banner of Light,"
in 1883:

"332 W. 51ST ST.,
"NEW YORK CITY, April 20, 1894.
"H. D. BARRETT, ESQ.,
"DEAR SIR:—Your favor of April 5th received,
and has remained unanswered because of pressure of business. None other has been received
by me. I sincerely wish it were in my power to

make a favorable reply to your request. This is
not the first time I have been asked to contribute
biographical matter with regard to Mrs. Richmond, and I have always felt constrained to refuse. Mrs. Richmond is a unique personage,
with, I imagine, a unique mission, and none can
give a true estimate of either herself or her work
until this work is closed. For that, a perspective
is required.

"I heard Mrs. Richmond for the first time
thirty years ago and more. I was not a Spiritualist then, but a materialist, nevertheless she
impressed me to a marked degree. Then came
a hiatus of twelve years. In the meantime I had
become convinced of Spiritualism, *i. e.*, the
spiritual origin of the phenomena. During the
past eighteen years I have heard Mrs. Richmond
hundreds of times in different places, both in
public and in classes. But time or places have
no consequence or importance for me. Besides,
my interest in her is chiefly esoteric and is concerned with her teachings on the Soul in Human
Embodiments. The only matter of possible interest I could furnish, therefore, would refer to
these teachings, and these are all set forth in her
works. As for an estimate of her esoteric work,
the time for that has hardly come. That these
esoteric teachings will one day be ruling ideas in
the world, I make no sort of doubt.

"About ten years ago, I wrote for the 'Banner' somewhat of an estimate of the work. I enclose the same, and you are welcome to make any use of it you like. Once I thought I could see somewhat clearly as to her work and place, but the problem became more and more difficult with time.

"To write about her understandingly, one should be of the councils of her guidance, and that is permitted to none of us. In any proper estimate of her work, her life and her teachings must go together, must complement and illuminate each other, and this must await the perspective of history.

"Let me mention one incident. It was in 1863 or '64 that Mrs. Richmond filled an engagement in Kingsley Hall, Chicago. It attracted wide attention. One day a locomotive exploded in the heart of the city, killing a number of people and wrecking several buildings. The affair caused great excitement. The following Sunday evening it happened that two engineers were chosen on the committee to select a subject for the speaker. They decided on 'Boiler Explosion,' and for an hour this young woman of twenty-three or four dicoursed on this subject. After the lecture, the engineers on the committee, well-known citizens, arose and remarked that in their opinion the subject had been most profoundly treated, and that the manner and matter betrayed intimate knowledge which could only be

gathered from long experience in practical engi-
neering.

" Fraternally yours,

"FREDERICK F. COOK."

The following is the article referred to in Mr.
Cook's letter:

MRS. RICHMOND, IN NEW YORK.

TO THE EDITOR OF THE BANNER OF LIGHT:

"Such outward circumstances as pertained to
Mrs. Cora Richmond's discourses in this city
during the month of January have been duly
recorded in the columns of the 'Banner,' and,
perchance, require no further statement. There
is, however, associated with her recent sojourn
among us much possessing deep Spiritual significance and to the end of setting this before your
readers as best I may I beg a little of your all
but too valuable space.

"Most events have two aspects—an outer and
an inner. Mrs. Richmond came as no stranger
to New York. During her Spiritual ministry,
now extending beyond a quarter of a century, she
has often filled protracted engagements here.
But I feel assured that never before was it her
privilege to make so profound, and, what I believe, so lasting an impression. Thirty years
ago she was a child-wonder; today she typifies a
transcendent Spiritual power. Once the gift of
which she is possessed was used to make men mar-

vel that such things could be; today this same angelic power, taking upon itself a broader and profounder significance, appeals to man's religious nature, and lays deeply and strongly the foundations upon which any Spiritual structure worth the building must rest. He who is at all conversant with the work done through this instrument—more particularly during the past decade—and does not perceive a clear and distinct order of progressive development, must be blind indeed. Steadily has she been kept in advance; deeper and deeper has become the meaning of her utterances; and what at first was strictly esoteric, because the masses are so easily blinded, by excess of light, through an enlightened and adapted course of preparation, has won its place among the accepted themes of discussion in the Spiritual household, while it is also that about which there is most desire to know, and that which, above all other messages from the world of souls, sustains the spirit during its uneven struggle with mortality.

"Surely any worthy work to be done by Spiritualists in the future must be done *apart* from the *facts* which Spiritualism presents. Say what you will, *facts* are not *forces*. Let us not mistake the external form for the living truth within. Facts may be suggestive of forces behind them, but in themselves they have no potency. What I mean is this: Given a *fact* of spirit origin, and unless there be *in you* a perception that corresponds to the intelligence that produces the *fact*, it has no Spiritual significance for you. Hence the *force* is not in the fact, but lies wholly in that occult realm that subsists as relation between giver and receiver. A fact is never anything more than a touchstone; you respond, or you do not respond, as may happen.

"I have made this seeming digression in order to lead the reader up to true appreciation of Mrs. Richmond's work. The *facts* of Spiritualism we have now had with us for a third of a century; but what of the *Spiritual* work accomplished? The *facts* with which we have thus far most concerned ourselves have rent us into a myriad of embittered factions—what unity there is, is in the higher realm of Spiritual perceptions, where the mere outward manifestation loses its significance as a Spiritual factor. Spiritualism as a so-called science, appealing to the senses, is not only a chilling concretion, but a source of ceaseless strife, because Spiritual truths will on no terms permit themselves to be bottled and labelled. But Spiritualism as a *religion*, uplifting the soul to the contemplation of Spiritual beatitudes, is a realm that shall vitalize the world; and it is from this side that the Spiritualism of the future is destined most potently to move upon and possess the world.

"From the first Mrs. Richmond has been an

instrument to convey the higher truths. Time was when Spiritualists, engaged in a bitter struggle with an aggressive theology, had little patience with any expressions savoring of a religious devotion. It had been the work of their lives to dethrone the God of theology, and having no conception of any other, they listened with ill-concealed resentment to the voice of prayer. However, what Spiritualists wanted or did not want made no difference to the guides of the child-medium, and the invocations breathed through her lips often lit a light never afterward to go out.

"Thus the work has gone on. Step by step has the movement been pushed forward and upward into a higher Spiritual or religious atmosphere, until today thousands of Spiritualists (whose sole reliance once consisted of a miscellaneous assortment of *facts*—mere *props*, which any well managed 'exposure' never fails to give a terrible shaking), have an inward experience to sustain them—a light of their own, kindled in spheres celestial, than which no 'exposures' can affect, no dross of earth in any form can dim.

"To *know* is one thing; to *feel* quite another. One is science, the other religion. Now mere knowledge has no element of good in it. It is only when *knowledge* has been translated into *feeling* that it becomes a moral force, or any enduring force whatsoever. Is it not true that on the *knowledge side* the world is growing daily more and more selfish and utilitarian? The poor may starve—what boots it? Have not the rich knowledge? Science teaches that the poor must go to the wall. Has it not discovered a law of 'the survival of the fittest,' behind which capital contentedly piles up its millions? By all means let us make Spiritualism a science, and marry it to this inexorable law of necessity, so convenient to put up as a screen when conscience would have a word to say. But I read Spiritualism terribly amiss if it has not come for the very purpose of tearing away this screen; of bringing man face to face, not with *insensate facts*, but with *burning moral obligations.*

"Spiritualists! there is a voice in the land, if ye would but heed it! It is the voice of the soul pleading for other souls—for the recognition of a wider brotherhood, a broader charity, a deeper conscience-work than any yet known. In this light, how petty our bickerings over *facts;* how ignoble our deridings and persecutions in the name of Truth and Justice. Truth and Justice forsooth! In the glare of that white light now rapidly approaching the earth, the dross of our pretensions will melt as snow before the sun; and if there be naught in us that is genuine, no love for our fellows, no charity for the weak or fallen, we shall stand forth as whited sepulchers, revealing only so many grinning and ghastly *facts.*

"Steadily have the guides of Mrs. Richmond turned the thought of the world inward. There has never been heard a word through her belittling the significance of the outward phenomenon in its appointed and appropriate sphere of usefulness; and their voice has been raised in warning only when it has been sought to make the phenomena cover the whole sphere of Spiritualism. On such occasions the reproof has been clear and definite. Again, when ignorance and malice have combined to stamp out mediumship, whatsoever its kind or nature, under the specious plea of 'purifying Spiritualism,' none has come to the defense of our spirit instruments more eloquently, none has pleaded their cause on higher grounds, and nothing has been to this persecuted class so great a source of strength in the hour of trial, as the words of cheer and comfort and defense spoken through these inspired lips. Thus it is that from first to last her inspiration has been consistent, wise and beneficent; and that it is culminating in a glorious harvest the experience of the past month most eloquently attests.

"To me the work of Mrs. Richmond during the past seven or eight years has been a most instructive study. Viewing it without prejudice —the rather with a strong spiritual sympathy— I have noted its adaptations as step by step it has advanced. It is because of this study that I feel a sort of right to be heard on this subject;

and it cannot be a matter of indifference to Spiritualists to know how such work as that of Mrs.
Richmond is pushed forward in this work-a-day
world.

"From my standpoint of observation I can say
without hesitation, that the past decade has witnessed wonderful changes. Utterances that ten
years ago would scarcely be tolerated, are now
not only received as matters of course, but sought
after with intelligent avidity. What even five
years ago was strictly esoteric doctrine is now
the corner stone of all her public teachings. Be
the question propounded what it may, the answer comes in the light of absolute soul existence
—in its relation not to fractional, but to integral
truths. The way to this victory has been spiritually wearisome; often during the toilsome march
the innocent medium has been made to feel those
slings and arrows which a prejudiced ignorance
alone knows how to bring to their greatest perfection. But wearisome or no, the work has
gone on, and the victory has been *won*. Never
before have I seen such audiences of Spiritualists as gathered in Republican Hall during the
Sundays of January just past. That many were
again and again turned away for lack of room
was by no means a source of surprise to me; but
that the basis from which every subject presented was treated should have proved so acceptable, was, indeed, a most gratifying result.

"To cut any portion of the Spiritualist household away from the physical basis of life has been no small task. Many portions still adhere to it tenaciously. But surely the work will not go backward. Once away from this material mooring, once the spirit feels itself launched upon its native element, and how quickly its pinions grow, how eagerly it soars aloft, with what thankfulness it breathes the upper air! However tentatively or suggestively merely the first notes may have sounded in the past, there is now free sweep along the entire gamut of the soul's inner revealings; and the symphony of existence in its absolute state, with all its exalted heights and passionate depths, is brought into this every day life with such rare skill and power of expression that none can fail to recognize the Master-hand in the performer; nor yet—unless he be blinded by pitiable human limitations—the power to solve this human riddle in the clear light of infinite love and justice.

"To me the deliverances of the guides during the sojourn of their beloved medium among us, has been deeply suggestive. Every topic was discussed, every question answered in the searching light of *spiritual reality*. To many Spiritualists, alas, this would mean that they talked about substantial spheres, organic forms and fixed relations generally. But I am devoutly thankful that there is a body of Spiritualists, daily augmenting in numbers, to whom *spiritual realities* have come to mean spiritual qualities; not inert matter, however refined, but throbbing aspirations, exalted ideals, infinite love and charity, and all those graces of the soul to which we give the name of Beatitudes. When all the world shall awake to these higher and deeper truths, this will be a new world; and when men and women shall truly live in the light of this new gospel, the peace on earth and good will to men, promised by the angels when the morning stars sang together, shall be fulfilled.

"Mrs. Richmond, remaining only one Sunday with her people in Chicago, immediately departed for California to minister to our friends there for a period of six months. That the Spiritualists of San Francisco and the Pacific Slope generally will duly appreciate the spiritual blessing thus sent into their midst, I cannot for a moment doubt, and I sincerely trust that what is now our temporary loss will prove their eternal gain.   "FREDERICK F. COOK.

"February 10, 1883."

We cannot better conclude this chapter—epitomizing, as it does, the work of our subject from the standpoint of those best qualified to judge— than by introducing the statement of Drs. Emmett and Helen Densmore, written by the latter. She is one of the brilliant and progressive women of our day, and with her husband, Dr.

Emmett Densmore, has been for years engaged in practical reforms having for their object the uplifting of mankind. Both have been intimate friends of our subject for many years, and both are students and earnest disciples of the Soul Teachings of the guides:

"There are several phases of Mrs. Richmond's genius that are interesting and most unusual. Indeed, as a whole, I consider her mediumship the most unique on the planet. She began public speaking when only twelve years of age, at which time her discourses were characterized by literary skill; in style they commanded the admiration of scholars and savants. Without education or training, as commonly understood, she has continued her public work during all the following years with never a break, except when obliged by illness to rest. She was an invalid for many years and often had to be carried to and from the place of speaking, sometimes under control during the entire time. The subject of the address is often selected by the audience after she has taken her seat on the platform, and it has been her custom to speak twice every Sunday during the year. It happened at one time that it was my good fortune to attend her ministrations for nearly a year, and I was always surprised by their excellence, whether the subject was chosen at the time by the audience, or by announcement the previous week. She always

spoke extempore, and upon all variety of subjects—political, religious, social, historic, and
philosophical. The discourses were seldom less
than forty minutes in length nor more than forty-
five. They consisted in a preamble, in which
the ground to be covered was carefully laid out,
the subject discussed from its various points of
view, followed by a summing up and ending with
a peroration. These discourses would do credit
to an able scholar or practiced divine who had
prepared his discourse with care during the week
and committed it to memory; never was there
hesitancy for a word, never a word illy chosen or
misplaced. They appeared perhaps too carefully studied, too methodical and unimpassioned
to reach the highest type of eloquence, but were
always faultless in gesture and intonation.

"These discourses are followed by an impromptu poem upon a subject chosen by some
member of the audience; and as there are usually
several subjects suggested by different members,
the one chosen was either voted for by the audience, or the various subjects were woven together
into one poem, thus precluding any possibility
of the medium having had any previous knowledge of the subject, or of having been able
to make any preparation. These poems are
quite unlike the discourses in point of artistic
expression, are often faulty in measure and
rhythm, but they are rich in poetic thought; and

if any person thinks this phenomenon is an easy
accomplishment without outside help, let such
person ask some skilful litterateur, scholar, or
orator to try and do as well.

"Another marked feature of Mrs. Richmond's
mediumship is the readiness with which she
passes from her conscious self to the inspired
state. At times when the conversation happens
to be upon unimportant subjects, and her part of
it apparently carried on by herself, if some one
introduces a difficult Spiritual or philosophical
question, at once without apparent change she
will give the most advanced thought, in the
choicest language, offer the most thoughtful
suggestions, and give the wisest conclusions for
consideration. To many of which, if questioned in her normal state, she could give no
answer nor lead the enquirer to any satisfactory
conclusion.

"Her prophetic power at times is also very remarkable — whether you question the oracle
through playing-cards, or the tea-cup, or the
crystal, matters not. She will startle the questioner by her knowledge of his past, which she
reads as from the book of his life, or by her
familiarity with the present as it lies all about
his consciousness, or as she reveals the future in
sombre or brilliant coloring, as the future facts
decree. While this is exercised not as a serious
performance, but as recreation to while away an

hour of entertainment, there are often revealed
in this way matters of the gravest import.

"Perhaps the most phenomenal phase of her
psychic power is the delineations of character
which she gives to persons whom she has never
seen, and of whose lives and fortunes she can
have no previous knowledge. This she does
standing behind the person and placing her fingers lightly on the temple, without looking at the
face or manipulating the head or forehead, as is
usual with phrenologists. In this position she
will give a more correct picture of the person
before her than his or her most intimate friends
could do, greatly surprising such person and all
the friends who happen to be present. She will
picture the struggles of life, the hopes and fears of
the future, the triumphs and failures of the past,
and give such promises of the future as she can
wrest from the stern decrees of fate. But whatever
the material fortune may be, over all is thrown
the sure release at last from all the seeming sorrows of life, when the body of death is cast off
and the paradise of the spirit is revealed. At the
close of the poem a name is given that shadows
forth the Spiritual quality of the life and the possible achievement to be reached before 'finis' is
written at the bottom of life's page. I have seen
large companies held breathless during such re-
citals; companies composed of men and women
who were not versed in Spiritualism, who would

not have believed that any manifestations of a supermundane character could have any interest for them, and who were perfectly astonished and unable at first to comprehend its nature or meaning.

"While all these phases of Mrs. Richmond's mediumship are wonderful, and would of themselves be sufficient to claim the attention of all thoughtful minds, the most marvelous still remains to be told.

"It has always been one of the most notable features of Spiritualism as a cult, that it has no formulated articles of faith, no system of philosophy underlying its organization—no organization, in fact. A belief in the existence of continued life after death, of an invisible world and the possibility of communication with its inhabitants, is all that is needed to constitute one a Spiritualist and is the only article of faith held by all Spiritualists. In consequence of this fact Spiritualism has escaped the common fate of new religions to become fossilized by the cramping tendency of formulated articles of belief. It is true there are some general contradictions to the orthodox creeds of established church faith held in common by orthodox churches; for example a literal hell, the vicarious atonement of Christ, salvation by grace alone, the divinity of Christ and the trinity; but it is also true that belief in these is fast dying out and are undergoing modification constantly within the churches themselves; while these creeds have not been changed by authority of synods or convocations, they are no longer preached, or belief in them insisted upon as necessary.

"It is also quite as noticeable a fact that the most rounded system of Spiritual philosophy that has ever been given to the world—a system that is consistent with itself; that accounts in a reasonable manner for the phenomena of the universe, answers to how and why, the whence and the whither, to the satisfaction of a rational being, gives at last a satisfying glimpse of the destiny of man on a basis that gives us order in the universe, a governing power that commands our reverence, excites our confidence, and exalts our spirits, has been given for the first time through the instrumentality of Mrs. Richmond. This was given years ago, before the doctrine of re-incarnation, Karma, the astral plane and other tenets of Eastern religious systems had shed their light upon the Western world though Madame Blavatsky and the formation of the Theosophical Society. These doctrines are fragmentary and unrelated, containing many half truths, but lacking the symmetrical perfection and satisfying nature of Mrs. Richmond's system which was given at a time when Madame Blavatsky was vigorously denying the doctrine of re-incarnation. Before hearing Mrs. Richmond's teachings, I be-

lieved the dead still live, that we can under
favoring circumstances communicate with them,
and that the invisible world is all about us, but I
could see no order or justice in the universe.
God seemed to me to be unable to do much for
the work of His creation; and spirits seemed to
be not much better off than mortals The teaching of physical science, with its cold and cruel
system of evolution, presented to my mind just
the conception which Prof. Drummond so characterizes in his recently published work, 'The
Ascent of Man,' as 'a picture painted only in
shadow, a picture so dark as to be a challenge to
its maker, an unanswered problem to philosophy,
and an ever standing offense to the moral nature
of man.' While Spiritualism offered me an improvement on theology, I found nothing to
answer the ever-recurring questionings that tor-
ment the enquiring mind until I found the system
of Spiritual philosophy which has been given
through this remarkable medium. I attended
one of the classes consisting of six lessons on
'The Soul in Human Embodiments,' and in that
teaching I found the truth that settled forever
my doubts, that opened a vista of creation, a
scheme of salvation for every human soul out of
the chaos of doubt which had enveloped my mind
since my first troubled attempts at adjusting the
affairs of the world to the possibility of there
being a Creator able and willing to supervise

them. I had studied various systems of religious philosophy, ancient and modern; I had turned to Western Theosophy, as taught by Madame Blavatsky, hoping to find a solution of the problem. Among them all I only found an occasional half truth, gleaming on the murky horizon. But here is an answer full of promise and potency which completely fills the chasm of a Godless universe. This is not the place nor time to give even a summary of this philosophy. It is to be found in Mrs. Richmond's published work, 'The Soul in Human Embodiments,' and will repay any one to read who has not yet found rest in Spiritual philosophy. One of the private doctrines taught is that we are not to take the say so of any one man or spirit as truth for one's self; that within the spirit of every human being is involved the truth; that as we grow in experience and expression we will perceive the truth; and until we do perceive it, it is not truth to us; that when we have made the necessary development we will always respond to the truth when we hear it spoken, or read it expressed by others, or see it from within without the help of the outward sign. This at once stamps it as divine, and differentiates it from all human methods of religious propaganda. The announcers of this philosophy evidently believe that truth is mighty and will prevail, and leaves mankind in no danger of missing it, through accident or perversity.

Through it all runs the same quality of the divine as contrasted with human ways and means.

"By their works ye shall know them, is the test of men and creeds. By this test the philosophy given through the instrumentality of Mrs. Richmond stands out from the shadow of creeds and formulated philosophy of all time, a safe and consistent light which in time will be seen by all."

It has been a rare treat to us to delve in this mine of friendship, and to review the history of past years through the pages of scores of letters from true and tried friends, for it proves to us that friendship is a gem whose lustre time and change can never dim, but, like the beautiful immortelles, shines forever fair and bright, both in the earth life and in spirit realms. The record of these kindly words and loving thoughts proves that the expressions of the human soul are not transitory and fleeting, like the material things of the world, but as enduring as the universe itself.

No adequate review of the life work of our subject can be made. As imperfectly as it is sketched in these pages, the reader will have gathered somewhat of its scope and meaning, the full measure of which must be for later years to chronicle, and for future generations to incorporate into their lives. When the *entire* system of Soul Teachings is given to the world in printed form—when the new social and spiritual state shall begin (already outlined in a practical plan by the wise teachers and guides to be incorporated into society whenever the world is ready), when the fruitage of all this planting by angel hands shall have ripened in human lives, then the world will know the full meaning of this life work.   To the reader we will say that we trust the book will be all that you have hoped it would be.   We have put our very *soul* into it, for we loved the work—yes, loved the life of which we were writing—loved the noble guides back of that life.   If we have failed to make the work all it should be, please consider the failure due to errors of the head, not of the heart. We have written from the standpoint of one who has been led to higher heights by the guides, therefore have appreciated both the medium and the guides in so far as our limited understanding enables us to do so.

CHAPTER XVII.

VISITATIONS, VISIONS AND EXPERIENCES WHILE UNDER THE CONTROL OF MY GUIDES.

BY CORA L. V. RICHMOND.

NO part of the life work chosen for me as a medium is *my* work (excepting that of being a willing instrument), yet it is made for me and is my *life work*. Whatever perfections that work may contain, the beginning, the scope, the accomplishment, the finality must be solely attributable to these spirit guides who have chosen me for their instrument. Whatever imperfections there may have been, I consider them wholly attributable to the lack of perfection in me. As an instrument, a pupil, an humble follower of the sublime teachings, I have been ever willing, ever ready, and, as far as I know, obedient.

My individuality has not been lost nor swallowed up in that of my guides or any of the spirit controls. On the contrary, my instruction, my individual thought and responsibility have been as much more carcfully preserved, retained and trained than if I had been under the training and guidance of eminent teachers on earth, as the system of teaching of the guides is higher than any earthly method and system.

As far as I am aware, I did not differ from other children, only as we all must differ one from another, except in a diffidence, a sensitiveness to the presence of strangers that was really painful. Whether it made me awkward, I cannot say, that it made me suffer extremely in childhood, and that the sensitiveness has continued to a great extent all my life, I am only too painfully aware.

I had had no dreams nor visions, and was not given to many imaginings in my youth. I do remember seeing small faces that appeared in miniature-like shape and then disappeared, but supposed everyone saw them, and if I spoke to my mother about the "little people," as I called them, she must have thought it a part of my play.

From the very first of my control, *i. e.*, the writing on the slate in little arbor, in Lake Mills, Wisconsin, to the present time, I have never been conscious of anything that transpired in the outward world during the time I was under con·trol. This state or condition has not changed since I became a medium. I could not through my own knowledge state or testify in court that I had ever spoken in public, ever delivered an address or poem in my life. While passing under control, I do not experience any peculiar

sensations or physical changes. Unconsciousness to physical surroundings and consciousness
of Spiritual presence being almost simultaneous.
The added or larger consciousness of spirit being
accompanied by a seeming expansion of all the
powers, and by great freedom of mind.

From the first I always saw (as soon as outward objects ceased to be visible, and without
any thought that outward things were passing
from me), spirit presences. As soon as I became
aware of these spirit presences and companions,
they were as real to me as though in human
form. They seemed to me as *natural*, in the
sense of true being, nothing uncanny or ghost-
like about them, but certainly, if as natural,
they never seemed the *same* as if in human form.
Whether I saw or perceived them, I did not
know, nor did I try to know in my younger
years.

Not only did I see or perceive spirits every
time I was entranced and the controls were using
my organism to write or speak, but I was distinctly aware of being a separate conscious iess,
out of, or not acting upon or through my own
body. *I went away* to all intents and purposes
having only a sympathetic "psychic" contact with
my organism. I visited people whom I knew,
and places with which I was familiar, also persons
and localities I had never seen in my normal
state; but my experiences were especially with

those in spirit life. I was as one of them, my father, grandparents, relatives, friends, many of whom I had never seen in earth life, were my companions in these seasons of inner consciousness.

My own instruction Spiritually was under tuition of these spirit friends, yet the teachings seemed to be superintended by one or more spirits, whom I afterwards knew as guides. I saw the scenes and conditions of spirit life, and passed the time, without being aware of time, that my organism was under the control of my spirit guides in repeatedly visiting the scenes, and renewing the lessons of spirit existence—adapted, of course, to my state and my ability to perceive or understand the scenes that I witnessed were relative to the condition of spirits whom I met. Visions were sometimes shown me, and I soon became aware that these were not panoramas, nor views of *things* separate from spirit *states*, but were related to and subject to spirits in their individual conditions. Nevertheless, the visions were most beautiful.

I will relate a few instances of each of the distinct kinds of classes of experiences while thus separated in consciousness from my body, and for convenience will classify them.

VISITING PEOPLE AND PLACES ON EARTH.

One of the earlier instances that I now recall, of my own consciousness or spirit being active in another earth place, while my body was controlled by a spirit, whom I was afterward assured by my earth friends, was addressing them all the time I was away, was as follows:

During the summer after I was twelve years of age, my father and I had visited Western New York; the controls, chiefly Mr. Ballou(Augustus, as we familiarly call him), and the German Doctor, and ''Shannie (now Ouina) had formed circles and left instructions for the people to continue their meetings and Spiritual seekings after we had returned to Wisconsin as they, the spirit controls, intended to bring me back the following year, and they wished the people to prove their interest by seeking Spiritual advancement, allowing their mediums an opportunity of being controlled, many of whom had become partially developed during our sojourn among them. One of these circles was formed in Dunkirk, New York. A few of those who attended that circle are still living in human form, and I meet them every year at Cassadaga, New York. After my father and I returned to my home in Wisconsin, my organism had been under control on one of the usual evenings for instruction and speaking from Augustus or the German doctor. On my return to outward consciousness, among other things I instantly recalled having been in Dunkirk, in the center of the circle that had been previously formed there. I had seen distinctly every member of the circle, but had also been perfectly aware that no one could see me, except one lady, who was clairvoyant, and who was visiting the circle that night for the first time. She saw me and described me so accurately that they all exclaimed, "Why, that is Clara," and a shadow fell upon them. Instantly, the clairvoyant, disturbed by their feelings, could see no more. Then I could clearly discern that they thought I had passed to spirit life, that my body was dead. While relating my experience to my parents I urged my father to write at once and inform them that I was not dead, that I was visiting them in spirit as I had many times before, but there had been no clairvoyant to see me at other times. My father wrote that night, but before the letter had reached its destination, he received a letter from either Mr. Palmer or Mr. Germond (the circle was at one or the other of these gentlemen's houses, which adjoined), wherein was written, "Cora was distinctly seen, and described by a seeing medium at our circle last night. What has happened?" Of course, it was explained when they received my father's letter.

Another instance: A lady friend in London, to whom I was much attached, was frequently aware of my visits. I could not only make her realize my presence, and could comfort her and allay any anxious thoughts concerning me, but I could make her know of some trifling, yet pleasing incident in my outward life, which I would have naturally told her had I seen her in bodily form. Once she wrote me in a letter, "I was very ill, dear, the night you came to me, and I know Dr. Rush and Mr. Ballou were with you. *I like you in the dress you showed me.*" I realized perfectly that I had been with her, that she was ill, that she had perceived my presence, and that of the guides whom she named, and I had wished, in a lighter mood, that she could see me in a new dress of the favorite material, and the color she liked me to wear. This has been fulfilled.

Another friend lived in Albany, N. Y. One Sunday the guides were speaking through me in a small town in the West. I visited this friend, saw her reclining on a couch in her room, and made her aware of my presence, at the same time calling her attention to a blue dress that *my body* was arrayed in, a shade that she very much admired, and had often wished me to wear. Before my letter could have reached her, telling her of my visit, I received one from her, in which she wrote: "I saw you plainly Sunday morning, and you appeared to me in the exact shade of blue that I like to see you wear."

My mother, always very intuitive, became very mediumistic after my powers as a medium were made known. After the decease of my father she returned to Hopedale, and later to my native place, Cuba, N. Y., where she resided until she passed to spirit life in the Winter of 1869. Every Summer, and sometimes more frequently, I would visit her, making my native place the center of my vacations, and often going at the Christmas holidays for a week or so. It was a favorite wish of mine to surprise her, but I never could. My home and work were then in New York city, and however tardy the train, or late the hour of my arrival, I would find her waiting for me, with a warm supper ready. I would say: "I did not write to you that I was coming." She would re ply: "No; but you came last night in spirit and told me that you were coming." It was useless to plan surprises to her while in my outward consciousness, for my truant spirit would reveal the secret. She was always aware of my state of health or happiness, and usually of my where-abouts, by this method of communion be-tween us.

In December, 1869, she was taken very ill. I was in Washington, D. C., and was then in very delicate health, but I became aware of her con-dition, and I insisted on going to her. "She wants me," I said; "her spirit will need me there to help the others." My spirit guides, seconded my desire to go. Laden with flowers, the gifts of kind friends at Washington, I took the train for Western New York. In the middle of the

Yours very Truly
Cora L. V. Richmond

night, while I was on the train, she came to me saying: "I am now released from my pain; they have sent for you." Her face was transformed into youthful beauty. Every line of pain and suffering was removed, and she seemed semi-transparent, so ethereal was her spirit form. On my arrival next day my sister and friends were greatly surprised to see me. They said, "We did not send you word at first, for we knew how frail you were, and did not wish to trouble you. When it was all over we thought we *must* send. How did you get here so soon?" I told them I had the message before they sent it, and knew the change must come.

My mother's spirit had said to me: "Don't look at the face of the body. Think of me as I was before I was ill and as I am now." So I wove the garland of flowers for the casket, and never looked at the face, from which the light of life had forever fled. *She*, my mother, was not there, but arisen. At the services, which were conducted by George Taylor, of North Collins, N.Y., my guides added another evidence of their power by controlling my organism to speak. Feeble as I was, and under circumstances usually so trying, meanwhile my spirit was conscious of being with my mother in her newly arisen state, and I was rejoicing with other friends in spirit life over her relief from earthly sufferings and her happy reunion with them.

Mr. Richmond, who is usually reporting the discourses, stenographically, while they are being delivered through my organism, frequently feels my presence as I am passing to or from my visits in spirit states. He often asks me on our way home from the services: "What were you doing during the discourse?"

My reply is: "I was away as usual, but in passing I touched your forehead, thus," illustrating by lightly touching his forehead with my finger. He would affirm: "That is why I asked you, for I distinctly felt your fingers upon my forehead." "How did you know they were mine?" I would ask. "Because they felt exactly as your fingers felt just now."

Mr. Richmond's mother, who is a member of our household, is often aware of my presence. During one of our visits to California, I was filling a six months' engagement in San Francisco, and it seemed that we would stay there another winter. In fact, we took it for granted, for not only had I been invited, but the audiences were very large, very enthusiastic, and most anxious to retain me there. One day in June, I was aware of seeing our mother in Chicago. She was sitting out of doors, in the shade, on the north side of the house, thinking of us. I stooped over and kissed her, and told her something which I in spirit thought was true. When I returned to my form in San Francisco, I said to Mr. Richmond:

"I have been home to Chicago. Mother was sitting in the garden, and I whispered to her something, and I'm so sorry, for *it is not true.* She will be so disappointed." "What did you tell her?" he asked. I replied, "I told her we would be home in October, and I know we are going to stay here."

In the next letter our mother wrote: "I felt your presence when I was in the garden (mentioning the day), and you whispered something to me *that was too good to be true.*" Then she wrote what it was, as recorded above. The result proved that I had better knowledge in that state than in my so-called normal condition. For we did go home, arriving there in October.

I might multiply these instances, *ad infinitum*, as they extend over the entire period of my life, from the age of eleven to the present time, but the above serve as illustrations. I may here explain that these visits to people who are in earth forms seem to be of short duration, and occur while I am passing to and from the more Spiritual states, or those more separate from material life.

I have often noted that those of whom I had previously been thinking, and concerning whom I was most anxious when in my outward state, were those whom I first visited in spirit. Yet I have also been aware of having visited people yet in earth life, whom I had never met in human form, and have afterward recognized them, on being introduced for the first time outwardly, as those whom I had seen in spirit. There are others whom I have seen in vision, yet have never met in person, and when we do meet here or hereafter, I shall know them I am sure. Nothing could better prove how spirit annihilates time and space; and may we not look forward to the time, that my guides assure us is coming, when the written word, often so long delayed and so anxiously looked for, shall no longer be necessary?

VISIONS.

Open vision of spirits came with my first control as a medium, whether sight or perception, or both. I cannot even now tell, and in early life did not know how to ask. I *saw*. The outer consciousness was usually entirely removed, and my sight of spirits and spirit scenes was when the organism was under control; but sometimes then, and in later years quite frequently, the inner vision was open when I was in my usual normal state. The outward vision and surroundings being no impediment to spirit sight. Nor did I have to close my eyes (with few exceptions) to shut out material objects, since what I saw appeared *through* the material forms, and, for the time, was more palpable. I had seen spirits both while in the inner state, as companions and friends, and while in the more outward state, when they were shown me; but by my own volition I could never see, nor can I now invoke this inner sight, nor induce this other state. The time, place, occasion, response to requests have always been governed by the spirit intelligences who speak through me, or who act upon my spirit or organism. I can only say the visions came, were experienced, and sometimes expressed to others while being seen (when they came in my normal or outward state). Friends and relatives, many of whom I had never seen in their earth life, were thus seen and described by me.

One of the first visions that made a lasting impression upon me was at the bedside of my father when he was passing from earth form. He had been to Western New York with me early in the season of 1853, and we had returned home to Wisconsin. Later, an aunt had accompanied me again to Western New York, as my father felt that he must stay at home and attend to some business preparatory to accompanying me wherever I might be required to go to "spread the glad tidings." No sooner had I arrived in Western New York, and the work of healing and speaking was fairly begun than the spirit control "Augustus" (as we called Mr. Ballou), said to my aunt through me: "You and the medium must instantly return to Lake Mills." Of course she wondered, as we had only been

in New York State a few days. He added, ''You
will both be needed there very soon.'' We did
return, and within a week or ten days were
summoned to the bedside of my father who had
been taken suddenly ill in the night. The spirit
physician through me aided the earthly doctor,
a friend, who was in attendance, but all proved
unavailing to retain the life in mortal form.

My vision was opened. I saw the attendant
spirit friends, most of whom I had seen in spirit
vision or visitations before. I saw all the people,
our family and friends, in earth form standing
around, and saw the form of my father in the
state of dissolution. A white, fleecy light, like
luminous vapor, was over the whole form, and
gradually concentrated at the head, the two
points of contact with the body being at the
head and heart. This luminous, cloud-like appearance took form and shape and stood erect
like my father's form; from the portion which
outlined the head I saw my father's face—
youthful, radiant, with an expression as self-
poised as though he had just entered from a
walk. He was not surprised at the change, and
as the spirit friends gathered around to greet
him, he seemed as much at home with them as
if he had seen them but yesterday. He turned
to me and said, (I cannot tell, nor could I then,
whether I thought there was a voice audible):
''I know where I am and what has happened.

Cora, tell ma not to grieve. It was so sudden I did not straighten up my affairs, but I will give her directions through you." And he did.

I had never been present in my still younger childhood at a "death bed," had no knowledge of the awful seeming of death to those who are not aware of our blessed light, and this, my first initiation into its sublime mysteries, was a revealment of what the *change really* is. So I can truly say that death has never had any terror for me. Since that time it has been my blessed privilege, sometimes amid great heart-longings and strain at the human parting, to stand beside the forms of many thus passing into spirit state, and always has the way been an "open way" to me; always have I followed or accompanied them with open vision; always have I known whether their spirits slowly or immediately became adjusted to the changed conditions.

These various visions of scenes at the door of spirit-life, of the transitions from human to spirit states would alone fill a large volume. The bewilderment, the surprise, the joy, the amazement of the arisen ones. The light and shadow of the individual conditions formed a part of the wonderful lessons shown me of what came to spirits in their added awakening.

The temptation to pause on this border-land is strong but is entirely set aside by the visions and experiences of the beyond. Let me here state once for all that I relate these scenes as they were *experienced*, and that the problem of their being "subjective" or "objective" was not considered when the visions or experiences oc- curred—and now I consider that mere specula- tions on those questions are utterly valueless.

Early in my visions of spirit scenes, I realized that there were differences and distinctions in my own state as well as in what was shown me, that *visions within visions*, or visions as illustra- tions might be shown me while I was experienc- ing the absence from outward consciousness, and might form a part of the lesson or series of lessons being given to me.

I must designate all that follows under the in- clusive word

EXPERIENCES.

I early became aware that the scenes surround- ing spirits were not geographical and fixed in location; although they were realities, they were not substance in the sense of being organic matter.

I saw shadowed spirits surrounded by what seemed to be their own shadowed atmospheres and within those atmospheres were the dim out- lines of their desires and wishes, ever taking shape and form yet ever baffling their attainment.

"There is no Hades," my teachers would say, "except this: The unconquered desires, appe- tites that have not been outgrown on earth. They are not desires and appetites in the spirit-life, but the *shadows* of them."

The spirit home of my father was with those congenial minds whose ideas he had so much admired on earth, tending toward a realization of human brotherhood; Robert Owen, and later Robert Dale Owen; Adin Augustus Ballou, (my spirit control), and finally Adin Ballou; not to mention the many whom he had never met on earth, to whose spirit presence he was attracted by similarity of ideas. I always found him near my control, Adin Augustus, yet apart, as though he did not wish his personal interest in me to mar or interfere with the work of the guides.

Many of my early visions and lessons in spirit life after my father passed on were personally conducted by him. When I wondered at not seeing him always with my grand-parents, and other relatives (his family) he said: "I am with them when I wish to be or when they desire it, but we each have Spiritual pursuits in which the others are not especially interested, and to which we are mutually adapted; therefore, why should we hinder each other by trying always to be together?"

I did not so fully understand this as I now do, for I have learned more of the true adaptations in spirit life. Works of philanthropy and help for others seem to be conducted on very different principles from those on earth. "We mutually help each other." My father would say, "I have known and still know many whom mortals account unworthy, who know more than I do in some directions, and sometimes they are better, more spiritually advanced than those who send them out of their bodies. The law of helpfulness in spirit is to give what we have to impart where needed; those who need us attract us to them as air is attracted to fill a so-called vacuum."

In my visions, and visits with my father he never seemed to have *things* or belongings, but I saw him always with people or engaged in helping others. "Where is your home?" I once asked him. "Wherever I am," he smilingly replied. "With those I care for or can help. Don't you feel at home with me?" he asked. "Oh yes, I am satisfied, but I wondered if you were always as I see you now?" He answered, "Yes, I am always with those who can aid me or whom I can aid in Spiritual ways, for that is our life."

Around my father I often saw a sphere or circle of amber light bordered with blue. One of my guides told me that this was his *aura* or atmosphere of spirit, and that I was enabled to perceive it as I was in sympathy with him.

When approaching any of my father's co-workers in spirit life, they appeared in similar auras, varying according to their individual states, and often with other interblending colors or tints.

After my mother passed to spirit-life, I saw

her frequently in my father's sphere, and saw him
in her "garden," for she seemed to have a garden
of flowers that were a part of *her home.* Those
flowers I knew were emanations from her own life
and spirit, and took such familiar forms as she
loved on earth. Rosemary, lavender, sweet peas—
all familiar and fragrant shrubs, and even aromatic
herbs. She told me these were her sources of
healing, and with odors or essences of these, her
spirit flowers, I found her able to heal the sick,
she said she needed these aids, and those whom
she had aided on earth seemed to need them also.
I saw her surrounded by the objects that she had
most cared for, even to the exact reproduction
of a particular chair, in which, in our home on
earth, she had loved to sit and sew or read. That
chair in her spirit home was under an arb r of
her favorite Morning Glory. A sense of the *home*
feeling that used to come over me when a child
whenever I was near my mother (whose absence
from home always made me feel homesick) would
return to me when I visited her in spirit. The
beauty of her flowers, the sweet scent of the
Rosemary and Lavender, the rare distillation of
her healing lotions, (distilled in the sunshine of
her spirit home), enraptured me; whether I remained there for hours or moments I cannot say,
but I always returned to my earth form with
kind of a homesick feeling after these visits.
Mother's care-taking, her intense sympathy, and

in her later life, her gift of clairvoyant healing, indicated her Spiritual adaptation while in earth life; so I found her spirit among those who are especially designated as "Healers," and who belong to the "Healing Sphere." I was at first disturbed that my mother and father were not *always* together. The same answer was given me as before: "When we need each other, we are together, but our work and adaptations are not the same in all directions."

From my mother's healing garden, I saw a most beautiful scene of hills and valleys, streams and forests tinted sometimes with the first delicate hues of Spring, sometimes flashing the gold and crimson banners of Autumn foliage, with deep-toned pines interspersed—exactly the view from our home in Western New York, that my mother loved so well. Here I met all the familiar faces, the old, old friends who had renewed their youth in this garden of immortals, some of whom always sent back by me messages of love to their friends whom they knew I would meet when I returned to my outward form.

My mother's home also opened upon a vista of blooming flowers and fountains, and beyond them was a pavilion of lilies where many met who were in the mother sphere, who had left their loved ones on the earth, to solve the problems of life of those who must still remain below, or to receive and bestow ministrations from higher spirits.   This lily pavilion seemed a true place of prayer and aspiration, where one would fain pause; yet ever for another uplifting.   I give now some of my experiences in the sphere of my spirit control and teacher.

ADIN AUGUSTUS BALLOU.

The most familiar presence, always excepting Ouina, the spirit state and sphere within which all of philosophical and ethical knowledge that I possess, of education, material or spiritual, (far too little manifested considering the Spiritual opportunities that have been mine), the presence into which I ever pass and through which, as a luminous gateway of mind and spirit, I am prepared for spirit instruction and for what is beyond instruction, is that of the genial, critical, philosophical, humanitarian, Adin Augustus Ballou.

I well remember when this spirit presence flashed upon me—very soon after my first control as a medium—how from the midst of relatives and friends who were crowding around, anxious to be recognized, and to have me bear a message to their loved ones upon earth, this young face shone out and smiled upon me, as I had seen it once before in the garden at Hopedale, when in my foolish fright at seeing a stranger I had run away.   Seeing him in spirit, I was not frightened nor had I any inclination to

fly from the genial presence, which won me from
the first by kindly frankness and afterwards by
matchless patience, teaching me the essentials of
outward knowledge by Spiritual methods, and
preparing me for the teachings of the higher
guides—his guides as well as mine—by primary
stages of Spiritual instruction, and of unfoldment
in the recognition of *perception*.

The knowledge that I was being taught without words, formulas or the usual adjuncts of
education, at first puzzled me. I no sooner had
a thought or a desire to know, than the response
came: "I am told, and you will soon perceive,"
he thought to me, (in this world would be *said*)
"that correct perception makes correct thoughts
and these in turn produce correct speaking and
doing." At that time he was teaching me principles and truths relating to spirit and matter.
Language and experience in forms of speech, in
fact, the use of words came to me in this manner,
as outgrowth of perception. "Principles and
perceptions, then *ideas* and then words—if one
must use them; in spirit we do not require them;
in your state of human consciousness they will
come to you as you need them," said my teacher.

There is not room within the limits of this
chapter to trace step by step those stages of progress, to give to others as was given to me, or
even to describe what could only be received in
a similar manner and state. I found myself

gradually in possession of knowledge of material things, of the philosophy of the existences and natural objects around me in earth life, without having learned in earthly schools or from books written by human hands.   How far this knowl edge would stand the test of technical criticism, I cannot tell.   I have never had the occasion to put it to the test. Since the knowledge displayed in the discourses is their. knowledge not mine. Whenever I have essayed music, it has come to me, and had I been able, had not my time been dedicated to the guides for their work through me, music would have been my choice.   Suffi- cient perception of it made it possible for me to soothe and interest myself for hours with music and sometimes to impart pleasure to others. My sense of form and color seems to have received sufficient discipline to make drawing and paint- ing easy, had I had time or occasion to pursue them.   My perception of music, form and color. however, have all come through Ouina and her realm.

This teaching of Adin Augustus led me step by step into the themes of philosophy and ethics or the principles of life, as the basis of thought and the methods of carrying out in practical ways the perceptions of the spirit.   While in that state, knowledge is not an *attainment*, but an unfoldment through perception.   Whenever I became aware of a wish to know, the knowledge

was ready for me, as easily received as is the
atmosphere of earth by inhalation; the capacity
for receiving knowledge having been unfolded in
any particular direction, the knowledge came as
directed by the volition of my teacher, to answer the need. The difference in the method of
gaining knowledge was not so noticeable to me
in my early life as in later years, when I became
outwardly more conscious of the usual methods,
and that they often hamper and fetter the spirit
in the very struggle that is made for knowledge.
The greater wisdom of the inner method will one
day be recognized in human life, when the struggle for attainment will give place to unfoldment;
inspiration will supersede dictation.

Adin Augustus bore with all my shortcomings,
explained the necessity first of clear perception,
then clear thinking, then clear statement. The
return to outward consciousness did not at once
bring with it the possibilities of thinking these
lessons, much less of stating them; and even the
continued training through many years has not
sufficed to make me confident that any statement
of mine concerning these vital questions will be
of value to others. To me the teaching has been
invaluable; often, when occasion requires, I find
myself in possession of knowledge in many directions that a life time of study in any one of those
directions would not have been sufficient to bring
to me.

The realm of mental, social and ethical philosophy, includes all of those of kindred minds and spirits who have sought to solve the social ethics of human life, and whose religion has been the welfare of mankind; whether seen in the light of co-operative human interests, Fraternal Association, or Christian Brotherhood. The underlying principles have been the same.

Didactic or empirical knowledge seems to have no place, even in the realm of science that impinges on this broad realm of philosophy. Perception takes the place of experiment. Discovery is but another name for knowing what is. The application to material uses being as readily perceived as the underlying principle. A spirit teacher perceives and moves upon a mind in earthly form, imparting some principle and its application, and the latter at once perceives and utilizes the principle.

Adin Augustus does not claim to be a scientist except in the broader realm of philosophy. From this standpoint I was taught the underlying principles of true science. Other spirits of scientific attainments while in mortal forms, some of whom were my friends in earth life, made me their pupil, revealing to me their methods of scientific research after their separation from human organisms. Prof. Robert Hare, Prof. J. J. Mapes, and others who were here interested in me, as a little girl, because of my mediumship. Their interest

in me was continued in their Spiritual states; I
was admitted to a knowledge of the change in
their methods of perceiving and pursuing their
favorite studies.   I shall never forget with what
radiant surprise the spirit of Prof. Mapes made
known to me his added power of perceiving truth,
his first awakening to the knowledge that spirit is
immortal as spirit, and not as an "added function
of matter" which had been his usual method of
explaining a continued Spiritual existence after
the death of the body.   "I now understand," he
explained to me, "why much that I knew on
earth came to me so easily, and why it was not
accounted 'scientific' by my associates *because I
did not learn it.*"

These attractive spirit reminiscences so allure
me that there is great temptation to go on, and
on, but I must not do so here. *Sometime* I may
take up my pen and not lay it down until I have
told all that is tellable of these experiences and
then feel as I do now that *nothing* of what really
was my experience *can be told*.

The absence of belongings, of things in those
inner realms, never occurred to me while in those
states, but in attempting to relate my experiences to earth friends, I found that I was at once
subjected to a system of questioning.   "How
did the world seem? Were there houses there?
Were there fields and streams and hills? What
did the spirits whom you saw wear?"   In utter

humiliation I was obliged to confess I had not noticed any of those things, and could not recall that I had either seen or missed them. It was often a great triumph in my human state when on my return I could tell them of something I had *seen*, although perfectly aware that what I saw might have been a vision shown me and not an "objective reality," as we are accustomed to say. *Thoughts* not *things*, *spirits* not *places*, *companionship* and *communion*, not *belongings;* these ever have been and must continue to occupy me most in the state to which I refer. When I asked Adin Augustus "how can I describe my experiences in this state when I return?" "Tell them as *it is*," he would reply, "no seeming will suffice. Spirit is spirit, and the sooner they know it, the better."

On and on he led me to fascinating and enthralling themes until the schools of philosophies merge into one grand whole, and the metaphysical and transcendental streams are traced back to their fountain heads through Plato and Socrates, back, back into their eternal source.

OUINA'S HOME.

By far the greater portion of my visions, and experiences in spirit states have been with Ouina, usually in the beautiful, seemingly boundless, indescribable realm known as "Ouina's Home," and through that to the realms beyond.

Through archways of perfect light, tinted with thousands of hues unknown to earth, or through cloudless ether—lighted by neither sun nor moon nor stars—but self-luminous, I ever pass, accompanied by Ouina, and after she came to me and became a part of my life, accompanied by my little girl—my little girl! The precious gift of motherhood brought my darling to me only to remain in earth form one sweet year, yet never since she came and stamped her image upon my heart and life have I passed into or out of the spirit state without seeing her first and last,—to greet me, to reluctantly let me return. I have seen her unfold in Ouina's home, one of her precious messengers, one of those appointed to bear the blessed tokens of life to those who need it.

Ouina's home is a sea of ether, crystal as no water ever could be, over which bend ethereal skies, tinted or azure, veiled in soft light or more luminous, as the occasion required. Here Ouina's thoughts and deeds take form, if beauteous things transparent as air and ethereal as sky and iridescent as thought can be called forms. The messengers appear like snow white doves or the snow birds she loved so well on earth. The "canoes" that seem innumerable are of pearly hue, and shaped like shells or flowers, drawn by snowy swans or doves. These bear spirit children to her abode when they pass from earth, and bear her messengers when they choose to thus embark on their missions of love. Innumerable islands, large and small, grouped or apart, like jewels set in a crystal sea, form the abodes or places of grouping for her children. Yes, children they are, who from loveless or loving homes, from poverty and squalor, or the sometimes greater poverty of palaces, have been gathered into this most beautiful, wonderful realm. How familiar it all is to me! How more, a thousand-fold, more real than any earthly scene. The island of pansies and violets, the island of lilies and forget-me-nots, of rose buds, of star beams, of pearls. Drawing near these beautiful blossoms, grouped or apart, instantly the separate flowers come near to me and I behold they are children, who wear their lovely thoughts like garments of flowers, fashion their deeds into these images of beauty. The archway of pearls formed of tears of sympathy, the bridge of forget-me-nots, fashioned of the thoughts of loved ones on earth for their darlings in Heaven. The rose buds, spirits folded in sweet thoughts and deeds of love.

There are guardians and teachers appointed by Ouina, through the sweet law of adaptation and affection. Mothers whose darlings are on earth, and who teach these little ones that they may the better reach their own from whom they are veiled; loving spirits, childless on earth, whose tender sympathies and tender adaptations have fitted them to be the companions and teachers of Ouina's little ones.

Nor could I always be certain which were the teachers, for many grown-up children were there, whom these child messengers could teach. I found myself among that number, and learned much of spirit lore from these sweet flower children in Ouina's home. This vision world, this dream of loveliness and harmony proved to be but the vestibule, or vast ante-room to inner and broader realms; yet a vestibule so wonderful that we might spend æons of that unending eternity, and never weary.

THE POET'S SPHERE.

Beyond or within Ouina's home of children, which seems as a bright and luminous borderland to what lies beyond, is the state or realm of poets; not that all poets are alike, nor that they necessarily, *by virtue of being poets* are in the same realm, but there is a particular quality of kinship in certain poets, and those idealists akin to poets—although they may have written no poems, certain of these are in one realm.

Across an interval of dream-like beauty, suggestive of Elysian fields, through which flow streams of crystalline waters, from whose banks arise fair slopes and sun-kissed mountains, through wooded stillnesses and wondrous tangles of bloom—an interval not of space nor time, nor sight, nor sound, but of all rapturing things of beauty, ardor, hope, harmony, love—in this realm Ouina led me. First as one might be led in fairy legend into an enchanted palace, or garden of paradise, afterward drawn thither by whatever in me responded to so much loveliness of theme and thought. I learned to know the way to where earth's idealists, prophets, dreamers had formed that sphere of their own hopes, set to the perfect rhythm of loving lives. Many whose lives were bright in ages past whose names I will not give, many unknown on earth whose lives were bright with all that poetry contains of perfectness, I met in that enchanted realm until the *perception* of somewhat that this realm holds is mine, unfolding evermore and with each experience until it seems to lead to the Soul of poetry, the Divine.

SPHERE OF MUSIC.

Ouina often has led me through an enrapturing state into the ideal sphere of music. Whether of sound or silence I cannot tell, but the surpassing experience has each time thrilled me with such exquisite joy, that for hours after my return to outward consciousness the sweetest sounds of earth would jar like discord on my spirit and silence alone seem endurable.

The sphere of Mendelsshon always awakens a perception of joyous and wondrous flight, as

though music were fashioned of wings of light.
I never experience similar spiritual raptures of
wings of ineffable and most ethereal lightless.
In contrast the music sphere of Beethoven affects
me like "deeps calling unto deeps," as winds and
waves would if their sounds were set to the
deep themes of the soul. There is no sorrow in
Beethoven's sphere, but a depth that stirs and
pervades until the music is lost in silence.

After Wagner's transition, I experienced a
desire to visit his sphere. Ouina led me (by
her loving volition) into a most entrancing and
ravishing prelude or preparation of mingled perceptions, like sights and sounds of aspirations
and prayers, of worship and love, until we came
into a theme of life, so grand in all its mighty
import, so full and complete in all its parts that
I thought there could be nothing beyond. So
perfectly from the smaller themes did the whole
gradually enkindle and arise; I could perceive
the fountains of the soul music awaken; the
streams from far-off mountains gleam and shine;
the ocean surge; the stars and suns arise and
shine with scintillant rays of ravishing sounds,
souls from out the infinite being become *exist-
ent* and *aware*—on and on—until I could bear
no longer the rapture of the Symphony Eternal.

So akin are all the arts, sculpture, painting,
poetry, and music, that in the ultimates of each
they blend; therefore, it was no surprise when I

found the sphere of artists, of those who made symphonies in marble and epics in form and color, was also one of the realms eternal leading from that rare vestibule, Ouina's garden of flowers.

Artists are creators, not imitators, and in their spirit states images do not suffice. The sphere of painters and sculptors, awakened in me a perception of lives, not forms, spirits quickened to the expression of loveliness by what is within grown lovely in the work for others.

The sphere of Raphael seemed to reflect but *one face*, yet many thousand lives which had been made glad by sweet pictured faces of his Madonnas, gave loving tribute of more lofty endeavors and more deeds prompted from within by the beauty of his works on earth. Thus perception of beauty becomes a strong incentive to beauty of life that is born of the soul of loveliness.

Ouina, my sweet child sage, my teacher whose presence thus revealed, made me aware that she could teach all that I could learn for as many ages as I had years on earth, Ouina, poetess and prophetess, led me to the sphere of the three-fold master of art,

MICHAEL ANGELO.

Whatever shaping of unyielding and insensate matter into perfect form, whatever ideal fashioning of thought into living themes, whatever maj-

esty and sublimity of moulding truth into human
lives, whatever conquest over human strife attained through great heart pangs and throes of
mighty anguish, whatever realization of ideals of
loveliness born of eternal soul possessions have
been mine—alas, too dimly and feebly perceived
by me—I have found in and *through* this surpassing realm! What living images of loveliness,
of names and themes most dear; what reminiscences of soul familiar faces gleaming in sudden
reproduction on the still, luminous background
of the past, faces yearned over in time and sense,
while torturing memory's empty urn in vainly
searching for their semblance in human visages
—all known and loved forever in this wonderful
soul state.   *Through* that realm, I say; for that
rare state but opens to a vaster, more divine and
more absolute kingdom, where Truth and Love
are eternal *Soul Possessions*.

THAT REALM BEYOND.

Beyond Philosophy, calm-browed and clear-
thinking; beyond Art in her three-fold splendor
of form, color and sound, to the Soul of Art,
which is the Eternal Essence of Beauty, into the
innermost, uttermost—ah, none can declare what
is innermost and uttermost, but all that can be
perceived in that transcendent state of the Soul
of the Eternal.

Religion, shaped on earth and in the spirit

states to the blindness or needs of mankind, frag-
ments of praise and worship born of the feeble
glimmerings through the human sense, all this
was unknown to my spirit, and seemed no part
of my experience or teaching. I had nothing to
unlearn. Perception of spirit had been imparted
to me. By growth and knowledge, perception of
soul was awakened and became, while in that
state and afterwards, a continual possession.

Perception of God, the All-Soul, the Infinite,
was mine. I was not taught it ; from within
it came, an unfolding consciousness of an innate
possession. No education of outward schools
or creeds had made or marred it, no partial
training in any peculiar modes of spirit teaching. As far as I can recall, as far as perception serves, no word or thought of *religion* had
ever been *taught* me; yet here in this state into
which I had been gradually permitted, or prepared to enter, was the one perception that
makes knowledge of the Infinite possible, the
one perception that makes the life of love and
devotion to others the only true service and
praise of God. Far be it for me to claim, even
in the smallest degree, this divine fulfillment;
but such perception is and has been mine in soul
as serves to make a perfect standard; an ideal
the realization of which is to be obtained; that
which in its fulfillment will make in this human
life the "Kingdom on earth as it is in Heaven."

WORKS OF CORA L. V. RICHMOND.

ENTIRE SYSTEM OF

Soul Teachings.

The entire Series of "Lessons in Soul Teachings" (including the "Soul in Human Embodiments" already published), making a volume of five or six hundred pages, will be ready for the public as soon as the requisite number of names has been secured to warrant issuing the book. One hundred names are already on the list; two hundred more are necessary to complete the guarantee list.

Will you kindly interest your friends to send in their names at once? Bound in cloth, price $5.00.

THE BOOK WILL CONTAIN

First Series of Six Lessons:
THE SOUL IN HUMAN EMBODIMENTS.

Second Series of Six Lessons:
THE WORK OF THE ANGELS, IN HUMAN LIFE AND AN-GELIC STATES.

Third Series of Six Lessons:
MESSIANIC CYCLES. THE MESSIAHS AND THEIR MESSAGE TO EARTH.

Fourth Series of Six Lessons:
THE BOOK OF THE MADONNAS.

Fifth Series of Six Lessons:
THE ANGELS OF OTHER PLANETS.

Sixth Series of Lessons:
ARCH ANGELS. CREATIVE ANGELS.

MRS. CORA L. V. RICHMOND,

STATION Y. - CHICAGO, ILL.

The Soul in Human Embodiments. Its Nature, Relations and Expressions through Matter.

A series of Lessons consisting of a condensed and comprehensive treatise on the Soul.

LESSON I.—The Nature of the Soul; Its Relation to God.

LESSON II.—The Dual Nature of God and the Soul.

LESSON III.—The Embodiments of the Soul in Human Form.

LESSON IV.—The Embodiments of the Soul in Human Form (continued).

LESSON V.—The Re-united Soul.

LESSON VI.—Angels, Arch-Angels and Messiahs.

LESSON VII.—Recapitulation.

Finely Bound in Cloth, $1.00.

Heaven's Greeting to Columbia.

FROM THE SPHERE OF THE POETS.

A Sermon in Song delivered impromptu, and reproducing the exact style of Longfellow, Whittier, Tennyson and Whitman. (A beautiful souvenir for the Columbian Year.)

Neatly Bound in Paper, 15c.
Extra Binding, 25c.

Also Lecture before the Philosophical Society of Chicago on the Mind, &c., with Criticisms and Discussion.

MRS. CORA L. V. RICHMOND,

STATION Y,   -   CHCAGO, ILL.

Psychopathy; or Spirit Healing.

A series of Lessons on the Relations of the Spirit to its own organism and the inter-relations of Human Beings, with reference to Health, Disease and Healing, *accompanied with Plates illustrating the Lessons.*

LESSON I.—The Physical and Spiritual Basis of Life.

LESSON II.—The Influence of the Spirit over the Organic Functions of the Body.

LESSON III.—The Influence of Food, Raiment and Surrounding Conditions and Atmospheres on the Human Organism.

LESSON IV.—Psychology, Mesmerism, Magnetism and Electricity as Healing Agencies.

LESSON V.—Social Life; including Marriage and Parentage.

LESSON VI.—The Actual Magnetic Poles and their Corresponding Nerve Centers; Their Relation to Psychopathic Treatment.

LESSON VII.—Volition.

LESSON VIII.—Resume.

Handsomely Bound in Cloth, $1.50.

Spiritual Sermons or Discourses on a Great Variety of Subjects.

Single Copies, 5c.; Postage 1c. Extra.

For all of the foregoing send orders, wholesale and retail, to

MRS. CORA L. V. RICHMOND,

STATION Y, — CHICAGO, ILL.